Cities and Nature
in the American West

THE URBAN WEST SERIES

Cities AND Nature

IN THE AMERICAN WEST

EDITED BY

Char Miller

UNIVERSITY OF NEVADA PRESS

RENO AND LAS VEGAS

THE URBAN WEST SERIES

Series Editors: Eugene P. Moehring and David M. Wrobel

University of Nevada Press, Reno, Nevada 89557 USA
Copyright © 2010 by University of Nevada Press
All rights reserved
Manufactured in the United States of America
Design by Kathleen Szawiola

Library of Congress Cataloging-in-Publication Data
Cities and nature in the American West / edited by Char Miller.
p. cm. — (The urban West series)
Includes bibliographical references and index.
ISBN 978-0-87417-824-1 (pbk. : alk. paper)
1. Urban ecology (Sociology)—West (U.S.)—History—20th century.
2. Urbanization—Environmental aspects—West (U.S.)—History—
20th century. 3. City planning—Environmental aspects—West (U.S.)—
History—20th century. 4. Nature—Effect of human beings on—West
(U.S.)—History—20th century. 5. Environmentalism—West (U.S.)—
History—20th century. 6. Social change—West (U.S.)—History—20th
century. 7. West (U.S.)—Environmental conditions. 8. West (U.S.)—
Social conditions—20th century. 9. West (U.S.)—History, Local.
I. Miller, Char, 1951–
HT243.U62W473   2011
307.760978—dc22   2010014696

The paper used in this book is a recycled stock made from 30 percent post-
consumer waste materials, certified by FSC, and meets the requirements
of American National Standard for Information Sciences—
Permanence of Paper for Printed Library Materials, ANSI/NISO Z39.48-1992
(R2002). Binding materials were selected for strength and durability.

19   18   17   16   15   14   13   12   11   10
5   4   3   2

CONTENTS

Campground

City

PREFACE

Cities and Nature in the American West was born of a profound sense of loss, personal and professional. All of its contributors were friends and admirers of Hal K. Rothman, a superb historian of the American West, who at forty-eight died way too soon. Shortly after his passing on February 25, 2007, I began contacting some of his colleagues to see if they would be interested in turning our collective grief into a celebration of Hal's dynamic scholarship in environmental and urban history. Their enthusiasm was palpable, their assent emphatic, reflecting the impact Hal had on so many of us.

That impact is seen as well in the range of topics their essays address. They are framed around some of the constituent elements of the western experience: the links between land, water, recreation, and city life.

It is also captured in these chapters' focus on the intense and reciprocal relationship between urban societies and the natural world in which they are located. Each author has probed this connection in a different way, but each is convinced that the only way to understand how and why cities in the western United States function as they do is to recognize the interplay between natural systems and human habitats that have transformed each other. The many landscapes analyzed in this volume are a vital meld, which on a daily basis we integrate into our lives and livelihoods: the places we inhabit and those we visit, terra incognita and home ground.

Teasing out these complicated interactions is at the heart of this project, which is why it is lovingly dedicated to Hal Rothman, who helped advance some of these arguments through his many books, articles, and commentary. Inspired by his work, *Cities and Nature in the American West* could not have been completed without its contributors' vivid engagement, for which I am grateful. I am grateful as well for the efforts of the remarkable staff at the University of Nevada Press, notably Director Joanne O'Hare, editors Matt Becker and Sara Vélez Mallea; the two anonymous reviewers; and former editor Charlotte Dihoff. Finally, for Hal's family— Lauralee, Talia, and Brent—we hope this anthology testifies, however incompletely, to his intellectual gifts, profound energy, and inspiring generosity. We miss him more than we can say.

Cities and Nature
in the American West

Into the West

CHAR MILLER

Where is the American West? It should be easy enough to locate on a map, but doing so requires identifying it in relation to other cardinal points on a compass—east defines west, and vice versa. That reciprocal relationship also demands a historical calculation: which West at what time? The Northwest Ordinance of 1787 had nothing to do with the states of Oregon and Washington, referring instead to the more than 260,000 square miles that sprawled west of Pennsylvania and north of the Ohio River; the post-Revolutionary generation's spatial imagination tracked only so far as the Mississippi River.

If there was no West Coast then, some now living on what is known affectionately or derisively as the "Left Coast" have their doubts about how best to identify their specific locale. A friend's daughter, who grew up in Oregon, informed her parents that she was heading west for college—to Montana. For her, the idea of the West as a place was more culturally derived than cartographically determined, a point Texas-native Rick Bass also makes in the title to his memoir about moving to Montana from the Lone Star State—*Why I Came West*. This fluid form of literary place making is manifest as well in that thickly settled fictional terrain, The Wild West. Backdrop to innumerable movies, literary home to upwards of 1,700 dime-store novels about Buffalo Bill, it is a mutable space writes Clive Sinclair: "We all grew up putting together our own little miniature Wests."[1]

Historian Frederick Jackson Turner believed too that the West was a moving target. In 1893 he declared that the western frontier had reinvigorated American democracy: the "existence of an area of free land, its continuous recession, and the advance of American settlement westward, explain American development." Embedded in his perception of that movement was a cultural assertion that allowed Turner to score points against the eastern-centered historians of his day. If the frontier determined the ebb and flow of the democratic impulse, he wrote, then the "true point of view in the history of this nation is not the Atlantic coast, it is the Great West."[2]

The truth of his perspective, he believed, was defined by the nature of settlement. As the frontier pressed west into the Great Plains, up and over the Rockies, across basin and range, and then into the Pacific coastal valleys, it recapitulated earlier, more primal conditions and thereby reenergized American political institutions and social life. "The peculiarity of American institutions," Turner observed "is the fact that they have been compelled to adapt themselves to changes in an expanding people," a westward course that set the stage for a final act of adaptation. In "the changes involved in crossing a continent, in winning a wilderness, and in developing at each area of this progress," the expansionary nation evolved "out of the primitive economic and political conditions of the frontier into the complexity of city life."[3]

Yet urbanization did not mark the end of the frontier, it was its catalyst; so recognized one of Turner's contemporaries, famed journalist Richard Harding Davis. In 1892, a year before Turner delivered his "Frontier Thesis" to the American Historical Association meetings in Chicago, Davis had roamed through Texas, Oklahoma, and Colorado; in search of the frontier crucible, he discovered that it had been hammered out on an urban forge.

Not that he was impressed with the cities through which he toured. Only Denver seemed anything like his New York City home, and he disdained the middling metropolises he visited, dismissing San Antonio as "ugly" and Oklahoma City as "a freak of our civilization." Anything smaller was almost beneath contempt: "seven houses in the West make a city," he snorted. But this well-traveled, if parochial, man understood from the transportation grid on which he journeyed and the U.S. Cavalry units with whom he rode—from the muddy mining communities he slogged through and the financiers and executives with whom he dined—that the contemporary western economy depended heavily on the urban tools of conquest and commerce. The federal government's fiscal subsidies and military power; the massive investment of outside capital to extract precious metals, harvest timber, and run livestock operations; and the steady stream of migrants—all were key agents linking these distant and disparate places into the wider metropolitan marketplace. Davis went west only to find what he had thought was peculiar to the east.[4]

The famed correspondent's startled discovery, historians have come to understand, was accurate as well for the broad sweep of American history. The eighteenth-century Dutch, English, French, and Spanish colonial empires were urban in their structure and political economy; they planted cities along coastlines, in deltas, and at river confluences and fall lines, from which they controlled their expanding hinterlands. That pattern was replicated in the early nineteenth century argued Richard Wade in *The Urban Frontier* (1959), a deftly titled analysis that took dead aim at Turner's provocative claims of the frontier's priority. For Wade, the dominant factor in the nation's construction was urbanization; Pittsburgh, Cincinnati, and Louisville determined the timing and character of trans-Appalachian settlement. Replicating this developmental process were the nation's first great western cities—New Orleans, St. Louis, and Chicago. Through their radiating lines of transportation (river and rail); webs of communication; voracious appetites for natural resources, grains, and other foodstuffs; and deep pockets, they opened up and organized the Mississippi River Valley and well beyond. In time, San Francisco, Seattle, and Los Angeles became the energetic hubs of a pan-Pacific trade network only two hundred and fifty years after Boston, New Amsterdam, and Philadelphia had acted as conduits for the movement of goods and people between European ports and the New World interior. There could be no margin without a center, no frontier without metropole.[5]

The central place of cities in the American West has intensified over time. That is partly the result of the region's explosive population growth dating from the late 1930s. Successive waves of in-migration—beginning with those fleeing the Great Plains Dust Bowl or who pushed out of the South as a result of the mechanization of agriculture, and accelerating with the wartime buildup of military bases, defense plants, and shipbuilding facilities across the West—brought millions of new residents. More joined them in the post–World War II boom, resulting in a surge in the construction of a new urban geography consisting of homes, shopping malls, offices, and the high-speed highways that linked them together. The demographic shift has continued unabated: since 1950, more than 18 million people have moved from the North and the East into the West (22 million headed south during the same time frame); the last half century has been witness to the single largest human migration in U.S. history.

Western cities have swelled as a consequence. In 1950, Los Angeles was the only city west of the Mississippi that ranked in the top ten of the nation's largest. Six others have joined it over the past thirty years, including Houston, San Antonio, Dallas, Phoenix, San Diego, and San Jose. These Sunbelt metroplexes, by spinning out new work and people, have sparked a rapid increase in the economies and populations of secondary and tertiary cities: nineteen of the fastest growing twenty-five are in the West. From Austin to Anchorage, Tucson to Denver, Salt Lake City to

Portland, the regional pattern of growth has been as profound as the national implications are significant. Currently one-third of all Americans live west of the Mississippi River, and demographers expect one-half will do so within twenty years. This represents, historian David Kennedy has observed, a "tectonic demographic shift," an observation that underscores his claim that this is "How the West Has Won."[6]

Among the things gained has been robust political power: as its population has grown so has its number of representatives in the U.S. House. It is not incidental that in 2007 a Californian became the Speaker of the House and a Nevadan the Senate majority leader. This demographic reality has had corresponding implications for presidential campaigns. With the uptick in western electoral votes, those running for the White House are compelled to take regional issues more seriously and do so as well because increasingly they or their running mates are from states west of the Mississippi; Nixon and Reagan (California); Johnson and the Bushes, father and son (Texas); Clinton (Arkansas); and in 2008 the Republican nominee, John McCain, hailed from Arizona. All roads appear to head west.

Actually, there is a concrete basis for that claim: the postwar construction of the U.S. interstate system, which closely tracked the routes of nineteenth-century intercontinental railroads, has sped up the growth of the western economy, tied its sprawling cities together, and facilitated the westward flow of an auto-centric people. They come looking for work and weather, for rest and recreation. And until the early twenty-first century they benefited from cheap energy to fuel their cars and power their air conditioners, along with plentiful water at minimal cost; agribusiness churned out food at a price the consumer easily could afford and construction companies built so many houses so rapidly that seemingly anyone could afford them. These veritable dreamscapes lured still others to the magical West.[7]

Joining the westward rush were many of the very historians who have been most engaged with probing the contours of these dramatic transformations of the region. Often born and trained in the East and or Midwest, they followed the sun to colleges and universities whose enrollments were increasing in tandem with the larger population; spikes in state-educational budgets and in institutional endowments, new campuses, well-funded laboratories and libraries—all located in a boomtown atmosphere—were heady inducements. Novelist David Lodge was right on mark when, in *Changing Places* (1979), he dubbed his fictional West Coast university "Euphoric State."[8]

Although Lodge had in mind the University of California at Berkeley, the appellation could have stuck at a number of other places, even one situated in as arid a landscape as the campus of the University of Nevada at Las Vegas. Certainly Hal K. Rothman, a gifted historian of the American West who hailed from the East Coast, thought he had died and gone to heaven when in 1992 he arrived in the city he later dubbed the "Neon Metropolis." There he found a challenging academic home and vibrant community, and made his considerable mark on each during his meteoric, all-too-short academic career that this volume commemorates.

Like his peers elsewhere, Hal brought to his analysis of the West in general, and Las Vegas in particular, a fresh perspective that helped him see patterns in regional development that might have been more difficult for the native born to discern. He later would rail against "carpetbaggers," those "hip intellectuals and grandstanding writers" who came to Sin City to write about its venality; all these "outside observers see is a reflection of themselves," he wrote, and their "renditions sound forced and stale to locals." But even as he adopted the language of an aggrieved insider, a reflection of his deepening affection for the place he now called home, Hal maintained the capacity to write penetratingly about its foibles, faults, and fears. "He embraced the city with passion and energy," William deBuys wrote after Rothman's death in 2006 from ALS, "and in short order he grew into it and it into him like two vines on the same wall."[9]

The same energy that drove Rothman's writing about Las Vegas, which included a wide array of books, articles, and newspaper commentary, fueled his equally prolific work on the history and present state of the U.S. National Park System; on tourism and recreation in the remaking of urban society, tribal communities, and rural life; on fire, water, power, labor relations, and environmental justice. Few could match his broad reach or intellectual curiosity, let alone the ferocious work ethic that defined and drove him. Even as he lay dying, with the aid of family, students, and friends, he wrote one column after another, and these have been gathered in the posthumously published *Playing the Odds: Las Vegas and the Modern West*. His magnificent study *Blazing Heritage: A History of Wildland Fire in the National Parks* also appeared after his death. The fact that either made it into print is almost miraculous; just as astonishing is that his mind could remain so open as his body was shutting down.

Yet Hal's strength at the end was consistent with his lifelong receptivity to innovative arguments and counterintuitive claims that recast contemporary historiographical debates. Making this case was the title to one of his many edited volumes, *The Reopening of the American West*. In its introduction, he noted that the collection's ten chapters offered "another look at issues that seem decided, that have been widely accepted and made part of the historical canon. Here we have a genuine reopening, a post–new western history approach to the environmental history of the American West, a series of articles that delves into the premises that underpin not only an older generation of scholars and thinkers, but also those who have redefined the field in the past two decades." To change how we conceive of the past requires us to reconsider our fundamental perceptions and preoccupations; to break new scholarly ground demanded a sympathetic ear, and flexible intellect— characteristics that distinguished Hal's best work.[10] *Cities and Nature in the American West* tries to emulate those qualities too. Its contributors, which include Hal's friends, colleagues, and collaborators, cover many of the fields that he roamed through and made his own. With him, they are particularly intrigued with locating, identifying, and defining the intersection of environmental, urban, and western history, from the Mississippi to the Pacific, from New Orleans to Seattle to Honolulu, encompassing as well the valleys of Napa, Silicon, and Yosemite. The goal has been to develop arguments that provide a deeper appreciation for the complex processes by which urban society has shaped and has been shaped by its sustaining environment; to explore how habitats human and natural have been grown together, or overrun one another, leading to changes in each that have been unexpected, seemingly inexplicable, or just plain ordinary. The politics of sugar and grapes, and oil and water; like the cultural representations embodied in pitching a tent, planting wildflowers, or selling the Great Outdoors; questions of social justice and resource exploitation, like the vagaries of municipal politics, the challenges of environmental inequity, and the pleasures of urban frolic; and the power to consume goods, services, and experiences—these are some of the entangled realities, and their historiographical implications, that this volume seeks to explicate.

In its first section, "Land," the decision of what crop to grow where, and who determines that choice, has had profound implications for the environment and the people who work it. This situation was particularly vexed in Hawaii. At the turn of the last century, Claus Spreckels was one of several San Francisco investors who recognized that the islands' soil and climate were perfect for producing vast quantities of cheap sugar for American consumers and that it would be relatively easy to transport the sweet stuff to Bay Area refineries, creating a trans-Pacific commercial corridor. But to secure enough acreage, significant quantities of irrigable water, and a pliable labor force, Jessica Tiesch observes, required a major investment in Hawaii's political structure. Spreckels did so as a cost of doing business in the islands, but the price exacted from land and its imported workers was steep. Sixty years later, the stakes were no less high, if for different reasons, in California's Napa County: as residential development spiked in the 1950s and 1960s, a consequence of white flight from San Francisco and the East Bay, it threatened the county's agricultural economy and rural ambience. Help came in the form of the Williamson Act, a 1965 legislative initiative granting counties the power to help conserve prime farmland, whose reach Napa extended by rezoning the entire valley as an agricultural preserve. In so doing, Kathleen Brosnan reports, the county protected its land resource in ways that its peers, particularly those in the South Bay, did not. Yet in privileging the wine industry and the symbiotic tourist business that grew up with it, the preservationist strategy committed the region to a single crop, with all the attendant problems that come with monocultural practices; it also boosted land values so that few if any winery workers could afford to live within easy reach, thus accelerating congestion, the very antithesis of a bucolic terrain. Growing wild-flowers could prove as ambiguous a project, Vera Norwood argues. Not that that was Lady Bird Johnson's intent: as First Lady, her commitment to beautification along the nation's interstates led her to advocate the banning of billboards and the planting of indigenous flowers. After her husband, President Lyndon Johnson, left the White House in 1969, she continued to promote these issues, but the native plants became her passion. Her desire to protect local landscapes—cultural and natural—was born of her love of place, as was the mechanism she selected to carry out her ambition, The Lady Bird Johnson Wildflower Center in Austin, Texas. The center's purpose is manifold: to conduct research on wildflower habitat and propagation; to educate landowners about how to seed their properties with natives; and to link this form of environmental activism with a wider movement seeking to preserve the regional in the face of global homogenization. Mass marketing the wild to urban consumers well versed in the cultural cache of going native is only one tension emanating from Johnson's program. But then it has never been easy, whether in Hawaii, California, or Texas, to balance to the demands of place, politics, and power.

Finding that equilibrium is every bit as complicated when discussing water in the American West, the topic of part two in *Cities and Nature in the American West*. Its nourishing flow, economic import, and aesthetic value cannot be gainsaid. That demands on it have escalated in a region into which so many people have crowded is equally clear. Take salmon, a species whose survival in the Pacific Northwest is open to question. Through a case study of Seattle, Matthew Klingle probes the anadromous fish's lifecycle, framed by its youthful passage downstream to the ocean and its later migration upstream to spawn, and its movement through a watershed that dams and development have compromised severely. By the late 1990s the endangered fish had "become an omen of urban growth gone amok." This wholesale reconfiguration of space and habitat, and the competing claims of salmon and people for water (and within that competition another pitting different social stratum with differing degrees of power and authority over one another) have proved disastrous. Tracing this disaster's sources is reasonably easy; much harder will be building a political commitment that sees in the restoration of the battered riparian habitat the salvation of the human community. The communal right to and responsibility for the urban waterfront has been every bit as contested in Portland, Oregon. With its economic development tied to the Columbia and Willamette rivers, which give Portland its physical form, "each major effort to adjust city to river or river to city" has generated new problems and required further adjustments. Whether to build docks and dams (or not), to construct floodwater channels, restore salmon runs, and/or plant a park in a mid-stream island that had been a gravel pit, writes William Lang, was part of the city's long-standing debate with itself about how best to relate to that pair of rivers lapping "at the edge of our lives and livelihoods." Critical to the conception of San Jose, California, now the nation's tenth-largest city, is a ready supply of potable water. That hardly makes it unique, but what is anomalous is the institutional means by which this fast-growing town has procured its essential waters. Since the mid-nineteenth century it has been served by an investor-owned, private purveyor, the San Jose Water Company (sjwc); it is the largest city in the country so situated. That fact alone is worth investigation, argues Martin Melosi, because it runs counter to the history of municipal services in the United States; public ownership of public utilities, especially of water, has been one means by which city government has expanded its operations and political importance. Not so in the formerly farm-rich "Valley of Heart's Delight," which has morphed into tech-savvy Silicon Valley, for reasons peculiar to the situation—deft management, daft rivals, a steadily growing and satisfied customer base, a weak or co-opted city hall, and good luck—have kept sjwc in business. So long has it endured that its unique status just might become an example to those touting water-privatization schemes here and abroad, an irony that might further roil the political waters.

A form of public ownership synonymous with the West that already has found its way around the globe is the concept of national parks, the subject of this collection's third section. Their physical construct dates from the March 1872 creation of the world's first national park at Yellowstone, which eighteen years later expanded with the inclusion of Sequoia, General Grant (now King's Canyon), and Yosemite national parks; the system itself was formally established with the National Park Service in 1916. What it was designed to accomplish, beyond its grand collection of magnificent sites and historic landmarks, its one-of-a-kind geological formations and picturesque tableau, has been the subject of considerable public debate and scholarly inquiry. The initial focus on the preservation of the grand jewels and the promotion of visitation into these unique wildlands, has shifted away "from a cultural affinity for scenic monumentalism to a more scientific understanding of ecological systems and natural habitat," observes Marguerite Shaffer. Capturing this evolution of ideas and policy is the transformation of the Park Service's response to bears: where once rangers built viewing stands so that tourists could watch the bears being fed, today park employees diligently dissuade human-bear interaction of any kind. By reading this change through the "lens of consumer culture," Shaffer argues we gain new insights into how wilderness and the wild have been "defined, packaged, and marketed as a consumer product and experience." Until we recognize how the bears and their performative function match up with our desires for spectacle, we will be unable to devise a strategy to live within and share these grand landscapes with them. As it is, we have a hard time sharing this terrain with ourselves: although the number of visitors to parks is down of late, you would be hard pressed to tell that from the traffic jams at the entrance to Yosemite, the crowds that gather along the Grand Canyon's south rim, and the sunbathing throng lying along Fire Island National Seashore. How to control access and egress is one thing, but it is another entirely to devise the infrastructure required to flush away these masses' effluent; while not a subject for the Park Service's snappy promotional brochures, plumbing is a critical backstage operation that the agency has spent much time assessing and refining. In their case study of how Yosemite has handled its wastes, Craig Colten and Lary Dilsaver reveal the park's traditional commitment to screening infrastructure and masking odors so as to be consistent with Frederick Law Olmsted's 1865 urging that such "inharmonious" features not detract from "the dignity of the scenery." His advice became holy writ, impelling park designers to build, move, and upgrade facilities in response to every new surge in visitation, shifting ever farther away from prime tourist sites; today they are located outside the park proper. These alterations led to the development of a systemwide policy regarding waste management, a concern for public health that had to meld federal environmental regulations and park aesthetics with the goal of ensuring that urban tourists, used to comforts of home, could enjoy an unsoiled, "natural" experience. What constituted that experience is the subject of Phoebe S. Kropp's analysis of the act of sleeping outside, which comes bundled with a host of symbolic elements. From Civil War bivouacking to the Adirondack camps that sheltered New York's elite; from hoboes who bedded down in Hoovervilles to the homeless who lay down near steam grates; from hardy hikers in the high country to the drivers of gas-guzzling recreational vehicles that lumber into valley campgrounds—each tells a complex tale about these types' putative relationship with nature, often set within a hierarchy of purpose and legality. The laws against urban camping, which define it as vagrancy or loitering, dovetail with class-defined notions that there is a "right way and a wrong way to camp," and reinforce a culture divide between conceptions of city and country.

Tracing the convergence of the built and natural environment frames the final section of *Cities and Nature in the American West* through analyses of one of the nineteenth century's key gateways to the West, New Orleans; the region's most populous twentieth-century metropolis, Los Angeles; and San Francisco, at any time arguably its most cosmopolitan center. Their urban monikers—the Crescent City, Shaky Town, and the City by the Bay—speak to their physical location and identify some of the defining features that bounded their growth. The Mississippi River established New Orleans's site and situation, leading its citizenry to chafe against some of the limitations that the massive waterway posed. Because "wild nature is a dangerous neighbor," writes Ari Kelman, "New Orleanians have struggled to reinforce the lines dividing their city from its environs." Levees to divert floods; pumps to drain the backswamp; and an "artificial river system" of gutters, drains, canals, and channels to capture runoff constitute an engineered landscape that provides residents with the illusion of safety until one of its constituent elements fails. Their misapprehension sinks whenever rampaging waters rush in to fill the void, only to bob back up as the fetid flood retreats, a resilience that will contribute to the next disaster's intensity. The same process is at work in Los Angeles, where the catastrophic seems ordinary. Some of these catastrophes are human in origin, others tectonic; regardless of source they reflect the inescapable link between these people and that place. Angelenos at times would have loved to escape that bond, Sarah Elkind notes, not least during the 1940s when the southland's vast oil deposits were targeted for the war effort. In the preceding decades, when the first strikes occurred, the community and corporations battled over their relative rights and responsibilities, and gains and losses. The city council swung between supporting anti-drilling measures and green lighting development, political behavior that became harder to maintain or justify in Pearl Harbor's wake. Still, as many of these projects were slated in residential neighborhoods, grassroots resistance could clash with an ambivalent city hall's desires to accede to the federal government's demands. As locals debated what the public good consisted of and who had the power to define it, the president and executive branch, along with major petroleum corporations, attempted to squelch the city's political process by claiming that wartime emergency overrode democratic dialog; patriotism trumped politics. This would not be the last time, Elkind cautions, that the federal government would wrap natural-resource policy in the flag.

The development of postwar ski resort communities was also something of a con job. William Philpott, in his examination of the marketing strategies that Vail Associates employed to build, then sell, the idea of a "Plastic Bavaria" in the American Rockies, argues that the construction of an instant town was akin to that era's packaging of Disneyland and shopping malls: in each case, consumers were lured by the prospect of an exotic experience that could not be replicated anywhere else; in buying into the notion that they could get away from it all at an exclusive resort, they were participating in the broader forces transforming contemporary culture. This was of particular significance in the West: high-country tourism, and the popular environmentalism that went along with it, became a key marker of the region's transition away from resource extraction to a service-based economy. But not all recreation took place far from the asphalt jungle. In the 1970s, San Franciscans brought to life what Andrew Kirk describes as an "alternative vision of pragmatic technologically enthusiastic environmentalism," aimed at urban New Age Americans. The brainchild of Stewart Brand and other creative figures revolving around the *Whole Earth Catalog,* this protomovement sought to harmonize ecological sensitivities with a love of technology, design, and urban recreation. Rather than head off to the woods, Brand and his cohorts wanted folks to go to a city park, and there revel in an innovative form of play, which they dubbed New Games. At its unveiling in October 1973, the New Games Tournament drew more than 6,000 participants in a valley across the bay from San Francisco. There, they balanced on beams while others tried to knock them off with gunny sacks; they learned the just-devised rules for "Caterpillar," "Planet Pass," and "Orbit," or piled into "Earth Ball" activities, in which the crowd shoved, chased, pulled, lifted, and otherwise moved the object with no point other than to have a blast. By establishing tentative links between "alternative sports, environmentalism, and urban social activism," New Games placed itself at the heart of a debate about the character of modern environmental culture at a time of rapid urbanization; its festive spirit suggested that the first step to restoring a more robust connection to our home communities was to reclaim our more playful selves.

This declaration of interdependence might seem to be a typical West Coast conceit: only in San Francisco, and its peer cities, was it possible to dream up a form of recreation that liberated the soul and society; only in these more laid-back environs could a new urban society be conceived. This assertion contains some Turnerian overtones: even after the closing of the frontier, the West's creative and democratic impulse lived on in the very cities that the great historian was convinced had signaled its demise. The West could not be the East.

Joel Tarr would concur: growing up in the dense, compact, noisy, industrial landscape of northern New Jersey, he confirms, made it difficult to embrace postwar western urbanism; he never felt comfortable as a student or professor in Tucson and Los Angeles, built as they were around automobility, suburban sprawl, and far-flung commercial nodes, linked together by high-speed highways. By 1967, Tarr had made his way back to the world of his parents, studying the industrial revolution's devastating environmental consequences in Pittsburgh and elsewhere, just as these archetypes of an older urban economy lost out to the new hubs of Sunbelt prosperity.

What Tarr left behind, Hal Rothman moved toward, finding in western cities a dynamism that matched his own. The energy and pulse of his adopted Las Vegas convinced him that he had seen the future—and that it worked. "A look down Las Vegas Boulevard, more widely known as the 'World Famous Las Vegas Strip,'" he asserted in the first sentences of *Neon Metropolis*, "revealed the triumph of post-industrial capitalism, information, and experience over its industrial predecessor. Billions of dollars from the world financial markets have been fashioned into a long line of multicolored casinos that lit the night sky. This spectacle of postmodernism, a combination of light and dark that owes nothing to its surroundings and leaves meaning in the eye of the beholder, is one of the largest private investments in public art anywhere." Its excess enthralled him because he recognized its historical importance: Las Vegas "produces no tangible goods of any significance, yet generates billions of dollars annually in revenue. Here is the first city of the twenty-first century."

Its putative preeminence led him to dismiss all comers: while visiting Minnesota, he made a point of stopping at the Mall of America, touted as the "biggest shopping center in the world." He left within minutes, reporting later that it reminded him of "a bad county fair," banal in its pretension, flavorless in its design. The genius of the Vegas Strip, by contrast, lay in its ability to transport the consumer. "You are never just shopping in Las Vegas. You are always making yourself into something new," he affirmed, which meant that in this once-minor oasis "[e]ntertainment and shopping have become the same thing. It is no longer about the goods but the way you acquire them." So saying, he situated the twenty-first century urban West at the nexus of desire, consumption, and experience; placed its service economies at the center of a postmodern culture; and asserted that these forces defined the region's site and situation, its present and future. This, he might have concluded with characteristic bluntness, is what the West has become.[11]

Notes

1. Clive Sinclair, *Clive Sinclair's True Tales of the Wild West* (New York: Picador, 2007); Tom Shippey, "Cowboys and Cowboys," *Times Literary Supplement,* July 11, 2008, 19; Rick Bass, *Why I Came West: A Memoir* (New York: Houghton Mifflin, 2008).

2. Frederick Jackson Turner, "The Significance of the Frontier in American History," in *Frontier in American History* (New York: Henry Holt and Company, 1921), 1–3.

3. Ibid., 3.

4. Char Miller, "Proving Ground: Richard Harding Davis in the American West," *Southwest Review* 90 (1), 2005, 13–28; Richard Harding Davis, *The West From a Car-Window,* edited by Char Miller (Dallas: DeGolyer Library & William P. Clements Center for Southwestern Studies, 2006).

5. Richard Wade, *The Urban Frontier: The Rise of Western Cities, 1790–1830* (Cambridge: Harvard University Press, 1959); Joel Tarr, ed., *Devastation and Renewal: An Environmental History of Pittsburgh and its Region* (Pittsburgh: University of Pittsburgh Press, 2005); William Cronon, *Nature's Metropolis: Chicago and the Great West* (New York: W. W. Norton, 1991); Gary Brechin, *Imperial City: Urban Power, Earthly Ruin* (Berkeley: University of California Press, 2006); Robert M. Fogelson, *Fragmented Metropolis: Los Angeles, 1850–1930* (Berkeley: University of California Press, 1993); Matthew Klingle, *Emerald City: An Environmental History of Seattle* (New Haven: Yale University Press, 2007).

6. David M. Kennedy, "Can the West Lead Us To A Better Place?" *Stanford,* May/June 2008, 47–53.

7. John M. Findlay, *Magic Lands: Western Cityscapes and American Culture After 1940* (Berkeley: University of California Press, 1992).

8. Char Miller, "Sunbelt Texas," in Robert Calvert and Walter Buenger, eds., *Texas Through Time* (College Station: Texas A&M University Press, 1991), 279–309. David Lodge, *Changing Places* (New York: Penguin, 1979).

9. Hal K. Rothman, *Playing the Odds: Las Vegas and the Modern West* (Albuquerque: University of New Mexico Press, 2007); Hal K. Rothman, *Neon Metropolis: How Las Vegas Started the Twenty-First Century* (New York: Routledge, 2002); Hal K. Rothman and Mike Davis, eds., *The Grit Beneath the Glitter: Tales from the Real Las Vegas* (Berkeley: University of California Press, 2002).

10. Hal K. Rothman, *Reopening the American West* (Tucson: University of Arizona Press, 1998), x.

11. Rothman, *Neon Metropolis,* xi; Rothman, *Playing the Odds,* 5–56.

Land

Sweetening the Urban Marketplace

California's Hawaiian Outpost

JESSICA TEISCH

In 1921, Elwood Mead, professor at the University of California and chair of California's Land Settlement Board, received a call from George P. Cooke, secretary of the Hawaiian Homes Commission (HHC). Born of an act of U.S. Congress, the HHC intended to resettle native Hawaiians on government land. By the early 1900s, it had become clear that only remedial measures could resurrect the "vanishing" Hawaiian race. HHC leaders believed that settling Hawaiians in agricultural communities on home lands would create a new yeoman—and more American—class of farmers that would offset the influx of Asian labor. Cooke wished to draw on Mead's land settlement expertise around the world and develop suitable lands for Hawaiian settlement.

The need to resettle native Hawaiians evolved from conditions set in place by California's interest in Hawaii two decades earlier—not only in annexation in 1898, but also in the profits that could accrue from a thriving sugar industry. Pulling Hawaii into a global economy via American imperialism meant growing sugarcane on an unprecedented scale; developing sophisticated irrigation, production, transportation, and marketing systems; hiring foreign labor; and addressing the native Hawaiian question. Californians facilitated the entry of Hawaii into a global economy and expanded their own Pacific sphere, but not without certain incongruities, including the creation of a poor, urban class of Hawaiians.

On August 24, 1876, a steamer from San Francisco docked at Oahu. The ship carried the message that President Ulysses S. Grant had signed the Reciprocity Treaty between Hawaii and the U.S. It also carried Claus Spreckels, a wealthy San Francisco sugar refiner, to Hawaii for the first time. Over the next decade, Spreckels built a sugar empire that tied Hawaii's commercial and political future to Californian capital, technology, markets, and expertise.[1]

The connection between rural and urban landscapes has been well explored in both theoretical works and monographs; one of the best iterations is William Cronon's *Nature's Metropolis* (1991). In it, Cronon explains the relationship between Chicago and its hinterlands through the exploitation of nature's commodities, which fed the region's burgeoning nineteenth-century industries—grain, lumber, and meat. Similarly, San Francisco capitalists linked its growing urban markets to the exploitation of nature, leading to the economic and social transformation of its Far West hinterlands, intricately connecting city and country, and forever changing the landscapes of both.

The Hawaiian Islands, located in the Pacific Ocean approximately 2,000 miles west of San Francisco, comprise eight principal islands ranging in size from 45 to 4,030 square miles. Made up almost entirely of lava flows, the land provides fertile soils that support sugarcane, a giant-stemmed perennial grass. Although most of the islands are subtropical, the climate ranges from tropical to almost arctic where mountains rise above 10,000 feet. The annual rainfall varies between 20 and 400 inches. One third of the archipelago is arid for almost the entire year, making irrigation a necessity for large-scale sugarcane cultivation.[2]

American interest in Hawaii began in the 1820s, when American whalers created a commercial outpost on the islands and Christian missionaries started to populate the islands. Not wishing to invest in the islands until they had implemented their Western ideas about law and property rights, Americans converted the Hawaiian Kingdom into a constitutional monarchy in 1840.[3] The 1876 Reciprocity Treaty promoted Hawaiian sugar by allowing its entry (as well as that of rice) duty free into the U.S. It in effect dedicated full government support for Hawaii's fledgling sugar industry, made it a one-crop economy, and attracted direct investment by Californians, who viewed the islands as a commercial and strategic gateway to Asia. Proximity to the Pacific Coast and efficient ocean transport made San Francisco sugar's natural market. The overthrow of the Hawaiian Kingdom and the establishment of the provisional government in 1893, followed by the islands' annexation by the U.S. in 1898, cemented this trend.[4]

Claus Spreckels, one of San Francisco's largest industrialists, became the islands' most influential investor. Born in Germany in 1828, he moved to California in 1856. With only one sugar manufacturer in San Francisco, Spreckels found the city an open market. In 1864, he incorporated the Bay Sugar Refinery, the first of his several successful sugar ventures that linked Hawaiian sugar production to California markets. Three years later, he expanded his operations and founded the California Sugar Refinery.[5]

After studying the process back in Germany, Spreckels designed a new method to make cube sugar, which marked him as the most efficient sugar producer on the West Coast. In 1869, one newspaper reported that Spreckels, by doubling the capacity of his establishment to 250,000 pounds of sugar every ten hours, "had bled his opponents, so freely that he foresaw their early retirement." The California and Hawaiian Sugar Refining Corporation at Crockett, which owned about 60 percent of raw sugar production in the Hawaiian Islands, provided Spreckels's major competition. Both companies depended on continuous shipments of raw sugar from Hawaii.[6]

Certainly without government support, fewer foreigners like Spreckels would find Hawaii a ripe opportunity for investment. He initially opposed the Reciprocity Treaty in the belief that lower or nonexistent tariffs on sugar would hurt his refinery. Working to protect his interests before the treaty went into effect; he traveled to the Hawaiian Islands and contracted with the Hawaiian planters for more than half of the entire production of sugar for the year.[7]

In 1878, like Chicago's capitalists who extended their reach into the Midwest's hinterlands in the nineteenth century, Spreckels—who viewed Hawaii as another Louisiana—returned to the islands and started looking for land on which to develop his sugarcane plantation. By ancient custom, land belonged to conquering chiefs and their constituents, and rights in land were revocable. During the reign of King Kamehameha III (1825–1854), the great *Mahele* of 1848 abolished Hawaii's feudal land system and divided lands among the king, government, and people. But by 1850, Crown lands could be leased or passed into the hands of private owners. Many Hawaiians lost their land as foreigners like Spreckels purchased land outright.[8]

Sugarcane had long been grown on the Hawaiian Islands. When Captain Cook encountered the islands in 1778, he found natives cultivating it in the valleys and lowlands. Until the 1860s, however, primitive technology and limited capital hindered Hawaiian sugar production. By 1875, only 10,000 acres were under sugar cultivation, mainly on Maui.[9]

Spreckels found this island an ideal region for a plantation. Maui spans 760 square miles and consists of two volcanic groups of mountains. Sugarcane, with irrigation, grows well in the volcanic red dirt. Plantations had already developed around the mountain bases. Samuel Alexander and Henry Baldwin—whose East Maui Irrigation Company constructed the island's first major irrigation channel, the Hamakua Ditch, in 1878—founded the first large plantation on East Maui. Other companies had staked claims on the west side. Spreckels planned to outdo these competitors, but two obstacles stood in his way: he owned neither land nor water rights.[10]

Spreckels purchased in 1878 an undivided interest in 16,000 acres of the Waikapu Commons and leased 24,000 acres of the adjacent Wailuku Commons Crown lands. His alliance with King Kalakaua and Walter Gibson, a former missionary who had carved out an empire on Lanai and a member of the Hawaiian legislature, was crucial to his acquisition of these Crown lands and his eventual purchase of more. Kalakaua and Gibson instituted an unprecedented regime of political corruption based on favors: Spreckels lent Kalakaua money and the king and Gibson, in turn, helped Spreckels increase his holdings. Later, in a corrupt deal, the legislature granted Crown lands to Spreckels in fee, which allowed him to develop his plantation without fears about titles to the land or the short period of his lease.[11]

Spreckels then applied for water rights, which, at that time, were owned by the kingdom and adhered to the land. Water could, however, be leased or sold separately, subject to other vested rights. Spreckels first unsuccessfully petitioned the ministry for the desired water rights. But the king, already in debt to Spreckels and dissatisfied with the cabinet, dismissed its members that night and replaced them with politicians more sympathetic to Spreckels's enterprise. The San Franciscan made the king a generous financial gift and loan. The new cabinet granted water privileges to Spreckels for thirty years, rationalizing that if the government could not afford to undertake large water projects, private capitalists should. This water deal gave Spreckels a few lasting and not altogether flattering monikers, including "the sugar king of Hawaii," "the power behind the throne," and "the maker and breaker of cabinets."[12]

After he had acquired land and water, Spreckels incorporated his holdings. In 1878, together with Herman Schussler—chief engineer of California's notorious water monopoly, Spring Valley Water Works—and other businessmen, Spreckels organized the Californian-owned Hawaiian Commercial Company. In 1880, he formed a partnership with William G. Irwin. Irwin & Company became one of the leading sugar agencies in the kingdom, serving as financier, merchant, exporter, importer, and marketer of Hawaiian Commercial Company's sugar. It also directly controlled one-third of the sugar crop on the islands and purchased the remaining two-thirds from other planters. In 1882, the Hawaiian Commercial Company reorganized as the Hawaiian Commercial & Sugar Company (HC&S) and joined the ranks of the "Big Five" sugar companies, which owned or controlled most of Hawaii's land, plantations, water, power, mills, transportation, and refineries—as well as exerted undue influence in financial and political matters.[13]

Spreckels's next step entailed building an extensive irrigation system that would meet the high water requirements for growing sugarcane. Employing white and Chinese laborers, Schussler harnessed the rivers of the wetter side of the island and brought water to the drier, western side with sixty-five miles of canals and tunnels. When completed, the thirty-mile long "Haiku ditch" delivered fifty million gallons of water daily, irrigating twenty times as much land as had been possible under previous methods.[14]

Spreckels not only revolutionized irrigation methods, but modernized sugar production in every way. His namesake plantation and company town, Spreckelsville, became a successful experiment in industrial agriculture. Deemed the largest sugar estate in the world by 1892, Spreckelsville spread over forty thousand acres and used only the most modern methods and machinery. In anticipation of high yields, Spreckels employed two men from San Francisco's Risdon Iron Works to design a sugar mill with a capacity of processing twenty tons of sugar each ten-hour day. Electric lighting, the first of its kind on Maui, facilitated plantation operations. Within ten years, Spreckels added three more mills and mechanized the sugar production process, from hauling cane to the mill to extracting the juice, reducing it to syrup, and producing dried sugar grains. The raw sugar was then packed and shipped to Spreckels's refinery in San Francisco.[15]

Just as the railroads revolutionized the Midwest's hinterlands, so too was transportation key to Spreckels's enterprise. Spreckels, however, developed his systems on a much smaller, local scale that aided his endeavors rather than benefiting the larger populace. Plantation transportation had previously consisted of mules and oxen. To reduce the costs of hauling sugarcane to the mills, foreign laborers constructed a narrow-gauge railroad through Spreckelsville. By the early 1880s, twenty miles of iron track ran at full capacity, connecting with the Kahului Railroad, a corporation whose stock HC&S controlled. This line transported the processed sugar to Maui's major port, where Spreckels owned his own landings, storehouses, and general store. In 1881, Spreckels and his sons organized the Oceanic Steamship Company; their two steamships and nine sailing vessels connected Hawaiian sugar to markets in America, Australia, and New Zealand, and effectively monopolized Hawaiian sugar traffic around the world.[16]

No matter how innovative, Spreckels's plantation could not have survived without a labor hierarchy based on race. Labor grew scarcer each year. Disease and introduced commodities, including liquor, brought about the destruction of the native economy, one based on subsistence cultivation and some interisland trade. Between 1778 and 1876, the Hawaiian population decreased from about 300,000 to 50,000. Planters tried to secure steady work from Hawaiians, but to many, Hawaiians seemed lazy or unwilling to work. The itinerant Mark Twain, visiting the islands in 1866, noted that, "the Kanaka race is passing away. Cheap labor had to be procured by some means or other."[17]

Because they couldn't rely on the free market—and since slavery would never curry public favor—planters sought contract labor, which became the engine of Hawaiian sugar plantations. The Royal Hawaiian Agricultural Society, founded in 1850 to represent planters' interests, and the Bureau of Immigration, formed in 1864, initiated the immigration of agricultural labor from China, Korea, Japan, the mainland U.S., Puerto Rico, Portugal, Germany, Norway, and Oceania. Between 1852 and 1900, foreign immigration steadily increased. First the Chinese and then the Japanese arrived. Portuguese, Germans, Norwegians, and Filipinos followed. After the Reciprocity Treaty, more than 55,000 unskilled immigrant workers entered Hawaii. Chinese labored in the fields; Japanese workers constructed irrigation ditches; and Hawaiians worked as teamsters. The plantation system could not have succeeded without this cheap labor supply and the division of labor it allowed.[18]

Yet squalid working conditions, feelings of tenancy, and low wages prompted many laborers to leave the plantation after their contracts had expired to seek better employment in the cities or acquire land of their own, as some Japanese did. "Sugar is still, and will long continue to be, King in Hawaii," one prominent sugar booster argued, "but it will take breadth of spirit and progressive intelligence in handling the labor question."[19] Upon visiting the islands, Frederick H. Newell, Director of the U.S. Reclamation Service, agreed. The dwindling number of laborers willing to work in the fields, compounded by the increasing demand for labor, posed "an almost impassable barrier" to the lifeblood of the sugar industry.[20] Hawaii's dependence upon a single industry, which rested upon the existence of a protective tariff and continuous influx of foreign labor, did not bode well for the continued prosperity of the islands.

The issue of contract labor raised questions on the national, territorial, and personal level. For Spreckels, contract labor related to the big political question of the day: annexation. Spreckels, who saw contract labor as the only viable system, believed that whites could not—and Hawaiians would not—work in the cane fields. If planters could not hire cheap labor, the plantations would fail. Spreckels thus advocated two unpopular positions: that Hawaii restore the monarchy, or that California annex it as part of its own state.[21]

The presence of contract or migratory labor, which formed the majority of Hawaii's population by the 1880s, posed its own problems. Producing what Newell called "an artificial condition of social and business life not conducive to settlement by whites," it stymied the ideal of a white agricultural class, intermediate between the sugar-owning corporations and the landless, migratory labor. Newell recommended dividing up the public lands and distributing them in small tracts to white citizens. Every possible effort, he concluded, "should be made by public and private interests to put upon the land the best obtainable men, who will live upon small farms, cultivate the soil and become independent, self-supporting citizens."[22]

Newell's dream of a society of small landholders did not, of course, mesh with Spreckels's vision. By 1885, Spreckels had reached the peak of his power in Hawaii. As the islands' largest sugar producer, he controlled almost the entire crop. He dominated the carrying trade between the islands and the Pacific Coast and exerted major political influence.[23] Together with his San Francisco partners and engineers, he had reengineered Maui's social, economic, political, and natural landscape and tied it neatly to San Francisco's commercial interests and its urban marketplace. His innovations forged many links in a vast industrial chain: the Spreckelsville plantation; the sugar agency of Irwin & Company; and the Oceanic Steamship Company.

Spreckels had founded the California Sugar Refinery in 1867, and by the late 1870s his Hawaiian plantation was sending it a steady stream of raw sugar. By 1881, his refinery sprawled over six square blocks in San Francisco, adjacent to the Southern Pacific Railroad tracks and San Francisco Bay. The company employed five hundred men—mostly of European origin, given the Exclusion Acts of the 1880s, which limited Chinese immigration—and produced nearly one hundred thousand tons of sugar annually. Throughout the decade, Spreckels patented new methods of making cube sugar, crushed sugar, powdered sugar, fine crushed sugar, and dry granulated sugar. In 1887, he reorganized the California Sugar Refinery as the Western Sugar Company, which, through rail and steam power, transported the refined sugar to major ports around the world.[24]

Yet in the mid-1880s, with his California refinery thriving, Spreckels's power started to ebb in Hawaii. Hawaiian planters, rebelling against Spreckels's monopoly, formed their own company, the California and Hawaiian Sugar Refinery Corporation. It located its headquarters in San Francisco and its refinery in nearby Crockett, and subsequent expansions made it one of the largest refineries in the world.[25]

Spreckels also suffered financial setbacks and a break with Kalakaua in 1886 over the negotiation of a large loan. A few years later, management problems and the deterioration of facilities at the Spreckelsville plantation weakened his grasp on Hawaiian sugar. In 1898, Spreckels's earlier fear that Hawaiian annexation would bring about the demise of the contract labor system throughout Hawaii was finally realized. He then lost control of the HC&S to the Maui sugar planters, Alexander & Baldwin. Spreckels eventually abandoned Hawaiian sugar for California-grown beet sugar, although other Californians continued to play prominent roles in developing the Hawaiian Islands through the nineteenth century and beyond.[26]

Yet despite vast economic growth, the sugar industry engendered troubling social inequities and raised heated debate over the future of white—and Hawaiian— settlement on the islands. These tensions led George P. Cooke—secretary of the HHC in Honolulu, millionaire rancher on Molokai, and former territorial senator— to contact Elwood Mead in December 1921. "I have been deeply interested in your book, *Helping Men Own Farms*," he wrote. "I firmly believe that the industrial development of Hawaii can be put on a more permanent basis, and one that will be more American."[27] The division and loss of native Hawaiian lands at the behest of the sugar industry, as well as the decline of traditional native livelihoods, had created a poor, urban class of Hawaiians. Cooke, like others before him, believed that settling Hawaiians on government-owned homesteads offered a way to simul- taneously "Americanize" the islands, preserve the Hawaiian race, and idealize an old, subsistence form of the Hawaiian economy while implementing commercial agriculture. Yet HHC home building, which used race as a motivating factor, proved to be more powerful in rhetoric than in reality.

At the time of annexation, Hawaii had ceded roughly 1.8 million acres of land to the U.S. Given the nation's interest in sugar growing, returning Hawaiians to the land was always favored over returning land to the Hawaiians. The HHC, in the spirit of other land settlement programs around the world in the late nineteenth and early twentieth century, intended to help native Hawaiians regain possession of Hawaiian Kingdom government and Crown lands. Once settled on government land, the HHC hoped that Hawaiians would make better livings than they would as wage workers and tenement dwellers in Honolulu and Hilo.[28]

Like Mead's land settlement plans in other parts of the world—such as Cali- fornia and Australia, where he had designed scientific, economically viable, state- run irrigation colonies—HHC fell short of its goals. While cloaked in humanitarian motives, the HHC was meant to assure stability and control over the public lands while undermining the power of native Hawaiians. The large sugar planters, for example, fearing the loss of productive public lands that they were leasing from the government, inserted a provision into the HHC Act that excluded the most fertile and commercially valuable island lands from settlement.[29]

To further darken prospects for Hawaiian rehabilitation, controversy surrounded the definition of "Hawaiian." An early bill stated that people with one thirty-second Hawaiian blood could apply for home lands. But the final act restricted eligibility for application to these lands to descendents with at least one-half Hawaiian blood, thereby dramatically decreasing the potential number of applicants leasing Hawai- ian home lands. It also confused traditional Hawaiian understandings of rank and genealogy. As a palliative measure, the HHC Act provided that 30 percent of the annual receipts from the leasing of sugar lands would be loaned to Hawaiian natives for homes, livestock, and improvements on their leased lands. Yet the final version of the act also decreased the duration of the leases from nine hundred and ninety-nine to ninety-nine years. What originally started as a Hawaiian rehabilitation scheme became little more than a way to prevent the breakup of large sugar estates.[30]

By the early 1900s, conditions had worsened for native Hawaiians. Sugar interests altered traditional land ownership and tenure patterns, threatening Hawaiians' taro-growing subsistence economy. In 1909, whites controlled more than half of the privately owned land in Hawaii; part Hawaiians, Hawaiians, and Asians together controlled only about a sixth. The majority of Hawaiians lived in new urban slums around Honolulu and Hilo, and their population was rapidly declining. In 1919, three years before Mead's first visit to the Hawaiian Islands, the number of "full-blooded" Hawaiians had dwindled to approximately forty thousand.[31]

The Hawaiian government had tried to settle Hawaiians on the soil prior to the HHC Act. After annexation, the U.S. Congress did not apply its extensive homesteading laws to the territory since an 1895 Hawaiian Land Act, which opened up public lands to native Hawaiians with 999-year leases, supposedly provided sufficient means to settle the small farmer. Many Hawaiians, however, could not meet the lease restrictions; others sold their land to non-Hawaiians. While government lands had been subdivided into small blocks of five to fifty acres and sold on a lottery basis, they often left the national trust upon terms more attractive to land speculators than to well-intentioned farmers. Other acts further alienated Hawaiian people from their land.[32]

The HHC emerged out of Hawaiians' desire for revitalization. The vision of "restoration through the land" resulted in the passage of the HHC Act, signed by President Warren G. Harding in July 1921. If the Hawaiian people, an HHC executive reported in 1922, "might again be placed upon the lands, where they could till the soil and form the nucleus of an independent citizen farmer class, and become self-supporting and raise healthy, happy families and become home-owners, new blood would be gradually infused into the race."[33]

The HHC Act designated, for its first five years, lands on Molokai and Hawaii for the return of native Hawaiians. It provided between 20 and 80 acres of agricultural land, 100 to 500 acres of first-class pasture lands, and 250 to 1,000 second-class pasture lands—a total of approximately 200,000 acres on Hawaii and Molokai combined—for each community. Settlers could lease lands for ninety-nine years with an annual rental for each tract of $1.00 per year.[34]

At the end of June 1922, Elwood Mead visited the Hawaiian Islands to investigate the rehabilitation project. After meeting with the HHC in Honolulu, Mead visited

Molokai and inspected the homesteads, gardens, and agricultural lands on which a few families had already settled. Seeing "nothing but commercial feudalism"—with Hawaiians and immigrant groups the pawns of the big sugar planters—he expressed pessimism about the entire project. His final report outlined recommendations and further plans for Hawaiian rehabilitation.[35]

One of the key sites for this social experiment occurred on Molokai, the "lonely isle," which covers an area of 261 square miles. It rises in the east nearly five thousand feet to a forested, rain-drenched peak. The arid, west end of the island rises only to about one thousand feet. The rich, red land between these peaks forms a saddle-like plateau about five hundred feet above sea level. It was this plateau that was to be homesteading country for Hawaiian natives. By 1900, Molokai's native population had dwindled to one thousand. This number, exclusive of the leper colony founded in 1864, remained stable. Nonetheless, the HHC hoped to repopulate and carve from the island a group of self-laboring Hawaiian cultivators.[36]

The rehabilitation process began in 1922 with the Kalanianaole settlement. The HHC chose homesteaders on the basis of at least 50 percent blood lineage and character. Many arrived from Honolulu, where they had held various jobs. In 1922, the HHC developed twenty-two farm lots, thirty-three residential lots, and twenty-five hundred acres of community pasture and grazing land. HHC experts completed surveys for roads, piped in water for irrigation, established a demonstration farm, and started to clear the land.[37]

The Kalanianaole settlement grew from modest beginnings. "No attempt is made," an HHC report announced, "to provide a small sugar plantation, or hand over a tract to be cultivated under the direction of a head luna while the homesteader sits on his lanai and smokes and sleeps." Instead, as in Mead's California settlements at Delhi and Durham, the purpose of the first Molokai settlement was to "HELP the home builder HELP HIMSELF." Yet since the government had not yet completed the colony's infrastructure by 1922, despite Cooke's protests, homesteaders moved to Kalanianaole under extreme hardship.[38]

The virulently anti-Asian Mead tied this ideal of self-labor to citizenship and nationality. "It is realized by practically every civilized country of the world today that proper settling of its people upon the land and rooting patriotism in the soil is the political and social problem that is most vital to the welfare of a nation," he reported in the Honolulu Star Bulletin.[39] The HHC implicitly advertised homesteading as a national imperative, one that implied the fulfillment of certain social, political, and racial ideals.

"[R]ooting patriotism in the soil" meant replacing traditional governments and cultures with American ways. Annexation in 1898 made American imperialism a fait accompli. Still, "rooting patriotism" did not mean forcibly displacing native Hawaiians, since Hawaiians were viewed as a new Hawaiian-American race. They inhabited a racial category that could, with intermixing, conform to the American one. And, with such low numbers, assimilation would occur rapidly. Nor did "rooting patriotism in the soil" mean leaving Hawaiians to their own devices. Hawaiian resettlement could be used to mold a new class of citizen farmers who would offset the influence of large numbers of Asian landholders. But only the HHC and government would bring to Hawaiians' attention the "true relation of land to the national life," Mead warned.[40]

Mead, working in the spirit of American Progressive reform, urged the Molokai settlements to follow sound business and scientific practices. First, he wanted agricultural experts, as they had in his California colonies, to run the settlements. These men would then transform homesteaders—plantation workers or previous wage earners living in Honolulu and Hilo—into skilled cultivators. He also wished to adhere to the basic principle that had guided his Closer Settlement policies in Australia: limiting the size of farms and homesteads. Individuals could increase their holdings as they gained more experience.[41]

Finally, Mead warned that one place could not be fully applied as a model for the next. California's Durham and Delhi settlements could not exclusively serve as a model for the HHC. Nor could the HHC's Molokai experiments be replicated exactly throughout the rest of the islands. Molokai's good water supplies, for example, made the region well suited for a homestead colony. Yet Molokai was "no guide" to future settlements because of the vast discrepancy in rainfall throughout the islands and their varied transportation systems and markets.[42]

With Molokai homesteading underway, Mead visited some of the HHC's projects on the island of Hawaii. His trip revealed mixed results. The Waiakea homesteads disappointed him. While a good road built by the territorial government passed through them, nearly every field showed neglect. The residence lots, by contrast, contained neat, attractive gardens. "Inquiries showed," Mead wrote, "that men who were subject to temptation, becoming dissipated in town, were leading orderly, sober lives."[43] On a visit to a dairy farm, Mead praised the beautiful herd of cattle and modern cream separators, capping machines, and churns. But when he interviewed a Chinese-Hawaiian who resided on the same land, Mead realized that irrigated cultivation had halted completely.[44]

Despite the variations that Mead witnessed in Molokai and Hawaii, he felt that the HHC's project had every chance of succeeding if they met certain conditions. The settlements needed small, irrigated tracts, hard-working settlers, government support, good transportation and markets, and most importantly, a capitalist mentality. After Mead's optimistic assessment of the HHC's future, the Honorable W. R. Farrington, chairman of the HHC, concluded that Mead's visit had been "of great value to the Territory."[45]

His confidence was premature. In early 1923, the HHC again called on the Californian for advice with the flailing settlements. Mead returned in April to Hawaii to examine the progress of the Kalanianaole and Palaau settlements on Molokai, identify solutions to the problems that plagued them, and help design future settlements.

The problems that the HHC homesteads faced resembled those in other newly developing regions—problems of technology, markets, transportation, and labor. Reliable irrigation in Kalanianaole, despite miles of piping, presented the first challenge due to mineral buildup. While the region's extremely fertile soil produced fruit and vegetables and supported cattle, hogs, and poultry, the unreliable water supply and infestation of crops by pests and diseases undermined even the most planned agricultural enterprises.[46]

Markets posed another dilemma. Although entering the Honolulu market was possible, small Asian homesteaders and truck farming glutted Molokai homesteaders' potential markets. Small markets at Kaunakakai, local ranches, and plantation camps provided few outlets and made systematic marketing difficult. Despite a decent road to the pier and a regular freighter service to Honolulu, one HHC employee complained that, "Where homesteaders have quit producing, it has not been their lack of interest, but rather the uncertainty of getting a return."[47]

Most troubling of all was the homesteaders' growing reliance on Molokai's pineapple companies. Many Hawaiians who could not make ends meet leased their holdings to large pineapple growers. The HHC's annual reports through 1927 show the homesteaders "working hard and enthusiastically." But once the pineapple companies started renting the homesteaders' land and hiring the homesteaders for wages, the self-labor ideal deteriorated. Other Hawaiian homesteaders employed Filipinos, Koreans, and Japanese to work in their own fields.

These problems worsened as the Hawaiian subsistence economy transitioned into a commercial one. One Hawaiian mourned that, "[Our] older system of cooperative work broke down almost entirely.... A commercial attitude grew up among the families, to the great regret of many of the people." One settler more sympathetic to earning a profit asked: "Why should we work, when we don't see the money?—it goes into other people's pockets." To the HHC, this attitude suggested a deep-seated antipathy towards work. One homesteader summed up general sentiment by asking, "What do you think I'd look like walking behind a plow?"[48]

The issue of self-labor related, once again, to the thorny racial issues. By 1905, more than 44,000 Chinese and 111,000 Japanese had immigrated to Hawaii to work in the sugarcane fields.[49] Asian immigrants competed with Hawaiians, push-ing them into menial positions or unemployment. While rehabilitating Hawaiians on the land presented a feasible solution to this influx of foreigners, identifying them as Americans raised complicated issues. Even though the HHC attempted to transform Hawaiians into American-style farmers, whites were still seen as a far more advanced race. Hawaiians, one visitor to Hawaii noted, "still lived in the stone age, knowing no metals, yet governmentally developed along feudal lines to a degree comparable to that of England a thousand years ago."[50] Even after annexa-tion, Hawaiians—technically Americans—held an indeterminate racial position.

Mead wisely sidestepped the issue of the Hawaiian race by voicing his nation-alist principles: "[N]o race that does not intermarry and mingle freely with the whites, is or can be a good American. It is not a question of political but social and economic domination."[51] Assimilation could solve the Hawaiian race problem. Many Hawaiians intermarried with whites and thus became more "white" them-selves, joining the increasingly powerful white society on the islands.[52] Hawai-ians also commingled with other groups, particularly the Japanese. "It seems safe to conclude," a U.S. government official claimed, "that the ultimate Hawaiian-American . . . will be something near one-third Japanese, one-fifth Filipino, one-ninth Portuguese, one-tenth Hawaiian, one-twelfth Chinese, [and] one-fifteenth Anglo-Saxon."[53] Yet as far as the HHC was concerned, such interracial mixing, which diluted the 50 percent native blood required to apply for HHC land, impeded its rehabilitation efforts.

Despite these issues, Hawaiian settlement proceeded. In 1924, the HHC opened more homesteads for settlement on Molokai. By 1924, 287 men, women, and children lived on HHC's Molokai lands. Although these settlements revealed the difficulties of putting city dwellers on farmland, Mead concluded in 1927 that the results of the HHC "have been so encouraging that the practically unanimous vote of the Legislature in favor of continuing this experiment seems justified." By 1929, 378 allotments out of 925 applications for land had been made on the islands of Molokai and Hawaii—a large increase given the number of those eligible for land.[54]

Despite Mead's optimism, the Molokai colonies floundered for many years. As Hawaiians intermarried, the 50 percent blood quota also decreased the num-ber of applicants to home lands. Yet the HHC continued its work, eventually fold-ing into the Department of Hawaiian Home Lands under the jurisdiction of the U.S. government.

Hawaii joined California's—indeed, the world's—economy in ways that con-firmed how capitalist growth took precedence over social equality, and how racial motives played into industrial development and agricultural settlement. From Spreckels's Maui plantation to Mead's consultations with the HHC, the history of the Hawaiian Islands in the late nineteenth and early twentieth century reveals how commercial development generated new racial hierarchies and inequities, while linking together the urban centers with the far hinterlands' resource exploitation. The modern yeoman ideal that Californians so persuasively, if not always successfully, exported around the world had little relevance to Hawaii's agricultural development and its indigenous peoples.

Notes

1. Jacob Adler, *Claus Spreckels: The Sugar King in Hawaii* (Honolulu: University of Hawaii Press, 1966), 3; Jacob Adler, "The Maui Land Deal: A Chapter in Claus Spreckels' Hawaiian Career," *Agricultural History* XXXIX.3 (July 1965): 155.

2. F. H. Newell, *Hawaii: Its Natural Resources and Opportunities for Home-making* (Washington, DC: Government Printing Office, 1909), 8–16; Doak C. Cox, "Water Development for Hawaiian Sugar Cane Irrigation," *The Hawaiian Planters' Record* LIV (1954): 175–80; L. H. Herschler, "Irrigation in the Hawaiian Islands," TS, Water Resources Center Archives, University of California, Berkeley, 1–9; M. M. O'Shaughnessy, "Irrigation Works in the Hawaiian Islands," *Transactions of the American Society of Civil Engineers* 54 (1905): 129–30.

3. Adler, *Claus Spreckels*, 16–17.

4. Sylvester K. Stevens, *American Expansion in Hawaii, 1842–1898* (New York: Russell & Russell, 1968); Hugh Craig, President of the Chamber of Commerce, San Francisco, in *California Illustrated. Hawaiian Edition* (1897–1898), 3.

5. William Woodrow Cordray, "Claus Spreckels of California." PhD Dissertation (University of Southern California, 1955), 2–16; "The California Sugar Refinery, Its Founder and His Work," *The San Francisco Merchant*, May 27, 1881, 9.

6. Quote from "The California Sugar Refiner, Its Founder and His Work," 9; California and Hawaiian Sugar Refining Corporation, *Something about Sugar* (San Francisco: California and Hawaiian Sugar Refining Corporation, 1925), 13.

7. Adler, *Claus Spreckels*, 3, 12; Carol Wilcox, *Sugar Water: Hawaii's Plantation Ditches* (Honolulu: University of Hawaii Press, 1996), 12–13; Cordray, "Claus Spreckels," 32–36.

8. "Spring and the Grocery Trade as viewed by leading businessmen," *San Francisco Weekly Journal of Commerce*, March 10, 1881, 6; Jacob Adler, "Maui Land Deal," 155–56.

9. California and Hawaiian Sugar Refining Corporation, *Something about Sugar*, 6, 9; W. P. Alexander, *The Irrigation of Sugar Cane in Hawaii* (Honolulu: Experiment Station of the Hawaiian Sugar Planters' Association, 1923), 1; "Sugar-Refining, The Early History of Sugar-making," San Francisco *Commercial Herald*, Jan. 15, 1880.

10. "The Sugar Industry of the Hawaiian Islands," Honolulu *Evening Bulletin*, Industrial Edition, Nov. 1901, 12; Wilcox, *Sugar Water*, 57, 114–16, 122–23; Hawaiian Sugar Planters'

Association, *Story of Sugar in Hawaii* (Honolulu: Hawaiian Sugar Planters' Association, 1926), 16–17; Dan Gutleben, *The Sugar Tramp, 1950, "Hawaiian Issue"* (San Francisco: Bay Cities Duplicating Company, 1950), 5; John W. Vandercook, *King Cane: The Story of Sugar in Hawaii* (New York: Harper & Brothers Publishers, 1939), 66–69.

11. Cordray, "Claus Spreckels," 36; Claus Spreckels, Plaintiff, vs. Hawaiian Commercial and Sugar Company, in the Superior Court of the State of California, in and for the City and County of San Francisco, no. 53,045, p. 2; Wilcox, *Sugar Water,* 56–58; Adler, "Maui Land Deal," 163; Adler, *Claus Spreckels,* 16–19.

12. Newell, *Hawaii,* 25; H. A. Wadsworth, "A Historical Summary of Irrigation in Hawaii," *Hawaiian Planters' Record* XXXVII.3 (Oct. 1933): 131–32; Cordray, "Claus Spreckels," 37–38; quotes from Adler, *Claus Spreckels,* 27.

13. Claus Spreckels, Plaintiff, vs. Hawaiian Commercial and Sugar Company, in the Superior Court of the State of California, in and for the City and County of San Francisco, no. 53,045, p. 2–3; Adler, *Claus Spreckels,* 12–13; Wilcox, *Sugar Water,* 16.

14. Adler, *Claus Spreckels,* 46, 49; Claus Spreckels, Plaintiff, vs. Hawaiian Commercial and Sugar Company, in the Superior Court of the State of California, in and for the City and County of San Francisco, no. 53,045, p. 2; Michael M. O'Shaughnessy, "Irrigation Works in the Hawaiian Islands," 134; Vandercook, *King Cane,* 69–70; Cordray, "Claus Spreckels," 36–39; Bristow Adams, "Sugar Irrigation in Hawaii," *Forestry and Irrigation* IX.3 (March 1903): 125.

15. Hawaiian Sugar Planters' Association, *Story of Sugar in Hawaii,* 58–63; Cordray, "Claus Spreckels," 39–40; Adler, *Claus Spreckels,* 70–71, 77.

16. Jesse C. Condé and Gerald M. Best, *Sugar Trains: Narrow Gauge Rails of Hawaii* (Felton, CA: Glenwood Publishers, 1973), 208–9; "The Sugar Industry of the Hawaiian Islands," 12; Adler, *Claus Spreckels,* 70–77, 105; Claus Spreckels, "Pacific Steamship Line," MS, Bancroft Library; J. D. Spreckels & Bros., *Ports of San Francisco, San Diego, Puget Sound, Portland, and Honolulu* (San Francisco: William C. Brown, 1889), 47.

17. "The Labor Situation in Hawaii." A paper read by Lorrin A. Thurston, before the Social Science Club of Honolulu. Honolulu: The Hawaiian Gazette Co., Ltd., April 1906, 9; Adler, *Claus Spreckels,* 6; quote from Mark Twain, *Letters from Honolulu Written for the Sacramento Union* (Honolulu: Thomas Nickerson, 1939), 51–52.

18. H. P. Baldwin, "The Sugar Industry in Hawaii," *Overland Monthly* XXV.150 (June 1895): 668; Herbert K. Marutani, "Labor-Management Relations in Agriculture: A Study of the Hawaiian Sugar Industry," PhD Dissertation (Honolulu: University of Hawaii, 1970), 11–13, 19–20; Adler, *Claus Spreckels,* 77, 233; Hawaiian Sugar Planters' Association, *Story of Sugar in Hawaii,* 25–32.

19. "The Labor Situation in Hawaii," 13–14, quote from 16.

20. Newell, *Hawaii,* 42.

21. Adler, *Claus Spreckels,* 231–233, 249; Cordray, "Claus Spreckels," 63; Marutani, "Labor-Management Relations in Agriculture," 11–20.

22. Newell, *Hawaii,* quote from 45, 46–47.

23. Cordray, "Claus Spreckels," 51–52.

24. Spring and the Grocery Trade as Viewed by Leading Businessmen," "The California Sugar Refinery, Its Founder and His Work," "The Laying of the Corner Stone," *The Daily Alta San Francisco,* May 29, 1881; "California Sugar Refinery," TS, Bancroft Library, University of California, Berkeley, 1; "The California Sugar Refinery, Its Founder and His Work," 10.

25. Cordray, "Claus Spreckels," 71–75.

26. Wilcox, *Sugar Water,* 114, 122; Condé and Best, *Sugar Trains,* 210; "The Sugar Industry of the Hawaiian Islands," 13; Hawaiian Sugar Planters' Association, *Story of Sugar in Hawaii,* 94; James D. Schuyler, *Report on the Water Supply, the Projected Storage Works, the Proposed Electric Power Development and the Prospective Business of the Wahiawa Water Co. Ltd.* (Los Angeles, 1903); James D. Schuyler, *Culture of Sugar Cane* (Oakland, CA: Jordan & Arnold, Printers, 1889); James D. Schuyler, "Report on Water Development for Oahu Plantation, Apr. 29, 1907," Schuyler 182, Water Resources Center Archives, University of California, Berkeley; "Memoir of James Dix Schuyler," *Transactions of the American Society of Civil Engineers,* 76 (1913), 2243–45; Joseph B. Lippincott, "Report on the Feasibility of Bringing the Waters of the Waiahole, Waikane and Kahana Streams through the Koolau Range to the Lands of the Oahu Sugar Company, Limited," Aug. 19, 1911, Lippincott 42.1, Water Resources Centers Archives, University of California, Berkeley; letters between Lippincott and the Oahu Sugar Company, July 6, 1911 to Jan. 6, 1912, Lippincott 42.2, Water Resources Center Archives; O'Shaughnessy, "Irrigation Works in the Hawaiian Islands," 129–37.

27. George P. Cooke to Elwood Mead, Berkeley, 7 Dec. 1921, carton 1, correspondence between Elwood Mead and Hawaiian Homes Commission, Elwood Mead Papers, Bancroft Library.

28. J. Kehaulani Kauanui, "Rehabilitating the Native: Hawaiian Blood Quantum and the Politics of Race, Citizenship, and Entitlement," PhD Dissertation (University of California, 2000), 3, 5; George Paul Cooke, *Moolelo O Molokai: A Ranch Story of Molokai* (Honolulu: Honolulu Star-Bulletin, 1949), 76; Marylyn Vause, "The Hawaiian Homes Commission Act, 1920: History and Analysis," Master's Thesis, University of Hawaii, 1962, 1.

29. Vause, "Hawaiian Homes Commission Act," 73, 116–17; James R. Kluger, *Turning on Water with a Shovel: The Career of Elwood Mead* (Albuquerque: University of New Mexico Press, 1992), 103–4.

30. Kauanui, "Rehabilitating the Native," 2–6, 46; Kluger, *Turning on Water,* 103–4; Vause, "Hawaiian Homes Commission Act," iv.

31. Kauanui, "Rehabilitating the Native," 85, 102; Alan Murakami, "The Hawaiian Homes Commission Act," in Melody MacKenzie, ed., *Native Hawaiian Rights Handbook* (Honolulu: Native Hawaiian Legal Corporation and the Office of Hawaiian Affairs, 1991), 44.

32. Kauanui, "Rehabilitating the Native," 86, 104; "Hawaiian Board Is Advised by Mead," *Berkeley, CA, Gazette,* July 26, 1922; Vause, "Hawaiian Homes Commission Act," 24–26.

33. Quote from Hawaiian Homes Commission, *Rehabilitation in Hawaii* (Honolulu: Bulletin of the Hawaiian Homes Commission no. 2, 1922), 3.

34. Hawaiian Homes Commission, *Rehabilitation in Hawaii*, 11–15.

35. Quoted in Kluger, *Turning on Water*, 104.

36. Felix M. Keesing, *Hawaiian Homesteading on Molokai* (Honolulu: University of Hawaii Research Publications, vol. I, no. 12, 1936), 25, 27.

37. Keesing, *Hawaiian Homesteading*, 27–28, 67.

38. Quote from Hawaiian Homes Commission, *Rehabilitation in Hawaii*, 21; Cooke, *Moolelo O Molokai*, 77; "Eight Chosen for Places on Molokai Land," *Honolulu Star Bulletin*, June 28, 1922; "Some Facts about the Haiku Homestead District, Haiku, Maui Co., Hawaii," carton 5, Elwood Mead Papers, Bancroft Library.

39. "Dr. Mead Airs His Views on Colonization," *Honolulu Star Bulletin*, June 28, 1922.

40. Kauanui, "Rehabilitating the Native," 66; "Ex-Soldiers to Colonize Rural Areas in Hawaii," *Los Angeles Herald*, Sept. 8, 1922; quote from Elwood Mead to the Hawaiian Homes Commission, Jan. 12, 1923, carton 5, Elwood Mead Papers, Bancroft Library, 2.

41. Elwood Mead to the Hawaiian Homes Commission, Jan. 12, 1923, 4–7.

42. Ibid., Jan. 12, 1923, 7, quote from 8.

43. Communication of Dr. Elwood Mead of the Bureau of Reclamation, Oct. 20, 1927, in Hawaiian Homes Commission, *Report of the Hawaiian Homes Commission to the Legislature of Hawaii* (Honolulu, 1929), 51.

44. "Record of visit to Waiakea Homesteads," ts, June 22, 1922, item 2, Hawaiian Homes Commission I, Elwood Mead Papers, Bancroft Library, 2–5.

45. "Dr. Mead Says Hawaii's Colonization Plan Has Every Chance of Success," *Sacramento Bee*, July 17, 1922; quote from Hon. W. R. Farrington to Elwood Mead, 6 July 1922, carton 1, Correspondence between Elwood Mead and Hawaiian Homes Commission, Elwood Mead Papers, Bancroft Library.

46. Keesing, *Hawaiian Homesteading*, 45–49.

47. Ibid., 56, 63–64, quote from 65.

48. Ibid., quotes from 91–92.

49. "The Labor Situation in Hawaii," 3–4.

50. U.S. Dept. of the Interior. William Atherton Du Puy, *Hawaii and Its Race Problem* (Washington, DC: Government Printing Office, 1932), 100.

51. "Notes of the Trip to Hawaii." Written in the Union Club, Honolulu, June 29, 1922, Hawaiian Homes Commission Report, 1922, Elwood Mead Papers, Bancroft Library, 1.

52. "Notes of the Trip to Hawaii," 1.

53. Du Puy, *Hawaii and Its Race Problem*, 115–17.

54. Keesing, *Hawaiian Homesteading*, 27–28, 67; quote from Communication of Dr. Elwood Mead of the Bureau of Reclamation, Oct. 20, 1927, in Hawaiian Homes Commission, *Report of the Hawaiian Homes Commission to the Legislature of Hawaii*, 13, quote from 51.

Crabgrass or Grapes

Urban Sprawl, Agricultural Persistence,
and the Fight for Napa Valley

KATHLEEN A. BROSNAN

"You could grow a really good crop of rutabagas here," David Whitmer, the Napa County agricultural commissioner, joked in 2004, "but nobody would come and watch you harvest them."[1] Instead, the Napa Valley hitched its fame and fortune to wine and the tourism that has accompanied it. Napans have engaged in commercial viticulture (grape growing) and enology (wine making) for almost 150 years. However, they had not yet achieved the current level of international renown in the 1960s when the urban sprawl that engulfed much of the San Francisco Bay region threatened their vineyards. In response to that trend, Napa County created an agricultural preserve to protect the vineyards, a measure that was both conservative and progressive. While environmental historians have tended to focus on developments in federal law in the post–World War II era, the agricultural preserve and subsequent Napa County ordinances (expanding the preserve, defining wineries, and limiting hillside vineyards) reaffirm the centrality of local law in defining land-use controls—controls that dramatically, directly, and immediately affected human interactions with the physical world while balancing competing economic and cultural interests. In this case, and despite the imperfections of their solutions, a county government and its committed populace have used local laws, when federal and state laws proved less effective, to preserve both agriculture and open space in one of the most densely populated regions in the United States.

Napa County lies to the north of San Pablo Bay, the northernmost extension of San Francisco Bay, and east of the Pacific Ocean and Sonoma County. For most outsiders, the heart of the county is the Napa Valley. Carved prehistorically by the Napa River and blessed with a Mediterranean climate of generous summer sunshine and cooling nighttime breezes, the valley has long been a center of agriculture. Nestled between the Mayacamas Mountains on its northern and western sides and the Vaca Mountains on the east, Napa Valley opens into the marshy deltas of the San Pablo Bay to the south. The valley, which begins at the foot of Mount St. Helena, the second highest peak in the Bay Area, is but one mile across at its northern end, travels only thirty miles in length, and reaches just five miles across at its widest. With the exception of a few smaller valleys, the remainder of Napa County mostly involves mountains or steep hills.[2]

As of the year 2000, some two-thirds of the county's population of 125,000 lived in the Lower Valley in the City of Napa and the recently incorporated community of American Canyon. Another 11 percent called the Upper Valley communities of Calistoga, St. Helena, and Yountville home. With a land area of 754 square miles, Napa had the lowest population density (165 people/mile) in the nine-county Bay Area. Sonoma County, Napa's neighbor to the west and perhaps the nation's second-best-known wine region, had the next lowest population density in the Bay Area, but it was 75 percent greater than Napa's. By contrast, the counties south of San Francisco Bay have experienced substantially greater growth. For example, Santa Clara County was once called "Valley of Paradise" and enjoyed a thriving agricultural economy. Santa Clara officials in the 1950s and early 1960s had hoped to alternate urban and agricultural zones, but the cities soon overwhelmed the farms. The area now bears the moniker "Silicon Valley" and has a population density of 1,303 people per square mile, almost eight times greater than Napa County. James Hickey, who was regional planning director for the Association of Bay Area Governments in the 1960s and director of the Napa County Conservation, Development, and Planning Commission in the 1970s and 1980s, wistfully observes, "There was some of the best agricultural soil in the world under the city of San Jose and they've pumped so much water out of it, they have about a foot or more of subsidence in some areas."[3]

Numerous scholars have discussed the emergence of the United States as a suburban nation following World War II, attributing growth on the urban fringe to revolutionary construction techniques that provided relatively inexpensive housing; federal programs that provided building loans and supported highway construction; and a newfound affluence that allowed working-class and middle-class whites to abandon older city centers, while discriminatory policies and other factors often precluded blacks and other minorities.[4] As Adam Rome observes, "Because the archetypical postwar subdivision was built on farmland, open-space advocates often argued that the nation was risking the loss of a vital productive resource."[5] The San Francisco Bay region proved a popular destination for many Americans who had moved there to work in wartime industries or traveled through the area as part of their military service. More and bigger suburbs began to clog northern California. Commentators worried about disappearing farms, but expressed their greatest fears for the loss of prime lands that grew specialty crops such as nuts, vegetables, and fruits, including wine grapes.[6] Nowhere was this problem more acute than in Santa Clara County. Filled with vineyards and orchards that produced a third of the world's prunes, the Santa Clara Valley had been known for its natural beauty and agricultural fertility.[7] Construction of the Stanford Industrial Park and other research facilities, however, prompted a six-fold population increase between 1940 and 1970. Two decades later, the continuous expansion of tract housing for some 1.5 million residents obliterated the agrarian landscape. As late as 1959, Santa Clara County held more than 73,000 acres of fruits and nut crops; by 1992, less than 1,900 acres remained.[8]

Historically, Napa and the other North Coast counties had been less populated than the communities on the peninsula south of San Francisco, due in part to the difficulties of access before the erection of the Golden Gate and San Francisco–Oakland Bay bridges in the late 1930s. Napa County received a demographic boost as military activity at the Mare Island naval shipyard attracted workers to the nearby City of Napa during World War II and the early Cold War. By 1960, however, Napa County's population still teetered below 66,000, and grew at a slower rate than all but two Bay Area counties. The only two counties growing at a slower rate than Napa County were Alameda and San Francisco, home to Oakland and the city of San Francisco, respectively. The already crowded cities had little room left for growth and newcomers spread suburbia into the adjoining counties.[9] Napa's North Coast neighbors, Marin and Sonoma counties, still possessed open spaces, farmlands, and pasturage, but the postwar suburban onslaught had begun to lurch across the Golden Gate Bridge. Marin's population almost tripled between 1940 and 1960, while Sonoma's population grew from 69,000 to 147,000. Planners in Napa County studied regional and local trends, and in 1966, they estimated that by the new millennium, the county population could exceed 210,000, a 223 percent increase over the 1960 figure.[10]

In the 1960s, Napa County was still home to diversified agriculture. Grape growing and wine making first became commercial enterprises in the 1860s, but Napans had always produced other crops, often in greater numbers and for greater profits. A century later, orchards were still interspersed among the vineyards, and cattle pasturage remained a more lucrative venture for some Napans until 1971. Nonetheless, by the mid-1960s, a long-term shift toward grapes as the valley's dominant product had crystallized. Lower returns for prune and walnut growers led many to uproot their trees and plant vines. Napa vintners and the University of California

Agricultural Extension agents expressed optimism for an expanding premium wine industry. Grape growers confidently planted new vineyards, although foreboding "suburban" storm clouds loomed on the horizon.[11]

Over the preceding decades, however, some Napan families had halved and quartered individual holdings to provide for their children and grandchildren, and on these smaller parcels, it had become increasingly more difficult to make a profit in agriculture. Many Napans fretted that the smaller parcels in the Napa Valley were susceptible to developers, and that once developers made inroads into their famous valley, patchwork patterns of subdivisions would ultimately undermine agricultural activity and attract an even larger wave of suburbanites than the planners predicted. They were eager to preserve their agriculture—and the open spaces and culture that it embodied. Santa Clara County offered the model that they hoped to avoid.[12] Outside commentators agreed. In 1965, the *New York Times* editorialized, "So great are the purely financial rewards of this kind of urban expansion that even the sundrenched Napa Valley . . . is seriously threatened. Vineyards are less profitable than subdivisions." Harold Gilliam, the San Francisco–based writer and environmentalist, worried, "The [Napa] Valley will become indistinguishable from sleazy suburban developments all over the Bay area."[13]

In Napa and across northern California, many small grape growers and other farmers and ranchers on the metropolitan fringe often struggled to pay taxes assessed on their properties' full cash value—value dictated by a speculative land market. "The process of shifting from agricultural to urban use is not instantaneous. Intermediate to the two uses is what might properly be called a speculative use of the land. The day-to-day agricultural activity still may be carried out; but the owner, if he is acting to optimize his return from the land, is weighing every present activity in terms of its effect on the potential returns from alternative uses."[14] Assessments were based, in part, on future returns to the land. Thus, speculation about urban conversions increased assessments. Large agribusinesses often resisted such economic pressures, but many small operators surrendered their lands to developers. "The resulting pattern was frequently one of premature land conversion, discontinuous development, and urban sprawl."[15]

Responding to this tax issue and to relatively uncontrolled urban sprawl, the California State Legislature passed the Land Conservation Act in 1965. Known as the Williamson Act, the law allowed qualified farmers to remove their properties from the speculative market by entering into contracts with the county government. The contracts restricted use of the land to agriculture for ten years. In turn, the county assessed the land on the basis of its agricultural value. In effect, both parties to the contract agreed that agriculture was the highest and best use of the land regardless of speculative possibilities. The contracts were extended annually unless the county or owner filed a notice of nonrenewal, giving the agreements a sense of perennation. The law applied to prime agricultural properties (Class I or Class II land as defined by the Soil Conservation Service Land-Use Capability Criteria) or alternatively to slightly inferior soils that grew specialized agricultural crops. In 1965, approximately 7.5 million acres of prime lands remained in California, and they seemed to be the ones most threatened by urban sprawl.[16] A subsequent amendment exempted land set aside under the Williamson Act from a policy which required assessment at 25 percent of market value, thus making agricultural conservation more attractive to property owners. By 1969, twenty-three counties, including Napa, had restricted more than 2 million acres of private property in California's agricultural districts.[17]

To implement the Williamson Act locally, the Napa County Board of Supervisors found a unique solution. In 1968, it rezoned the entire Napa Valley into an agricultural preserve, including some 23,000 acres of Class I, II, and III soil. The path to this solution, however, had followed a circuitous and hotly contested course, creating some rifts within the valley that never healed. The movement to taper growth to a more reasonable rate began in September 1961 when the state highway commission announced a freeway bypass through the valley. The proposed highway would cut through choice vineyards and around the key viticultural community of St. Helena. Given estimates of population growth, the commission anticipated completion of the highway in 1974. An alliance of residents formed the Upper Napa Valley Associates (UNVA) to stop the highway. The extension agent supported their conclusion that this highway construction would undermine a wine industry on the brink of exciting new success. The state highway commission informed residents that the construction of the highway depended upon developments in the county. If subdivisions filled the valley, a highway would follow to service the new homeowners. Santa Clara County provided the UNVA with one model of all that could go wrong, but its members also found an example close to home, having witnessed the disappearance of hundreds of acres of prunes and vines on the northern edge of the City of Napa. Although the lost vineyards did not produce the premium wines that became the valley's standard, their demise seemed to confirm that urban sprawl was a real and imminent threat.[18]

The UVNA counted among its members some landowners, vintners, conservationists, residents of the valley's four urban areas, and wealthy San Franciscans who had weekend homes in the valley. They "realized that winemaking and the land were inextricably linked" and began to talk to their neighbors about creating a permanent agricultural zone to protect the vineyards.[19] Shortly thereafter, conservationist William Bronson published an article proposing the designation of the "Napa Valley National Vineyard." Bronson analogized his proposal to the national park precedent, suggesting that the federal government purchase private holdings of forty thousand to fifty thousand acres in the Upper Napa Valley and prohibit any nonagricultural structures.[20] Such a plan seemed unlikely. Most property owners probably would resist such sales. Moreover, even with the repeal of Prohibition, there had been resistance within the federal government, particularly the U.S. Department of Agriculture at various times, to supporting the wine industry. Napans' confidence in an expanding market niche was confirmed when U.S. sales of dry table wines surpassed the sales of sweet dessert wines for the first time in 1967. Yet a strain of neoprohibitionism persisted in the United States, leading Congress to enforce a series of restrictive laws on labeling and distribution.[21]

Nonetheless, Bronson's idea gave new impetus to other preservation efforts. When a proposal was made to create a subdivision within the historic To Kalon vineyard (which the Robert Mondavi Winery subsequently purchased), UNVA members concluded that the county needed to change its zoning laws and began to work with the county's planning commission to devise a plan that would conserve vineyards and preclude tract houses and highways. Environmental historians have tended to focus primarily on federal laws in explaining postwar environmental policies and changes in land use, including farmland preservation efforts, even when they acknowledge the foundational role of grassroots movements.[22] And in many ways, the federal government has played a major role in the wine industry over time. While the wine industry is more heavily regulated in other countries, the nation-state has been a central player in the U.S. industry from land grant institutions that provided research, through Prohibition and its repeal, to the creation of an appellation system.[23]

Yet, in reality, the general-purpose local government has been the principal institution for reconciling the competing interests of the landowner, his or her neighbors, and possible speculators. Historically, local officials, often advised by planners and other professionals, have attempted to resolve conflicts by adopting and administering land-use regulations with which landowners must comply. Officials are not passive arbitrators; in setting policy, they inherently elevate certain land uses over others. Thus, local laws profoundly and more immediately influenced how individual property owners use the natural resources within their possession.

Before 1900, nuisance laws, fire regulations, vice laws, health and safety codes, and exercises of eminent domain provided local governments with some limits on what uses landowners adopted.[24] In the twentieth century, governments exercised greater powers over land use through building and related codes, subdivision regulations, general plans, and zoning ordinances. Under municipal law, local governments theoretically are creations of their individual states and their powers were to be construed narrowly, prompting those whose interests were not favored by policies to frequently challenge the exercise of local authority as an overextension of the police powers.[25] In reality, American courts have recognized and supported local governments, even when they have acted beyond the limitations of their charters. Since the U.S. Supreme Court confirmed in 1926 that the federal constitution did not preclude local governments from segregating uses and creating special districts, every state court has affirmed the general practice of zoning. California courts have given local officials the greatest latitude in protecting favored uses and natural resources. Early zoning ordinances viewed the single-family house as the highest use and assumed that the simple segregation of uses would push nonconforming uses away and force the market to conform to unchanging rules. In reality, however, it has proven difficult to predict future demands, and market forces that contradicted the ordinances tended to create great political pressure for changes to the ordinances.[26] Before 1968, most zoning had regulated uses, setbacks, housing densities, and building heights. By 1968, some Napans were prepared to expand the parameters of their county's zoning scheme.

UNVA members worried that the Williamson Act, in and of itself, was an inadequate solution because it was a voluntary program. Even with the tax advantages offered by the Williamson Act, farmers could do whatever they wanted with their property. Over the long run, this state law had limited effectiveness across California. Despite penalties for premature development, contracts were frequently broken because the profits from land sales were so great. Additionally, some counties suffered from the loss of tax revenue, while California's largest landholders benefited disproportionately from the law. In the late 1960s, the National Cattleman's Association successfully lobbied to expand the law to cover all agricultural land. Consequently, by 1970 only 30 percent of the land protected by the Williamson Act included prime farmland. Most of the reserved land was discontiguous and distant from urban areas.[27]

In the end, the Williamson Act was perhaps most effective in that it encouraged some Californians to contemplate the preservation of agriculture. In the Napa Valley, this state law perhaps proved most successful. The UNVA pushed for zoning changes that would compel the farmers to accept the Williamson Act protections. In 1967, the county planning commission, with the UNVA's urging, held hearings on an ordinance to increase the minimum lot size in unincorporated county lands on the valley floor from one to twenty acres. Months of heated debate followed. The divisions within the county were neither clear nor obvious.[28] Republicans and Democrats fell on both sides of the debate. The wine industry, which was to be protected by this zoning, had never been a monolithic entity whose members necessarily shared the same values or economic status. In the 1960s, grape growers greatly outnumbered vintners. Some growers produced their own wine, while others sold it to vintners. Vintners might have owned wineries, but some made their wine at one the valley's cooperatives. Some vineyards were small and family owned; others were controlled by large corporations. The same was true of the wineries. Moreover, the bulk of Napa County's population resided in the Lower Valley, and many residents there had, at best, tangential relations to the wine industry.

The vintners who supported the zoning plan included Jack Davies, a relative newcomer to viticulture who had reopened the historic Schramsberg winery in the 1960s, and Louis M. Martini and his son, who had made wine in the valley since the 1930s. Most proponents did not think of themselves as environmentalists. They simply wanted to preserve a traditionally rural way of life and a system of viticulture that was carving a niche in the premium market and responding to a growing U.S. demand for table wines. Other members of UNVA were at the forefront of an open space movement. Adam Rome describes such people as "grassroots activists and government officials [who] saw the difficulty of acquiring open space as part of a larger problem—uncontrolled growth."[29] They perceived the once-celebrated postwar housing boom as an ecological disaster.

Leading the opposition were Louis Stralla and John Daniel. Stralla had owned and operated various properties for bulk wine production for thirty years. Daniel had inherited the Inglenook estate from his great-uncle and its founder, Gustave Niebaum, and had continued to produce premium wine there. A few years earlier, in 1964, Daniel shocked the valley when he sold his vineyards and winery to United Vintners, which was part of Allied Growers, a huge conglomerate that primarily produced bulk wines and soon cheapened the Inglenook name. Daniel still remained an influential member of Napa society as a board member of the St. Helena branch of the Bank of America, which financed many wine ventures. Stralla and Daniel argued that the preserve would diminish land values in both the long run and the short run. Some observers suggested that Stralla and Daniel actually seemed to believe the county planned to confiscate their property. They were joined in their opposition by some small landholders who hoped to sell to developers for a profit that they had never enjoyed in agriculture, and others who simply wanted to subdivide their land and build houses for their children. More than two thousand property owners signed petitions opposing the preserve.[30]

These opponents voiced objections grounded in the constitutional argument regarding property rights that defined most resistance to open-space and environmental regulations. Many commentators have associated this property rights movement in the American West with the rise of Ronald Reagan and the Sagebrush Rebellion of the 1980s. Adam Rome alternatively suggests that the issue originated in postwar suburbia at the end of the 1960s. In the Napa case, it began a bit earlier in a predominantly rural county. Mel Varrelman, a young high school teacher and part-time policeman in 1968 who was elected to the Napa County Supervisors fourteen years later, recalls the battle over the preserve as one of the "first classic property rights versus public responsibilities" issues in the nation.[31]

In the end, the only opinions that mattered were those of the five members of the Napa County Board of Supervisors. They concluded that the highest and best use of the land was not necessarily dictated by what was most immediately profitable. They voted unanimously in favor of the zoning change and locked into agriculture some twenty-three thousand acres of contiguous, unincorporated county lands on the valley floor. The opponents, led by John Daniel, filed suit, first unsuccessfully seeking an injunction to block implementation of the zoning ordinance and then challenging its constitutionality as an excessive exercise of the county's police powers. The California Court of Appeals upheld the ordinance. No further appeals were pursued, in part because Daniel, the main litigant, died unexpectedly just days before the final ruling.[32]

The agricultural preserve was both conservative and progressive. Many Napans feared change and the new social elements that might accompany greater urbanization. The preserve also constituted an attempt to maintain an economy and a way of life threatened by urban encroachment and to some extent the modern consumerism it represented. In the tradition of American agrarianism, the board of supervisors confirmed that in the valley, agriculture was again the highest and best use of the land. Yet the new ordinance also was an innovative and unique zoning scheme for agriculture. It served as a precursor to urban and suburban open-space regulations, and constituted an abrupt break from the primal elevation of individual property rights. The preserve's proponents did not seek to create "an ecologically beneficial place," but they provided much more than a cursory stopgap to suburban sprawl. And if they rejected some of the modernity associated with urban America, they also recognized that only wine grapes and the "urbane" consumer culture it employed provided the best chance to sustain the preserve. Viticulture offered an economic base that few, if any, other crops could.[33]

Napa County crafted the first agricultural preserve as a solution to the problem of urban sprawl, but a growth-control movement had emerged already in the

United States and in California in particular in the 1960s. For the most part, this movement took place in exclusive suburban communities where residents saw metropolitan growth as a threat to their property values and quality of life and actively engaged in the local political process to thwart new development. Nearby Marin County, for example, enjoyed a mixture of suburbs, agriculture, and parkland, but with a population density that was significantly higher than Napa's. So, in 1966, just as in Napa five years earlier, a grassroots movement there stopped a proposed highway and the development it promised to bring. In 1971, Marin officials eventually adopted and formalized this revolt against urban sprawl in an ambitious countywide zoning plan. The plan identified three permanent land-use zones: a city-centered corridor along Highway 101; an inland rural corridor reserved for agriculture; and a recreation corridor along the Pacific shoreline. In many ways, the plan worked. Since its adoption, property values in Marin County have skyrocketed while the population only grew by thirty thousand in the last three decades of the twentieth century.[34]

In 1968, however, proponents of the Napa agricultural preserve fretted about its inherent fragility. While vineyards were more valuable than orchards, such lands still "did not trade for a lot of money."[35] More significantly, the preserve and the ordinance that created it could disappear in thirty days if any three county supervisors voted for a new zoning law. Instead, over time, the supervisors and the county voters who elected them became increasingly more committed to the protection of open space and vineyards. In 1979, the supervisors strengthened the zoning scheme by increasing the minimum lot size within the preserve to 40 acres. They next expanded the preserve to include adjacent hillsides that were within the Napa River watershed, increasing the preserve's acreage to approximately 30,000 acres. Eventually, the minimum lot size peaked at 160 acres. At the same time the voters, the majority of whom lived within the county's urban areas, passed initiatives which suggested that they did not want to leave land management issues solely to the political processes of the board of supervisors. Measure A, adopted in 1980, limited residential growth in unincorporated areas of the county to 1 percent of the current population—a substantially lower growth rate than in the rest of the Bay Area. The county's conservation, development, and planning department controlled growth by closely monitoring the number of building permits issued. Within Napa County's five incorporated cities, council candidates frequently and successfully ran on slow growth, proagriculture platforms, and the cities have persistently maintained rural-urban limits in an effort to contain growth.[36]

In 1990, Napa County citizens reaffirmed their commitment to agriculture and open space when they overwhelmingly supported Measure J, an initiative that froze all county zoning laws until the year 2020 unless two-thirds of the voters agreed to changes through specific ballot initiatives. To date, county residents have approached such changes with both practicality and a sense of the importance of place. In one case, a restaurant had continued its business within the agricultural preserve as a preexisting nonconforming use. When the restaurant's owners hoped to provide outdoor seating by utilizing a large porch, voters approved. However, when developers attempted to subdivide the Kirkland Ranch property within the unincorporated county lands southeast of the City of Napa, more than 80 percent of the voters rejected the project.[37] Addressing Measure J, a recent editorial observed, "From one perspective, this is democracy run amok, micromanagement of private property decisions that may be of small consequences to the public. From another, Measure J is the key to preservation of the county's open spaces and agriculture. It also keeps the decision-making on land use decisions out in the open, and land use decisions are at the heart of county politics. Finally, it has the positive effect of keeping us all in the role of stewards of the county's future."[38]

This commitment to the agricultural preserve and open space reflected a growing postwar environmental ethos, but it also relied on the exponential success of Napa's wine industry in the last three decades of the twentieth century. In the 1960s, as the preservation efforts were taking hold, Napan vintners and their agricultural advisors anticipated new opportunities, particularly given changing consumer tastes and improvements in the quality of their products following World War II. Few, however, could have predicted the economic boom that lay ahead. It had taken decades to overcome the effects of Prohibition. In 1966, after leaving his family's operations at the Charles Krug winery, Robert Mondavi had opened the first new large winery since the repeal of Prohibition. He joined, and quite frequently led, other members of the Napa Valley Vintners Association in their continued efforts to emphasize the quality afforded by the valley's superior *terroir,* and to define their niche in the premium wine market.[39] The vintners employed graduates from the viticulture and enology program at the University of California, Davis, and adopted suggestions from the school's scientists regarding grape varieties, climate, and fermentation. They cast wine as a part of the good life, and lured to the valley for tastings residents and tourists from the Bay Area and more distant locales.[40]

The Napa Valley became "the spiritual center of wine growing in America."[41] In 1976, the region took center stage in the global market when a Paris wine shop owner arranged a blind tasting between French and California wines. To most observers' surprise, the French judges selected two Napa Valley vintages as the best red and white wines. Napa had not usurped France as the world's premium wine producer, but the results conveyed to consumers that certain Napa wines merited inclusion with the world's best. The chair of the Napa County Board of Supervisors claimed, "We represent the only county in the United States which has within its boundaries an internationally recognized wine industry."[42] A handful of wineries in the 1960s morphed into 164 wineries by 1989 and some 300 by the new millennium. Napa wines earned high prices and brought prestige to their producers. More and more land was turned over to vineyards within Napa County. By the year 2000, wine grapes accounted for 98 percent of the county's gross agricultural production. There are now more than 45,000 acres in grapes—more land under cultivation than in any previous year under diversified agriculture.[43]

The wine boom combined with the agriculture preserve to create a unique success in the Napa Valley, but it came with some unexpected costs. These factors contributed to a scarcity of viable vineyard land. Vineyards occupy approximately 9 percent of the county's lands as of 2007, and it is estimated that less than 3 percent of the remaining land is suitable for grape production. In 1967, Napa vineyards sold for between $500 and $3,000 per acre; by the end of the century, the price often exceeded $200,000 per acre. Substantial financial resources were needed to join the industry—to buy land, plant vineyards, build winemaking facilities, and wait the necessary three to five years for a product mature enough for sale. In the 1960s and 1970s, many industry insiders, former cellar rats who learned the business in the vineyards and wineries, opened their own operations and joined the old-timers to build Napa's reputation. In the 1980s and 1990s, new owners often included corporations or individuals who had made fortunes in the high-tech industries or other enterprises, but brought no winemaking experience to their new ventures.[44]

Given the scarcity of lands within the agricultural preserve, these new ventures looked to the surrounding mountains. Hillside vineyards once had been a part of Napa viticulture but, after Prohibition's repeal, had remained relatively ignored until 1980. Those who wanted the cachet of the Napa sobriquet needed the hills.[45] Deforestation followed in certain areas, although large stands of trees are still found throughout Napa County. In 1980, heavy rains on a newly deforested hill drove an avalanche of silt to the valley floor, blocking the main traffic artery. During a 1989 rainstorm, two thousand tons of sediment from a cleared hillside flowed into the Bell Canyon reservoir that supplies the city of St. Helena, turning the water red. Thin hillside soils were especially susceptible to erosion. By 1987, the California State Water Quality Control Board identified the Napa River as an "impaired" water body. Sediment filled gravel beds, smothered fish eggs, and changed water temperature and oxygen content. Diversions and road crossings hampered steelhead trout migrations. The explosion of vineyards arguably contributed to a loss of biodiversity. A third of Napa's native species were rare or endangered. Remaining oak woodlands competed with grapes for soil moisture. Regeneration became difficult because of fire suppression methods where vineyards mingled with forests.[46] The dedication of more acres to grapes contributed to pest infestations. Phylloxera, a sap-sucking insect indigenous to North America that feeds on grapevines and nearly destroyed the world's commercial wine industry in the nineteenth century, returned in the late 1980s. It forced the replanting of half of Napa's vineyards, although the infestation was attributable to historical choices about rootstock as well as the wall-to-wall planting of vines.[47]

Agricultural Commissioner David Whitmer believes such criticisms are over-stated: "I think it's only about 8 or 9 percent of the acreage of the county is in wine grapes. The rest is in other uses. And the largest of that is native vegetation, so we still have a tremendous amount of ecological resources and biodiversity here."[48] Except for the pest infestations, however, these environmental problems would have been as bad or worse with greater urbanization. Some difficulties, such as diversions and road crossings, are attributable to other economic activities. Increased tourism accompanied this wine boom. The supposedly bucolic character that the preserve seemed to enhance made Napa an increasingly popular destination. In the postwar West, Hal Rothman argues, tourism generally served as a replacement economy.[49] This was not case in the Napa Valley. Tourism formed a truly symbiotic relationship with the wine industry. They were inherently dissimilar, but intimately connected and mutually beneficial activities. Agriculture is dirty, hard work requiring patience. Tourists prefer clean places, take things at a leisurely pace, and want instant gratification. Viticulture dominated the valley, but tourism facilitated its growth. By the early 1980s, an estimated 2 million people visited Napa Valley annually and spent $136 million.[50] The demographic character of Napa's tourists was as important as the money they spent. Vintners tapped baby boomers with disposable income who earned more than the median family income.[51] Vintners wanted visitors who would purchase premium wines when they returned home.

Tourism studies solicited by the city of St. Helena (1983) and the Napa Valley Foundation (1984), however, exposed concerns about tourism's impact. Tourist-oriented businesses replaced establishments that served locals. Residents debated the meaning of these changes. Some complained about higher rents, the difficulty in finding necessities, and the expulsion of old-timers. Others believed that St. Helena was too rooted to lose its small-town character. Residents worried that the changes related to wine tourism might undermine the agricultural activities. In a pattern consistent throughout the valley, 28 percent of St. Helena's employed residents worked in agriculture (almost all viticulture by this time) or wine production (which included guest services at wineries). Another 15 percent held jobs in the retail sector, a higher percentage than most small agricultural towns. Throughout the 1980s and 1990s, tourism remained the fastest growing sector of the local economy.[52]

Other complaints surrounded traffic. In the early 1960s, the state's proposal for a freeway through the Napa Valley helped trigger the agricultural preserve. Given the absence of significant population growth, the state had abandoned its highway plan. Consequently, the narrow valley possessed only two north-south arteries, and for most of their length, both were only two lanes wide. Between 1977 and 1986, daily traffic across the valley increased 34 percent overall, and at certain intersections it almost doubled. Weekends presented the worst problems. Most visitors came by private vehicle for one day only. Traffic jams were frequent occurrences. Transiency taxes and sales taxes covered St. Helena's costs for additional staff for traffic control, but left the city with little additional revenue.[53]

Wine industry employees contributed to the congestion. The valley lacked public transportation, and workers traveled to and from their jobs in private cars. As intended, the agricultural preserve stalled urban sprawl, slowed population growth, and in turn ensured the expansion of the wine industry and tourism. Zoning laws that created the preserve, however, limited building locations for affordable housing. Except for the recently incorporated American Canyon, the county's cities (Napa, Yountville, St. Helena, and Calistoga) strained against their rural-urban limits while housing prices rose. Across the unincorporated and protected areas of the valley, and to the chagrin of many, "McMansions" appeared on the large-acre holdings that were beyond the means of most workers.

Increasingly, many workers lived at the valley's southern end in the more plebeian cities of Napa and American Canyon, which received fewer visitors and was 30 percent and 17 percent Hispanic, respectively, by the year 2000. Others increasingly lived outside the county. Nearly all persons working in Napa County lived there in 1960. Two decades later, some 87 percent still resided there. By the turn of the twenty-first century, county officials estimated 30 percent of Napa workers commuted from other counties and they expected the rising trend to continue.[54] Agricultural workers and visitor-related employees who earned substantially less than the tourists represented a disproportionately large share of the commuters. This pattern is common in resort areas but not in most agricultural regions. It also has been a frequent result of the growth-control movement which protected exclusive suburban enclaves from development and closed the doors, whether intentionally or not, to the poor or working class, as had happened in nearby Marin County.

Disparities in wealth, population density, and race in Napa County added to the tensions between the Upper Valley (where most vineyards were located) and the Lower Valley (where most Napans lived).[55]

Worries about tourism also led to questions about the relationship of the new wineries to agriculture. As Hickey emphasizes, wine involves "a kind of industrial processing" of an agricultural product. Because wine production was directly related to grapes supposedly grown locally, zoning ordinances had not treated it as a nonconforming use.[56] In 1974, the V. Sattui Winery opened in a commercial zone on the edge of the preserve. At that time, it offered picnic grounds and a deli but owned no vineyards and produced no wine. For Napans concerned about the integrity of the preserve and the viticulture it protected, V. Sattui also seemed to constitute a dangerous precedent. Other wineries provided restaurants, art exhibits, and summer concerts. Some wineries sold food items at least tangentially related to the idea of wine as part of cuisine, but other items seemed to have a more tenuous connection to grapes. Critics noted that the Niebaum-Coppola winery sold binoculars, board games, and bocce balls, and highlighted co-owner Francis Ford Coppola's movie memorabilia.[57] Growers were particularly concerned that wineries in Napa could make wine from grapes grown beyond the county's borders. Eventually the planning commission and the board of supervisors took up the question of how to define a winery. The growers lobbied for a definition that categorized wineries and limited their activities according to the timing of their inception. Facing a loss of revenue, vintners objected. A compromise ordinance in 1990 simply required that all new wineries obtain 75 percent of their grapes from Napa vineyards. Some commentators suggested that the policy amounted to "screw the new guys," but Varrelman, a county supervisor at the time, points out that it was difficult for government to undermine the substantial financial investments of established wineries by telling them to do business in a different way. Moreover, the established wineries generally had easier access to grapes grown in Napa County. If new wineries, which lacked such access, used outside agricultural products, then they arguably constituted industrial operations with no relationship to Napa and thus undermined the county's agricultural base.[58] In the end, the ordinance did nothing to slow proliferation of wineries (nearly three hundred by the year 2000) or the waves of tourists (5 million annually by 2000).

The wine industry's success prompted another attempt to preserve the county's environment; this time, by checking unrestrained agricultural expansion. In 1991, Napa County adopted a law regulating vineyard development on the hillsides. Although all human activity results in erosion and some erosion occurs naturally, the law was an effort to reduce sediments in county streams and to improve water quality. The ordinance required the filing of erosion control plans for slopes greater than 5 percent and required setbacks from streams. The county's conservation, development, and planning department did not extend building permits for any slopes greater than 30 percent. Napa is the only winegrowing region in the United States to adopt such restrictive policies. Nonetheless, a 1999 lawsuit by the local residents who belonged to the Sierra Club questioned the adequacy of the erosion control plans. (The national Sierra Club did not join the lawsuit.) These litigants argued that the intense agricultural activities in a relatively small area had already pushed the watershed to the limits of its capacity. Agricultural Commissioner Whitmer countered that only 3 percent of the county's remaining undeveloped land was suitable for grape growing, and its development as vineyards would not increase agriculture's impact significantly. A subsequent settlement required the county to enforce the California Environmental Quality Act. Unless a vineyard qualified for an exemption, its owner needed to complete an environmental impact report explaining how the operation would contain ecological damage. The Napa County Resource Conservation District now reviews the environmental impact reports for new properties, but the law did not apply to established vineyards unless they were redeveloped.[59]

Some critics have questioned the zealousness of the litigants because it alienated growers who had previously been willing to work with environmentalists to improve Napa Valley.[60] Certainly some wine industry participants revel in the image of a gentleman farmer, but many have taken positive steps to protect the environment and viticulture. Some growers have joined local officials and other Napans in the Napa Sustainable Winegrowing Group that works to identify and employ "winegrowing practices that are economically viable, socially responsible, and environmentally sound." Other landowners have "donated" more than 50,000 acres to the Land Trust of Napa County through conservation easements and outright property transfers. Almost 6,700 vineyard acres are involved, including sizable contributions from V. Sattui and Niebaum-Coppola, operations frequently criticized for promoting tourist activities separate from wine production. These property owners have demonstrated a commitment to open space and environmental protection, but also recognized that such sustainable measures give them an environmentally friendly image that has marketing advantages.[61]

Conclusion

In the beginning, the agricultural preserve helped a wine industry on the brink of new economic success. In the end, the viticulture experienced success beyond most predictions, and its strength has allowed the agricultural preserve to continue. Napa County stalled the urban sprawl that has defined much of northern California. A series of local laws and ballot initiatives have shaped a landscape of vineyards and open spaces intermixed with wineries and McMansions. These policies attempted to balance competing demands on the land, and debates often have stirred underlying tensions based on class, race, profession, and location over the past four decades. Nonetheless, however imperfect their solutions, the local populace and their local governments have pursued unique paths in preservation and exhibited a persistent, far-reaching, and shared sense of place that transcends other divisions.

Notes

1. David Whitmer, Napa County Agricultural Commissioner, interviewed by author, 16 June 2004, Napa, California, 14 (tape recording and transcript in author's possession).

2. *History of Napa and Lake Counties, California* (San Francisco: Slocum, Bowen & Co., 1881), 4–7; Marguerite Hunt and Harry Lawrence Gunn, *History of Solano County, California and Napa County, California* (Chicago: S.J. Clarke Pub. Co., 1926); and Napa River Watershed Task Force, Phase II, Final Report, Prepared by the Napa County Board of Supervisors by Moore Iacofano Goltsman, September 2000, 1–5.

3. James Hickey, former Napa County Planning Commissioner, 14 July 2004, Napa, California, 7 (tape recording and transcript in author's possession). Also see U.S. Census Bureau, State and County QuickFacts, http://quickfacts.census.gov/qfd/states/06000.html (accessed 10 May 2007); and Warren A. Beck, *Historical Atlas of California* (Norman: University of Oklahoma Press, 1974).

4. There is a vast literature on suburbia. See, generally, Kenneth T. Jackson, *Crabgrass Frontier: The Suburbanization of the United States* (New York and Oxford: Oxford University Press, 1985); Adam Rome, *The Bulldozer in the Countryside: Suburban Sprawl and the Rise of American Environmentalism* (New York: Cambridge University Press, 2001); Robert Fishman, *Bourgeois Utopias: The Rise and Fall of Suburbia* (New York: Basic Books, 1987); Elaine Tyler May, *Homeward Bound: American Families in the Cold War Era* (New York: Basic Books, 1988); Robert A. Beauregard, *When America Became Suburban* (Minneapolis and London: University of Minnesota Press, 2006); and Dolores Hayden, *Building Suburbia: Green Fields and Urban Growth, 1820–2000* (New York: Pantheon Books, 2003; reprint, New York: Vintage, 2004).

5. Rome, *Bulldozer in the Countryside*, 123.

6. Regarding farmland losses, see Curtis C. Harris Jr. and David J. Allee, "Urbanization and its Effects on Agriculture in Sacramento County, California, Part 1: Urban Growth and Agricultural Land Use," Giannini Foundation Research Report No. 268 (December 1963), 1–2; James P. Degnan, "Santa Clara: The Bulldozer Crop," *The Nation* 200 (March 8, 1965): 124–137; "The Saga of San Jose: Santa Clara County Shows How to Balance Farms with Factories," *Fort-*

night (February 18, 1949): 10; Marvin Kottke, "Changes in Farm Density in Areas of Urban Expansion," *Journal of Farm Economics* 48 (December 1966): 1290–97; Raymond F. Dasmann, *The Destruction of California* (New York: Macmillan, 1965), 120–38; and Tim Lehman, *Public Values, Private Lands: Farmland Preservation Policy, 1933–1985* (Chapel Hill: University of North Carolina University Press, 1995), 98–99.

7. *The Chapter in Your Life Entitled San Francisco and the California it Centers* (San Francisco: Californians Inc., 1947), 35; and Blair Tavenner, *Seeing California: A Guide to the State* (Boston: Little, Brown & Co., 1948), 307.

8. Regarding Santa Clara County, see John Findlay, *Magic Lands: Western Cityscapes and American Culture after 1940* (Berkeley: University of California Press, 1992), 101–154; and Stephen J. Pitti, *The Devil in Silicon Valley: Northern California, Race and Mexican Americans* (Princeton: Princeton University Press, 2003), 128–29, 173. Also see www.census.gov/population/cencounts/ca190090.txt (accessed 10 May 2007); and *California Fruit and Nut Acreage, 1959* report, 5, and 1992 report, 10. *Cry California* ("The Journal of California Tomorrow") dedicated a special issue to matters of suburbia and open-space preservation, and proved particularly critical of "San Jose's Self-Destruct Policies," *Cry California* 5 (Fall 1970): 8–17. San Jose is the Santa Clara county seat.

9. See census figures at www.census.gov/populations/cencounts/ca190090.txt (accessed 10 May 2007).

10. "Population Data of Napa County," Napa County Planning Department, 28 November 1966. Regarding Bay Area urbanization and its implications, see Donald Joseph de la Pena, "Vineyards in a Regional System of Open Space in the San Francisco Bay Area: Methods of Preserving Selected Areas," (master's thesis, University of California, Berkeley, 1962), 50; and "Draft Environmental Management Plan for the San Francisco Bay Region," Association of Bay Area Governments, December 1977, Vol. II, 3. Also see census figures at www.census.gov/populations/cencounts/ca190090.txt (accessed 10 May 2007).

11. Napa County Department of Agriculture, Crop Reports, 1943, 1961, and 1973; and James V. Lider, Napa County Farm Advisor, "Farm Advisor's Report on 1965 Grape Crop in California's Major Grape Counties," *Wines & Vines* 47 (February 1966): 21.

12. Hickey Interview, 6; and Mel Varrelman, former supervisor, Napa County Board of Supervisors, interviewed by author, 13 July 2004, St. Helena, California, 8 (tape recording and transcript in author's possession).

13. "The Green Legacy," *New York Times*, editorial, 9 January 1965, 24; and Harold Gilliam, *San Francisco Sunday Chronicle*, 14 March 1965, quoted in Irving Hoch and Nickolas Tryphonopoulos, "A Study of the Economy of Napa County, California," Giannini Foundation Research Report No. 303 (August 1969): 57. See census figures at www.census.gov/populations/cencounts/ca190090.txt (accessed 10 May 2007).

14. Curtis C. Harris, Jr., and David J. Allee, "Urbanization and its Effects on Agriculture in Sacramento County, California, Part 2: Prices and Taxes of Agricultural Land," Giannini Foundation Research Report No. 270 (December 1963): 6–7.

15. California Legislature, *Joint Committee on Open Space Land, Preliminary Report* (Sacramento, March 1969), 10, quoted in Ralph B. Hutchinson and Sydney M. Blummer, "The Williamson Act and Wine Growing in the Napa Valley," California State Polytechnic College (Pomona, 1970), 1. Also see B. Bruce-Briggs, "Land Use and the Environment," in *No Land is an Island: Individual Rights and Government Control of Land Use* (San Francisco: The Institute for Contemporary Studies, 1975), 1–13.

16. Hutchinson and Blummer, "The Williamson Act," 2–4; and J. Herbert Snyder, "A Program for Agricultural Land Use in Urbanizing Areas," *Journal of Farm Economics* 48 (December 1966): 1306–1313.

17. Hoch and Tryphonopoulos, "A Study of the Economy of Napa County, California," 59; and Hutchinson and Blummer, "The Williamson Act," 7–11.

18. Varrelman Interview, 6–7; and summary of various articles from the *St. Helena Star* from 1962 through 1964, cited in Charles L. Sullivan, *Napa Wine: A History from Mission Days to Present* (San Francisco: Wine Appreciation Guild, 1994), 266–67.

19. Ann Schwing, interviewed by author, 10 June 2004, Archer Taylor Preserve, Napa County, California, 6 (tape recording and transcript in author's possession); Hickey Interview, 5; and James Conaway, *Napa: The Story of an American Eden* (New York: Houghton Mifflin, 1990), 83.

20. William Bronson, "A Proposal: The Napa Valley National Vineyard," *Cry California* 1 (Summer 1966): 14–16; and David Graves, interviewed by author, 9 July 2004, Saintsbury Vineyards, Napa, California, 10 (tape recording and transcript in author's possession).

21. *Wines & Vines* 50 (April 1968), 24; and Thomas Pinney, *A History of Wine in America: From Prohibition to the Present* (Berkeley: University of California Press, 2005), 38–39, 351, 366–67.

22. See, for example, Lehman, *Public Values, Private Lands;* Rome, *Bulldozer in the Countryside;* Richard N. L. Andrews, *Managing the Environment, Managing Ourselves: a History of American Environmental Policy* (New Haven: Yale University Press, 1999); Hal K. Rothman, *The Greening of a Nation? Environmentalism in the United States since 1945* (Fort Worth: Harcourt Brace, 1998); Samuel P. Hays, *Beauty, Health, and Permanence: Environmental Politics in the United States, 1955–1985* (New York: Cambridge University Press, 1987); and Richard H. K. Vietor, *Energy Policy in America since 1945: A Study of Business-Government Relations* (New York: Cambridge University Press, 2004).

23. For a discussion of these and other examples, see Kathleen A. Brosnan, "'Vin d' Etat': Consumers, Land, and the State in Napa Valley," in Gwyn Campbell and Nathalie Guibert, eds., *Wine, Society, and Globalization: Multidisciplinary Perspectives on the Wine Industry* (New York: Palgrave Macmillan, 2007).

24. William Novak argues that there is a long history of governmental regulation that undermines notions of American individualism, particularly as embraced within property ownership. Instead, he argues that Americans lived in a well-regulated society in which individuals bore responsibilities to their neighbors. The traditional legal doctrines of *sic utere tuo*

("use your property in a way as to not harm others") and *salus populi* ("the good of the people is supreme") held sway throughout the nineteenth century. William J. Novak, *The People's Welfare: Law & Regulation in Nineteenth-Century America* (Chapel Hill: University of North Carolina Press, 1996), 14, 17, 44–48.

25. Edwin A. Gere, Jr., "Dillon's Rule and the Cooley Doctrine: Reflections of the Political Culture," *Journal of Urban History* 8 (1982): 271–98; Kenneth F. Payne, "The Entrepreneurial Powers of Local Governments: Dillon's Rule Revisited" (PhD diss., University of Massachusetts, 2003); Gerald E. Frug, "The City as a Legal Concept," *Harvard Law Review* 93 (1980): 1057–1154; and Gerald E. Frug, "The Geography of Community," *Stanford Law Review* 48 (1996): 1047–1108.

26. Robert C. Ellickson and A. Dan Tarlock, *Land Use Controls: Cases and Materials* (Boston and Toronto: Little Brown and Co., 1981), 39–61; and *Village of Euclid v. Amber Realty Co.,* 272 U.S. 395, 47 S. Ct. 114 (1926).

27. Hickey Interview, 5; and Lehman, *Public Values, Private Lands,* 99–100. See also Gregory C. Gustafson and L. T. Wallace, "Differential Assessment as Land Use Policy: the California Case," *Journal of the American Planning Association* 41 (1975): 379–89; and David E. Hansen and Seymour I. Schwartz, "Prime Land Conservation: the California Land Conservation Act," *Journal of Soil and Water Conservation* 31 (1976): 198–203.

28. Hickey Interview, 5; and Sullivan, *Napa Wine,* 298–99.

29. Rome, *Bulldozer in the Countryside,* 135. Rome suggests that the momentum shifted toward open-space regulations in 1970, but indeed Napa County was ahead of the trend and the first place to apply such notions to agricultural land.

30. Hickey Interview, 5; and Conaway, *Napa,* 82–92.

31. Varrelman Interview, 6; and Rome, *Bulldozers in the Countryside,* 11. Also see H. E. McCurdy, "Public Ownership of Land and the Sagebrush Rebellion," *Public Studies Journal* 12 (1984): 483–90.

32. *San Francisco Chronicle,* 11 April 1968, 6. Hickey Interview, 6.

33. Graves Interview, 8; Varrelman Interview, 6–7; Hickey Interview, 7; and Hutchinson and Blummer, "The Williamson Act and Wine Growing in the Napa Valley," 13. Also see Michael G. Dalecki and C. Milton Coughenour, "Agrarianism in American Society," *Rural Sociology* 57 (1992): 48–64; Eric T. Freyfogle, *Agrarianism and the Good Society: Land, Culture, Conflict, and Hope* (Lexington: University Press of Kentucky, 2007), 1–7; Paul Thompson, "Agrarianism and the American Philosophical Tradition," *Agriculture and Human Values* 7 (1990): 3–8; and David B. Danbom, "Romantic Agrarianism in Twentieth-Century America," *Agricultural History* 65 (1991): 1/-12.

34. Louise Nelson Dyble, "Revolt against Sprawl: Transportation and the Origins of the Marin County Growth-Control Regime," *Journal of Urban History* 34 (November 2007): 38–66.

35. Graves Interview, 9.

36. Whitmer Interview, 10; Hickey Interview, 3, 19, 26–27; and Varrelman Interview, 9.

37. Whitmer Interview, 10; Varrelman Interview, 9, 15; and Graves Interview, 16.

38. *American Canyon Eagle* (California), 23 May 2007, at http://www.americancanyon eagle.com/articles/2007/05/23/opinion/editorial/iq_3961851.txt, accessed 29 May 2007. Growers and other landowners have taken private steps to ensure the county's rural character is protected. The Land Trust of Napa County has overseen the protection of more than 47,000 acres in 113 transactions since 1977, through conservation easements, Land Trust ownership, or transfers to resource agencies. Approximately 5,100 vineyard acres are included in conservation easements. See http://www.napalandtrust.org/framewho.html, accessed 1 May 2007. Also see Schwing Interview, 6–20.

39. A French term, *terroir* describes those physical characteristics of a place, such as soil, water, sunshine, temperature, and exposure, that distinguish vineyards and their products. James E. Wilson, *Terroir: the Role of Geology, Climate and Culture in the Making of French Wines* (Berkeley: University of California Press, 1999), 22–56.

40. Wineries of Napa Valley, survey compiled by Irene W. Haynes; "Napa Valley Vintners: the Early Years, 1943 to 1958," scrapbook and photo album; Interview of Robert Mondavi by Ina Hart and T. E. Wilde, 29 December 1978, Vol. III, 209–11, and Interview of George Deuer by Bernard Skoda, 19 June 1974, Vol. I, 130, in Interviews and Reminiscences of Long-Time Residents, the Napa Valley Wine Library Association, St. Helena Public Library ("NVWLA"). Also see James T. Lapsley, *Bottled Poetry: Napa Winemaking from the Prohibition to the Modern Era* (Berkeley: University of California Press, 1996), 47–51, 137.

41. *Wine Spectator,* April 1979, 13.

42. Testimony, John Tuteur, chair, Board of Supervisors of Napa County, before United States Department of Agriculture, Department of the Treasury, Bureau of Alcohol, Tobacco, and Firearms, Public Meeting in the Matter of Proposed Regulatory Definitions of Appellation of Origin, San Francisco Hyatt Regency, San Francisco, California, transcript, 228, NVWLA. For descriptions of the Paris tasting and its consequences, see *Time,* 7 June 1976, 58; and "Cabernet Sauvignon: An Assessment of Supply and Demand," Grape Intelligence Report, George M. Schofield, St. Helena, July 1989, 1–2, NVWLA.

43. Wineries of Napa Valley, Survey; James Conaway, *The Far Side of Eden: New Money, Old Land, and the Battle for Napa Valley* (Boston: Houghton Mifflin, 2002), 1–6; Napa River Watershed Task Force, 1–10; Napa County, Crop Reports, 1967, 1971, and 2001; *California Nut and Fruit Acreage,* 1919–1953, 1971–1981, and 2001; and http://napachamber.com/agpreserve.html, accessed 1 May 2007.

44. Varrelman Interview, 3; Hoch and Tryphonopoulos, "A Study of the Economy of Napa County, California," 36; Anne McLachlan, "The Wine Grape Industry of Napa, California, 1964–1979," (master's thesis, Birbeck College, University of London, 1980), 2; and Conaway, *The Far Side of Eden,* 1–6. A 2003 study, for example, indicated that vineyard owners who plant cabernet sauvignon grapes will invest more than $127,000 per acre in the first three years before they produce a viable crop. Costs include labor, fuel, lube, repairs, material, rootstock, and clones. Edward A. Weber, Karen M. Klonsky, and Richard

L. De Moura, "Sample Costs to Establish a Vineyard and Produce Grapes (Cabernet Sauvignon): North Coast Region: Napa County," University of California Cooperative Extension (2003), 14.

45. Napa River Watershed Task Force, Phase II, Final Report, prepared for the Napa County Board of Supervisors by Moore Iacofano Goltsman, September 2000, 1–3.

46. B. A. Garrison, "A Strategy for Conserving Oak Woodlands in Vineyard Landscapes," California Department of Fish and Game, Lands and Facilities, Administrative Report #2000–1 (2000), 4–10; Napa River Watershed Task Force, 4; Juliane Poirier Locke, *Vineyards in the Watershed: Sustainable Winegrowing in Napa County* (Napa: Napa Sustainable Winegrowing Group, 2002), 32–36, 47, 51.

47. *Integrated Pest Management: Field Handbook for Napa County* (Napa: Napa Sustainable Winegrowing Group, 1997), 2; Napa County Department of Agriculture Crop Report, 1999, and "Cabernet Sauvignon: An Assessment of Supply and Demand," 2–3.

48. Whitmer Interview, 15.

49. Hal K. Rothman, *Devil's Bargain: Tourism in the Twentieth-Century American West* (Lawrence: University Press of Kansas, 1998), 10–28.

50. "Study of Tourism in St. Helena," prepared for the city of St. Helena, California ([San Francisco]: Environmental Science Associates, Inc., December 1983), 11–12; and "Napa Valley Tourism Project," Prepared for the Napa Valley Foundation (San Francisco: ESA Planning and Environmental Services, November 1984), 5, 14, 18.

51. "Planning for Travel and Tourism in Napa County," 15 February 1990, prepared for Napa County Board of Supervisors by Dean Runyan Associates, 65–67. The Napa Valley Conference and Visitors Bureau (NVCVB) unapologetically attempts to identify and cater to the very wealthiest consumers. Annual Report, 2000/2001.

52. "Study of Tourism in St. Helena," 1, 3–5, 22 (quotation); and "Napa Valley Tourism Project," 5, 14, 18. Also see, for example, "Annual Planning Information, Napa County," 1984–1985, 1988–1989, and 1994," (San Francisco: State of California, Employment Development Department); and "Projections and Planning Information," 2001, 6.

53. "Study of Tourism in St. Helena," 17; "Planning for Travel and Tourism in Napa County," 19, 82; "Napa Valley Tourism Project," 10, 25–26, 29; Annual Report, 2000, NVCVB; and Hutchinson and Blumner, "The Williamson Act and Wine Growing," 3–5.

54. "Napa Valley Tourism Project," 24; "Annual Planning Information, 1984–85," 5; "Annual Planning Information, 1994," 14; "Projections and Planning Information, 2001 Updates," A-2; and *New York Times,* 12 December 2001, E1, 14. James Conaway describes locals' resentment: "They felt it while sitting in a long line of cars on Highway 29, looking up at once pristine slopes dense with conifers and chaparral, studded now with 'steroid houses,' 'muscle houses,' 'McMansions,' all contemptuous names for places built not to live in but as monuments to finance, visited by absentee owners." Conaway, *The Far Side of Eden,* 7. See also http://www.bayareacensus.ca.gov/cities/AmericanCanyon.pdf and http://www.bayareacensus.ca.gov/cities/Napa.htm, accessed 10 May 2007.

55. "Napa Valley Tourism Project," 30; "Planning for Travel and Tourism in Napa County," 101, 104; Graves Interview, 18; and Varrelman Interview, 11. See, more generally, James S. Duncan and Nancy G. Duncan, *Landscapes of Privilege: The Politics of the Aesthetic in an American Suburb* (New York: Routledge, 2004); and Fishman, *Bourgeois Utopias.*

56. William H. Friedland, "Agriculture and Rurality: Beginning the 'Final Separation'?" *Rural Sociology* 67 (2002): 358; and Hickey Interview, 8.

57. Conaway, *The Far Side of Eden,* 268–69; and Sullivan, *Napa Wine,* 349.

58. Varrelman Interview, 16–17; Hickey Interview, 11–16; and Graves Interview, 12. Also see Napa County Winery Definition Ordinance, Environmental Impact Report, prepared for the county of Napa, by LSA Associates, Point Richmond, CA, December 1989; Friedland, "Agriculture and Rurality," 357; and Sullivan, *Napa Wine,* 351–52.

59. Chris Malan (one of the litigants), interviewed by author, 21 July 2004, Napa, California (tape and transcript in author's possession), 20; Whitmer Interview, 24; Paul Roge, "Monitoring Erosion Control Strategies of Vineyards in Napa County," Water Resources Center Archives, Hydrology (2004), 4–11; *Santa Rosa Press Democrat* (CA), 3 November 1999; *St. Helena Star,* 13 December 2001; Napa River Watershed Task Force, 10–12; and Locke, *Vineyards in the Watershed,* 39.

60. Varrelman Interview, 21–23; and Graves Interview, 15–17.

61. www.nswg.org, accessed 10 May 2007; www.napalandtrust.org, accessed 10 May 2007; and Locke, *Vineyards in the Watershed,* 15.

Natives' Return

LBJ's Texas White House and Lady Bird's Wildflowers

VERA NORWOOD

When Lady Bird Johnson passed away on July 11, 2007, she was laid to rest next to her husband in the private family cemetery on the Hill Country ranch on the Pedernales River that had served as the "Texas White House" during Lyndon Johnson's presidency and had been their home since the 1950s. Press coverage and memorial tributes to Mrs. Johnson mentioned her love of the place and went on to chronicle her contributions to highway beautification, wildflower preservation, and various other conservation initiatives, as well as her role as a key advisor and emotional support for her husband throughout his political career. Since his death in 1973, Johnson's legacy has been the subject of much scholarly attention; we are now just beginning to understand Mrs. Johnson's legacy. In this essay I examine how Lady Bird, aiming to make her mark as First Lady, used her attachment to the Texas Hill Country ranch to engage a larger national and international environmental agenda of her own.

Hal Rothman's fine book, *LBJ's White House "Our Heart's Home,"* probes the meanings of the ranch for Johnson during his presidency. Their reference to the place as "our heart's home" suggests that Lyndon and Lady Bird shared a sense of the importance of the ranch to their lives before, during, and after the presidency. There were not only personal but political reasons why LBJ decided to buy a dilapidated ranch in the Hill Country. His family was from the area and his purchase of the ranch on the Pedernales River was a homecoming but, as Rothman notes, a homecoming of one who had risen from a poor, rural background to a seat of national and international power. The ranch and Johnson's improvements of it became a physical embodiment of the history of the man: "The ranch became a symbol of Johnson—his presidency, his roots, his belief in the ability of people to achieve their dreams."[1] Rothman and others have linked Johnson's history on the land with his support for the conservation movement as part of his "Great Society" initiatives. Johnson cast himself as a "conservation farmer" and the ranch as a model of scientific range management. Rothman argues that "Johnson understood poor people and ambition, and he respected practices that developed the land: agriculture, animal husbandry, and similar economic endeavors" and these views led to his vision of the ranch as representing not only remedies for the nation's ills during the tumultuous 1960s, but also for poverty he encountered in developing countries. This very regional place then participated not only in national agendas but also international initiatives like the "Green Revolution."[2]

Yet Johnson experienced some difficulty in having the ranch serve as a pure expression of western regionalism and as an expression of American power as a nation and in the world. The Johnson persona on the ranch was very much the modern cowboy. He enjoyed giving visiting dignitaries and reporters joy rides around the ranch in his convertible. His rural roots were ridiculed in the press after one ride in which it was reported he sped down ranch roads throwing empty beer cans out the window. Although the Johnson team did what they could to repair the image of LBJ as "litterbug," the alternative narrative which pictured the president and Lady Bird strolling the ranch picking up "beer cans and other refuse" was believed by some to damage his image as a powerful figure. This was especially so since this particular tale hit the press as Lady Bird was beginning to articulate her ideas for her beautification programs.[3]

Lewis L. Gould's biographies of Mrs. Johnson, *Lady Bird Johnson and the Environment* and *Lady Bird Johnson: Our Environmental First Lady* provide a comprehensive history of how she came to the decision to make beautification, especially of the highways, her primary initiative as First Lady. As Gould notes, both Johnsons saw the beautification agenda to be integrally a part of the War on Poverty and the construction of the Great Society. Parks and gardens in blighted urban areas improved the quality of life and developed community as well as providing jobs for local residents. They worked together on the various legislative and fund-raising efforts that emerged during Johnson's tenure in office. Gould documents Lady Bird's increasing collaboration with Stewart Udall, secretary of the interior and influential conservationist, to enhance the president's understanding and embrace of such quality-of-life initiatives in his own agenda, to the point of being the first president to include a call to improve and conserve the natural beauty of America in a State of the Union address. She understood that dubbing the effort a campaign on "Natural Beauty" gave a "feminine aura" to the whole endeavor and that having the president's visible backing provided a masculine authority to the project.[4] While they may have worked in tandem, gender issues were clearly at play for both as they collaborated to bring the values of the Texas Hill Country onto national and international stages.

The role the ranch played in LBJ's legacy, though, is complex. On one hand, Johnson's efforts to make the ranch a model operation, coupled with the very modern forms of connectivity (telephones, satellite dishes, televisions, airplane landing strips) needed by the president rendered it, in Rothman's words, a "fusion of the modern world with traditional America" which offered "a symbol for being grounded, for having roots in a genuine world that differed from the head-turning pull of politics and high society." On the other hand, those roots doomed the legacy. When LBJ identified the ranch and Texas with his brand of western cowboy independence "and made a claim for their place in the nation" he "played off of national myths that were rife in popular culture." This was the era of the western film, but Johnson the man and his ranch, Rothman argues, became "anachronistic" as the 1960s "need for a place" was replaced "by an emphasis on the need to wander" in the 1970s and beyond.[5] Rothman makes a convincing case for the failure of LBJ's vision to carry into the late twentieth century and the future. But Lady Bird had a hand in making the place as well. It was she who referred to the ranch as "our heart's home" and she had her own history on the property itself, in Texas and as First Lady. A look at that history suggests a somewhat different legacy for the Texas White House, one which places it squarely in contemporary environmentalism.

LBJ may have been the rancher and farmer of the family but Lady Bird was the gardener. Born and raised in a small town in East Texas near the Louisiana border, she remembered enjoying the outdoors as a child and often recounted memories of her love of the wildflowers on her walks through the countryside. As an undergraduate at the University of Texas she carried her appreciation for local flora to Austin. After her marriage she and her husband had residences in Austin and Washington, D.C., and she developed into an avid gardener with a deep interest in how to grow native wildflowers. When LBJ determined to buy the Pedernales ranch in the Texas Hill Country in 1950, Mrs. Johnson did not at first embrace the hardscrabble, run-down place, but she quickly took over the ornamental landscape design. In the 1950s she began her efforts to plant beloved native wildflowers, particularly the Texas bluebonnet, along the river and later on the landing strip added after Johnson became president, and she had wide expanses of ranchland seeded with natives. She was also a member of local civic organizations, including the garden club, and worked on beautification efforts in the region and the state.[6] These endeavors grew from as gendered a history as did her husband's. The landscape of wildflowers scattered from ranch to road to highway to national monument and beyond bears the legacy of that history.

Mrs. Johnson, and her effort to link her regional interests in native-plant preservation with her support for national agendas such as the antilitter and antibillboard campaigns, was as conscious of the power of her office and the meanings of being a southern and western woman as was her husband and his effort to forge a modern cowboy presidential persona at play on a national and international stage. For her, the issue was not only what the flora of Texas had to contribute to the beauties of the nation, but also how the diverse landscapes of America offered a global model for valuing the local in an increasingly cosmopolitan world. Lady Bird espoused a regionalism that at once supported and resisted nationalism and globalization— and this balancing act was articulated from her role as the landscape designer, as LBJ's First Lady, in the place they called their "heart's home."

One of the most common images of Lady Bird is of her sitting in a field of Texas bluebonnets. Jean Andrews's naturalist account, *The Texas Bluebonnet,* is a hymn to the native flower and its role in defining Texas as a regionally distinctive state in the larger United States.[7] The book credits Lady Bird Johnson as one of the key defenders of the bluebonnet in the late twentieth century and illustrates that history with a composite image of Johnson overlaid on a field of bluebonnets growing alongside a highway in Texas. Andrews offers a brief history of how the bluebonnet came to be the state flower. That history demonstrates that Mrs. Johnson inherited a tradition of women's engagement with defining the valued landscapes of Texas. In 1901 the state legislature considered a number of plants for designation as the state flower, and the elected officials were clearly concerned with picking a flower that reflected the state's rising influence in the nation as well as its regional landscape. The cotton boll had some favor because it was "the white rose of commerce." The prickly pear did not get very far. The bluebonnet, nominated by the National Society of the Colonial Dames of America in the State of Texas, won the designation as state flower when the women made their case by bringing to the floor of the legislature a classic still life painting of bluebonnets by Miss Mode Walker—suitable for hanging in any drawing room in the country. This native wildflower branded Texas as a distinctive place whose flora embodied the beauty of an America increasingly proud of its natural glories. Throughout the early twentieth century the women of Texas continued working to protect native flowers and to use them to beautify local roadsides.[8]

Deeply rooted herself in place, Mrs. Johnson inherited the mantle of those Colonial Dames and the garden club women who followed them by taking on responsibility for reminding a nation of the aesthetic values of its natural heritage. Keying off the powerful symbolism of "America the Beautiful," she became a leading voice for quality of life initiatives that included antilitter and antibillboard campaigns, city beautification and public park projects, and—most importantly for her regional interests—wildflower plantings along the ever-burgeoning national high-way system. The issue was not only what the flora of Texas had to contribute to the beauties of the nation, but also how the diverse, locally specific regions of America could be posed in resistance to the monolithic spaces associated with the interna-tional style of architecture which had been layered across the twentieth-century American landscape in buildings and public gardens. This was true even of her work on monumental Washington, D.C., when she worried that plans for beautify-ing Pennsylvania Avenue would ruin the distinctive feel of the space by importing "clipped European trees." These concerns carried throughout her life. In her 1993 coffee table book, *Wildflowers Across America,* she and her coauthor (the horticul-turalist Carlton Lees) specifically took note of the intrusions of the international style in urban landscape designs.[9] Thus, we need to understand this image of Lady Bird in a field of bluebonnets as a statement of resistance to an aspect of modern global culture, a statement grounded in equal parts national exceptionalism and regional pride. Just as her husband used the Texas cowboy stance in opposition to a rapidly changing, increasingly global world, so Lady Bird cast herself as a western Dame speaking for the values of garden and landscape traditions centered in the American West.

Scholarly literature contrasting national with global culture stresses the extent to which "culture" and "society" have been defined as a "bounded entity occupy-ing a physical territory mapped as a political territory (predominantly the nation-state) and binding individual meaning constructions into this circumscribed social, political space." Such embeddedness in place is threatened by forces of globaliza-tion that "deterritorialize." Cultural critic John Tomlinson considers the infiltration of local cultures by such forces of connectivity as transportation systems, radio, television, and mass-produced goods, and concludes that "embodiment and the forces of material circumstance keep most of us, most of the time, situated, but in places that are changing around us, gradually, subtly, losing their power to define the terms of our existence." This is "sometimes met by countervailing tendencies to re-establish the power of locality."[10] Such resistance in defense of nation is certainly what Mrs. Johnson was doing in her campaign to reclaim "America the Beautiful" by re-territorializing space for native plants.

Tomlinson is not necessarily engaged, however, in a critique of globalism's ten-dency to compress and connect the world. He also argues that "the penetration of localities which connectivity brings is . . . double-edged: as it dissolves the secu-rities of locality, it offers new understandings of experience in wider—ultimately global—terms."[11] Mrs. Johnson offers an example of how such doubleness plays out in one individual's life. She was a citizen of the world: wife of one its most powerful leaders, she routinely flew around the globe and was very much a player in international media markets through her ownership of radio and television stations. Like many privileged world citizens, she took for granted and actively pursued the many mundane aspects of global infiltration into daily life. But she also participated in what Tomlinson posits as one of the most significant, reflective understandings of global connectivity—environmentalism.

One of the first expressions of late twentieth-century globalism arose out of a post–World War II awareness in America of the extent to which human action was affecting, in very troubling ways, not only home and country but the entire planet. Mrs. Johnson was drawn into and became an influential voice for a circle of Americans deeply worried about the environment; of specific regions, the nation, and the world. Johnson was of the generation who read Rachel Carson's *Silent Spring;* her husband inherited the Kennedy administration's popular embrace of environmental politics; she consulted with and supported such cosmopolitan environmental leaders as Stewart Udall and Laurence Rockefeller.[12] In this context, a field of bluebonnets growing by the highway represented the salvage of a globally threatened biodiversity. Wildflowers transcended national boundaries by suggesting an expansive symbolic function for a beauty identified as critical to the preservation of a worldwide, universally beloved landscape in which regional distinctiveness was the key.

What emerges is a regionalism whose value as a cultural construct is, in fact, the extent to which its meanings can be stretched to include a dynamic, tangled set of relationships between nation and world. A very specific kind of localism helps makes this contradictory, unstable set of values work. If the Texas White House defined LBJ as a cowboy on a ranch, and the ranch and the cowboy were rendered anachronistic by their very rootedness and ties to tradition, the place had a very different meaning in regard to Lady Bird. Mrs. Johnson retired with her husband to the ranch at the conclusion of his presidency, and from that place she launched a campaign in defense of native plants that put her and the Texas Hill Country in the center of emerging efforts to figure out how best to protect cultural and natural landscapes worldwide. To understand her legacy it is critical to consider how she valued a wildflower and to place that value within the synergistic landscapes of home, region, nation, and world.

Lady Bird loved the flowers of her home, and asked questions of them and about them from her earliest childhood.[13] Her attachment to a place was most often expressed through reference to its plants. By the time she was First Lady, she had a clear answer for the difference between wildflowers and tame ones: wildflowers "fit" a place; they are able to thrive and grow because the climate, soil, companion plants, pollinators, and the like meet their needs. Unlike "tame" flowers, they do not depend on human horticulture to provide extra water or nutrients, to shelter them from wind, or sow their seed. Unlike weeds (which display many of the same characteristics as wildflowers), they compliment and enhance biodiversity; they are not so aggressive that they take over their fellow plants. Wildflowers were a key identifier of region for her because their spread across a landscape defines locale.

There are two kinds of wildflowers under her rubric—natives and recent arrivals. Native plants are endemic to a place; a series of them grouped in communities often defines distinctive qualities of the region. These are the plants with long tenancy—with "roots." Lady Bird often used a specific historical moment of arrival—such as when the first Spanish or Anglo explorer arrived in the Texas Hill Country and saw fields of such plants—to illustrate the virtues of a native wildflower. That historical priority to European arrival is one of the simplest defining characteristics of a native plant—which is always also wild. Thus, even though Lady Bird worked with the state highway department in Texas to develop methods for mass plantings of nursery-bred bluebonnets along the highway, they remained wildflowers. The assumption being that, once there, they can take care of themselves.[14]

Tame plants may become wild as well. Lately we have become quite familiar with the invasive tendencies of exotics like purple loosestrife in the East and pampas grass along the western coasts. These plants may be wild and they may even flower, but they are not wildflowers. They are weeds. Wildflowers can be imported plants—ones en route from somewhere else—that fit gracefully into a region, embed in it, and add to its biodiversity and distinctive quality. They also remind us that plants do not stand still. They follow likely trails as surely as animals, they hitchhike shamelessly, and they even ride along in moving vans to bring a little reminder of somewhere else into a new place.[15]

Borrowing from the cultural anthropologist James Clifford, who has studied the issues of dwelling and travel in tourism and cultural performances, a field of wildflowers may represent at once "roots" and "routes"—deeply embedded, place-based communities and traveling cultures. Such "Persian carpets," as Lady Bird loved to call them, define a particularly cosmopolitan version of localism, one that makes room for relative newcomers, including Lady Bird herself who had to come to embrace the Texas Hill Country. Thus a region, while remaining highly localized because of the specific physical demands of its terrain and climate, may also reference the sort of eclectic connectivity and diversity associated with mobility.[16]

Mrs. Johnson's contributions to this interactive dance between region, nation, and world culminated in the establishment of her most visibly enduring legacy—The Lady Bird Johnson Wildflower Center. Originally titled the "National Wildflower Research Center," the buildings, gardens, and wildlands are direct ancestors of the Pedernales ranch, the Texas White House. In 1971 LBJ turned the ranch over to the National Park Service, with the stipulation that Mrs. Johnson would have the use of the house for her lifetime. After her husband's death, Mrs. Johnson took the ranch in a new direction. In an interview in 1987 she commented that "I am pleased to say I am not personally responsible any longer for a single cow. The Park Service keeps some around to give atmosphere for the tourists."[17]

No longer a model of modern agriculture, the Texas White House became identified with Lady Bird's interest in preserving and cultivating native plants in the landscape. During the 1970s and 1980s she began using the ranch for research into the germination and growth of wildflowers. From that effort grew her vision of a center whose mission she described as a place for ensuring that development would include making "a conscious effort, as we built, to preserve and make use of our native plants . . . So I thought I might establish a center which would encourage people to incorporate wildflowers into the development grid, distribute information about how this can be done, call attention to how practical—for example, as a means of saving water—it is to landscape with native species."[18] The first center was built in the early 1980s on property Mrs. Johnson donated on Austin's east side. Fundraising for the new center made use of the Texas White House. Reminiscent of LBJ's grand barbeques for national and international guests while he was president, Mrs. Johnson held a "County Fair" benefit for the center at the ranch in 1984, attracting 1,000 guests—many of whom flew in aboard planes landing on the air strip—and concluding with a group sing of *America the Beautiful*. As the center grew, there was a push to move to a larger forty-two-acre site, in part because the center had difficulty growing plants of the Hill Country on Austin's east side, and the new site was on the city's west side, on the edge of the Hill Country landscape ecosystem.[19]

Over the last twenty-five years the center has maintained the initial mission of encouraging use of native plants in developed landscapes, but has also expanded its range in keeping with emerging concerns about protection and restoration of plant biodiversity. The center's current site offers several critical environmental landscapes that are at the forefront of efforts to preserve plant diversity in the context of urbanization. One grid of the center targets suburban Austin. Demonstration and theme beds offer the public ideas for how to landscape their own backyards. In 1999 the center purchased 136 acres south of the original forty-two-acre plot to control housing developments slated for the area; the land was then set aside to support the newly established Center for Landscape Restoration. The Wildflower Center began to explicitly pursue standing in plant conservation and endangered species protection with a stated goal of moving to a greater focus on ecological issues. The new acreage references the growth of "ranchettes" in Austin: suburban homesteads of one to forty acres carved out of remnant ranchland. Here the questions have to do with how to restore native grasslands, and the center offers the public an opportunity to tour research sites addressing land-management practices, such as the effect of fire on restoring native prairie. Finally, the center engages the public in efforts to protect and preserve habitat for endangered species like the Texas wild rice, which grows in only one place along a stretch of the San Marcos River popular with urban inner-tubing fans.[20] For Austin and the region, the center has become a key definer of what constitutes the appropriately settled Texas Hill Country landscape. At the same time, the center makes clear that its efforts involving a network of botanical gardens, research groups, and activist organizations espouse an increasingly common twenty-first-century message of the value of regional plants in a global environmental context. The Wildflower Center (and the ranch from which it springs) has become a site participating in the creation of what Tomlinson refers to as a "world memory," grounded in the specificity of localism usually identified with nationalism—but now also applied to native green landscapes anywhere in the world.[21]

The specific sort of localism upon which this tangle of regional/national/global culture depends continues to be reset by the plants themselves. Johnson and her comrades imagined a cosmopolitan community of natives and migrant flowers in a dynamic landscape. Their decades-long attempts to nurture the plants have, however, forced a less romantic view of how to maintain the diversity at the heart of those Persian-carpet landscapes Mrs. Johnson loved. Not every plant lives happily by the roadside, or in a concrete river channel, or even in carefully constructed refugia at the local botanical garden. Relocated plants may also hybridize and such interbreeding leads to a loss of diversity. Rare natives can be "loved" to death by all sorts of transportation.

As the center became more engaged in ecological research, staff began to emphasize, in a newly reflexive manner, their role in the global effort to preserve and restore landscapes threatened by just the sorts of mobility represented by those highways Mrs. Johnson had earlier seen as the route to salvation of native plants. In an interesting mixture of rootedness and mobility, the center began to tout by the 1990s the critical importance of maintaining boundaries. Plants were not seen as so easily "carted" around by human hands. The center used its publications in order to alert the public to what it termed as the "silent crisis" of plant extinctions and loss of diversity due to "urban development and road construction, agriculture and ranching, and habitat fragmentation and pollution." A 2001

issue of the center magazine, *Native Plants,* devoted to endangered and threatened species, provided advice for gardeners in responsible consumption of native
plants, including the caution that "irresponsible collection of seed and plants from
the wild by gardeners, collectors and retail companies adds to the decimation of
entire populations." Center publications continue to emphasize the importance
of discovering how to restore landscapes of home and highway, and displays of
seed packets for sale in the center store warn about the threats to plant diversity
in sowing native seed outside its typical range. Appropriate sorts of traveling by
native plants continues to be a theme, however. In 2006 the magazine reported
on the center's collaboration with the city of San Antonio to restore an urban
stretch of the San Antonio River by replanting with natives commonly found one
hundred miles north in a protected stretch of the river. *Ex situ* conservation is
an acceptable way for plants to travel as well, as the center ships seeds of native
plants from West Texas to the Royal Botanical Garden in Kew for storage as part
of the Millennium Seed Project. And virtual mobility is encouraged through the
center Web site's invitation to Austin residents to electronically surf the world of
native plant preservation, including links to a variety of activist initiatives in support of global biodiversity. [22]

There remain cautionary tales to be drawn from the center's brief history. Lessons learned from the plants themselves about the difficulties with the metaphor
of wildflowers and their seemingly easy spread along all sorts of disturbed terrain
have not translated into a broader reflexive stance in regard to the center itself as
an exemplar of the intrusions of globalization into locale. The architecture of the
center is truly stunning. All the stone in the buildings is local and much of the
wood is recycled from older buildings demolished around Austin. But the style of
the buildings and the gardens makes reference to the history of migration in the
region—somewhat to the Spanish mission period, but especially to the architecture and agriculture of later settlers with German and English backgrounds. The
architecture references the history of the Pedernales ranch, which was located in
the heart of German settlement in the Hill Country and harks back to the Johnsons'
use of ranch barbeques to stage reenactments of waves of European arrivals. In this,
the center gestures toward Mrs. Johnson's shared interest with her husband in the
history of Anglo-American settlement of Texas, what Hal Rothman refers to as the
Texas "xenophobia about mythic roots."[23]

Native American history is limited to a small artificial spring just inside the
entrance. The indigenous, relatively mobile peoples who preceded European
contact are not perceived to have left quite the same sort of architectural or
botanical marks on the land as later European migrants.[24] Although the center is

concerned with reaching a more diverse demographic, the founding moment was Lady Bird Johnson's drive to preserve the distinctive plants of America in their regional diversity. While the plants represent roots and grounding, the architecture is firmly evocative of a historically narrow version of routes and roads. Anglo-American mobility thus serves to build a national culture that has envisioned regional embeddedness as a trait easily achieved by the "right sorts" of travelers, those who sing the virtues of "America the Beautiful." The center is only beginning to address the question of the plant values and beloved landscapes of the urban human communities that constitute the ever more diverse megalopolis of twenty-first-century Austin, Texas.

A related problem for the center is its own footprint in Austin. It sits on the Edwards Aquifer recharge zone, Austin's key water source. And, since its construction, it has been one of the magnets drawing residential development out, contributing to Austin's sprawl. These issues have been apparent since the land was purchased. In response, the center was designed to make little or no draw on Austin's water supply, and tours highlight the importance of water conservation and protection of the Edwards Aquifer recharge zone. Although staffed at the center work with Austin citizen groups on such development problems, this history continues to divide environmentalists who otherwise share very similar values, challenging the center to take more leadership in Austin's plans for growth. Mrs. Johnson's "Keep America Beautiful" campaigns of the 1960s and 1970s have been criticized for their failure to recognize the more fundamental environmental challenges that growth and urbanization pose—and this contradiction in the goals and effects of the Wildflower Center site well illustrates that problem.[25]

Much scholarly commentary on globalization assumes a historically linear shift (sometimes lauded but more often criticized) from the regional to the national, which is then displaced by equally problematized forces of connectivity and proximity erasing regional and national historical memory with a flood of integrated electronic information and marketing systems. Momentum for such change is laid at the door of post–World War II America and its influence on the world, with the clear understanding that globalization is often synonymous with Americanization. Reflecting on the world she witnessed during her time in Washington, Mrs. Johnson remarked in 1963: "As I travel around the world with Lyndon, I often think of the funny old sign on my daddy's store, 'Thomas Jefferson Taylor, Dealer in Everything.' Now science and time and necessity have propelled the United States to be the general store for the world, dealer in everything. Most of all, merchants for a better way of life, I hope."[26] In "taming" wildflowers for mass roadside plantings, helping to make their seeds more commercially viable, and supporting the development of a market for "native plants," Mrs. Johnson certainly engaged in merchandising regionalism in service to nationalism (cum globalism) as a "better way of life," ironically wedding the virtues of place to the ills of global capitalism.

It is easy to read the commodification of native plants through such a lens, but this reading denies the continued agency of region, of specific places. For, as Mrs. Johnson and her followers suspect, wildflowers might have another way of regarding their current fortunes—one often posed as a fundamental mode of resistance to the de-territorializing forces of globalization. No matter how forces of connectivity and proximity may deny realities of time and space, a walk through the Hill Country savannah of the Wildflower Center, Lady Bird's re-creation of the native plants and landscapes of her home on the Pedernales River, illustrates Tomlinson's assertion that "locality continues to exercise its claims upon us as the physical situation of our lifeworld."[27]

In the end, Hal Rothman argues that LBJ's rootedness in both a time and a place meant that the ranch and the man failed to carry much influence into the twenty-first century. Mrs. Johnson, however, reinvented the ranch as a cosmopolitan model of our environmental future. The Lady Bird Johnson Wildflower Center makes a claim on our interest because of the synergies it contains: its location in an urban setting embodies all the complications and contradictions of post-twentieth-century globalization, while its stubbornly material existence, the fundamental localism of these plant communities, symbolizes the endemic, naturally distinctive places in which we live day to day.

Notes

1. Hal K. Rothman, *LBJ's Texas White House: "Our Heart's Home"* (College Station: Texas A&M University Press, 2001), 5.

2. Rothman, *LBJ's Texas White House*, 98. The "conservation farmer" quote is on p. 151. On Johnson and conservation see also Martin Melosi, "Lyndon Johnson and Environmental Policy," in *The Johnson Years, Volume 2: Vietnam, the Environment, and Science* (Lawrence: University Press of Kansas), 113–49.

3. Rothman, *LBJ's Texas White House*, 204.

4. Lewis L. Gould, *Lady Bird Johnson and the Environment* (Lawrence: University Press of Kansas, 1988), 61. See also, Gould, *Lady Bird Johnson: Our Environmental First Lady* (Lawrence: University Press of Kansas, 1999). For Mrs. Johnson's sense of how her beautification work fit into the political goals of the Great Society, see her speech to the Yale Political Union on October 9, 1967, "Beautification and Public Welfare," *Social Action*, vol. 34 (May 1968): 21–27.

5. Rothman, LBJ's Texas White House, 263, 5.

6. Gould, *Lady Bird Johnson*, 6–23; Rothman, LBJ's Texas White House, 155.

7. Jean Andrews, *The Texas Bluebonnet* (Austin: University of Texas Press, 1986).

8. Andrews, *The Texas Bluebonnet*, 13–14. For a history of Texas women's continuing efforts in support of native plants and natural beauty into Mrs. Johnson's lifetime see, Gregory T. Cushman, "Environmental Therapy for Soil and Social Erosion: Landscape Architecture and Depression-Era Highway Construction in Texas," in Michel Conan, *Environmentalism in Landscape Architecture* (Washington, DC: Dumbarton Oaks Research Library, 2000), 45/-70?.

9. Gould, *Lady Bird Johnson and the Environment*, 99. Lady Bird Johnson and Carlton B. Lees, *Wildflowers Across America* (New York: Abbeville Press, 1993), 272.

10. John Tomlinson, *Globalization and Culture* (Chicago: University of Chicago Press, 1999), 28.

11. Tomlinson, *Globalization*, 30.

12. Gould, *Our Environmental First Lady*, 36.

13. For the development of her love of flowers see her account of her youth and years in the White House, Lady Bird Johnson, *A White House Diary* (New York: Holt, Rinehart and Winston, 1970), her contributions to *Wildflowers Across America*, and the Gould biography, *Lady Bird Johnson and the Environment*.

14. For an example see Lady Bird Johnson, *Texas—A Roadside View* (San Antonio: Trinity University Press, 1980), 24. For the early history of the Texas roadside planting programs see Conan, *Environmentalism*.

15. See the section in *Wildflowers* on the distinction between native and introduced plants, 34–62.

16. James Clifford, *Routes: Travel and Translation in the Late Nineteenth Century* (Cambridge: Harvard University Press, 1997). Mrs. Johnson's opening essay in *Wildflowers Across America*, "Wildflower Adventures," lays out her enchantment with "the wonderfully romantic" ways in which flowers spread across and move through various landscapes, 23–34.

17. The interview is in Bill Gilbert, "In from the Fields, Wildflowers Find a New Welcome Among Gardeners," *Smithsonian* vol. 18 (April 1987): 42.

18. Gilbert, "In from the Fields," 42–43.

19. On the "Country Fair" benefit see "Over 1000 Attend Center's 'Country Fair' Benefit," *Wildflower: Newsletter of the National Wildflower Research Center* vol. 1 (Summer 1984); Gould, *Environmental First Lady*, 125.

20. See the center's guidebook, *Lady Bird Johnson Wildflower Center: Native Plants and Native Places* and the center Web page www.wildflower.org.

21. Tomlinson, *Globalization*, 103.

22. For a sense of the shift to ecological issues see the 1999–2001 issues of the center magazine, *Native Plants*. Quotes on endangered species are from vol. 18, (Winter 2001) 3, 6. For the collaboration with San Antonio see Roddy Scheer, "Urban Renewal," *Wildflower*, (Winter 2006).

23. Rothman, *LBJ's Texas White House,* 169.

24. As Rothman notes, the tall grass prairies encountered by the Europeans were the work of "ten thousand years of cyclic fire and nomadic use" by native tribes, including the Apache and Comanche, *LBJ's Texas White House,* 10–13.25. Gould, *Environmental First Lady,* 125.

26. Gould, *Lady Bird Johnson,* 27.

27. Tomlinson, *Globalization,* 149.

Water

Fishy Thinking

Salmon and the Persistence of History
in Urban Environmental Politics

MATTHEW KLINGLE

When the flood waters came, Jennifer Forrey knew what to blame.

The weather was only partly at fault. On the evening of December 14, 2006, a powerful low-pressure system slammed into the Pacific Northwest, delivering heavy rainfall and hurricane-force winds. Some two million residents from southern British Columbia to Oregon lost power for days, some for weeks. At least eight people died and damage estimates ran into the tens or hundreds of millions. Forrey was one of the many victims. She and her partner, Jack Lawless, fled their West Seattle home at the height of the gales. When they returned, they found their newly renovated basement filled with water and their seventeen-foot aluminum boat floating in the driveway. The mangled garage door dangled in its tracks.

Another likely suspect was Pilchuck Construction, a private contractor rerouting natural gas lines in the neighborhood. Workers had left dirt and gravel piled on the street near storm drains, but that alone was not enough to cause the severe flooding. In Forrey's opinion, the real problem was the cloth filters mandated by state authorities to prevent construction debris from damaging endangered salmon habitat downstream. Across Seattle, almost 350 homeowners and businesses reported that drains blocked by clogged filters had led to extraordinary flooding. In the recriminations that followed the so-called Hanukkah Eve Wind Storm, city officials accused builders of not removing the filters. Alan Justad, a representative for Seattle Public Utilities, retorted, "we hadn't gotten complaints about these inserts until this big storm." In the minds of Forrey and other waterlogged Seattleites, the blame came down to one culprit: salmon.[1]

In the spring of 1999, the National Marine Fisheries Service tried to stop ebbing Chinook salmon runs. Seattle and its neighbor to the south, Portland, Oregon, were now the first urban areas in the United States to face an Endangered Species Act listing. Endangered salmon had become an omen of urban growth gone amok. In the words of then-mayor Paul Schell, salmon were also "the fish that might save Seattle"—provided that Seattleites learned to stop and even roll back sprawl. If Seattle needed saving, however, salmon were an expensive indulgence. As James Vesely, editorial editor for the *Seattle Times,* explained soon after the 1999 federal edict, residents needed to expect "major confrontations of property rights, tough limitations on recreation time and space, and residential development." "Likewise," he continued, "political careers and campaign strategies" would revolve on who could "deliver a salmon campaign that ignites the hearts of voters." No wonder that many since have questioned the premise behind Schell's naïve assessment since salmon have divided northwesterners from the beginning of American rule in the former Oregon Country, if not before.[2]

Ultimately, the debate over salmon is less about the fish than about one of the oldest and most enduring conflicts in American society: the longing for community. For more than a century and a half, disputes over salmon have figured into almost every argument in and around Seattle over how to balance society and environment. A century ago, the terms of the debate revolved around improving nature to improve society by redirecting rivers, leveling hills, filling estuaries, and luring industry. By millennium's end, restoring nature propelled discussions over redefining human community. The story of Seattle's salmon suggests a more complicated view of how history, human and nonhuman, creates and splinters the idea of community through time. Paying attention to the persistence of the past can suggest how, if Seattleites think historically, they might be able to rebuild a city that is home to salmon and people, too.

The paths that connect past to present stretch back into the epoch before human time, beginning with the unique evolutionary adaptation called anadromy, a trait shared by all species of Pacific salmon, members of the genus *Oncorhynchus.* The rising and falling of the ocean, coupled with the advance and retreat of great Pleistocene Era ice sheets, cut ancestral salmon off from either salt water or fresh, in alternating cycles, compelling them to migrate between the two for survival. Pacific salmon thus became anadromous: born in freshwater, maturing at sea, and then returning to spawn and often die in lakes and streams. Other pressures also directed salmon evolution. Drenched by seasonal rains and snow, the Pacific Northwest's volcanic soils leached minerals out to sea. The salmon, in a fashion, returned this wealth to the terrestrial realm in their fatty tissues to provide their progeny with trace elements necessary for proper physiological development. Without dead salmon, living salmon would not be anadromous.[3]

Anadromy is also what made salmon valuable to human beings and vulnerable to changes that humans made in their habitat. The diverse Indians of Puget Sound venerated salmon as a reliable source of food and numinous power. They timed their seasonal subsistence rounds on the arrival of particular species, and told stories to one another of what happened if humans offended salmon or took them too greedily.[4] Yet moderation was not the motto for the Americans who invaded Puget Sound. The Americans eventually exploited the fisheries of Puget Sound for commercial profit, but they used salmon for statecraft first. The founding territorial governor of Washington, Isaac Ingalls Stevens, realized this in the treaties he negotiated with the many bands of Puget Sound Indians in 1854–55, promising them payments for their ancestral lands and the unrestricted right to fish, hunt game, pick berries, and harvest shellfish in their "usual and accustomed places" on any "open and unclaimed lands." By letting Indians continue, in some fashion, their seasonal subsistence rounds, he hoped to reduce the costs of maintaining them on reservations while providing white American settlements, at the request of labor-starved mill operators and farmers, a proximate and well-fed workforce. Stevens's plan soon fell apart because whites viewed the treaties and the Indians who signed them instrumentally. For their part, Indians came to resent the treaty and reservation system because they understood their rights literally and continued to fish and hunt, often under the threat of imprisonment by state authorities, beyond reservation boundaries. Federal officials did little to protect their Indian wards once they left their assigned reserves, choosing instead to side with white sport anglers who complained that unchecked development and unregulated commercial fishing were ruining Puget Sound's salmon fisheries.[5]

Sportsmen had reason to whine when it came to habitat loss. From the late 1890s, when the Klondike gold rush brought capital and migrants to Puget Sound, through the 1920s, Seattle was one of the nation's fastest growing cities, but demography was not the only force changing geography. An assortment of entrepreneurs, corporations, city engineers, and state agencies, often working at cross-purposes but all driven by an ethic of improving the natural world to release its energies for profit or reform, remade the physical face of Seattle and its environs. Muddy tidelands ringing the city's waterfront became solid land for docks and railway terminals, filled in with sawdust, ship ballast, or debris from the massive hydraulic regrades that leveled many downtown hills. The U.S. Army Corps of Engineers dug the Lake Washington Ship Canal that connected Puget Sound to Lake Washington. The canal lowered the lake's water level by almost ten feet, thereby becoming its sole outlet. City and county engineers transformed the sinuous and slow-moving Duwamish River, the city's largest, into the linear Duwamish Waterway, a river manufactured for industry. Seattle acquired the Cedar River, the largest tributary to Lake Washington, for its exclusive source, turning part of its flow into city reservoirs and the rest directly into the lake to help supply the water-hungry Ship Canal locks. Indeed, by the 1920s, almost every major waterway in central and southern Puget Sound was either diverted for municipal water, agriculture, or hydropower— or uncurled and dredged to reduce floods and improve navigation. At the same time, cities around the sound built combined sewer systems that turned creeks into sanitary and storm drains. In the case of Lake Washington and Seattle, the completion of the Ship Canal and Duwamish Waterway, coupled with filling estuaries and tide flats, altered an entire watershed that once drained more than 4,100 square miles.[6]

Changing the waters meant changing the original salmon runs too. Migrating fish now had to navigate confusing ladders at the Lake Washington Ship Canal locks, survive rising levels of pollution along industrialized rivers, or find other streams to replace those blocked by dams and culverts. As populations declined, state fisheries managers relied upon artificial propagation to sustain dying runs while expelling those who had the weakest political backing from the fisheries. Indians and recent immigrants, especially those from southern and eastern Europe, were the targets. And just as the engineers and industrialists were putting the final touches on their renovations to Puget Sound, the state fish commission, in 1920, after a series of contentious public hearings, banned commercial fishing in the waters off Seattle. Some of those excluded from the fishing grounds took to poaching even as white sportsmen celebrated their successful salmon conservation campaign. Eddie Bauer, the outdoorsman turned retail magnate, boasted in 1928 "Seattle fishermen are fortunate to have at their very door the finest salt water fishing in the country."[7] Another sporting goods vendor, Ben Paris, hosted the first fishing derbies in the early 1930s to attract more customers to his hunting and fishing store. Salmon derbies quickly became a durable part of Seattle's summertime culture. One enthusiast asked if there was any other place where sportsmen could "catch salmon off the docks, or under the shadow of a skyscraper?" Left unasked was who had suffered in the name of conservation. Many local commercial fishermen, barred from their former fishing grounds, now turned to thievery instead. Poaching along the Duwamish and around Elliott Bay was commonplace in the 1920s and 1930s, and many arrested by state fish wardens had Italian, Greek, Slavic, or Japanese surnames. Some were likely Indians fishing off reservation too.[8]

Victory by sportsmen did not mean that all was well with Seattle's salmon, however. Miller Freeman, publisher of *Pacific Fisherman,* the largest and most important trade journal of its kind, warned in 1934 "that every salmon stream from the Sacramento to Puget Sound is being most seriously affected by power projects, irrigation, denuding of the forests, pollution, etc." Freeman, long a tireless crusader for fish, also embodied the contradictions of the crisis he saw coming. He was an unabashed cheerleader for urban growth and backed the construction of the Mercer Island Floating Bridge, which connected the nascent suburbs on Lake Washington's eastern shores to Seattle in 1940. Freeman loved open space as much as he loved salmon fishing, and he soon joined the suburban exodus to the Eastside so his children would see "nature and beauty and life beyond the city streets." After the war, he purchased an old strawberry field once cultivated by Japanese American farmers north of downtown Bellevue as a gift for his son, Kemper, who turned it into Bellevue Square, the region's first suburban mall.[9]

When the younger Freeman opened the shopping center's doors in 1946, he welcomed thousands of eager customers. Many had moved to Seattle during the Second World War to work in high-paying defense jobs, staying afterwards to work in the burgeoning Cold War industries, like Boeing, the mighty aeronautical firm that now dominated the region's economy. The engineers, pilots, designers, and industrial laborers also stayed, in part, because of the region's scenic charms. They settled in the Lake Washington suburbs as Miller Freeman had, driving demand for better and faster transportation. In 1962, the Evergreen Point Floating Bridge opened, giving the Eastside its second link to Seattle. Three years later, the bridge was jammed with commuters, and Bellevue surpassed Seattle to become the state's fastest-growing city. Growth soon posed some major problems for the region, the most notable being the 1958 election that created the Municipality of Metropolitan Seattle, or Metro, the regional agency charged to build sewers and rescue Lake Washington from unchecked pollution. Yet Metro had not so much restrained growth as redirected and accelerated it by making still more suburban development possible. One local writer predicted, in 1965, that if growth continued unchecked, Seattle could "become the Northwest version of Los Angeles, only without the saving grace of constant sunshine to make the nightmare barely bearable." Attempts to rein in sprawl, as in so many places across the nation at the time, met with mixed success at the polls.[10]

Despite the severe turbulence following Boeing's near-fatal crash in the early 1970s—when the company slashed more than 60,000 jobs and the regional economy, still dependent upon Cold War largesse, plummeted—Seattle and its environs continued to expand. And salmon paid the price for growth. State fisheries scientists had warned, as early as 1948, that "the effects of civilization and real estate development" were ruining salmon habitat around Seattle.[11] Even those projects designed to save some locations, like Metro's sewers, which removed suburban sewage and septic tank runoff from Lake Washington, only displaced treated waste to other locations, like the industrialized Duwamish River or Puget Sound. Even as Lake Washington rebounded, thanks to Metro's efforts, sport anglers predicted that the sewers would spell "death for a tired old river," the polluted Duwamish. But sportsmen and fisheries managers alike were unwilling and unable to confront the full enormity of habitat destruction, continuing to rely upon hatcheries as a convenient cure-all, a position supported by most sportsmen and commercial operators, who blamed one another for diminishing stocks. The advent of postwar environmentalism brought with it another camp demanding salmon solutions: people living next to disappearing urban creeks and streams. When developers associated with Northgate Shopping Center began construction on new apartments in 1969, homeowners living next to Thornton Creek in northeast Seattle created the Citizens for the Preservation of Thornton Creek and reminded the state fisheries department of its legal obligation to protect spawning grounds.[12]

In the middle of these expanding debates, the unpredictability of nature itself seemed to play an ironic role when, in 1970, massive runs of returning sockeye salmon astounded scientists and anglers alike. The actual reasons for the surprise were biological as well as political. In 1917, just after the Ship Canal's completion, state fish wardens released hatchery-reared sockeye fry in Lake Washington and the Cedar River. Additional plantings followed, in 1935 or 1937, with the hope of establishing a new fishery by artificial means since sockeye, unlike other anadromous salmon, can spend up to two years in lakes as juveniles before heading out to sea. Modest numbers returned to spawn until 1967, when the number jumped from 45,400 to 190,000, prompting the first-ever commercial season on the lake the following year, with a recreational angling season declared three years later.[13] Fisheries managers could only claim partial credit for the seeming miracle. Reduced pollution, thanks to the Metro sewers, also boosted the populations of *Daphnia,* a tiny freshwater crustacean favored by juvenile sockeye. In a final twist, dredging along the lower Cedar River to alleviate flooding inadvertently produced clean gravel beds and clearer currents, perfect for spawning sockeye.[14]

But the unexpected success of Lake Washington's sockeye only further entangled the region's salmon disputes, and the knots were Gordian. The Cedar River, the lake's largest tributary, became the focus of the conflict because the river could not serve all of its consumers. The Army Corps needed more water from the Cedar River to accommodate burgeoning recreational boat traffic in the Ship Canal, the city of Seattle demanded more for its citizens, and fisheries advocates called for more to sustain spawning salmon. A *Seattle Times* reporter, writing in 1970, put the problem in stark terms: "one million sockeye will be competing with one million human beings for the pure, clean water of the Cedar River—and there isn't enough for both."[15]

Nor was there enough to satisfy even older legal claims. Puget Sound Indians now had the legal power of their restored treaty rights. Federal Judge George H. Boldt ruled, in 1974, that the signatories of the so-called "Stevens Treaties" had retained the right to fish in all of their usual and accustomed places. They were also entitled to the opportunity to take up to one-half of the entire catch. Boldt later ordered state fish and game officials to adopt a new fisheries management regime, which effectively made Indians co-managers of the region's fisheries. At first, the Boldt Decision seemed simply to be a fight between Indian and white anglers over who had the right to catch fish, where, and in what numbers. Those authorities charged with protecting Seattle's utilities knew better. The city-owned dams on the Skagit River, some seventy miles north and built in the 1930s, provided inexpensive hydroelectric power for Seattle customers; they were also efficient salmon-killing machines. The same could be said of the water spigots in every Seattle home since the city's water department had blocked spawning salmon from swimming above the municipal intake at Landsburg since 1901 out of fear that the rotting carcasses would contaminate supplies. Farther upstream, the water department allowed commercial logging within the watershed boundaries, a policy it had pursued since the early 1900s to pay for watershed maintenance and land acquisition. Silt and debris from denuded hillsides and logging roads spilled into the river, choking salmon spawning beds and elevating water temperatures above tolerable levels.[16]

Facing potential lawsuits to do more for salmon, the city created a habitat conservation plan for the Cedar River watershed in 1995. Habitat conservation plans, designed by Congress that same year as an exception to the 1973 Endangered Species Act, permitted nonfederal property owners who had sufficient cause to receive "incidental take" permits indemnifying them if they killed or injured federally protected flora or fauna. In the plan's first draft, the Seattle water department proposed limiting logging and building a new $25 million sockeye hatchery to mitigate destroyed habitat after meeting with county, state, federal, and tribal agencies. Diana Gale, the water department head, expressed hope that participants would "transcend jurisdictional boundaries" and help construct "one of the nation's premiere environmental restoration success stories."[17]

Any optimism soon evaporated. Seattle Public Utilities, the agency that subsumed the city's former engineering and water departments in 1997, wanted to maintain the old policy of cutting trees to pay for watershed operations. Several major environmental organizations lined up in opposition. For environmentalists, the Cedar River was a wilderness despite its long human history, almost 10,000 years, because of its "old growth" forests: the mature stands of Douglas fir, red cedar, and hemlock that once blanketed the Pacific Northwest. But old growth here was more of a political canard than an ecological fact. Only about 15 percent of the total watershed contained trees older than two hundred years. The majority of acreage, covered with second-growth forest ranging between thirty and eighty years old, had come back thanks to earlier reforestation efforts or natural processes. The ecological or historical complexities did not matter to old-growth advocates, who were then locked in a bitter struggle over the fate of logging ancient forests on public lands throughout the Pacific Northwest. That war's icon was the northern spotted owl, but in this skirmish, the emblem was the various species of Pacific salmon.[18]

For some wilderness campaigners, the proposed hatchery for the Cedar River was as abhorrent as chainsaws in the watershed's forests. Since the 1970s, hatcheries had become anathema to many environmentalists and sport anglers as mounting scientific evidence pointed to the detrimental effects of artificial propagation, ranging from diluted genetic diversity of wild stock to increased susceptibility to disease. In a letter to Stan Moses, chair of the Muckleshoot Indian Tribe's fish committee, the Sierra Club's Charlie Raines said the first priority was "maintaining and restoring ecosystem function (wild salmon and habitat) with artificial measures as a last resort."[19] Focused on upholding their treaty rights, the Muckleshoot disagreed. As Moses had explained to the Washington Environmental Council, "habitat restoration in the lower Cedar River by itself cannot satisfy our treaty rights." "The Muckleshoot Tribe does not have the luxury of fishing for only native or wild stocks," he observed, "thanks to the massive re-development of the Lake Washington basin since European settlement." With the specter of still more growth, the Muckleshoot could not tolerate the Sierra Club's binary logic.[20]

The Muckleshoot did not trust Seattle Public Utilities either because the problem facing salmon was not saving the trees alone. The Cedar River was Seattle's faucet and the city's utility managers turned it on and off depending upon consumers' needs. As a result, when demand was at its highest in summer and fall, the waters of the river ran low and warm. It was a deadly combination for salmon returning to spawn. The fish required cool temperatures and ample volume, and the Cedar was now an unreliable river for the fish, which made it an unreliable river for Indians, too. The Muckleshoot wanted full access to the watershed as co-managers, and as tribal chair Virginia Cross explained, by "locking gates on roads that lead into the watershed with no consideration of the Muckleshoot's subsistence," the city violated federal law. In exchange for backing the salmon hatchery, the Muckleshoot expected to receive guarantees in the Habitat Conservation Plan for hunting, fishing, and ceremonial visits to the watershed in perpetuity.[21]

Curiously, by pushing for the salmon hatchery, the Muckleshoot now allied themselves with their longtime adversaries, white recreational anglers, many of whom were unwilling to concede that they might have to live with a diminished resource. Frank Urabeck of Trout Unlimited argued that "habitat restoration projects were very much experimental with little documented success to date," whereas removing blockages faced by spawning salmon, such as the Ship Canal locks, or using hatcheries were more likely to succeed. Other sports fishers claimed that environmentalists were out to destroy their avocation. John C. Evensen, writing to the Seattle City Council, said that artificial propagation would benefit everyone and "not just the rich elitists."[22]

All sides now leaned upon consumer entitlements in their appeals, yet no appeals were as odd as those made on behalf of saving putative wilderness. Members of an ad hoc group, Protect Our Watershed Alliance, offered creative ways to pay for preserving the Cedar River's forests, one scheme calling for bottling and selling Cedar River water under the label "Seattle Rain." Another suggestion, titled "Save Your Watershed for One Latté a Year," exhorted Seattleites to "give up that one latté . . . or make it one beer, or a pack of cigarettes or maybe forgo that cheap video" to gain "a green watershed, one with fewer roads and more trees." The new mayor, Paul Schell, elected in the autumn of 1997—perhaps swayed by the public outcry, but more likely making a calculated political decision—announced early the following year that watershed management would not be subsidized by logging what he called a pristine area.[23]

A wealthy real estate developer and former University of Washington dean, Schell—with a snow-white head of hair and a personality that even supporters found detached and academic—was a fervent backer of "Cascadia," an invented region running from the Oregon-California border to southern British Columbia. He believed that Cascadians were "united by a love of the outdoors and reverence for the environment passed to us from the native people." Seen another way, it was the old mantra of Seattle's growth-crazed boosters now wrapped in flashy and progressive green packaging.[24] At first, environmentalists were convinced. Ed Zuckerman of Washington Conservation Voters said the mayor "surprised us in the strength of his words and his language," but the admiration was fleeting. With Schell's blessing, Seattle Public Utilities suspended discussions on maintaining minimum stream flow and refused to eliminate the proposed hatchery. The decision enraged all parties. The Muckleshoot again threatened to sue. Prominent fisheries biologists and environmental engineers belittled the reliance on hatcheries for "diverting limited financial resources from broader salmon and river recovery goals."[25] The environmental group American Rivers, following the official announcement placing the Chinook salmon on the endangered species list, added the Cedar to its own annual ranking of the nation's ten most imperiled waterways. Smaller utilities districts dependent upon Seattle's water feared higher rates and limited supplies. "We should not forget that people are as much a part of the environment," warned the head of one suburban water district, "as are the spotted owl, salmon, and trees."[26]

Finally, after almost three years of debate, Seattle Public Utilities issued its final habitat conservation plan in April 2000, a staggering thousand-plus page document with management plans for fourteen endangered bird, fish, and mammal species, including the Chinook salmon. (It omitted plans for another sixty-nine "species of concern.") Subsequent amendments halted all commercial logging, called for removing of 38 percent of existing logging roads in the watershed, and opened the Cedar River above the intake at Landsburg to migrating fish for the first time since the city completed its water supply system. The agency also pledged to help restore and protect fish habitat in the lower Cedar River, improve fish passage through the Ship Canal locks, and to fund further studies of Chinook and sockeye populations in Lake Washington. The total cost of the plan was almost $78 million. The sockeye hatchery remained and the city retained the right for an incidental "take" of threatened and endangered species to ensure sufficient water supplies for Seattle customers. The Muckleshoot Indian Tribe had the access it wanted for hunting and ceremonial purposes, but tribal leaders were concerned that the annual minimum river flow was inadequate, and prepared to mount a lawsuit against the city. Sports anglers split over the necessity of the hatchery.[27]

In the end, as one disgruntled citizen remarked, the plan was "a gutless, political choice following the path of least resistance," one designed to empower "a bunch of biologists measuring and monitoring ad infinitum. Nature is not static and will not be preserved," he concluded.[28] Such comments were strangely prescient, yet restoration advocates had reason for confidence: by the late 1990s, Seattle was booming again. With plentiful jobs at businesses old and new, like Boeing, Microsoft, and Amazon.com, a new wave of migrants discovered what writer and British émigré Jonathan Raban had discovered in the "new last frontier"—a world metropolis "built in a wilderness and designed to dazzle." Surveys backed Raban's breathless prose. A Seattle Times poll in 2000 found that almost two-thirds of all respondents would live nowhere else, with four out of ten listing the environment as the reason.[29] According to Emily Baillargeon Russin, a native who had left and come back at the height of the high-tech bubble, Seattleites now had "an emerging sense of the city as a vast personal playground." Her observation was an old one, and it did not include all citizens. Russin's Seattleites were mostly middle class and upwardly mobile residents, influenced by the lingering elements of 1960s counterculture, who had embraced an upscale environmentalism as a lifestyle choice.[30]

Those on the edges of nouveau riche and green Seattle, who did not buy their Gore-Tex jackets at REI or their organic produce at Puget Consumer Co-op Natural Markets, saw their city not so much a playground as a dump. Kristine Wong, an organizer for the Community Coalition for Environmental Justice, had unsuccessfully tried to convince local and national environmental activists converging to protest the 1999 World Trade Organization meeting in Seattle to connect with the city's poor and minority communities. The activists rebuffed Wong's efforts to put environmental justice on the agenda because few in the "overwhelmingly white mainstream non-governmental organizations" wanted to hear her opinion. After all, she explained, most Seattleites defined "the environment as forests, trees, [and] salmon" without considering how recent immigrants or Native Americans depended upon "contaminated fish" for sustenance.[31]

Perhaps no place symbolized Wong's frustration better than South Park, an enclave of modest homes and apartments sandwiched between Interstate 5, Seattle–Tacoma International Airport, and the Duwamish Waterway. In 1990, the South Park district had one of the city's lowest median household incomes, about $20,000 per household, and the city's largest concentration of nonwhite residents, nearly 40 percent. Life expectancy there was almost nine years less than for other Seattleites. Despite attempts to clean up the Duwamish, improvements could not remove contaminants imbedded in the riverbed: heavy metals like mercury, polychlorinated biphenyls (commonly known as PCBS), and dioxin, to name a few. Fifteen years later, little had changed. A 2005 study by Seattle's Community Coalition for Environmental Justice reported that the U.S. Census tracts along the Duwamish corridor had three common characteristics: the lowest household incomes, highest percentage of minority households, and largest number of federally designated toxic Superfund sites and sites under consideration. State health officials, beginning in 2000, started warning children and pregnant women to limit their consumption of Puget Sound and, later, Lake Washington fish, particularly salmon. As South Park resident Debbie Carlin observed, "people can't afford to move . . . that doesn't mean they choose to deal with all the pollution and stuff they dump down here."[32]

Salmon and other aquatic creatures now carried the pollutants of South Park, the lower Duwamish, and all of Puget Sound with them into almost every neighborhood in Seattle and King County, stored in the fatty tissues that fueled their epic spawning runs. The 1999 endangered species listing drove home an important biological point: almost everywhere that water flowed to the sea was potential salmon habitat. As federal and local agencies scrambled to come up with new regulations after the endangered species listings, they imposed tight restrictions to err on the side of caution. Federally funded low-income housing developments held up until contractors assessed the effects of each project upon nearby salmon habitat. Costs for other construction projects, from highway expansion on the car-clogged Eastside to new light-rail train tracks planned to ease gridlock, increased exponentially the closer the construction was to wetlands or spawning streams. Dogs could no longer play in the Sammamish River in Marymoor Park in Redmond, near Microsoft's plush corporate headquarters, when Chinook salmon spawned. One reporter summed up the cumulative effects of the salmon listing: "think of the spotted owl on a much grander scale, touching on every industry instead of just one."[33]

The editorial board of the *Seattle Post-Intelligencer,* responding to the original endangered species listing, said sarcastically that Seattleites had it coming to them since they had "long been the state's most vocal proponents of saving the environment in other people's back yards." It was "poetic justice" for Seattleites "to show their willingness to do the same." Seattle political leaders had tried to meet the challenge, if partially and with an eye on political expediency, with the habitat conservation plan for the Cedar River. Now, they had to address the salmon problem in their own backyard. The former mayor, Paul Schell, inaugurated the Urban Creeks Legacy project in 1999 to restore four of Seattle's largest remaining streams: Pipers Creek, Taylor Creek, Longfellow Creek, and Thornton Creek, the latter paved over at its headwaters in the 1940s to build the Northgate Mall. Denise Andrews, urban creeks coordinator for Seattle Public Utilities, explained that restoring the city's streams centered on "recreating nature as best we can." But even Schell, a real estate developer, underestimated the financial and political cost.[34]

James Fallows, writing in the *Atlantic Monthly* in 2000, rightly noted that the choice was not to save the salmon but a way of life. The recent high-tech boom had put a strain on the region's capacity to absorb growth. The newly wealthy and newly arrived wanted to live close to the water and trees—the very places that spawning salmon needed most. When Seattleites talked about saving salmon, they often failed to separate three intertwined but contradictory goals: protecting the salmon as a charismatic species, maintaining fisheries to sustain Indians and commercial fishermen as well as consumer demand, and preserving the habitat necessary for salmon to thrive. Each group had its own agenda and its own solution, but no one group was willing to curtail its own behavior. "The debate about whether this transformation should be undone," Fallows said, "is worth carrying out on its own terms—not on the backs of the fish."[35]

To Fallows, the Indians of Puget Sound might have replied that burdens of res-toration should not be on their backs either since, as they had argued for decades, they suffered the most when salmon began to disappear. The cooperative arrange-ments negotiated through the Boldt decision had worked reasonably well, embold-ening the treaty tribes to win access to public and private shellfish beds in addi-tion to the fishing grounds, a move that generated a new round of recriminations.[36] These victories would be hollow if there were no salmon to catch and if all the clams were poisoned by heavy metals and sewage, so treaty Indians began to angle for power over habitat restoration as well. Court decisions and legal scholarship suggesting that the treaty fishing right rested upon "three other rights: the right of access, the right of equitable apportionment, and the habitat right" bolstered their confidence and in early 2001, eleven western Washington treaty tribes filed a law-suit against the state of Washington to repair shoddy road culverts.[37] As state and tribal attorneys prepared their cases, the Muckleshoot Indian Tribe, whose juris-diction encompassed the Cedar River and Lake Washington, reached a $42 million accord in late 2006 with the city of Seattle that included the controversial sockeye hatchery, now deemed critical given the uncertain effects of global warming on salmon runs. The accord also guaranteed tribal access to watershed lands for hunt-ing and gathering. Environmental groups, hunters, and the Washington Depart-ment of Fish and Wildlife, which was not a party to the agreement, were incensed.[38]

Rand Little, a senior fish biologist for Seattle Public Utilities, explained this position three years earlier, in 2003, saying "we need the full meal deal: the habitat and the hatchery" since the city was "not in the fisheries business" but only "trying to do what everybody wants." It was a compromise position that, if read in a differ-ent and cynical light, bolstered farming, construction, and other business interests to avoid making even tougher choices. As one reporter explained, if "salmon can be raised in hatcheries, why bother protecting their wild cousins?"[39] Seattle was in the fisheries business, had been for some time, and it could not easily buy itself out. The city's 2003 comprehensive recovery plan demonstrated why. Focusing on the habitat needs for Chinook salmon across Seattle's many fresh and saltwater envi-ronments, it put city government squarely behind salmon restoration. As many had predicted, it made for good politics and the new mayor, Greg Nickels, linked his administration to the fish. "When we see salmon swimming upstream to spawn," he said in a glossary summary of the plan, "we can't help but be moved by their struggle to continue the cycle of life."[40]

That struggle made for even stranger, more convoluted politics by century's end because, as Seattle city council member Richard Conlin complained, "ecosystems are complicated and developments are complicated." To make the life of salmon easier, city leaders had to weigh the costs of making Seattleites' lives harder. New fish-friendly building codes, introduced in early 2006, were even more stringent than earlier measures. Property owners would have to replace native plants and gravel, and would be restricted from home improvements within one hundred feet of the water's edge. Public parks and golf courses faced limits on applying fertilizer or pesticides within fifty feet of wetlands or salmon habitat. Developers would be obligated to restore creeks previously stuffed into pipes and culverts. Angry homeowners and contractors, still riding the housing boom, vowed "to race to beat the change," but lost in their complaints and speechifying was the fact that these squabbles were largely among those who had done well in the booming nineties. Seattle had sold its charms too well. By the end of the decade, even middle-income families were finding it difficult to purchase homes in Seattle, thanks to what Knute Berger, an editor for the *Seattle Weekly*, called "the new meth"—the region's addiction to growth. He posed a difficult question: was Seattle "strictly a commercial zone where everything is for sale to the highest bidder? Or are there other community values that need to be asserted?"[41]

When it came to community, the city's affluent still asserted their values most forcefully, just as they had in the past. In Montlake, a formerly middle-class district adjacent to the Olmsted-designed Washington Park Arboretum where home prices now pushed past the million-dollar mark, residents united to oppose a proposed $4 billion-plus expansion to the Evergreen Point Floating Bridge. If approved, the new super span would slice through the neighborhood. Since the opening of the original bridge in 1962, motorists on the fourteen-mile stretch of bridge and highway squeezed onto four lanes of stop-and-go traffic. By 2005, the commute from Seattle to the Eastside was worse than the reverse. The proposed new bridge, which may be as large as eight lanes across, will likely be one of the most contentious public works projects every undertaken in Seattle's history. But why was a new bridge necessary, anyway?[42]

One reason was the gridlock that choked the bridge every weekday, thanks to expanding homes and businesses like Microsoft's corporate campus in Redmond. But another reason was that Miller Freeman's grandson, Kemper Freeman, Jr., had renovated the aging Bellevue Square shopping mall into a premier destination. Now, he wanted to transform Bellevue into a full-blown city rivaling Seattle, complete with high-rises and a proposed $70 million performing arts center. The younger Freeman learned his ambition "on the farm," the Bellevue home his grandfather Miller Freeman had built back in the 1920s in the middle of the now-paved-over strawberry fields, which was once tilled by Japanese farmers. To guarantee that Bellevue thrived, he lobbied state legislators for 1,400 miles of additional highway lanes and tried to quash plans for regional mass transit. "I have a greater vision for Bellevue," Freeman said in 2005, because his city was only "in the adolescent stage of its urban growth."[43]

For Freeman, an expanded Evergreen Point bridge would help Bellevue skip its awkward phase, but studies suggested that the current span's 350-plus drains, designed to remove storm water for motorists' safety, were hazardous for salmon. Tattered brake pads, leaky gaskets, worn transmission lines, and overfilled gas tanks spattered onto the bridge deck in concentrations that, at their highest during rush hour, exceeded state standards for acute or episodic levels of mercury, lead, copper, and other contaminants. Subsequent research found that the composition of pollutants entering Puget Sound's watery mazes was even complex than previously believed. A "toxic stew" of antidepressants, fire retardants, caffeine, and birth control hormones, to name just a few ingredients, seeped into nearby streams from septic tanks, storm sewers, driveways, and dumps, eventually making its way into the sea.[44]

It was an ominous finding for restoration advocates spending thousands of hours and millions of dollars removing garbage, planting native trees, replacing logs and gravel, recreating stream beds, and unclogging culverts to entice salmon back. Now, restoration alone was not enough thanks to the collision of human culture and salmon evolution. Those species best adapted to spawn in the small creeks and coastal tributaries commonly found in Seattle and other Puget Sound cities, like coho or silver salmon, were at the greatest risk. Coho timed their returns to match the autumn rains, the same showers that washed pollutants deposited on city streets and sidewalks into urban streams, stunning the fish with a toxic burst, and causing them to flail about on the surface in what one biologist called "the Jesus walk" before dying. In one study, 88 percent of the coho observed in one creek died this way. At the time, federal biologists had labeled Puget Sound coho as only a "species of concern," yet their troubles were an unpromising sign of things to come.[45]

By the beginning of the new century, most scientists conceded that the best hope was partial rehabilitation. The cumulative effects of the past continued to pile up, like commuters stuck in traffic on Seattle's snarled highways, and the cars were bringing still more trouble. The threat of climate change posed potentially devastating effects for Puget Sound salmon: increased air and water temperature, diminished snowpack, decreased stream flows in the summer, increased flooding in the winter, and rising sea levels. Some changes were already proving positive for some species. Chum or dog salmon were more tolerant of temperature swings; they were now the region's most abundant species. Most changes, however, placed all salmon species in far greater jeopardy. Calling salmon "wild" in this environment strained the definition of the word, yet restoration advocates remained hopeful, if chastened. As local environmentalist Judy Pickens concluded, after watching coho flailing and dying in city creeks every autumn, "if we get [salmon] back and they don't spawn, then all we have is one long controlled aquarium."[46] A group of fourteen prominent ecologists, fisheries biologists, and environmental engineers concurred with Pickens, arguing in an open letter that unless greater efforts were made to reduce or eliminate runoff "it is far more likely, with the arrival of millions more newcomers and concomitant high-impact development, that the health of Puget Sound will continue in its precipitous decline." Another 2007 study sponsored by the Washington State Department of Ecology and the U.S. Environmental Protection Agency determined that uncontrolled runoff was incontrovertibly the largest source of the worst pollutants entering the sound.[47]

If Puget Sound was becoming a poisonous fishbowl, who was to blame and who would benefit from protecting what is left of the region's waterways and open spaces? A walk along the city's beaches in West Seattle, near Fauntleroy Creek's outlet into Puget Sound, suggests one answer. There, stuck in the mud and rocks, framed against the snow-capped Olympic Mountains, are signs warning visitors not to catch and eat fish or shellfish, especially after a heavy rain. The signs are in as many as eight languages: English, Spanish, Russian, Chinese, Vietnamese, Laotian, Khmer, and Tagalog. Similar signs appear along the banks of the Duwamish River and all around Elliott Bay, standing as semaphores to the region's history.

The signs point to an important historical truth. Salmon are no longer the fetish of white sportsmen or Indian activists alone. The fish are, in a very literal sense, the city, and fights over salmon say less about the fish and more about the human combatants living in and around Seattle. An environmental prerogative for one group was often an environmental wrong for another. Complicating this new political reality was the dynamic structure of the physical world, which constrained some choices and opened other avenues for political action. Individuals and groups may have imagined themselves as operating as independent actors yet, as always, they were part of a larger and more entangled and interdependent history. And the full consequences of that history were on display by the century's end. Political and economic power determined whose position had the greatest credence, but no one could escape the past.

But if salmon are Seattle's potential savior, they will serve as such only if residents begin to think historically instead of nostalgically. To think nostalgically is to wish for what might have been or never was. After all, nostalgia, defined from the original Greek, is a sickness for an imaginary home. To think historically, however, is to see the past as a different place, the result of complex causes and effects unfolding in particular locations through time. For Seattle, then, salmon may help to point the way to community. Sensitive to changes in temperature and aquatic chemistry, the fish are nevertheless remarkably resilient and adaptable as long as they have clean, cool, and unobstructed waters in which to spawn, seasonally abundant food, and the ability to elude predators. Moreover, if waters are suitable for salmon, they are likely also suitable for other wildlife and people too.

The very complexity of repairing salmon habitat in urban Puget Sound will also require that diverse people come together to determine how best to have their fish and, perhaps, someday eat them safely as well. The latest cost estimates, upwards of $12 billion as of late 2006, including pollution reduction and habitat protection, are far too modest. Given the scale of this challenge, restoration will not be a matter of picking an arbitrary point in the past, eradicating nonnative species, turning creeks back into their beds, and watching nature return. Restoration instead will likely be a historical kind of process, more akin to amelioration, and as such, it will need to address social justice as much as environmental degradation. At its best, restoration might compel citizens to confront the consequences of the amenities they enjoy today. Someone somewhere will eat tainted salmon—or suffer the consequences of cleaning or restoring one stream at the expense of another. Such projects raise the unavoidably moral question of what makes a sustainable community, and how to remake places to cherish without rubbing away painful histories citizens would do well to remember.[48]

Because of salmon, more than any other issue, Seattleites are finally talking to one another again about community and the environment—even if shouting is more common than dialogue. Recent developments suggest that salmon may indeed be a fish to save the city and its region. The Puget Sound Partnership, launched in 2007, is the largest of the many collaborative efforts to include citizens and agencies from the local to the state to the tribal level. The partnership proposes managing salmon habitat across the entire region, treating the sound as both an ecological and political entity. Its goals are ambitious, but in the words of inaugural chair, former U.S. Environmental Protection Administrator William Ruckelshaus, the partnership hopes to convince citizens that protecting Puget Sound is "important to them and there's some economic benefit to them to improving the place where they live." Even Ruckelshaus, however, cannot escape the enormity of saving Puget Sound. For his part, he no longer indulges his passion for salmon fishing thanks to his work on behalf of the fish and their habitat. "I feel so guilty," he said. "It's ruined it."[49]

Still, any attempt to bring back some semblance of former salmon runs will not simultaneously yield community and ecological health unless participants think historically. And that will require them to confront the contradictions of wanting salmon and the good life at little or no burden to themselves. "As a nation we want convenience and abundance," wrote Hal Rothman, "but we want it without risk." The genius of environmentalism was to make risk measurable and bearable, but its assurances came with other costs that many were not willing to pay. The tendency to be green, Rothman archly concluded, comes most naturally "when it is inexpensive—economically, socially, and culturally."⁵⁰ The ongoing saga with salmon in Seattle is a poignant reminder of what that trade-off can cost over time for humans and nature alike. But the salmon crisis just might also restore the other promise of environmentalism—the sense that all things are connected.

Seattle may yet someday be a place where its residents see long commutes and poisoned waters, neglected neighborhoods and tainted fish, even flooded basements and ruined streams as all part of a tangled past that constantly intrudes upon a messy present and uncertain future. Yet this new ethic of place, one grounded in history and guided by historical thinking, may be possible. If and when it arrives, it may be small consolation to citizens like Jennifer Forrey, left with a flooded basement and damaged garage. But when it does, it might force her and other Seattleites to think about what making a home truly demands.⁵¹

Notes

Adapted and excerpted from Matthew Klingle, *Emerald City: An Environmental History of Seattle* (New Haven: Yale University Press, 2007). I am grateful to Yale University Press for their permission to reprint this material here. Thanks to Connie Chiang, Char Miller, and Jay Taylor for their comments and suggestions.

1. For details on the storm, including Forrey's complaints, see *Seattle Post-Intelligencer,* December 15, 19, 29, 2006, January 15, 2007.

2. For quotations, see *New York Times,* April 19, 1998; *Seattle Times,* August 30, 1999. For the history behind the crisis, see Joseph E. Taylor III, *Making Salmon: An Environmental History of the Northwest Fisheries Crisis* (Seattle: University of Washington Press, 1999). For critiques of salmon as unifiers, see John M. Findlay, "A Fishy Proposition: Regional Identity in the Pacific Northwest," in *Many Wests: Place, Culture, and Identity,* eds. David M. Wrobel and Michael C. Steiner, (Lawrence: University Press of Kansas, 1997), 37–70; and Taylor, "Regional Unifier or Cultural Catspaw: The Cultural Geography of Salmon Symbolism in the Pacific Northwest," in *Imagining the Big Open: Nature, Identity and Play in the New West,* eds. Liza Nicholas, Elaine M. Bapis, and Thomas J. Harvey (Salt Lake City: University of Utah Press, 2003), 3–26.

3. Thomas P. Quinn, *The Behavior and Ecology of Pacific Salmon and Trout* (Seattle: University of Washington Press, 2005), 5–36. The Latinate scientific names for these Pacific

salmon species are pink or humpback salmon (*O. gorbuscha*), sockeye salmon (*O. nerka*), coho or silver salmon (*O. kisutch*), chum or dog salmon (*O. keta*), Chinook or king salmon (*O. tshawytscha*), steelhead trout (*O. mykiss*), and sea-run cutthroat trout (*O. clarkii*). Two other species of *Oncorhynchus* are masu (*O. masou*) and amago (*O. rhodurus*) salmon, both found in the west Pacific. Atlantic salmon are *Salmo salar*.

4. For Indians and fisheries in the region, see Taylor, *Making Salmon*, 13–38. For details on specific Indian practices and names around Seattle, many with connections to salmon and the natural world, see the exhaustive atlas compiled by Coll Thrush and Nile Thompson in Thrush, *Native Seattle: Histories from the Crossing-Over Place* (Seattle: University of Washington Press, 2007), 209–55.

5. Alexandra Harmon, *Indians in the Making: Ethnic Relations and Indian Identities around Puget Sound* (Berkeley: University of California Press, 1999), 72–217.

6. Seattle's population jumped from 3,533 in 1880 to 315,312 in 1920. For details on these changes, see Klingle, *Emerald City*, 44–118.

7. Quotation from *Seattle Times*, July 31, 1928. For fisheries closings, see "Before the State Fisheries Board," Order No. 18 (1921), box 2, Hearings of State Fisheries Board, vol. H7, Department of Fisheries, Administration Library, Acc. 74-12-1115, Washington State Department of Fisheries Records (henceforth WSDF), Washington State Archives, Olympia (henceforth WSA); and "Test of Duwamish Closing," *Pacific Fisherman* 18 (February 1920): 30. For poaching, see the *Annual Reports of the State Fish Commissioner* from 1917–1927, WSA.

8. H. L. Dilaway, "Trout Fishing," *The Northwest Sportsman* 1 (April 1932): 2–4, 7. For Ben Paris's store, see *Star*, September 3, 1935. For arrest records, see *Annual Reports of the State Fish Commissioner: Twenty-Eighth and Twenty-Ninth, 1917–1919* (Olympia, WA, 1919), 162; *Thirtieth and Thirty-First* (1919–1921), 202, 293–94; *Thirty-Second and Thirty-Third* (1921–1923), 44–45, 104; *Thirty-Fourth and Thirty-Fifth* (1923–1925), 63–64, 128; *Thirty-Sixth and Thirty-Seventh* (1925–1927), 123–24, 203, WSA. For other accounts of poaching, see *Seattle Times*, October 1, 6, 11, 1928.

9. Miller Freeman to Henry Ramwell, American Packing Company, December 18, 1934, box 4, fol. 44, Miller Freeman Papers, Special Collections, University of Washington Libraries; Freeman, *The Memoirs of Miller Freeman, 1875–1955* (Seattle[?], 1956), 107–8. For Freeman's anti-Japanese activities, see David A. Neiwert, *Strawberry Days: How Internment Destroyed a Japanese American Community* (New York: Palgrave Macmillan, 2005), 48–69, 91–94, 111–40. There is no direct evidence that Freeman launched his tirades against the Japanese with the intention of taking their land, but he certainly benefited from his campaign. For the Freemans' postwar real estate activities, see Neiwert, 205–17, 224–28; and Robert F. Karolevitz, *Kemper Freeman, Sr. and the Bellevue Story* (Mission Hill, SD: Homestead Publishers, 1984), 74–121.

10. Rillmond Schear, "Seattle—1984," *Seattle Magazine* 2 (May 1965): 26–27. For antisprawl efforts, see Patrick Douglas, "Building a City: The Ins and Outs of Forward Thrust,"

Seattle Magazine 5 (January 1968): 29–32; and Walt Crowley, *Routes: An Interpretive History of Public Transportation in Metropolitan Seattle* (Seattle: Crowley Associates, Inc., 1993), 43–62; and Klingle, *Emerald City*, 234–36.

11. "Report on the Condition of the Spawning Tributaries of the Lake Washington Watershed," 1948, box 0061-23, Lake Washington-Cedar River, 1929–54, Stream Improvement and Hydraulics, WSDF, WSA.

12. For Metro and the Duwamish, see *Seattle Times*, October 26, 1959; Klingle, *Emerald City*, 203–29. For Thornton Creek, see Thor C. Tollefson to Fred H. Weber, May 18, 1971; William H. Rodgers, Jr., to Tollefson, August 8, 1969, box 1010-103, Stream Improvement-Lakes-Washington-Thornton Creek, 1949–1971, WSDF, WSA.

13. For sockeye plantings, see *Twenty-Eighth and Twenty-Ninth Annual Reports of the State Fish Commissioner, 1917-1919* (Olympia, WA, 1919), 89, WSA; L. A. Royal and Allen Seymour, "Building New Salmon Runs" *Progressive Fish Culturist* 52 (1940): 1–7; Andrew Paul Hendry, "Sockeye Salmon (*Oncorhynchus nerka*) in Lake Washington: An Investigation of Ancestral Origins, Population Differentiation and Local Adaptation" (PhD diss., University of Washington, 1995), 1–13, 135–39. The anadromous sockeye planted in Lake Washington were evolutionarily distinct from indigenous kokanee or land-locked sockeye observed by earlier fisheries scientists. The latter population of fish, if they were indeed kokanee, was likely trapped in the lake after the last major glacial period.

14. *Seattle Times*, November 22, 1970. For pollution and sockeye, see W. T. Edmondson, *The Uses of Ecology: Lake Washington and Beyond* (Seattle: University of Washington Press, 1991), 38–43; Stephanie E. Hampton, Pia Romare, and David E. Seiler, "Environmentally Controlled Daphnia Spring Increase with Implications for Sockeye Salmon Fry in Lake Washington, USA," *Journal of Plankton Research* 28 (April 2006): 399–406. For dredging, see Starlund and Biggs to Winters, King County Engineer, September 22, 1964, box 0061-23, Lake Washington-Cedar River, 1962–64, Stream Improvement and Hydraulics, WSDF, WSA.

15. *Seattle Times*, November 22, 1970.

16. *U.S. vs. Washington* 384 F. Supp. 312 (1974). For the trial and aftermath, see Charles Wilkinson, *Messages from Frank's Landing: A Story of Salmon, Treaties and the Indian Way* (Seattle: University of Washington Press, 2000), 51–62; and Harmon, *Indians in the Making*, 230–34.

17. Diana Gale to Margaret Pageler, April 3, 1996, box 83, fol. 1, Margaret Pageler Files, Legislative Department, Seattle Municipal Archives (henceforth SMA).

18. For human activity, see Lynne M. Getz, *Cedar River Watershed Cultural Resource Study* (Seattle: City Water Department, 1987), Special Collections, University of Washington Libraries. For forest structure, see *Cedar River Watershed Habitat Conservation Plan for the Proposed Issuance of a Permit to Allow Incidental Take of Threatened and Endangered Species* (Seattle: April 2000), 3.3-1–3.5, SMA.

19. Charles C. Raines to Stan Moses, May 6, 1997 (copy), box 75, fol. 1, Margaret Pageler Files, Legislative Department, SMA.

20. Moses to David Mann, April 4, 1997 (copy), box 75, fol. 4, Margaret Pageler Files, Legislative Department, SMA. For an analysis of Moses's observation and the ways that treaty Indians manipulated white environmentalist sentiment, see Coll Thrush, "City of the Changers: Indigenous People and the Transformation of Seattle's Watersheds," *Pacific Historical Review* 75 (February 2006): 112–17.

21. Virginia Cross to Bridgett Chandler, November 1, 1996; Moses to Mann, April 4, 1997, box 75, fol. 1, Margaret Pageler Files, Legislative Department, SMA.

22. Frank Urabeck to Seattle City Council, July 7, 1999, box 30, fol. 5, Nick Licata Files; John C. Evensen to Jan Drago, March 1, 1998, box 27, fol. 6, Jan Drago Files, Legislative Department, SMA.

23. Jo Ostgarden, "Fish, Trees and Clean Water," *Cascadia Times* (July/August 1998): 3–4; *Seattle Times*, April 20, June 23, 1998; "Save Your Watershed for One Latté a Year," (c. 1997), box 3, fol. 11, Peter Steinbrueck Files, Legislative Department SMA.

24. Paul Schell, "Cascadia: The North Pacific West" (paper presented at the meeting of the North American Institute, Seattle, October, 1992), 4, as quoted in Findlay, "A Fishy Proposition," 60. For Cascadia's history, see Janet Johnson, "Cascadia: It's As Much a State of Mind as a Geographic Place," *Seattle University News* (Spring 1994): 21–23.

25. John Daniels, Jr. to Schell, April 20, 1999, box 90, fol. 5, Margaret Pageler Files; Susan Bolton, et al. to Schell, February 18, 1999, box 3, fol. 11, Peter Steinbrueck Files, Legislative Department, SMA.

26. Pageler and Schell to Rebecca Wodder, American Rivers, April 9, 1999, box 3, fol. 13, Peter Steinbrueck Files; Ron Speer to Schell, July 21 and April 22, 1998, box 90, fol. 5, Margaret Pageler Files, Legislative Department, SMA.

27. For the various changes to the HCP, see Resolution 29977 (July 12, 1999) and Resolution 30091 (December 6, 1999), Seattle City Clerk's (Comptroller) Files, SMA.

28. Robert F. Roth to Pageler, June 2, 1999, box 105, fol. 15, Legislative Department, Central Staff Analysts' Working Papers, SMA.

29. Jonathan Raban, "The New Last Frontier," *Harper's Magazine* 287 (August 1993): 48; *Seattle Times*, May 21, 2000.

30. Emily Baillargeon Russin, "Seattle Now: A Letter," in *Reading Seattle: The City in Prose*, ed. Peter Donahue and John Trombold (Seattle: University of Washington Press, 2004), 250. For consumerism and environmentalism, see Andrew Kirk, *Counterculture Green: The Whole Earth Catalog and American Environmentalism* (Lawrence: University Press of Kansas, 2007); and Jeffrey Craig Sanders, "Building an 'Urban Homestead': Survival, Self-Sufficiency, and Nature in Seattle, 1970–1980" (paper presented at "The Place of Nature in the City in Twentieth-Century Europe and North America," German Historical Institute, Washington, DC, December 3, 2005, copy in author's possession).

31. Kristine Wong, interview by Monica Ghosh, July 28, 2000, WTO History Project, http://depts.washington.edu/wtohist/ (accessed May 2, 2005), Special Collections, University of Washington Libraries.

32. For South Park, see *Seattle Post-Intelligencer,* October 3, 1994; *Seattle Times,* February 24, 1994; Ian Ith, "The Road Back: From Seattle's Superfund Sewer to Haven Once More," *Pacific Northwest: The Seattle Times Magazine* (October 2, 2004): 22–29; *Seattle Times,* September 18, 2005. In 1990, demographic were 15 percent Hispanic, 13 percent Asian-Pacific Islander, 9 percent African American, and 3 percent Native American. For the 2005 CCEJ report, see *Seattle Post-Intelligencer,* August 25, 2005. According to the 2005 study, Seattle's citywide income average was $45,736, and the average percentage of minorities in the surveyed neighborhoods was 30 percent. For contaminated fish, see *Seattle Post-Intelligencer,* July 30, 2000, June 24, 2002, January 15, 2004, and October 27, 2006; see also "Final Report, State Board of Health Priority: Environmental Justice" (Olympia, WA: Committee on Environmental Justice of the Washington State Board of Health, June 13, 2001). For the 1994 comparison, see *Seattle Post-Intelligencer,* October 3, 1994; *Seattle Times,* February 24, 1994.

33. *Puget Sound Business Journal* (September 25–October 1, 1998): 33. For the details listed here, see *Seattle Post-Intelligencer,* April 21, 2000; *Seattle Times,* July 25, 1999, August 9, 1999, May 28, 2000.

34. *Seattle Post-Intelligencer,* March 14, 1999; *Seattle Times,* August 17, 1999.

35. James Fallows, "Saving Salmon, or Seattle?" *Atlantic Monthly* 286 (October 2000); 20–26; see also Taylor, *Making Salmon,* 237–57.

36. For the relevant case law, see *U.S. v. Washington,* 873 F. Supp. 1422 (1994); *U.S. v. Washington,* 898 F. Supp. 1453 (1995); *U.S. v. Washington,* 909 F. Supp. 787 (1995); and 157 F.3d 630 (9th Cir. 1998). For the latest agreement between private shellfish cultivators and treaty tribes, see *Seattle Times,* July 6, 2007.

37. Quotation from O. Yale Lewis III, "Treaty Fishing Rights: A Habitat Right as Part of the Trinity of Rights Implied by the Fishing Clause of the Stevens Treaties," *American Indian Law Review* 27 (2002–3): 311. For the lawsuit, commonly known at Boldt Phase Three, see *Seattle Post-Intelligencer,* January 21, 2001. For the relevant cases cited by Lewis, see *U.S. v. Washington* 443 U.S. 658 (1979); *U.S. v. Washington* 506 F. Supp. 187 (1980); and *U.S. v. Washington* 759 F. 2d. 1353 (9th Cir. 1985).

38. *Seattle Post-Intelligencer,* March 28, April 22, November 4, 2006.

39. *Seattle Post-Intelligencer,* October 1, 2003, March 30, 2004.

40. Quotation from "Chinook in the City: Restoring and Protecting Salmon Habitat in Seattle" (Seattle, 2004), SMA. For the larger plan, see *Seattle's Blueprint for Habitat Protection and Restoration* (Seattle: City of Seattle, December 2003), SMA.

41. *Seattle Post-Intelligencer,* March 6, 2006; *Seattle Weekly,* July 19, 2006.

42. *New York Times,* March 5, 2006; *Seattle Times,* April 26, 2005, June 11, November 6, 17, 2006; *Seattle Post-Intelligencer,* October 31, 2006.

43. *Seattle Post-Intelligencer,* April 6, 2005. For road building, see *Puget Sound Business Journal,* July 9, 1999; *King County Journal,* April 16, 2004.

44. *Seattle Post-Intelligencer,* April 9, 2003, April 6, 2006; and Frank Colich, "Trace Metals Concentrations in Storm Water Runoff from the Evergreen Point Floating Bridge in the

Seattle Washington Area" (poster presented at the 2003 Puget Sound/Georgia Basin Research Conference, copy in author's possession).

45. D. H. Baldwin, J. F. Sandahl, J. S. Labenia, and N. L. Scholz, "Sublethal Effects of Copper on Coho salmon: Impacts on Non-overlapping Receptor Populations in the Peripheral Olfactory Nervous System," *Environmental Toxicology and Chemistry* 22 (2003): 2266–74; J. P. Incardona, T. K. Collier, and N. L. Scholz, "Defects in Cardiac Function Precede Morphological Abnormalities in Fish Embryos Exposed to Polycyclic Aromatic Hydrocarbons," *Toxicology and Applied Pharmacology* 196 (2004): 191–205; and J. F. Sandahl, D. H. Baldwin, J. J. Jenkins, and N. L. Scholz, "Comparative Thresholds for Acetylcholinesterase Inhibition and Behavioral Impairment in Coho salmon Exposed to Chlorpyrifos," *Environmental Toxicology and Chemistry* 24 (2005): 136–45.

46. *Seattle Post-Intelligencer*, February 6, 2003. For global warming, see Climate Impacts Group, University of Washington, *Uncertain Future: Climate Change and its Effects on Puget Sound* (Olympia, WA: Puget Sound Action Team, October 2005), http://www.psat.wa.gov /Publications/climate_change2005/climate_home.htm (accessed January 15, 2006). For the challenges of restoration, see *Restoration of Puget Sound Rivers*, eds. David R. Montgomery, Susan Bolton, Derek B. Booth, and Leslie Wall (Seattle: Center for Water and Watershed Studies in association with University of Washington Press, 2003).

47. *Seattle Post-Intelligencer*, November 8, 2006; see also Douglas Beyerlin, et al. to Puget Sound Partnership, c/o Puget Sound Action Team, October 26, 2006, at http:// seattlepi.nwsource.com/dayart/pdf/stormwater20061108.pdf (accessed January 13, 2008). For recent studies, see *Seattle Post-Intelligencer*, November 30, 2007; and *Control of Toxic Chemicals in Puget Sound: Phase 1: Initial Estimate of Loadings*, Publication No. 07-10-079 (Seattle and Olympia: October 2007).

48. William R. Jordan III, *The Sunflower Forest: Ecological Restoration and the New Communion with Nature* (Berkeley: University of California Press, 2003), 28–53; and Andrew Light, "Restoring Ecological Citizenship," in *Democracy and the Claims of Nature*, ed. Ben A. Minteer and Bob Pepperman Taylor (Lanham, MD: Rowman & Littlefield Publishers, 2002), 153–72.

49. *Seattle Times*, May 20, 2007.

50. Hal K. Rothman, *The Greening of a Nation?: Environmentalism in the United States since 1945* (Fort Worth: Harcourt Brace College Publishers, 1998), 5.

51. For more on the "ethic of place," see Klingle, *Emerald City*, 265–80; see also Charles F. Wilkinson, "Toward and Ethic of Place," in *The Eagle Bird: Mapping a New West* (New York: Vintage, 1992), 132–61.

One City, Two Rivers

Columbia and Willamette Rivers in the Environmental History
of Twentieth-Century Portland, Oregon

WILLIAM LANG

At a regular Portland City Council session in late December 1909, Mayor Joe Simon called for a vote on an ordinance aimed at controlling nuisances in the city's harbor. A steadfast ally of waterfront commercial interests, the mayor prodded the councilors to fix what he saw as a social and an economic problem. They responded by unanimously passing the ordinance, which made it unlawful "for any person to keep, anchor, moor or maintain, or permit the keeping, anchoring, mooring or maintaining of any boathouse, house boat, scow house or scow dwelling used for human habitation within the harbor limits of the City of Portland as now established." Tensions had increased between shipping businesses at the Stark Street dock on the river's west side and a legion of river denizens, who had been accused of dumping debris, managing floating whorehouses, running thievery rings along the waterfront, and generally behaving in an unsightly manner. Tension had also developed between the waterfront interests and the public, which saw the private control of the city's dock facilities as a purloining of one of Portland's great assets—its direct access to the Willamette River. In an era of Progressive reform, city policies chipped away at private business privileges: first in 1910, when voters approved a referendum to create a Commission of Public Docks to build and maintain public docks; and second in 1911, when the city council ended a decades-long privatizing of city streets by owners who had blocked off streets to create special entrances to their docks and warehouses.[1]

The city council's focus on the Willamette River harbor early in the twentieth century was timely and appropriate. Little happened in Portland at the time that did not have at least an indirect connection to the Willamette or the Columbia rivers. The Columbia, the "Great River of the West," had been the key to economic development in the Oregon Country since the founding of Astoria at the river's mouth in 1810. The Columbia connected the region, a vast 259,000-square-mile drainage basin, to the world. The Willamette, a 187-mile tributary that drains an 11,000-square-mile basin, flows north to the Columbia and divides the city of Portland into westside and eastside districts. These rivers have profoundly shaped the city. Like rivers that have created urban centers throughout history, the Columbia and Willamette have had a physical impact on Portland's industrial, commercial, and residential districts—providing the city with wealth and opportunities to flourish, and offering their waters for navigation, recreation and aesthetics, and disposal for urban detritus. These three primary uses have dominated Portland's twentieth-century relationship with its rivers, especially the Willamette. The Columbia-Willamette seaway project, which scoured a navigation channel from Portland to the Pacific Ocean, made the city a commercial entrepot. The riversides and lowlands in the metropolitan area offered opportunities for recreation, natural areas, and parks. Both rivers offered their substantial flows to wash away nuisance effluent generated by industrial and municipal activities. These relationships between rivers and city are symbiotic, each affecting the other and influencing Portland's development as a "working city." The relationships pulled and pushed Portland, forcing the city to embrace the riverine landscape or ignore it, to abuse it or restore it. No relationship followed a straight or singular path, and each major effort to adjust city to river or river to city forced multiple adjustments and helped create new conditions that raised yet new concerns and problems. Like thousands of other river cities in the world, however, Portland is best understood as a human community in intimate connection with a dynamic part of the natural world.[2]

Portland began its urban life in the 1840s as the best and farthest upriver anchorage on the Willamette for deeper-draft ships. By the 1860s, it had outdistanced rival harbor towns on the river, its rudimentary docks handling produce and raw materials from fertile western valleys, precious metals from interior mines, and a bustling group of steamboat and cartage industries. Portland shippers sent Oregon wheat to Liverpool as early as 1867. By the 1880s, the city had become the dominant Pacific Coast shipping point north of San Francisco, sending out shipments of wheat, wool, lumber, and other natural resource products from the city's busy riverside docks. At the dawn of the twentieth century, Portland dominated the Pacific Northwest as the region's wealthiest and commercially productive city. "The Willamette River with its ships and bridges," historian Carl Abbott concludes, "has been the unifying factor in the development of Portland. The river is a key for understanding the city's history, economic functions, and geographic distribution of activities."

Three bridges spanned the Willamette by the first decade of the twentieth century, connecting the original westside city with a sprawling eastside that grew quickly and expansively by the 1920s. A network of streetcar tracks tied new city additions on the rolling landscape east of the river to the city's commercial center, a gridwork of twenty-some blocks west from the river and more than thirty blocks stretching along the river's north-northwest contour. The city's designers had squeezed out the most corners they could from the limited area beneath the sharp thousand-foot escarpment of the West Hills by plotting two-hundred-foot square commercial blocks. By the early twentieth century, formidable docks set on pilings lined the westside riverfront, extending the city's frenetic business activity directly into the Willamette River. The docks, freight terminals, warehouses, and distribution centers made Portland. As a city booster claimed in 1913, "Portland is . . . the city of DESTINY . . . with the finest Fresh Water Harbor in the WORLD, where RAIL can MEET SAIL."[3]

Commercial development on the Willamette and Columbia rivers led the way. By the 1920s, docks dotted both sides of the Willamette, with several major terminals, each with direct rail connections and efficient motor transport roadways. The construction of river-level bridges in Portland tended to concentrate larger docks along the northern, downstream edge of the city. Ocean-going ships traveled one hundred miles up the Columbia and an additional fourteen miles up the Willamette to Portland's harbor, giving the city a competitive edge over Puget Sound ports (Seattle's docks were 144 miles from the sea and Tacoma's 175 miles). As early as 1872, the U.S. Army Corps of Engineers had designated the Columbia-Willamette a major seaway that deserved to be considered as a single navigational unit. Corps dredges and snag boats cleared debris from the rivers and scoured out sandbars, trying to establish a twenty-foot deep navigation channel. During the 1890s, the state-created Port of Portland Commission worked strenuously to clear an adequate shipping channel on the Willamette, while the corps dredged the Columbia. By 1908, the corps had established a harbor line in Portland to mark the limit of river development, detailed two new dredges and three other craft to maintain the lower Willamette, and committed itself to establishing a twenty-five-foot channel from harbor to sea. In 1912, Congress authorized development and maintenance of a three-hundred-foot wide and thirty-foot deep Willamette-Columbia navigation channel, from ocean bar to Portland docks.[4]

Portland's population nearly tripled during the first three decades of the twentieth century; booming first between 1906 and 1912, again during World War I because of shipbuilding, and then during the booming 1920s, topping out at roughly 300,000 residents in 1930. Port activities had created much of the employment growth, in part because the city sank more and more investment into the harbor. By 1934, the northern section of the Willamette River harbor, downriver from the city's northern-most bridge, had attracted nearly 70 percent of the city's industrial employment. Intensive improvement of the seaway and harbor created the conditions for growth. The U.S. Corps of Engineers dredged the shallowest sections of the Columbia downriver from the mouth of the Willamette and the Willamette's particularly troublesome lower river bars. By the early 1920s, the corps had plowed through the bars, using their two powerful dredges, the *Multnomah* and the *Wahkiakum,* and constructed several dikes, driving sixty- to one-hundred-foot pilings into the riverbed and extending a two-tiered breakwater some twelve hundred feet from the riverbanks at three critical locations. The Port of Portland dredged the harbor and built sizable terminals, while the Commission of Public Docks raised property taxes and invested more than $30 million to build terminals, dry docks, and "the most modern elevator in the world for grain [that] will handle 10,000 tons of bulk grain in an hour." Dock facilities included cranes capable of lifting fifteen thousand tons and special bunkers for sulphur and phosphate, facilitating total trade that "was greater in volume than the entire export and import trade of the State of Washington, including Seattle and Tacoma with foreign countries." These investments built a generative engine that drove the economy through the first half of the century. When the *Oregonian* asked Portland businessmen in 1950 what most influenced the city's twentieth-century economy, they offered a simple and direct answer: the river and its port.[5]

The port depended on an efficient navigation system, which required re-shaping the Columbia and the Willamette. One of the most significant deterrents to navigation on the Willamette split the river channel in the heart of the industrial district—Swan Island, a 270-acre marshland that hugged the east bank of the river, sending the river's strongest flow to the shipping channel on the east side of the island, smack against an extensive wetland, Mock's Bottom, itself a marshy littoral beneath a steep bluff. Steamboat captains had long complained about the giant "s" curve they had to navigate at Swan Island. "The main channel of the river on the East side of Swan Island," the city council heard in 1907 testimony, "is so crooked and contracted to such a width as to absolutely prevent the vessels coming up the river from seeing any other vessels coming down the river." Compounding the danger were log rafts, which constituted more than 50 percent of river traffic and were "sometimes a quarter of a mile in length, and entirely out of control of the tow boat and no way of checking their momentum or even altering their course in any reasonable distance." It was a recipe, the boat captains argued, for disaster and tie-ups that frequently crippled river traffic. The solution required reconfiguring the river by dredging a new shipping channel to the west side of Swan Island, dumping the dredge spoils on the island, and creating a land-filled link from the island to the river bank.[6]

By 1919, a mayor-appointed task force—the so-called Committee of Fifteen—began work on a coordinated approach to harbor improvement. The committee made two significant recommendations. It advised the Port of Portland to absorb the Docks Commission and create a unified agency to develop the harbor. It also suggested that the port purchase Swan Island for development. Voters approved the purchase of Swan Island from an assortment of owners and the docks merger, although the latter was not achieved until the 1970s. Nonetheless, the realignment of the shipping channel was a major alteration to the river and a project that fell to the Port of Portland, with the aid and advice of the Corps of Engineers. By 1928, dredges had scoured out a new shipping channel, filled portions of Swan Island with spoils, and created a causeway that connected the island to the river shore. Attaching Swan Island to the riverbank blocked the river flow and created a back-flow basin, which additional dredging deepened to accommodate large ships. Reconfiguring Swan Island improved Portland's harbor considerably by assuring that larger ships could efficiently navigate the Columbia-Willamette seaway and also creating a modern boat basin and dry dock facility in the heart of the industrial area. The new Swan Island also housed the city's first municipal airport, which opened for business in late 1928.[7]

Directly across from Swan Island, the city saw land that beckoned as a potential recreation and aesthetic parkland. The focus was Guild's Lake, a four-hundred-acre wetland on the west bank of the Willamette that had also drawn interest for industrial development. In 1903, the city could imagine both uses, but a grand plan created by John Olmsted, son of landscape designer Frederic Law Olmsted, strongly suggested that the area become parkland. Olmsted's city plan, which met with general acceptance, also identified Swan Island and Ross Island as potential parks. It also coincided with a multiyear effort by businessmen and city boosters to create an exposition to commemorate the centennial of the Lewis and Clark Expedition. By 1904, the exposition committee had settled on Guild's Lake as the site for the Lewis and Clark Centennial and American Exposition and Oriental Fair. The fair offered a perfect opportunity to tout the city and create riverside pleasuring grounds in a city that had concentrated on building docks and wharves and assigned less than 2 percent of its land area to public parks. On June 1, 1905, Portland's world fair opened to forty thousand fairgoers, who marveled at an engineered lake environment that re-cast the wetlands into a movie-set landscape, dominated by a massive and ornate exhibition hall and other buildings full of exotic and promotional exhibits on the Northwest and Pacific Rim regions. The June-to-October fair drew an estimated 800,000 visitors, who took in the riverside environment and fantastic constructions and heard about Portland's bid to become "The Gateway to the Pacific," a term that conjured the long-idealized wealth of trade with China.[8]

Another recreational development on the river—Oaks Amusement Park—opened, in competitive fashion, one day earlier than the Lewis and Clark extravaganza. The amusement park took advantage of another wetland, this one miles up the Willamette from Guild's Lake at the far southern edge of the city. Billed as "Portland's Coney Island on the Willamette" and tucked in tight to the Sellwood residential district some two miles upriver from the center of Portland, Oaks Park featured riverside swimming and boating areas, thrill rides, and dance and skating pavilions, set on river pilings. The park's developers, the Oregon Water Power and Railway Company, selected the site because it took advantage of a shallow section of the river where a narrow isthmus jutted out into the Willamette and was just fifteen minutes from the city on the company's trolley line. Oaks Park quickly became a preferred recreational destination for Portlanders, drawing more than 300,000 visitors per year, and remains today the oldest continuously operated amusement park in the nation. In 1915, on the Columbia River, the Portland Electric Company developed an expansive swimming park that also drew thousands during the summer months on the company's trolley line. A little over a decade later, developers created Jantzen Beach on Hayden Island in the Columbia River, a forty-acre amusement park that included the West's largest roller coaster, huge swimming pools, and expansive picnic grounds. The marshy lowland site for Jantzen Beach required substantial protection from the Columbia's spring freshets, which threatened to swamp the area. The Corps of Engineers built an extensive dike along the northern edge of Hayden Island to constrain the river.[9]

Riverside recreation areas, even those that provided a substantial economic return to private developers, always remained susceptible to higher value use, especially as industrial land. There is no better example of this symbiotic relationship between recreational and industrial uses than the fate of the Guild's Lake fairgrounds after the close of the Lewis and Clark Exposition. Attendees on the fair's "Portland Day," September 30, 1905, received a promotional tag with the legend, "Portland great! Portland fine! Five hundred thousand in nineteen nine." It was an ambition not reached until the end of the century, but it expressed the optimistic view that they were on the brink of a new era, and for some investors it would begin at the fairgrounds, at Guild's Lake. Even before the exposition closed, investors had purchased portions of the fair site for industrial use. A scheme quickly developed to fill in the Guild's Lake wetlands with sluiced material from the West

Hills above the exposition site, using high-pressure hydraulic "monitor" nozzles that literally blasted terraces from the steep hillside. The terraces fulfilled city planners' and real estate developers' dreams for high-value homesites, while sluicers dumped thousands of cubic yards of fill into the Guild's Lake wetlands, creating a flat industrial area at "a uniform elevation of 32 feet above low water stage," and eventually 20,000 feet of river frontage. By 1913, the *Oregonian* newspaper reported that Guild's Lake had been "transformed from a muddy unattractive sheet of water into a modern up-to-date industrial center." It and other marshy places along the river, where proximate rail and dock facilities existed, drew developers' attention. As the city's newly created planning commission commented in 1919, lowland riverside areas were "a series of swamps" that begged for filling. The glorious fair site had given way to commerce and industry.[10]

By the early 1920s, commerce and industry dominated thinking about Portland's relationships to the Columbia and Willamette. Investments in industrial river landscapes came rapidly as Portland's population burgeoned and demand for shipping facilities boomed. Portland business interests considered development of the Columbia River navigation to the interior regions, east of the Cascade Mountains, as critical to the city's prosperity. The Corps of Engineers had worked on improving navigation on the Columbia for decades, beginning with construction of two massive jetties at the mouth of the Columbia, then building canals and locks at the Cascades in the Columbia River Gorge in 1896 and between The Dalles and Celilo Falls in 1915. The improvements facilitated safe passage of large ships to Portland on the Columbia-Willamette seaway and passage of drayage boats and barges up to the mid-Columbia. The canals and locks, however, proved disappointingly inefficient. They were not large enough and competition from the railroads diminished their effectiveness. Shippers wanted a bigger causeway, with more capacity and reliability, and that meant big dams and huge reservoirs to create slack-water navigation. High wheat prices during World War I prompted Portland interests in the early 1920s to lobby Congress for upriver improvements, what W. B. Dodson of the Portland Chamber of Commerce called "a new vision of the possibilities that might be won from the water resources of the Columbia River." The heart of the "new vision" was the marriage of navigation and hydropower, for Dodson and others knew that "each dam must have a by-product of power or irrigation to warrant the expense"—in essence a multipurpose dam. In late 1920, a favorable ruling by the Interstate Commerce Commission over contested shipping rate differentials between Puget Sound and Portland ports had the effect of giving "Portland an advantage of about 40 cents per ton on grain," which firmly attached the city to the grain-growing areas on the mid-Columbia and lower Snake rivers.

Mid-Columbia River interests joined with Portlanders to advocate for a dam at Umatilla Rapids, an especially difficult section of the river that blocked upriver traffic. The Bureau of Reclamation studied the potential for an irrigation and navigation dam, but their 1922 report returned disappointing news for Portland shippers: the bureau's cost-benefit analysis concluded that building a dam at Umatilla Rapids could not be justified. The Portland Chamber of Commerce persisted, but it was the Great Depression and Franklin D. Roosevelt's New Deal public-works program that finally secured the first of the big dams on the river. Just forty miles upriver from the mouth of the Willamette, Bonneville Dam swamped Cascade Rapids, created the first slack-water navigation section on the Columbia, and brought an enormous volume of hydroelectricity to the metropolitan area. The dam also initiated nearly four decades of dam building on the Columbia and Snake rivers that, by 1975, created a slack-water navigation route from Portland to Lewiston, Idaho, some 475 miles from the ocean in the middle of the region's most prosperous wheat-growing area.[11]

The development of the Columbia had a profound effect on Portland. The government's electrical marketing and power distribution agency, the Bonneville Power Administration, located its headquarters in the city in 1938. The power generated by Bonneville facilitated the location of three large shipyards in the metropolitan area at the onset of World War II, bringing the first significant national-scale heavy industry to Portland. The Kaiser shipyards on the Willamette and Columbia rivers—in North Portland, Swan Island, and Vancouver, Washington—attracted thousands of new workers who helped pioneer new, more efficient methods for building tanker ships, Liberty-class vessels, and small aircraft carriers. In September 1942, the Oregon shipyard on the Willamette built and launched a Liberty ship in fourteen days. Aluminum reduction plants on the Columbia, one at Vancouver and a second east of Portland at Troutdale, pulled even more power from Bonneville and established a light-metals industry that remained an important component of the regional economy until the 1990s. Demand for housing prompted the creation of the nation's largest wartime housing project—Vanport—on 650 acres of Columbia River floodplain in North Portland. More than 40,000 people lived in Vanport during the height of wartime shipbuilding, making it Oregon's second-largest city from 1943 to late 1945. Most were young, and many were African American—over 18 percent of the residents. After the war, as white war workers left in droves, Vanport's population dropped to 20,000, more than 25 percent of them African American. On Memorial Day 1948, a railroad dike designed to keep the Columbia River at bay broke under pressure from flood-stage flows—registering more than thirteen feet above flood stage at Vancouver—and in a few hours the wartime houses that had rested on simple foundations were adrift, with an estimated twenty deaths and thousands left homeless. Vanport lay in ruins, a mass of rubble, mashed houses, and collapsed buildings. After the disaster, the area remained undeveloped until the 1970s, when the city reclaimed the former townsite as recreational parkland, with a car-racing track, municipal golf course, and expansive playfields.[12]

The transformation of Columbia River floodplain into Vanport and finally to parkland is an example of the symbiotic and even reciprocal relationships Portland has always had with its rivers. Up the Willamette at the southern edge of the harbor area, another important riverine landscape went through a similar transformation, beginning as parkland and ending up as industrial space. Ross Island, a complex of four nearly contiguous islands covering approximately three hundred acres just downstream from Oaks Park, had been highlighted in Olmsted's 1904 master plan for Portland as a perfect park site. Originally homesteaded in 1850 by Sherry Ross, the island complex served the family as farm and pasture lands and even a short-lived location for an orphanage operated by the Ross family. Because the islands divided the river into two separate channels for more than a mile, the corps decided to exclude it from regulation when it set the harbor line. It meant that nearly any activity could take place, as long as it did not impede upriver navigation.[13]

At the turn of the century, it was not clear how the islands might be developed. In 1912, the city eyed the islands as potential parkland and tried to purchase the property from heirs of the original owners, but a public bond measure failed, leaving the islands' fate uncertain. In 1926, when a new, high bridge connected Portland's southwest and southeast districts and sparked more development, a consortium of politically well-placed investors paid more than $200,000 for the Ross Island property to develop it as a gravel quarry. The Ross Island Sand & Gravel Company quickly received construction permits and approval from the dock commission to establish a pre-mix concrete business on the east bank bluff opposite the islands. Within a decade, the company became the largest of its type in Oregon.[14]

The Ross Island Sand & Gravel Company radically transformed the islands. Their proximity to Oaks Amusement Park, a substantial wetlands, and residential neighborhoods made it a potential nuisance, and city interests had never quite given up on rescuing the islands for parkland. They could do little to prevent the gravel company from restructuring the islands, however, beginning with the clear-cutting of half the trees, the building of a causeway that connected two of the islands with a causeway and restricted river flow, and the use of power dredges to mine the Pleistocene-era gravels. The gravels made a nearly perfect aggregate for construction concrete, and the islands literally built the modern city by giving up their foundations for streets, roads, highways, low-rise buildings, and skyscrapers. The company prospered, and by the 1970s it had supplied nearly 40 percent of Portland's construction concrete.

In 1972, as company officials claimed that the islands could offer another "20 to 25 years of material," it faced increased scrutiny and its first restrictions. Federal environmental legislation—the Clean Water Act and the National Environmental Policy Act—forced Ross Island Sand & Gravel Company to acquire permits to continue operations, a process that offered the city an opportunity to reassert its interest in acquiring a portion of or all the islands as an ecological reserve to enhance the nearby 140-acre wetland the city had purchased in 1969. The required Environmental Impact Statement revealed that Ross Island, even in a compromised condition, represented significant habitat for wildfowl, including bald eagles, 37 mammal and 135 bird species, and "an aesthetically pleasing green island in an area of deteriorating aesthetic values." The company stalled and dragged its feet on acquiring the necessary permits, worried that it could not meet conditions and remain profitable.[15]

In 1977, after more than five years of wrangling with the city and the Corps of Engineers, Ross Island Sand & Gravel Company prevailed because of its "important economic role in the community." Nonetheless, the city extracted a verbal promise from the company owner, Robert Pamplin, to donate or sell the islands to the city as parkland in an unspecified number of years. Mining continued unabated and with serious environmental consequences until 1979, when the state of Oregon required the company to restore part of the lagoon with 20 million cubic yards of fill. The company resisted the order until 2001, when the city stepped in to intercede for company owner Robert Pamplin Jr. and secure a better agreement that would honor his father's promise to donate the islands. In 2007, the Ross Island Sand & Gravel Company tentatively agreed to donate forty-five acres to the city for environmental purposes. That agreement, however, came only after the city agreed to pay the company to take millions of cubic yards of material excavated from the enormously expensive and ambitious "Big Pipe" project that would create a deep-tunneled series of sewer connectors. Ross Island's gravel built the city and left a compromised riverine landscape that will be filled with tailings from the city's deepest innards.[16]

The "Big Pipe" project, which began a long-delayed fix for Portland's ailing sewer infrastructure in 2001, faced up to the city's historic use of the Willamette as a waste stream. The new sewer project will cut a tunnel—14 feet in diameter and 70 feet below ground level some 4 miles long on the west side of the river, and a 22-foot-diameter matching tunnel 150 feet down running 6 miles along on the east side—to pipe sewage away from the river. The project will dramatically reverse the historic practice of mixing sewage and river flow that dominated the city's decades-long neglect of the Willamette River.[17] As early as the 1920s, sewers that emptied directly into the river along the city's waterfront backed up into businesses and residences whenever the Willamette's volume edged toward flood stage, a nearly annual event during the spring freshet flow and when winter rains swelled the river's tributaries. The city paid for sewer projects through user taxes, and mayors had not been eager to push sewer projects over paving streets or adding street lighting. By 1923, the issue could no longer be shelved, and property owners on the waterfront created an assessment district to fund the Front Street Intercepting Sewer and Drainage System Project, the city's largest public works project to date. An *Oregonian* writer summed up the situation aptly in 1924: "If this evil [sewer discharge] is not checked early in its growth our 'Beautiful Willamette,' will become as repulsive to the eye and nose as some river flowing through industrial cities of the old world and will be deserted by its abundant fish."[18]

City Engineer Olaf Laurgaard drew up an ambitious plan to completely restructure the city's connection to the Willamette in the center of the commercial district. His plan called for acquiring a fifteen-block swath of land along the river for public purposes, including building a seawall to keep the river from flooding downtown streets, constructing a public market building, and developing an urban railroad and public esplanade along the river. Begun in 1926 and completed in 1929, the massive project created a 5,400-foot seawall that became the city's interface with the Willamette. Construction included establishing a new harbor line, building massive gravel-filled cribs along the waterfront, and a gravity-type concrete wall and esplanade on top of the cribs at street level. The seawall kept the river from inundating the city's low-lying portside streets, and the sewer interceptor helped divert sewage from the Willamette. It was a historic project and a testament to Portland's desire to improve the river's water quality and beautify the waterfront, but it could not clean up the river.[19]

Five years after completion of the seawall, a 1934 report concluded that "from the standpoint of fish life, there is an absolute barrio of denuded water" in the Portland harbor, "where oxygen loving forms of life cannot exist." The following year, the Columbia River Fishermen's Association threatened to bring suit against Portland and other cities that dumped sewage and threatened commercial fishing on the Willamette and Columbia rivers. By 1938, scientists had detected dangerous levels of E. coli bacteria. Mayor Carson spearheaded a public campaign to support bond measures to build sewage plants, warning that "sooner or later this condition must be remedied" and conducting a dive into the river in a deep-sea diving suit to peer through muddy water to publicize the dire need and secure a win for his initiatives in the election. Carson's stunt may well have helped, for the voters approved creation of the Oregon State Sanitary Authority (OSSA) in 1938. The OSSA labored diligently, but with limited enforcement authority, and made some headway in addressing conditions. But two decades later one of its biologists, Glen Carter, found that "fish kills were common in the river [with] massive rafts of decaying algae . . . and a thick layer of bacterial slime . . . [on] much of the river bottom and shoreline." The pollution in Portland harbor was so bad during the 1950s that a two-foot waterline swath of tar and grease marred Navy ships that visited the city in June for the annual Rose Festival. "The mighty ships would steam downriver with sailors hanging over the sides in boatswain chairs," Carter remembered, "each grasping a bucket of solvent and a stiff brush to remove the rings of Oregon tar and grease. Soon after the ships had departed, [we] would receive a phone call from the U.S. Coast Guard's officer of the day in Portland, complaining that the agency was not aggressive enough in enforcing oil spill laws and regulations."[20] Tom McCall, the anchor of a local TV station news program, called attention to the river's condition in the early 1960s. In 1967, now as Oregon's governor, McCall initiated a "Willamette Greenway" program to revive the river's sustaining role in the state's most populous region. More important for Portland, McCall took personal charge of the Willamette's cleanup by pushing for stringent laws and establishing an executive office to oversee progress and ensure effective enforcement of regulations designed to limit industrial pollution, especially from pulp mills in the mid-Willamette Valley. The initial success led the *National Geographic* in 1972 to feature the river's resuscitation on its cover and comment: "Now Chinook spawn even below once-deadly outfalls. Little untreated waste ever enters the stream. Transgressors have learned that laws won't bend."[21]

McCall's focus on the Willamette led to Oregon's embrace of forward-looking environmental policies, but a steady population growth through the end of the century, an increase in pesticide and fertilizer runoff from upriver agricultural areas, and the advent of water-thirsty, high-technology industries kept the Willamette and Columbia rivers at environmental risk. During the 1990s, a series of governmental and legal actions put the city on notice: it had to do something about the deteriorating ecological condition of the Willamette River. A lawsuit brought by environmental organizations in 1991 forced the city to sign an agreement with the state to commit more than a billion dollars and twenty years of construction to keep raw sewage from spilling into the Willamette River. Portland used a combined sewer outflow system that piped rainfall runoff to the river. Whenever heavy rains drenched Portland, something that happened on average more than one hundred times each year, the resulting torrent carried sewage into the river. By 1996, residents had become sufficiently engaged to form Willamette Riverkeeper, an organization "dedicated solely to the protection and restoration of the Willamette River . . . [through] improvement of habitat and water quality on the Willamette."

The organization began conducting monthly monitoring of river conditions for public information. In March 1999, the National Marine Fisheries Service listed two anadromous fish species in the river under the Endangered Species Act, requiring the city and state to remedy conditions. Just over two years later, in December 2000, the Environmental Protection Agency identified a section of the Lower Willamette River in Portland's industrial district as a Superfund site, noting dangerous levels of polychlorinated biphenyls, heavy metals, pesticides, and petroleum products in the water and riverbed. As one politician remarked, the EPA designation was a "shot across the bow to the development community" in the city.[22]

By the end of the twentieth century, it had become clear that no single use of the Willamette and Columbia could be allowed to threaten the river's ecological health. Portland wrapped itself in "green" politics and progressive policies that established it as a leader in environmentally friendly growth. Nonetheless, the three historic relationships that had dominated the twentieth century remained in place. Plans to deepen the navigation channel to forty-five feet and improve port facilities in the early twenty-first century echoed those of a century earlier, while city authorities and corporations worked to minimize the costs and scope of the EPA-prescribed cleanup of the Portland harbor. River advocates could point to remarkable changes along the city's waterfront. The 1930s-era seawall and plans for an esplanade, for example, had faded by mid-century when the city approved building a six-lane highway along Front Street, blocking easy access to the river. By 1974, city planners re-thought the highway and at the urging of park supporters decided to rip out the highway and bring back the idea of an esplanade. They resuscitated part of the Laurgaard plan for the waterfront and built a riverfront park for public events, naming the area in honor of Governor Tom McCall. In 2001, the city dedicated a 1.5-mile-long eastside esplanade right at the river's edge that provides stunning views of the city's downtown skyline, naming it for Portland's modern reformist mayor, Vera Katz.[23]

Portland's twentieth-century relationships with its two rivers were utilitarian, with politicians, business interests, and the public seeing their rivers primarily as resources. Rarely did anyone argue for preserving any part of the Columbia or Willamette in the metropolitan area as an unmanipulated stream. Yet no one quite let go of the idea that the rivers at Portland's doorstep were part of nature. Periodically, the politicians and public turned attention to conservationist policies. Even the Port of Portland, the public agency most responsible for making the Willamette an industrial river, touts winning multiple environmental awards from the American Association of Port Authorities. An official of Portland's Sierra Club chapter claimed in 2000 that "the Willamette is kind of the nation's Every River. Virtually every problem that's affecting rivers in the U.S. is present in the Willamette watershed. . . . a lot of hope for what happens in the world is in the Willamette." In December 2001, the city took up that idea and initiated one more broad-gauged effort to embrace the Willamette and Columbia to "ensure a clean and healthy river system for fish, wildlife, and people." The "River Renaissance Strategy," unveiled in 2001, sets the city on a new course that pledges to learn from Portland's experience in the twentieth century: "The waters of the Willamette and Columbia Rivers lap at the edge of our lives and livelihoods. They course amid skyscrapers and parks, docks, port terminals, warehouses and neighborhoods. Linking east and west, the Willamette is Portland's true city center and the Columbia our gateway to the Pacific, and beyond."[24] The new initiative is both nostalgic and visionary, its principal statement a paean to how Portland wants to engage its rivers.

Notes

1. Ordinance # 20545, December 23, 1909, Portland City Council Documents Folder 108, 1910, Portland City Archives, Portland, Oregon, [PCA]. On Mayor Simon and his interests in dock companies and other political relationships, see E. Kimbark MacColl and Harry H. Stein, *Merchants, Money, and Power: The Portland Establishment, 1843–1913* (Portland: The Georgian Press, 1988), 416–19.

2. Carl Abbott, *Portland: Planning, Politics, and Growth in a Twentieth-Century City* (Lincoln: University of Nebraska Press, 1983), 11.

3. Abbott, *Portland*, 21, 249; L. M. Lepper, President, Greater East Side United Improvement Clubs Assn. to H. R. Albee, Mayor of Portland, October 4, 1913, General Records, Mayor's Correspondence 1913, A2000-003, 1707-08/2, Box 2, Folder 40, PCA.

4. William F. Willingham, *Army Engineers and the Development of Oregon: A History of the Portland District of the U.S. Army Corps of Engineers* (Portland: USACE, 1983) 18, 22–24, 53–54, 71–74; Reed, *North Pacific Division*, 8; "Executive Summary," Study of Rail and Water Terminal Facilities and Feasibility of Unification at Portland, Oregon, Day & Zimmerman Report No. 2863, December 29, 1930, 2012–30, Folder 59/20, Executive Summary, page 28, PCA.

5. "The Improvement of the Lower Willamette and Columbia Rivers, Ore. and Wash." Before the Committee on Rivers and Harbors, House of Representatives, 67th Cong., 2nd sess., February 16, 1922 (Washington: GPO, 1922), 3–5, 8–12; Memorandum: Willamette and Columbia Rivers Navigation, April 1922, RG 77, 1910–1938 General Correspondence, Entry 36, Box 6, Folder Dredges, National Archives, Seattle Branch [NARA-Seattle]; MacColl, *The Growth of a City*, 555; Abbott, *Portland*, 119–20.

6. L. M. Lepper, President, Greater East Side United Improvement Clubs Assn. to H. R. Albee, Mayor of Portland, October 4, 1913, General Records, Mayor's Correspondence 1913, A2000-003, 1707-08/2, Box 2, Folder 40, Auditor's Collected Reports, 2012–30, 05-10-16/2 Box

48, folder 7, Annual Report of the Commission of Public Docks For the Year ending November 30, 1919, 18; Report on the Economic Elevation of Flood Protection Works at Portland Oregon, Roger G. Dieck, Engineer, February 6, 1920, RG 77, 1910–1918 General Correspondence Entry 36, Box 6, Folder Technical Reports, [NARA-Seattle]; Kathleen D. Tucker, "'We Want Smokestacks and Not Swamps:' Filling in Portland's Guild's Lake, 1906–1925," (master's thesis, Portland State University, 2005), 67–69; *Oregon Journal*, June 5, 1920, as quoted in MacColl, *Growth of a City*, 230.

7. *Oregon Journal*, December 9, 1921; U.S. Army Corps of Engineers Report, Rivers and Harbors Committee, Document No. 10, 69th Cong., 2nd sess., 1927, 1669–1671; MacColl, *Growth of a City*, 233, 249 ; Oregon, Day & Zimmerman Report No.2863, December 29, 1930, 2012-30, Folder 59/20b, pages 217–19, PCA; Jewell Lansing, *Portland: People, Power & Politics, 1851–2001* (Corvallis: Oregon State University Press, 2003), 315.

8. Carl Abbott, *The Great Extravaganza: Portland and the Lewis and Clark Exposition* (Portland: Oregon Historical Society, 2004), 18, 51–52; MacColl and Stein, *Money, Merchants, & Power*, 357.

9. Tucker, "We Want Smokestacks," 2; Bryan Aalberg, "Oaks Amusement Park," *Oregon Historical Quarterly* (Summer 2003): 252–54.

10. MacColl, *The Growth of a City*, 77–80; *Oregonian*, September 28, 1913, as quoted in Tucker, "We Want Smokestacks," 57; Lansing, *Portland*, 309; River and Harbor Improvements in Oregon and Washington. Hearings, held before the Committee on Rivers and Harbors, House of Representatives, 65th Cong., 1st sess., December 13 and 16, 1918 (GPO, 1918), 10–11; Charles Cheney, *Report to the City Planning Commission*, June 1919; Day & Zimmerman Report No.2863, Executive Summary, Folder 59/20, pages 2–8, PCA.

11. Annual Report of the Commission of Public Docks For the Year ending November 30, 1921, 34–35, Auditor's Collected Reports, 2012-30, 05-10\16/2 Box 48, folder 7, PCA; E. G. Hopson, "Report on Five Mile Dam Project," August 1922, p. 3, Box 1, Elmer Dodd Papers, Oregon Historical Society, Portland; W. B. Dodson, talk before Inland Empire Waterways Assn., October 20, 1937, Box 3, Folder Portland Chamber of Commerce, Pacific Northwest Waterways Papers, Whitman College Archives, Walla Walla, Washington. On the potential for agricultural development and irrigation from damming the Columbia, see J. A. Krug, *The Columbia: A Comprehensive Report on the Development of the Water Resources of the Columbia River Basin* (Washington: Bureau of Reclamation, 1947), 274–75. On damming of the lower Snake River, see Keith Petersen, *River of Life, Channel of Death: Fish and Dams on the Lower Snake* (Lewiston, ID: Confluence Press, 1995).

12. MacColl, *The Growth of a City*, 561–66, 571–73; Day & Zimmerman Report No. 2863, 2012-30, Folder 59/20B, pages 208–9, PCA. On Vanport see, Manly Maben, *Vanport* (Portland: Oregon Historical Society Press, 1987); and Albert P. Heiner, *Henry J. Kaiser: Western Colossus* (San Francisco: Halo Books, 1991), 127–30.

13. MacColl, The *Growth of a City*, 245–47; Willingham, *Army Engineers and Portland*, 53-56.

14. *Oregonian,* April 4, 1972; U.S. Army Corps of Engineers, *Final Environmental Statement: Ross Island* (Portland: U.S. Army Corps of Engineers, Portland District, 1973), iii, as quoted in Nicholas Deshais, "Created by Catastrophe, Damaged by Development: How Ross Island made Portland," (unpublished MS, 2006, in author's possession), 28–29.

15. Report of the Ross Island Task Force, 1977, as quoted in Deshais, "Created by Catastrophe," 35; *Oregonian,* June 4, 6, 10, 19, 2007.

16. *Oregonian,* January, 27, 2001; October 5, 11, 2006; May 26, June 2, July 8, September 12, 2007.

17. *Oregonian,* January 4, 2007, February 20, 2007, May 14, 2007.

18. Laurence Hodges's commentary in *Oregonian,* September 12, 1924, as quoted in MacColl, *The Growth of a City,* 319.

19. Olaf Laurgaard (City Engineer), ASCE Paper on Front Avenue Interceptor Sewer Project, 1–29, A1999–004, Box 1, Folder 1/1, PCA; MacColl, *The Growth of a City,* 315–17.

20. Charlton Food and Sanitary Laboratory, "Preliminary Report," October 5, 1934 (Portland: Chamber of Commerce), as quoted in MacColl, *The Growth of a City,* 544–47; Abbott, *Portland,* 115–16; James V. Hillegas, "Working for the 'Working River': Willamette River Water Pollution, 1926–1962," (master's thesis, Portland State University, 2009), 61, 91–103; Glen D. Carter, "Pioneering Water Pollution Control in Oregon," *Oregon Historical Quarterly* (Summer 2006): 259, 268–69.

21. Brent Walth, *Fire at Eden's Gate: Tom McCall and the Oregon Story* (Portland: Oregon Historical Society Press, 1994), 198–200, 327–31; Ethel A. Starbird, "River Restored: Oregon's Willamette," *National Geographic* (June 1972): 816–35; Stewart Udall, "Comeback for the Willamette River," *National Parks* 42 (March 1968): 4–8. On the success or failure of McCall's campaign, see N. Mullane, "The Willamette River of Oregon: A River Restored?" in Anontius Leanen and David A. Dunnette, eds., *River Quality: Dynamics and Restoration* (Boca Raton, FL: Lewis Publishing, 1997), 65–75; and W. L. Graf, "Damage Control: Restoring the Physical Integrity of America's Rivers," *Annals of Association of American Geographers* 91 (March 2001): 1–27. For the broader context of McCall's Willamette River anti-pollution crusade, see William G. Robbins and William Cronon, *Landscapes of Conflict: The Oregon Story 1940–2000* (Seattle: University of Washington Press, 2004), 248–80.

22. http://willamette-riverkeeper.org/about1.htm (accessed June 1, 2007); *Oregonian,* March 11, 17 (quotation) 1999; *Civil Engineering News* 70 (September 2000); 24–25.

23. Abbott, *Portland,* 216; *Oregonian,* September 4, 1999, November 13, 2000, February 20, 22, 2007; Lansing, *Portland: People, Power and Politics, 1851–2001,* 459–60.

24. Port of Portland, Environmental Fact Sheet, October 2003; www.portofportland.com/Notices/aapa_award_HTM.htm; Kim Murphy, "Polluted Willamette River Sullies Image of a Green Oregon," *Los Angeles Times,* April 8, 2000; Department of Planning, City of Portland, "River Renaissance Strategy," December 2004.

Private Water

The Curious Case of San Jose's Water Supply

MARTIN V. MELOSI

San Jose, located in Santa Clara County, California—the "Valley of Heart's Delight" and then "Silicon Valley"—became an incorporated city in 1850, the same year that California entered the Union. San Jose was the state's first capital and now is the third largest city in the state and the tenth most populous in the country. For the first several years of its history, San Jose depended on artesian wells for its water. Beginning in 1866, the San Jose Water Company established the first citywide water supply system, and to this day a large portion of the city's water is provided by a private company.

The persistence of a private water company in San Jose—regarded as the oldest invester-owned water utility in California—bucked the trend in providing water in urban America from public systems since the 1830s. This is a very big deal because municipalities in the United States from the nineteenth century to quite recently coveted public control of many city services—water being the greatest prize. In the last decade or so efforts to privatize water supply systems in the U.S.—a trend more popular in Western Europe and elsewhere—largely have failed to occur. The resolute belief that water supply service is a mainstay of municipal power and municipal revenue has been difficult to undermine. Yet San Jose, and a very few others, have viewed this issue differently.

This chapter asks: What accounts for the long history of a private water company in San Jose? What did it take to resist the historical forces that shifted many private services to public ones in the nineteenth and twentieth centuries? And what does the relationship between San Jose Water Works (later San Jose Water Company) and the city of San Jose tell us about the development and evolution of this community?

Public Ownership of Waterworks in the United States

While the fear of fire always loomed, the startling impact of an epidemic increased public pressure for improved water supplies in nineteenth-century American cities. Fear alone, however, was insufficient to lead towns and cities to abandon traditional sources of water and familiar methods of acquiring it (water carriers, wells, and cisterns). A community needed a political commitment, fiscal resources, and access to new technology. Most American cities and towns drew their supplies from wells, springs, or ponds, and did not have extensive distribution systems, if at all.

While communitywide water-supply systems developed slowly, in 1801 Philadelphia became the first to complete a waterworks and municipal distribution system sophisticated even by European standards. The necessary health, economic, and technical factors converged to produce what became a model for future systems.[1] The Philadelphia waterworks, however, was an anomaly, since it did not spark an immediate nationwide trend. Inexperience in dealing with such a major project helps to explain why urban population growth exceeded construction for so many years. In 1800 there were 17 works for an urban population of 322,000; in 1830 there were 45 works for 1,127,000 urban Americans. The great majority of the waterworks were located in the Northeast, with considerably fewer in the old Northwest and upper South.[2]

In absolute terms, the number of waterworks multiplied at an accelerated rate from 1830 to 1880. During the 1850s and 1860s, however, the number did not keep pace with the chartering of new cities. Urban population rose at a faster rate than the number of waterworks until 1870, when the trend began to reverse itself. Some communities experiencing modest growth continued to rely on wells and other local supplies or expected private companies under franchises to provide water service. Yet even cities undergoing rapid expansion were leery of the capital investment required for citywide systems. By the 1870s the trend toward more public water supplies was evident. There was a slow shift from private to public ownership in the period (9 of 45 public in 1830) with relative parity by 1880 (of 599, 293 were public, 306 private).[3]

The crucialness of adequate supplies of water to meet the needs of citizens, commercial establishments, and industry—and the emerging mandate of cities to protect the public health—meant that authorities in the largest urban areas wanted centralized systems under their direct control. Boosterism was an additional motivation, since an effective water system was a powerful promotional tool to enhance a city's economic base. While many water companies had been profitable, capital investment in the more modern systems was steep, and operating costs were on the rise. Private service, therefore, was gradually phased out in several communities. In addition, public control of the water supply enhanced the authority of city govern-ment vis-à-vis the legislature or rival cities, thus private owners often were under pressure to sell.

The desire of city leaders to convert private systems into public, or to build new public systems, rested on the ability of cities to incur debt to fund major projects and to sustain the high costs of operating water systems. As the nineteenth cen-tury unfolded, city finances underwent changes in scope and complexity which ultimately made the development of public water systems achievable. The impetus was blunted temporarily by the Panic of 1873, when retrenchment and conservative fiscal policy brought on a "pay as you go" philosophy. Also, until 1875, waterworks franchises were designed to be attractive to induce private companies to deliver water and to provide an adequate number of hydrants for fire protection.[4]

In developing citywide water-supply systems in this era, substantial public investment proved difficult for all but the largest and most fiscally sound cities. If the legislature was not withholding extension of greater authority, the council was debating the wisdom of increasing the city's bonded indebtedness or engaged in partisan debate. Going back at least to 1855, the percentage of public water systems tended to vary with the general financial health of the cities, at least until the 1880s when other issues also influenced decisions. In addition, municipal indebtedness had steadily grown in order to finance several improvements, including water supply. By 1860, municipal debt was three times the federal debt and almost equal to the aggregate state debt. Liberalization of charters and other fiscal changes also provided opportunity for cities to finance water-supply systems, especially begin-ning in the 1860s. In most cases, a combination of local circumstances and the experience of other cities influenced the shift from private to public.[5]

Water supply was the first important public utility in the United States and the first municipal service that demonstrated a city's commitment to growth. Officials and urban boosters promoted a variety of improvements in competition with rival communities. Along with sanitarians and municipal engineers, they supported ser-vices to improve health conditions and to secure bragging rights about the cleanli-ness of their cities.[6] City leaders concluded that control of the sanitary quality of its water service would be difficult if the supply remained in private hands. The push for municipal ownership, therefore, had as much to do with the desire to influence the growth of cities as to settle disputes with private companies over specific defi-ciencies. The "political nature" of water was important.[7]

Major cities tended to support public systems earlier than other classes of cities. In 1890, more than 70 percent of cities with populations exceeding 30,000 had public systems. In 1897, forty-one of the fifty largest cities (or 82 percent) had public systems. Since most of the urban population was located in the larger cities, it was not surprising that while only 43 percent of all American cities had public waterworks in 1890, 66.2 percent of the total urban population was served by public systems. The Midwest showed the greatest propensity to public systems by the end of the 1890s, which coincided with its efforts at reform of business regulation. Emerging industrial states along the Great Lakes showed strong support for public systems, as did agrarian states. For the East, the total was 42 percent, the South 38 percent, and the West 40 percent.[8]

Several factors account for the political and economic climate that favored public systems in the late nineteenth century: improved fiscal status of cities, cooperation between large cities and state legislatures in developing or expanding services, skepticism of private companies to deliver services, and broadening regulatory power with respect to public utilities. Most importantly, between 1860 and 1922 municipal debt increased from $200 million to more than $3 billion. Legislatures were more lenient in allowing cities to float water bonds than incurring other forms of public indebtedness, since they were stable and demonstrated a good payment record.[9]

Public systems became more widespread as criticism of private companies mounted. In some cases, a change in political environment worked against private companies, especially if reform-minded leaders criticized the franchisee as a source of corruption. In other cases, poor performance by the private company set off reconsideration of service delivery. Initially, waterworks franchises extended for long durations, offered tax exempt status for the company, and did little to regulate price. By World War I, fourteen states limited the length of a contract under provision of general law, but eighteen states still allowed perpetual franchises.[10] While as many as 850 new waterworks franchises were let during the 1880s, they were not as generous as those in the past. The length of the franchise was usually a central point of debate, since a perpetual contract gave officials virtually no control over the waterworks company. Other key concerns included the ability to manage rates and the option to purchase the waterworks if the company did not live up to its obligations. Cities had unique leverage with respect to rates. During the 1890s, rates charged by private companies were 40–43 percent higher than rates charged by municipal works. Unlike private companies, cities could take a loss on operations and use taxes to make up the difference. Rate flexibility sometimes gave cities an advantage in keeping private companies from overcharging, and often made the threat to terminate the franchise quite real.[11]

As public systems became more competitive, sensitivity to liberal water contracts often resulted in a call for municipal ownership. In some cases, a concern about local control was more persuasive than a demand for municipal ownership. Fresno, California, had considered municipal ownership since 1876, and reconsidered it after a major fire in 1882. But the city did little more than install public wells and hydrants in the 1880s, and the private Fresno Water Works continued delivery to residential areas. In 1889 a small group petitioned the city board of trustees to shift to municipal ownership, but the majority of Fresnans favored small government and low taxes and had not lodged major complaints against the private company. When the local water and power companies went bankrupt, they were reorganized in 1902 by a local utility magnate, and were purchased by national corporations in the 1920s. Only then did the demand for municipal ownership intensify. (See table 6.1 on decline of privatization from 1830–1924.)[12]

A few cities, such as San Francisco, resisted municipal ownership. The widespread belief that the city's water supply was clear and wholesome checked the demand for a change in control. Nearby San Jose also obtained most of its water from a private company, and has continued to do so to the present. We will explore why San Jose was an exception later.[13]

During the 1890s, a combination of factors shifted momentum decisively toward municipal ownership in most major cities. These included dissatisfaction

TABLE 6.1
Public v. Private Ownership of Waterworks, 1830–1924

Year	# Works	Public	Private	% Public	% Private
1830	45	9	36	20	80
1840	65	23	42	35.4	64.6
1850	84	33	51	39.3	60.7
1860	137	57	80	41.7	58.3
1870	244	116	128	47.5	52.5
1880	599	293	306	48.9	51.1
1890	1879	806	1073	42.9	57.1
1896	3197*	1690	1490	52.9	46.6
1924	9850	6900	2950	70	30

*Includes 17 undocumented systems
Source: Waterman, Elements of Water-Supply Engineering, 6.

with private companies, questions concerning the quality of the supplied water, high rates, and local interest in controlling services. By then cities had increased authorization to erect, lease, purchase, and operate waterworks, lighting plants, and in some cases, street railways. Opportunities to issue bonds beyond previous authorized limits and tax-granting status produced additional capital.

Progressive Era reforms were employed to sanction purchases or to grant new franchises. Between 1891 and 1901 permission to own, erect, and purchase water or lighting plants had been extended to municipalities in twenty-four states. California and Kansas passed very general laws allowing for municipal ownership. Several cities had ownership clauses in their new charters.[14]

The trend toward public water systems in the United States persisted throughout the twentieth century. Figures in 1990 indicated that almost 84 percent of all American cities relied on public systems.[15] Contrarily, the global trend toward privatization of water supplies and water supplies management that exploded in recent years has yet to occur in the United States. In 2003, only 5 percent of American cities had privately owned systems.[16]

San Jose and Private Water

Between the time that Spanish settlers established Pueblo San Jose in 1777 and the 1850s, the area depended on *acequias*—ditches—by building small dams across creeks to supply water. In 1854, the first artesian well was drilled, and groundwater became a mainstay of the first capital of California. Foundry owner Donald McKenzie and two partners founded the San Jose Water Company on November 21, 1866, taking advantage of the abundant artesian water that others had first tapped. The company was granted an exclusive franchise by the city of San Jose and the town of Santa Clara (until 1895 when it built its own waterworks) one year earlier. Under its provisions, the franchise ran for twenty-five years, but allowed the city to purchase the service and its assets after the expiration date. The San Jose Water Company was obligated to provide water for fire protection, and rates were to be set by the city council.

Demand for service increased rapidly, and the company reincorporated on December 12, 1868, with a substantial increase in capital stock. By the 1870s the company was becoming profitable, and began to expand access to water sources beyond artesian wells to include surface water. The artesian wells provided abundant water through the late 1860s, but during dry periods several wells failed. The company continued to purchase water rights, and soon the Santa Cruz Mountains became important to watershed development and Los Gatos Creek, in particular, draining the mountain area, became a focus of attention. By 1880 the total area of the watershed available was fifty square miles, with a capacity of 500 million gallons in the receiving reservoir. The system was thus supplied by gravity with water from the mountains in the area of Las Gatos and by pumping from wells.[17]

On January 26, 1888, President Edward Williams of the waterworks assured the mayor and city council that despite the fact that consumers "have been accustomed to use [water] lavishly and without regard for the season of the year . . . it is a fact that there has always been a sufficient supply of water, which is ready at any moment—in case of fire." He added: "With our present increased reservoir capacity, and pumping machinery, and our source of supply—we can *truthfully* say that no City on the Pacific Coast, of the same size, is so well protected, and nowhere is there such a splendid supply of pure water for domestic purposes."[18]

Despite Williams's assurances that it could provide necessary water supplies to the city, the San Jose Water Company also began to move in on competitors to increase its control of the water market, buying Los Gatos Manufacturing Company (which owned Los Gatos Water Company) in 1890 and later Mountain Spring Water Company (1899).[19] There were some, as early as the turn of the century, who feared an emerging "water octopus" that held the city in its clutches. This was an interesting turn of events considering that the company was regarded as well-run and had cordial associations with prominent citizens and the city government.[20] Others not so well connected to the powers that be obviously were wary of the local company.

Indeed, the water company was never free of critics and rivals during its long and virtually unprecedented existence as a private water company. In 1903, for example, Bay Cities Water Company wanted to divert artesian water from Santa Clara Valley (Smith Creek, Ysabel Creek, and Bonita Creek) into the watershed of Coyote Creek for use by its customers in Oakland. In this so-called "Coyote Creek Battle of 1903–1905," San Jose Water Company joined forces with local ranchers and the *San Jose Herald* in opposing the effort of outside companies to control water rights to Coyote Creek.[21] A *San Jose Herald* editorial claimed: "THE DIVERSION OF THIS WATER WILL RUIN FARMS AND ORCHARDS; DESTROY REAL ESTATE VALUES IN CITY AND COUNTRY; IMPOVERISH CITY AND COUNTY TREASURIES; DRIVE MERCHANTS AND MANUFACTURERS OUT OF BUSINESS AND THROW WAGE WORKERS OUT OF EMPLOYMENT."[22] More cynically, a story in the *San Jose News* asserted: "Compared to the San Francisco monopoly the San Jose Water Company is of as much consequence as a bunch of tar weed tied to the tail of a kite on a windy day, but nevertheless the local dictators of the price of aqua pura have apparently defied competition from any source."[23] Ultimately, an injunction against

Bay Cities was upheld in the California Supreme Court, which also upheld San Jose's rights to the water in Coyote Creek.[24]

Competitors for the water supply were one source of concern to the water company; the other was attacks by those favoring municipal ownership of water services. Historical accounts suggest that a serious antifranchise and municipal ownership campaign was not mounted until 1938. Yet contemporary sources suggest that such pressure was chronic, especially by those claiming that the company charged excessive rates for water. In *The Union Label* (July 1905), Louis Montgomery, secretary of the Municipal Ownership League, attacked the notion of a franchise as an opportunity for a few to make "large fortunes" at the expense of the municipality. "There is no value to a stream of water, no matter how pure or great if there is no one to use it," he stated. "It follows therefore that the value lies in its use and control . . . The people exclusively use it, they should have the exclusive control."[25]

Trust, therefore, rested with municipal government to provide better and cheaper service than an avaricious private company—an argument stated time and again throughout the country in this period.[26] An ironic twist in the "Coyote Creek Battle of 1903–1905" was Bay Cities' claim that San Jose Water Company (and San Francisco firm, Spring Valley Water Company, who also coveted water in Santa Clara Valley) was a monopoly who intended to impede competitors![27]

In the 1920s the controversy over municipal ownership of the waterworks intensified as a result of several pending changes in the water supply and administration of water resources in Santa Clara Valley. Application for a rate increase by San Jose Water Works in 1924 (the first since 1914) appears to have precipitated another round of debate over the "water monopoly."[28] Councilman D. M. Denegri, who opposed the rate hike, proposed that the city own its own water distribution system, connecting it with the Hetch Hetchy project. Hetch Hetchy Valley in Yosemite National Park was drained by the Tuolumne River—a water source which San Francisco had designs on for several years. After a bitter environmental struggle, O'Shaughnessy Dam on the Tuolumne was completed in 1923 with its water serving San Francisco, San Mateo, and Alameda Counties, and parts of the San Joaquin Valley. In 1924 officials in San Jose were queried about their interest in obtaining Hetch Hetchy water. However, the city did not yet have a pressing need for imported water as was the case with San Francisco and neighbor to the south, Los Angeles, which had tapped the Owens Valley.[29] The debate over a new water supply—and a municipally owned waterworks—spilled over into the 1930s.[30] The consistent stance of the San Jose Water Works continued to be that they provided excellent service, abundant water, and were strongly linked to the community. A flyer appearing in the *Los Gatos Star* on January 1, 1925, affirmed that 75 percent of the stockholders lived in Santa Clara Valley and 95 percent lived in California. "It is not often," it stated, "that the control of a public utility is so closely confined to the place where it operates. This unusual condition makes San Jose Water Works, very distinctively, a Santa Clara County institution."[31]

By the end of the decade talk of a municipal system and the selling of the company remained in the air. But the city was not the only interested party. San Jose Water Works was acquired by General Water Works and Electric Company in October 1929, as part of an effort by eastern utility holding companies to buy water companies and other utilities. Consummated amidst the 1929 Wall Street crash (October 24, 1929, was "Black Thursday"), its purchase was typical of business consolidations through holding company acquisitions happening in several areas in the 1920s. There was to be no change in local management in San Jose, but the assertions of the value of a hometown company providing necessary services was certainly weakened by the purchase.[32]

Equally, if not more significant for San Jose Water Works in 1929, was the formation of the Santa Clara Valley Water Conservation District (later the Santa Clara Valley Water District), established to manage some of the water resources of the area. Falling of the water table and problems of subsidence were noted in the 1920s, which was bad news particularly for local growers. An engineering report in 1921 stated that construction of dams to percolate water back into the aquifer was the solution—a rather bold idea for the time. Voters turned it down twice. But in 1929, the California legislature passed the Jones Act—named after Herbert C. Jones, a major figure in California water history—which set up a new type of water district that omitted provisions for bonds (later added to a 1931 law), and the SCWCD was subsequently approved.[33]

Improvements were to take the form of several dams, reservoirs, and pumping stations. Economic growth, more than conservation, likely made the formation of the district popular with city and county officials.[34] One historian has noted that the San Jose Water Works "probably welcomed the creation of a water conservation district" because it kept the company from having to develop new sources of water on its own. The "mutually beneficial business relationship" between the new public agency and the private company, she concluded, allowed the waterworks to continue to grow and prosper.[35] Indeed, pressure to provide adequate capital expenditures had weakened the ability of private water companies throughout the country to stave off municipal ownership. In San Jose, the SCWCD may very well have helped the waterworks avoid public takeover in the long run, since the company—wittingly or unwittingly—was becoming integrated into a water system not totally dependent on a single entity, public or private.

Despite the perceived advantages of the conservation district to the waterworks' future, the 1930s represented the most intense battles over public ownership in the company's history. What had changed? The makeup of the city council? The eroding of the waterworks' political clout? Poor service delivery? The answer is not readily apparent, although the fact that the waterworks was now owned by a New York company certainly played some role. Forces favoring municipal ownership continually charged the water rates for the city were too high. There was also, of course, competition for available water supplies from the potent agricultural interests in the "Valley of Heart's Delight," which still dominated the economy. In 1932, the city council instructed the city manager and city attorney to initiate condemnation proceedings against the water company and to obtain a valuation of its property to force a sale to the city. In response, the waterworks voluntarily reduced rates on January 1, 1933, and stated that it was willing to "talk price" with the city. However, the water company refused the city's offer, and the council dropped plans for a water-purchase bill from the subsequent ballot.[36]

In 1934 the city council, having momentarily turned away from direct purchase of the waterworks, contracted with Water Properties Company Ltd. of Arizona to supply San Jose with water from the American River along with thirty-nine other cities and towns in California. The plan called for the participating communities to become joint proprietors in the company after purchasing water for thirty years.[37] This amounted to a run around the waterworks to accomplish municipal ownership in a new way. Voters were presented with the contract in a ballot on May 7, 1934. Proponents raised the specter of the New York interests: "Keep Wall Street Profits for San Jose" without raising taxes or issuing bonds. "Water Properties Company, Ltd., gives to the City of San Jose its water distribution system to own and operate for ever."[38]

From the point of view of San Jose Water Works, "The proposed contract would for thirty years turn over the water destiny of San Jose to a group unfamiliar with local needs and conditions. It would subordinate San Jose's interests to the factions, disputes, and litigation sure to arise from the proposed jumbling of forty cities' water projects in this scheme." It added that other cities had not found the project acceptable, and that Water Properties Company Ltd. was neither "a public enterprise nor a public corporation subject to adequate regulation."[39] State engineer Edward F. Hyatt sided with the waterworks, viewing the plan "not financially feasible." Somewhat ironically, opponents of the scheme (especially directors of the waterworks) branded Water Properties as "a foreign private corporation" in much the same way that supporters of the plan had characterized San Jose Water Works.[40] Voters rejected the proposal by a thin margin (240 out of a total of 11,758 ballots), which in itself did little to clarify public sentiment over public ownership.[41]

But there was to be no stopping the city council from exploring municipal ownership of the water system in San Jose throughout the decade, including the possible purchase of Hetch Hetchy water from San Francisco.[42] In a letter from city manager C. B. Goodwin to the city council on November 4, 1935, Goodwin outlined five reasons why municipal ownership was necessary: (1) water rates were too high; (2) water was too hard; (3) interest rates were currently low, thus favoring a purchase of the waterworks; (4) San Jose was the largest city in the state in which the water system was not publicly owned; and (5) there was some danger of inflation that would increase the rate base. The options he presented to the council included acquiring the whole system, acquiring part of the system, or building a new system for San Jose alone. He believed that the best option was to acquire the whole system "if the right price could be agreed upon."[43]

In 1935 plans to build a municipal system through federal grants was considered and then dropped. Once again, in that year, the cost of a municipal system was explored to determine a purchase price, and again the waterworks had no interest in selling.[44] The sparring continued into 1936 and 1937.[45] A test poll conducted by the *San Jose Mercury Herald* (sometimes *San Jose Mercury*) in early 1937 indicated an overwhelming majority for municipal ownership—78 percent by the close of the poll.[46] The poll seemed to reinvigorate the city council to move on the waterworks again, but all the communities in the central Santa Clara Valley—especially San Jose and Los Gatos—were not in agreement on what kind of plan would suit their needs. H. G. Mitchell, orchardist and secretary of the East Side County Water District, argued that a takeover of the waterworks by San Jose might leave areas outside the city limits (currently served by sJww) "obliged to accept any sort of service or rates that might be imposed upon them." He concluded that if the waterworks was to become a community-owned service, "it should be through the means of a Metropolitan Water District."[47] But a plan for a San Jose–Los Gatos municipal utility district was defeated at the polls largely because of San Joseans' opposition.[48]

The debate over municipal ownership was getting significantly complicated in 1937—communities in Santa Clara Valley were increasingly at odds over the benefits of municipal ownership, the waterworks was predictably opposed to a change, and groups like the Citizens' League on Government and Taxation of Santa Clara County (Citizens' League), questioned a potentially arbitrary bond election without clear knowledge of the company's value and also questioned what the league believed to be unfounded assumptions about the inferior quality of the current supply or the level of the rates.[49]

But after a rancorous campaign, the latest effort to take over the waterworks failed when a bond issue to be used to purchase it went down to defeat in 1938. By a vote of 14,402 to 2,394 (six to one) voters turned away the latest and most vigorous effort by the city council to purchase the waterworks. As a *San Jose Evening News* editorial noted (the *Evening News* opposed the bond issue), "The surprise in yesterday's election was not that the water bonds were beaten, but that the majority against them was so large." The editorial suggested that recent bond proposals had met a similar fate, and that "this is not a good time to submit bond measures." The larger issue, it suggested, was that the voters were not asked directly to vote on municipal ownership. Whether by confusion or impulsive preparation for the election by the city manager and the council, there was not enough inertia in the bond issue vote to turn voters in a new direction.[50]

Harold Gilliam in the *San Francisco Chronicle* viewed the defeat as politics, pure and simple, with well-financed antimunicipal ownership forces creating a "buzz saw" that voters would not challenge.[51] The Citizen's League—beyond its firmly held belief that "political management is rarely, if ever, as efficient and economical as private management"—may have had its finger on the concrete issues that swayed the voters when it noted that the bond issue came "despite the lack of any wide-spread demand for public ownership." Rates had been lowered rather than raised by the waterworks, supplies seemed adequate, bonded debt would only add to the current tax burden, the current "serious business recession" did not favor public ownership, and there was a potential for inconvenience if the city decided simply to duplicate the waterworks system instead of absorb it.[52]

In addition, as Leslie Parks suggested, one factor working against the bond issue was that citizens of Santa Clara Valley had recently voted for the construction of five new conservation dams and had little reason to be concerned about their water supply at the moment. Also, Ralph Elsman, elected as chairman of the board and president of the San Jose Water Works in 1937 (who also became president and general manager of the state's largest privately owned water utility, California Water Service Company in 1939) was effective in working behind the scenes through a variety of community contacts. Particularly important was Parks's observation that since the mid-1930s at least a close relationship existed between progrowth forces that dominated city government (increasingly identified with new city manager Anthony P. "Dutch" Hamann, who became the most aggressive force for annexation in the city's history) and the directors of the water company—both benefiting from San Jose's rise as an urban-industrial center out of its days as a center for agriculture and related activities. By the time General Water, Gas and Electric liquidated its controlling interest in the San Jose Water Works it held since 1945, company stock increasingly returned to local ownership. Local stockholders obviously would support the continuation of the private company.[53]

Yet circumstances change. As droughts and fears of droughts challenge comfortable beliefs about existing supplies, as new residents poured into the valley, and as progrowth advocates reconsidered the value of a municipal water system, controversy was on the horizon again in the 1950s. The years 1948 and 1949 were two of the driest years in California history. Farmers, in particular, began to get nervous. The advantage of tapping Hetch Hetchy water again found supporters. The city council considered bringing waterworks employees under civil service in case the waterworks came under city control. The antis defeated this measure, but the upcoming city council campaign in 1950 pitted pro- and antimunicipal ownership candidates against each other over the water issue.

Alden Campen, a property manager, and Robert Doerr, a high school teacher, ran for city council on a municipal ownership platform, and gained support particularly among agricultural interests. Ralph Elsman stated publicly that there was no water shortage to be concerned about, but Campen and Doerr printed a pamphlet stating that "Ralph Elsman—Water Works Czar—Pumps Water YOU OWN Into Million Dollar Profits." In turn Campen and Doerr were charged by the Committee for the Preservation of the American Way of Life, in good 1950s fashion, as "sowing the seeds of Socialism in our midst." The results of the election were ambivalent for public ownership. Campen was defeated, but Doerr was elected.

The idea of a public waterworks was not just the platform for "left-leaning" proponents, therefore. Some progrowth advocates in the city council—even before the 1950 campaign—saw public ownership of the water system as enhancing the city's financial status; lowering rates and possibly becoming profitable in its own right. Dutch Hamann would mount his own campaign to purchase the waterworks. It was somewhat ironic that the progrowth notions that had supported Elsman's claim of the value of private water were being turned on their heads in favor of public water. The council had pro- and anti- elements in the 1950s, however, and little changed.

In 1960 the proposed annexation by the town of Los Gatos of some 10,345 acres—much of which included the Santa Cruz Mountain watershed—raised concern, leading Doerr to propose a study on the purchase of the waterworks. The purchase was deemed feasible. Hamann ultimately supported ownership of the waterworks after Los Gatos achieved its annexation goal. But proposed changes in the city charter to help make public ownership possible were defeated in 1961 and 1962 thanks in part of the waterworks' opposition.[54]

Complicating matters was the question of supply for the fast-growing Santa Clara County in these years. The SCVWCD provided wholesale supplies, but there were a variety of retail dealers in the area—but not necessarily working within county lines. Cities to the north of San Jose were using Hetch Hetchy water from

San Francisco, but San Jose was barred from it (under federal law) as long as it maintained a privately owned water company that sold water for a profit. County supervisors believed that they were the party most able to provide imported water and favored utilizing state water from an aqueduct close to San Jose, while the water district wanted federal water via another route into the valley. A compromise was consummated in the 1960s that would allow state and federal water to be imported, cities in the north part of the county would continue to get Hetch Hetchy water, and a new Santa Clara Valley Water District would accept input from the county supervisors and the old water district. Most importantly, the compromise recognized the regional nature of water supply, although it did little to help resolve the fate of private water in San Jose.[55]

In 1961, San Jose "got its foot in the door" with the purchase of the Evergreen Water Company, which was a small, private firm serving a few hundred people in the Evergreen area. The city almost sold the company to the waterworks the next year, but held on to it by a thread. Hamann tried to use the momentum of the purchase to get the council to support municipal ownership, but failed. The promunicipal ownership forces in place in 1958 were no longer in control of the council, and he faced the opposition of the San Jose Mercury as well. Despite the fact that municipal systems (other than Evergreen) were selling water cheaper than San Jose Water Works, public support for municipal ownership was missing. It seemed that a comfort level existed with the privately owned company that time and opposition had been unable to overturn—despite many efforts. This was not a concrete reason, perhaps, but certainly a product of historical momentum. Helping to maintain that position were a large number of progrowth advocates inside and outside of government who saw little value in a public system, and certainly possessed political leverage that the water company had courted for years.[56]

The year 1966 saw another attempt at a municipal system. Yet the same opposition parties, public ambivalence, and especially high interest rates foiled the effort. Financial consultants Stone & Youngberg stated that it was not feasible for the city to make the purchase with current interest rates up to 1.5 percent above normal.[57] Another challenge was made in 1972, three years after progrowth Dutch Hamann had retired. But there was no new strategy on either side, and the story played out as expected. The dwindling of progrowth supporters on the city council certainly dimmed enthusiasm for a public water system, and other city priorities shifted the battleground to other issues.[58] The passage of Proposition 13 in 1978 certainly was influential.[59] Through this "People's Initiative to Limit Property Taxation," the maximum amount of any ad valorem tax on real property could not exceed 1 percent of the full cash value of the property. By limiting revenue to the state, public-sector initiatives faced little chance of success. A new bond issue to purchase the water system was now out of the question. In the approching years of the Reagan era, publicly sponsored programs would face "outsourcing" and "privatizing"—not congenial for promoting municipal ownership.

Yet the story of the San Jose Water Works does not end with a clear private-sector victory. By 1974 there were three, albeit small, municipal water systems operating in the city of San Jose: Evergreen, North San Jose, and Alviso. Evergreen Water System served an area of about 18 square miles in that year. North San Jose served about 4 square miles and Alviso about 20 square miles, compared with about 138 square miles in metropolitan San Jose served by San Jose Water Company.[60] San Jose Water Company (the name changed in 1983), since the 1990s at least, also has been constrained by slow- or no-growth realities in its service area. As a *San Jose Mercury News* story stated in December 1992: the company "has survived financial panics, eathquakes, depression, drought, takeover attempts and political challenges. Now, it is threatened by slow strangulation."[61] The combination of significant decline in water use plus limits to the physical expansion of the city forced sjw Corporation—the holding company formed in 1985 of which San Jose Water Company is a wholly owned subsidiary—to attempt to obtain a percentage of California Water Service Company, which is the state's largest investor-owned water company. In addition, sjw Corporation has diversified to move into real property and other investments. This strategy was deemed necessary since there was little area within its existing territory for expansion.[62]

Conclusion

So what does this long history of San Jose and its private water company tell us about this historical anamoly—private municipal water in a publicly dominated world? In some respects, San Jose Waster Company (San Jose Water Works) survived because of a sustained period of economic and physical growth in the Santa Clara Valley. The area's population explosion, it relentless physical expansion, and its relentless transformation from a valley of orchards to Silicon Valley offered consistent opportunities for the water company to seek and serve customers and maintain its financial solvency for more than one hundred years. But the company did not persevere without challenges to its control and to its very existence.

At a distance it appears that San Jose Water Company had no real competitors and survived in a world of content consumers. A closer look suggests that the challenge of municipal ownership was unremitting since the nineteenth century. But why did municipal ownership fail here when it succeeded in an overwhleming number of other places in the United States? There are several reasons. First, the company never lost its customer base to rival private companies or from bad management and practices. Even when rates were regarded as high, the company responded by lowering rates or asserting that rates were fair. Because the franchise required that the city council and then the railroad commission set rates, this removed—or at least softened—a political issue that had hurt other private companies; that is, a third party between consumers and retailers was responsible for determining the value of the commodity. Second, when water supplies were challenged by dry spells and growing demand, new sources were discovered or the company convincingly argued that supplies were plentiful. Ironically, the formation of a public entity, the Santa Clara Valley Water Conservation District, helped to undergird potentially dwindling supplies by providing new infrastructure—dams and reservoirs—and financing new sources available to the citizens of San Jose and the valley, thus relieving the company of constant pressure to seek new water supplies on their own. Third, groundwater never became so scarce or so threatened by pollution or competitors as to remove this option from use. Bay Cities tried to capture groundwater, but the company—aided by the city and other supporters—fended them off. Again, public enitites came to the aid of a private company—if even unwittingly. In addition, scvwcd's plan for recharging the aquifers directly benefitted the water company. Fourth, support also was readily available within government circles and the business community, helping to shield the water company from takeover. As stated earlier, the "political nature" of water was important.

The momentum of successful service, plentiful supply, complementary support from a public entity like the scvwcd, and continued political engagement made the San Jose Water Company difficult to take down. Timing was everything—recession, depression, high interest rates, and Proposition 13 worked against public ownership. And certainly public perception played a role as well; the company was never successfully portrayed as a "water monopoly" in the eyes of the public—at least not an unwelcomed one. The moniker never stuck long enough for the voting public to abandon the water company in any bond election. The image of the San Jose Water Company usually focused on success, not failure—either by its backers or detractors. It was rarely if ever viewed as weak or moribund.

The historical context in which the San Jose Water Company found itself from 1866 to the present trumped the national swing toward municipal ownership in the nineteenth and twentieth centuries. Whether changing circumstances will lead to a new era of privatized water in the United States in the next several years remains to be seen. San Jose Water Company, however, bucked a long-standing trend, although it did so through amaze of issues not easily replicated by others.

Notes

Several years ago I began collecting material on San Jose's municipal services and infrastructure originally to be used in *The Sanitary City* (2000). However, until now, I have not had the occasion to tell at least part of the story of the fascinating growth of an important western city and my home town. This special volume dedicated to our dear friend and colleague Hal Rothman seemed to be the most fitting place to offer this new piece of work.

The overall structure for this section comes from Martin V. Melosi, *The Sanitary City: Urban Infrastructure in America from Colonial Times to the Present* (Baltimore: Johns Hopkins University Press, 2000).

1. John C. Trautwine Jr., "A Glance at the Water Supply of Philadelphia," *Journal of the New England Water Works Association* 22 (Dec. 1908): 421, 425; Michal McMahon, "Fairmount," *American Heritage* 30 (April/May 1979): 100–101; Michal McMahon, "Makeshift Technology," *Environmental Review* 12 (Winter 1988): 24–26; Donald C. Jackson, "'The Fairmount Waterworks, 1812–1911,' at the Philadelphia Museum of Art," *Technology and Culture* 30 (July 1989): 635; City of Philadelphia, Department of Public Works, Bureau of Water, "Description of the Filtration Works and Pumping Stations, Also Brief Historical Review of the Water Supply, 1789–1900" (1909), 57–59; Edward C. Carter II, "Benjamin Henry Latrobe and Public Works," *Essays in Public Works History* (Washington, DC: Public Works Historical Society, 1976); Jane Mork Gibson, "The Fairmount Waterworks," *Bulletin of the Philadelphia Museum of Art* 84 (Summer 1988): 9–12; Ellis Armstrong, Michael Robinson, and Suellen Hoy, eds., *History of Public Works in the United States* (Chicago: APWA, 1976), 232–33; "Golden Decade for Philadelphia Water," *Engineering News-Record* 159 (Sept. 19, 1957): 37; Martin J. McLaughlin, "Philadelphia's Water Works from 1798 to 1944," *American City* 59 (Oct. 1944): 86–87.

2. U.S. Bureau of Census, *Census of Population: 1960*, vol.1, *Characteristics of the Population* (Washington, DC: Department of Commerce, 1961), pt. A, pp. 1–14–15, Table 8; Waterman, *Elements of Water Supply Engineering*, 6; Harrison P. Eddy, "Water Purification—A Century of Progress," *Civil Engineering* 2 (Feb. 1932): 82; J. J. R. Croes, *Statistical Tables from the History and Statistics of American Water Works* (New York, 1885), 4–69.

3. Waterman, *Elements of Water Supply Engineering*, 6.

4. Letty Donaldson Anderson, "The Diffusion of Technology in the Nineteenth-Century American City," (PhD diss., Northwestern University, 1980, 102–4, 117); Letty Anderson, "Hard Choices," *Journal of Interdisciplinary History* 15 (Autumn 1984): 218; Joel A. Tarr, "The Evolution of the Urban Infrastructure in the Nineteenth and Twentieth Centuries," in *Perspectives on Urban Infrastructure*, ed. Royce Hanson (Washington, DC: National Academy Press, 1984), 30–31.

5. M. N. Baker, "Public and Private Ownership of Water-Works," *The Outlook* 59 (May 7, 1898): 79; Anderson, "Diffusion of Technology," 108.

6. Tarr, "Evolution of the Urban Infrastructure," 26. John Ellis and Stuart Galishoff, "Atlanta's Water Supply, 1865–1918," *Maryland Historian* 8 (Spring 1977): 5–22.

7. Cornelius C. Vermeule, "New Jersey's Experience with State Regulation of Public Water Supplies," *American City* 16 (June 1917): 602; Ernest S. Griffith, *A History of American City Government: The Progressive Years and Their Aftermath, 1900–1920* (Washington, DC: University Press of America, 1983), 86–87; Maureen Ogle, "Redefining 'Public' Water Supplies, 1870–1890 *Annals of Iowa* 50 (Spring 1990): 507–30; Gregg R. Hennessey, "The Politics of Water in San Diego, 1895–1897," *Journal of San Diego History* 24 (Summer 1978): 367–83.

8. Committee on Municipal Administration, "Evolution of the City" *Municipal Affairs* 2 (Sept. 1898): 726–27; Ernest S. Griffith, *A History of American City Government: The Conspicuous Failure* (Washington, DC: University Press of America, 1983), 180; Anderson, "The Diffusion of Technology in the Nineteenth-Century American City," 106; *The Manual of American Water-Works* (New York, 1897), f-g.

9. Anderson, "Diffusion of Technology," 106, 108, 112; Tarr, "Evolution of the Urban Infrastructure," 26, 30; Baker, "Public and Private Ownership of Water-Works," 78.

10. Anderson, "Diffusion of Technology" 122; Henry C. Hodgkins, "Franchises of Public Utilities as They Were and as They Are," *JAWWA* 2 (Dec. 1915): 743.

11. Anderson, "Diffusion of Technology," 115, 119, 121.

12. Todd A. Shallat, "Fresno's Water Rivalry," *Essays in Public Works History* 8 (1979): 9–13.

13. A. S. Baldwin, "Shall San Francisco Municipalize Its Water Supply?" *Municipal Affairs* (June 1900): 317–28; Clyde Arbuckle, *History of San Jose* (San Jose: Memorabilia of San Jose, 1986), 301, 486–87, 501–9.

14. "The Recent History of Municipal Ownership in the United States," *Municipal Affairs* 6 (Winter 1902–3): 524, 529; Anderson, "Diffusion of Technology," 122–23; M. N. Baker, "Municipal Ownership and Operation of Water Works," *Annals of the American Academy* 57 (Jan. 1915): 281.

15. Todd, *The Water Encyclopedia,* 351.

16. Martin V. Melosi, "Public Goods versus Privatization: The Development of Water Supplies in the United States" (unpublished paper).

17. *San Jose Water Company: 125th Anniversary,* Sharon Whaley, ed., (San Jose: San Jose Water Company, 1991), 3–5, 8–9; U.S. Bureau of the Census, *Statistics of Power and Machinery Employed in Manufactures,* v. 17 (1880), 174; Doug Hayward, "The quiet giant—and your money: Water—does it belong to the people?" *East San Jose Sun* (December 28, 1965); Glory Anne Laffey, "Water Management and Urban Growth in San Jose, 1846–1870," (master's thesis, San Jose State University, June, 1982), 47, 74–75; San Jose Water Works, *Nine Men and 100 Years of Water History: The Story of the San Jose Water Works* (San Jose: San Jose Water Works, March, 1967), Archives, San Jose Historical Museum; Philip Schuyler, "The San Jose Water Works," *Western Construction News* 2 (October 10, 1927): 44.

18. Edward Williams to the Mayor and Common Council, January 26, 1888, Box 02307, Archives, San Jose Historical Museum.

19. *San Jose Water Company: 125th Anniversary,* 8–9; "Company Organized in 1866, Has Had Intersting Growth," *San Jose Evening News* (April 3, 1937), San Jose Water Works Notebooks, San Jose Water Company.

20. Leslie Sayoko Parks, "A History of the San Jose Water Company" (master's thesis, San Jose State University, 1983), 50–51. See also Clyde Arbuckle, *History of San Jose* (San Jose: Memorabilia of San Jose, 1986), 501–9.

21. *San Jose Water Company: 125th Anniversary,* 11–12.

22. Editorial, *San Jose Herald,* October 8, 1903, San Jose Water Works Notebooks, San Jose Water Company. See the notebooks for extensive newspaper coverage of this and other issues of interest to the water company.

23. "Water Company May Have Competition," *San Jose Evening News,* July, 1906, San Jose Water Works Notebooks, San Jose Water Company.

24. Parks, "A History of the San Jose Water Company," 61–62.

25. "Advantages of Owning Our Own Water System," *The Union Label* 3 (July 24, 1905): 1. See also J. R. Lewis and Louis Montgomery to Mayor and Common Council of the City of San Jose, March 19, 1906, and City Attorney to Lewis and Montgomery, February 26, 1906, Box 02307, Archives, San Jose Historical Museum; "Appeal to Honest Stock Holders of Water Co.," *San Jose Times,* March 5, 1907, and "Mayor and Common Council: Are They Servants of the People, or Are They the Agents of the San Jose Water Company," *San Jose Times,* February 6, 1907, San Jose Water Works Notebooks, San Jose Water Company. Note: Montgomery's comments do not necessarily reflect a prolabor position on municipal ownership of the waterworks. For example, an article in *The Union,* Sept. 5, 1910, (on Labor Day), stated that "Organized labor has a deep interest in the water supply and the members of the 63 labor bodies here rely upon the company that is supplying us with this great necessity."

26. See Melosi, *The Sanitary City,* 177–48.

27. "Claim Water Co. is a Monopoly," *San Jose Evening News,* August 21, 1906, San Jose Water Works Notebooks, San Jose Water Company.

28. In 1912 regulation of water utility rates passed from San Jose City Council to the state railroad commission. In 1916 the original charter of incorporation for San Jose Water Company expired, and the name changed to San Jose Water Works with the new company assuming all franchises. See *San Jose Water Company: 125th Anniversary,* 13. Note: Missing from this official company history were many of the controversies surrounding the municipal ownership debate. See also Seonaid McArthur, ed., "Water in the Santa Clara Valley: A History," *Local History Studies* 27 (California History Center, DeAnza College, 1981), 14.

29. Glenna Matthews, "'The Los Angeles of the North:' San Jose's Transition from Fruit Capital to High-Tech Metropolis," *Journal of Urban History* 25 (May 1999): 468; "San Jose Rate for Water Up," *San Francisco Chronicle,* October 30, 1924; editorial, *San Jose Evening News,* January 14, 1926; "Hetch Hetchy Water Urged for San Jose," *San Francisco Chronicle,*

November 11, 1924; "San Jose Right in Resisting Water Corporation's Demands," *San Jose Evening News*, April 26, 1924, San Jose Water Works Notebooks, San Jose Water Company.

30. "Efforts to Obtain Hetchy Water Here Being Opposed at Modesto," *San Jose Mercury*, June 19, 1930, San Jose Water Works Notebooks, San Jose Water Company.

31. "A New Year Endeavor," *Los Gatos Star*, January 1, 1925.

32. *San Jose Water Company: 125th Anniversary*, 16; "N.Y. Company is Declared Purchaser of Water System," *San Jose Mercury*, April 2, 1929; "Talk of Selling San Jose's Water System Brings out Big Variety of Opinions," *San Jose Evening News*, March 15, 1929; "Water Purchase to Link S.J. with Big Utility Firm," *San Jose Mercury*, May 9, 1929; "$5,100,00 Sent Here to Close Water Co. Sale," *San Jose Mercury*, October 26, 1929, San Jose Water Works Notebooks, San Jose Water Company. Note: In 1931 San Jose Water Works was reincorporated with an increase in its authorized stock. "Local Water Co. is being Reorganized," *San Jose Evening News*, Oct. 24, 1931, San Jose Water Works Notebooks, San Jose Water Company.

33. Matthews, "'The Los Angeles of the North,'" 468.

34. See Santa Clara Valley Water District, *The Story of the Santa Clara Valley Water District* (June 1978), California History Center, De Anza College, Cuopertino, California; "Formation of Valley Water Conservation District is Approved by Huge Majority," *San Jose Herald*, November 6, 1929, San Jose Water Works Notebooks, San Jose Water Company. See also McArthur, ed., "Water in the Santa Clara Valley: A History."

35. Parks, "A History of the San Jose Water Company," 80, 85.

36. City Manager to City Council, May 15, 1933, City of San Jose, Box 1538; San Jose Water Company, *Annual Report, 1932*; "Our City Should Own Its Own Water Supply," *San Jose Evening News*, October 29, 1932; "Council Moves to Force Sale of S.J. Water Works to City," *San Jose Mercury*, Nov. 1, 1932; "Council Starts Action to Buy Water Company," *San Jose Mercury*, Dec. 20, 1932; "Water Works Asks City Delay Suit: Ready to Talk Price," *San Jose Evening News*, Janaury 6, 1933; "Water Works Will Refuse City's Offer," *San Jose Evening News*, May 15, 1933; "Council Drops Plan for Water Purchase Ballot," *San Jose Mercury*, May 23, 1933, San Jose Water Works Notebooks, San Jose Water Company.

37. "San Jose Signs 30-Year Contract for Municipal Water Purchase," *San Jose Mercury*, March 6, 1934; Louis Ashlock, "10,000 to Get Jobs by Huge Water Plan," *San Jose Evening News*, March 9, 1934, San Jose Water Works Notebooks, San Jose Water Company.

38. "Vote Yes" flyer (1934); P. C. Edwards, "San Jose Voters to Decide on Water Promotion Scheme Declared 'Gold Brick' Offer," *San Jose Evening News*, May 4, 1934, San Jose Water Works Notebooks, San Jose Water Company.

39. Letter to Pacific, Gas & Electric employees from H. S. Kittridge, president of San Jose Water Works, May 2, 1934, San Jose Water Works Notebooks, San Jose Water Company.

40. "Vote Down This Fantastic Water Scheme!" (1934), San Jose Water Works Notebooks, San Jose Water Company.

41. "City Rejects Water Supply Plan by 240; Re-Elect Cuncilmen," *San Jose Evening News*, May 8, 1934, San Jose Water Works Notebooks, San Jose Water Company.

42. "City Negotiates for Hetch Hetchy Water from San Francisco," *San Jose Mercury,* March 3, 1937; F. G. Cahill, Manager of Utilities, City and County of San Francisco, to C. B. Goodwin, Oct. 12, 1937, City of San Jose, Box 1538.

43. C. B. Goodwin to City Council, November 4, 1935, City of San Jose, Box 1538.

44. "Municipal Water Plans Dropped by City Council," *San Jose Mercury,* Sept. 3, 1935; "Council Paves Way for Public Owned Utilities," *San Jose Mercury,* Oct. 8, 1935; "Move to Acquire S.J. Water Works Launched by City," *San Jose Mercury,* Nov. 5, 1935; "Water Works Won't Sell to City," *San Jose Evening News,* Nov. 21, 1935; "San Jose Bids $4,500,000 for Water Company," *San Jose Mercury,* Dec. 6, 1935; "Water Works Turns Down Offer," *San Jose Evening News,* Dec. 21, 1935, San Jose Water Works Notebooks, San Jose Water Company; Citizen's League on Government. And Taxation of Santa Clara County to Mayor and City Council, November 25, 1935, City of San Jose, Box 1538; H. S. Kittridge to C. B. Goodwin, November 21, 1935, City of San Jose, Box 1538.

45. T. A. Hopkins (Consulting Engineer) to C. B. Goodwin, January 21, 1936, and "Comparative Costs of Acquisition and Operation of Proposed Municipal Water System for the City of San Jose, California," City of San Jose, Box 1538; "City Gets Water Plans," *San Jose Evening News,* March 6, 1936; "Council Hears Pro and Con on Municipal Water System," *San Jose Mercury,* July 25, 1936; "Water Company Again Refuses City Sale Price," *San Jose Mercury,* Feb. 20, 1936; "Water Company Announces Rate Cut," *San Jose Evening News,* Nov. 10, 1936; "Does S.J. Want Water Works?" *San Jose Evening News,* Dec. 8, 1936; San Jose Water Works Notebooks, San Jose Water Company.

46. "Water Poll Vote 81 Per Cent in Favor of City-Owned System," *San Jose Mercury,* Feb. 1, 1937; "80 Per Cent Favor Municipal Ownership, Test Poll Shows," *San Jose Mercury,* Feb. 2 , 1937; "Council Launches Move to Buy Water Works," *San Jose Mercury,* Feb. 9, 1937; San Jose Water Works Notebooks, San Jose Water Company.

47. H. G. Mitchell to San Jose City Council, April 3, 1937, City of San Jose, Box 1538.

48. "Utility District Defeated; City Water Plan Speeded," *San Jose Mercury,* Nov. 24, 1937; "East Side Opposes City's Buying Water Co.," *San Jose Evening News,* April 5, 1937, San Jose Water Works Notebooks, San Jose Water Company.

49. See J. Lester Miller to City Council, May 15, 1937; Miller to City Council, May 27, 1937; Ralph Elsman, Chairman of the Board, San Jose Water Works, to Richard French, City Council and C. B. Goodwin, City Manager, Dec. 15, 1937; Elsman to French and Goodwin, March 9, 1937; M. J. Vertin, Los Gatos Chamber of Commerce to City Council, May 15, 1937, City of San Jose, Box 1538. See also San Jose City Council Minutes, Dec. 16, 1937, March 21, 1938.

50. "Election Results," *San Jose Evening News,* May 3, 1938. See also "Water Bonds Out; Brooks is Beaten," *San Jose Evening News,* May 5, 1938, San Jose Water Works Notebooks, San Jose Water Company.

51. Harold Gilliam, "San Jose—Woried City in a Thirsty Valley," *San Francisco Chronicle,* July 16, 1950, 1.

52. J. H. Jamison, Director of the Citizens' League to City Council, February 25, 1938, City of San Jose, Box 1538.

53. Parks, "A History of the San Jose Water Company," 96–97, 111–17; *San Jose Water Company: 125th Anniversary*, 19.

54. Gilliam, "San Jose—Worried City in a Thirsty Valley," 1–2, 11; Parks, "A History of the San Jose Water Company," 119–41, John Spalding, "Buying Water Works Said 'Feasible' in City Report," *San Jose Mercury,* Sept. 12, 1961; Doug Hayward, "Water Works Grows and Prospers," *San Jose Sun,* Dec. 15, 1965. See also McArthur, ed., "Water in the Santa Clara Valley: A History," 75.

55. See Matthews, "'The Los Angeles of the North,'" 469–70. According to Matthews, in 1996 42 percent of Santa Clara Valley's water came from local reservoirs, 23 percent from the federal central Valley Project, 19 percent from a state project, and 16 percent from Hetch Hetchy water. See p. 469.

56. Parks, "A History of the San Jose Water Company," 142–45.

57. "Interest Rate Balks Water Co. Purchase," *San Jose Mercury,* Aug. 23, 1966; "Water Works Series Brings Out Strong Views," *East San Jose Sun,* January 12, 1966; "San Jose Water Activity—Higher Rates and Too Many Districts are Some of the Problems," *San Jose Sun,* Nov. 9, 1966; Parks, "A History of the San Jose Water Company," 145–48.

58. Philp J. Trounstine and Terry Christensen, in *Movers and Shakers: The Study of Community Power* (New York: St. Martin's Press, 1982), discuss San Jose Water Company as one of the interlocking institutions and boards of directors in the San Jose political and economic community. See pp. 73, 121–22. More on the political economy and water in Santa Clara Valley can be found in Richard A. Walker and Matthew J. Williams, "Water from Power: Water Supply and Regional Growth in the Santa Clara Valley," *Economic Geography* 58 (April 1982): 95–119.

59. See Parks, "A History of the San Jose Water Company," 149–61; Stone and Youngberg, *Preliminary Report: Acquisition of San Jose Water Works* (Oct. 1971); "Danger of Jumping into the Water Works," *San Jose Sun,* August 8, 1973.

60. Operations Analysis Division, Office of Fiscal Affairs, *Physical Facility Narrative Profile: City of San Jose* (San Jose, Sept. 30, 1974), 20.

61. Ron Wolf, "San Jose Water Co. Charts an Unusual Course to Growth," *San Jose Mercury News,* December 7, 1992, 1E.

62. Ibid., 1E, 9E; SJW Corp, online http://www.sjwater.com; Parks, "A History of the San Jose Water Company," 165ff.

Campground

Performing Bears and Packaged Wilderness

Reframing the History of National Parks

MARGUERITE S. SHAFFER

Traffic in paradise. We were inching along at two miles an hour in a line of cars, vans, and campers that seemed endless. Ahead a park ranger was directing traffic in the midst of pandemonium. Cars were veering off to the side of the road, skidding to a stop, and people were jumping out and running across the street with kids and cameras trailing wildly behind. The experience was unsettling. This was a mob scene—something you might expect to see in Hollywood or New York City. I couldn't help but wonder if I was really in the middle of Yellowstone National Park—one of America's premier wilderness destinations—it felt more like a Brad Pitt and Angelina Jolie sighting. But no, this was a "bear jam," National Park Service slang for what happens when tourists spot a bear in Yellowstone.

The spectacle of bears in Yellowstone is not a new one. As Alice Biel chronicles in her recent book *Do (Not) Feed the Bears,* the bear has long been a celebrity in Yellowstone National Park. And Biel is quick to point out the contradictions of idealizing a "human fed, garbage eating animal" as a wilderness icon.[1] Staged bear feeding originated in the 1890s at the Fountain Hotel, a high-end hotel financed by the Northern Pacific Railway, located near the Old Faithful Geyser. Yellowstone administrators quickly institutionalized the idea by transforming garbage dumps into amphitheaters at other major hotels in the park. At the Old Faithful Inn, Park Service employees built an elevated feeding platform for the bears, known as the "Lunch Counter," which was surrounded by log benches arranged in a semicircle. An even more elaborate feeding station was constructed at Otter Creek featuring seating for 250 people and a reinforced concrete feeding platform with running water for cleaning. By the 1920s when more and more tourists began to drive through the park, bears begging for food by the roadside became a common sight.

Park Service employees nicknamed one bear Jesse James for his routine of "holding up" automobiles near West Thumb. Horace M. Albright, Yellowstone's first National Park Service superintendent, formally sanctioned these kinds of wildlife shows; he established a "buffalo show coral" and a menagerie for wildlife viewing during his tenure as park superintendent. He also frequently posed for publicity photos feeding the bears while escorting celebrities and high-ranking government officials through the park. Albright argued that the NPS had a "duty to present wildlife as a spectacle" for the pleasure of park visitors.[2]

Environmental and administrative histories of Yellowstone National Park have tended to disregard the performing bears. Rather the national parks, Yellowstone first and foremost, have served as the premiere examples in the larger history of environmental preservation. Beginning with Roderick Nash's *Wilderness and the American Mind,* the history of the national parks has been used to document the story of wilderness and wildlife protection. Tracing the value of wilderness as it evolved from a cultural affinity for scenic monumentalism to a more scientific understanding of ecological systems and natural habitat, the major milestones in this historical narrative include: the establishment of Yellowstone as the first national park set aside "for the benefit and enjoyment of the people;"[3] the split between conservationists and preservationists in the unsuccessful battle to preserve the Hetch Hetchy Valley in Yosemite; the successful fight to prevent the damming of Echo Park in Dinosaur National Park; and the articulation of Aldo Leopold's land ethic, culminating in the passage of the Wilderness Act in 1964, which provided for "outstanding opportunities for solitude or a primitive and unconfined type of recreation."[4] And although historians have been quick to point out the flaws and limitations of these early preservation attempts, Yellowstone National Park and the other national parks that followed are still lionized as the harbingers of what would become the baseline of modern-day environmentalism.[5] The result of this history is that the national parks, despite a complicated past, have emerged in the public imagination as icons of wilderness and the poster children of the environmental movement. The story of performing bears in Yellowstone, however, suggests a different history.

Although bear feeding has long since fallen out of favor with the emergence of more scientific, ecologically based park management policies, the story of Yellowstone bears mirrors a much larger story about the promotion and display of nature in the national parks. Specifically, this is a story about defining and promoting wilderness as a consumer experience and giving wildlife and monumental scenery celebrity status. Whether talking about the bears in Yellowstone, Yosemite's Half Dome, or Lookout Point at the Grand Canyon, over the past century visitors have been conditioned by the Park Service to understand wilderness in consumerist terms. As one National Park Service policy report from the 1950s explained, "wilderness also needs to be regarded as a quality—defined in terms of personal experience, feelings, or benefits." In other words, according to the Park Service, wilderness was as much a particular place as it was a "state of mind."[6] Although much of the Park Service promotional literature juxtaposed park wilderness to urban industrial culture, the Park Service has conceptualized wilderness using the very same consumer values and ideals that underlie its urban industrial counterpart.

What happens if the history of national parks is viewed not through the lens of environmentalism, but rather through the lens of consumer culture? This essay explores the origins and implications of National Park Service practice and policy to frame wilderness in consumerist terms. If we tell the story from this perspective, the history of national parks reveals the process by which wilderness has been defined, packaged, and marketed as a consumer product and experience. In effect this history tells the story of how nature set aside in the parks was transformed into a standardized, nationally advertised, brand-named consumer product— *wilderness*. The milestones in this history highlight the process of branding, packaging, and marketing rather than the development of protecting and preserving. Although much of this history has already been told in various places, retelling the history of national parks from this perspective, I think, calls into question the concept of wilderness manifested by the national parks.[7] What follows then is an attempt to reframe the history of national parks and in the process to shed new light on the environmental ideals and impulses they have come to embody and reflect.

Branding National Park Wilderness

Wilderness began to attain a kind of celebrity status as a consumer experience at the same moment that manufacturers and distributors began to standardize, brand, and mass produce goods for a national market.[8] In the decades after the Civil War the nation's transcontinental railroads, following in the footsteps of other national corporations, began to package the national parks as brand name tourist attractions. Northern Pacific, the Atchison, Topeka and Santa Fe, and the Great Northern all created elaborate marketing campaigns to sell the scenic wonders along their lines, specifically developing and promoting national parks. Northern Pacific set the precedent when it dispatched celebrated landscape painter Thomas Moran and noted photographer William Henry Jackson to accompany Ferdinand V. Hayden's geological survey of the Yellowstone region in 1871. The resulting paintings and photographs were displayed in the Capitol while Congress debated the proposal to set aside Yellowstone as a public park "for the benefit and enjoyment of the people."[9] Moran's large landscape paintings, which resulted from his watercolor sketches done during this trip, became iconographic images of what would become Yellowstone National Park. William Henry Jackson's photographs reinforced this imagery. Through this kind of artistic imagery, which depicted unpeopled, monumental natural landscapes at their most awe inspiring, wilderness took on a kind of romantic ideal and spectacular appeal. Simultaneously, these artistic views were widely disseminated in tourist brochures, guidebooks, postcards, magazines and other promotional material advertising wilderness views in the same manner as everyday consumer products. These promotional images straddled the boundaries between art and advertising, embodying a kind of commercialized sublime that imbued wilderness with the allure of consumer desire.

Other major railroads followed suit, commissioning painters and photographers to document and dramatize the western scenic wonders along their lines. Railroads reproduced these images in promotional brochures and guidebooks, which were widely distributed in stations and railroad offices throughout the country. Railroads also distributed a slew of brochures and guidebooks publicizing this image of pristine wilderness populated by rugged individuals and picturesque Indians.

But railroads went beyond using alluring imagery to advertise national park wilderness, they also elaborately packaged park wilderness. Northern Pacific, Santa Fe, and Great Northern sought to design and standardize their respective parks into packaged tourist experiences. In the process they defined wilderness in consumer terms; like other corporations seeking to sell brand-name products, they refined and highlighted the characteristics of wilderness tourists could expect. The Yellowstone Park Hotel Company, financed by the Northern Pacific, promoted Yellowstone as a wilderness wonderland. From the trademark "tally-ho" stage coaches that met passengers at the Gardiner station to the rustic luxury of the Old Faithful Inn, the Yellowstone Park Hotel Company sought to create a recognizable and desirable tourist product or park wilderness experience. A tour of Yellowstone wilderness promised deluxe service on the Northern Pacific's "Yellowstone Park Line," geothermal wonders, and sublime scenic views accented by distinctive luxury hotels and a carriage escort. The Fred Harvey Company, in partnership with the Santa Fe, used a similar strategy in the Grand Canyon, promoting the park as a land of enchantment replete with sublime scenery, domesticated Indians, and frontier romance. Blending references to the region's Spanish and Native American past, Santa Fe/Harvey defined the wilderness experience in primitive terms. Whether gazing at the canyon from the balcony of the El Tovar hotel, or sampling Navajo and Hopi crafts at Hopi House—a miniature Indian Pueblo—or descending into the canyon from the rustic Hermit's Rest, tourists were encouraged to imagine their foray into the canyon as a kind of "Columbian encounter" with nature.[10] The Great Northern followed suit in Glacier National Park packaging the park as "the crown of the continent," a kind of "American Alps" nestled along the Continental Divide.[11] Tourists were met at Great Northern's Glacier Park Station by a group of Blackfeet Indians who ushered them to the Glacier Park Hotel, a luxury log palace tricked out with an open campfire, mission style furniture, Navajo rugs, and Japanese lanterns. From there tourists could choose to stop over at the park's nine Swiss chalets situated within hiking distance of each other, or they could travel to the interior of the park and stay at one of the park's teepee camps or the more upscale Many Glacier Hotel. Great Northern marketed Glacier as a kind of civilized frontier wilderness experience; pristine wilderness, Old World civilization, frontier ambiance, and manifest destiny were all rolled into one. By World War I, the national parks—Yellowstone, Glacier, Yosemite and the Grand Canyon being the most prominent—had been transformed into brand-name tourist attractions that offered up a mythic wilderness for display, pleasure, and recreation.

Packaging Park Wilderness

What railroad corporations began, the Park Service reinforced in defining a management strategy for the parks. The National Park Service Organic Act, passed in 1916, which officially established the National Park Service as a government agency responsible for administering the national parks, set the priorities by calling for the Park Service to both "promote and manage . . . national parks, monuments, and reservations." Selling the parks and the wilderness they protected went hand in hand with administering the parks as government properties. The language of the act is revealing. It called for the Park Service to "conserve the scenery and the natural and historic objects and the wildlife therein and to provide for the enjoyment of the same in such manner and by such means as will leave them unimpaired for the enjoyment of future generations."[12] From the start, park policy was set to focus on conserving (not preserving) scenery, wildlife, and nature for the "enjoyment" of the people. Secretary of the interior, Franklin K. Lane, who oversaw the establishment of the passage of the Organic Act, envisioned the national parks as "playgrounds of the people," offering "a great economic asset which had theretofore been entirely overlooked by the Federal Government."[13] And the new director of the Park Service, Stephen Tyng Mather quickly assumed the responsibility of putting this policy, which environmental historians have called "aesthetic conservation" or "façade management," into practice.[14]

Mather brought with him notable credentials as a Sierra Club member and outdoor enthusiast, but more importantly he brought exceptional experience in marketing and public relations.[15] After graduating from the University of California, Berkeley, he had done a brief stint at the *New York Sun*, where he learned the newspaper trade and made connections in the world of journalism; he then took a job with his father at the Pacific Coast Borax Company. It was there that Mather made his name as the originator of the "20 Mule Team Borax" brand name. He went on to make his fortune and his reputation as a "genius of publicity" in the borax business, first at Pacific Coast Borax and then at his own Sterling Borax Company.[16] While working for Pacific Coast Borax, Mather not only honed his skills in advertising and sales, but he also excelled at using direct testimonials, give-away contests, and promotional events to promote the product. He once offered a dollar prize for every customer who succeeded in having a letter published in the newspaper about the use of borax in his or her home. He even went so far as to stage a live twenty-mule team rig with a skinner and a swamper that traveled from city to city across the Midwest to gain publicity and promote the brand. He would bring to the Park Service his connections to the newspaper world, his understanding of advertising, sales, and public relations, and his organizational skill and energy; and he drew on all of these skills to promote the parks and effectively package wilderness as a National Park Service product.

Mather's management policy sought to support the efficient and sustainable use and conversation of wilderness through sightseeing and recreation. In taking over the Park Service, Mather clearly articulated the central issues facing the parks. The national park problem, he argued, "consists chiefly in making these national playgrounds available and useful to the people. Means of getting to them and living in them economically when one gets there must be systematized better than they have been . . . A great deal is to be done, all with the view of getting the largest benefit to the people out of the parks." He concluded, "We hope the time will come when an annual visit to a national park will be part of the routine of the average American family."[17] NPS policy worked to maximize public use and appreciation of wilderness. Just as Mather had sought to put a box of Pacific Coast Borax in every home twenty years earlier, he now hoped to make tourism in the national parks a national pastime enjoyed by every American. The goal was to maximize public use of the parks and appreciation of wilderness by publicizing park wilderness, facilitating transportation to the parks, and systematizing park concessionaire policy. In other words, advertise, standardize, and distribute (or in the context of Park Service wilderness—make more accessible).

Mather's initiatives mirrored the tactics of companies like Proctor and Gamble, Gillette, and Kodak in creating and marketing new consumer products for an expanding national market.[18] During his first two years as director, Mather went on a series of highly publicized park tours, speaking to chambers of commerce, wilderness groups, automobile associations, and other interested organizations to disseminate his ideas about developing the parks and making them more accessible to the American people.[19] He met with railroad representatives to negotiate reduced rates, suggesting that they issue "park tour tickets which [would] enable tourists to buy tickets at the starting point for a definite tour of national parks, all accommodations paid for and arranged in advance." In addition, he asked the roads to include information about the parks in their tourist brochures.[20] He also encouraged the construction of a national park highway that would link the western parks, making them more easily accessible by automobile.[21] The result of these endeavors was to further define national park wilderness as consumer landscapes.

Although a more scientific, ecologically based approach to wilderness preservation would begin to emerge in the 1930s and 1940s under the auspices of the short-lived NPS Wildlife Division, early development and management of the parks had clearly situated national park wilderness in a consumerist frame. At the end of Mather's tenure, Horace Albright tallied up the accomplishments of the Mather era: "1,298 miles of roads, 3,903 miles of trails, 1,623 miles of telephone and telegraph lines, extensive camp grounds, sewer and water system[s], power plants, [and] buildings."[22] The development of national park infrastructure, management of desired wildlife species, and promotion of park scenery took precedence. During its formative years, the Park Service managed and defined wilderness by building roads, trails, parking lots, and campgrounds, stocking lakes and streams with sport fish, ranching bison, elk, and deer herds, killing off predator species such as cougars, coyotes, and wolves that threatened the "charismatic megafauna,"[23] encouraging recreational activities such as golf, tennis, and swimming, and promoting winter sports such as skiing and sledding. As the first official policy statement for the Park Service dictated, "Every opportunity should be afforded the public, wherever possible, to enjoy the national parks in the manner that best satisfies the individual taste."[24] NPS park management policy in the postwar era would further solidify these consumerist aims.

Under subsequent National Park Service directors, Park Service policy would begin to place increased emphasis on preserving "natural conditions" in the parks. A more scientific approach to wilderness preservation was gaining credence both within the Park Service and among the broader circle of wilderness advocates.

Despite this growing interest in wildlife habitat and ecosystem management, the Park Service continued to follow Mather's directive, developing the parks as stages for the display and consumption of the spectacle of wilderness. Although park tourism waned during the 1930s, New Deal programs such as the Works Progress Administration (WPA) and the Civilian Conservation Corps (CCC) expanded the tourist infrastructure in the national parks. Not only did the CCC build new roads and trails in the national parks, adding scenic pullouts, campground facilities, and ranger kiosks, but it also sought to expand and develop a national infrastructure for outdoor recreation, further linking wilderness to urban consumer desire. However, it would take the combination of postwar abundance and the growing popularity of the automobile to fully position national park wilderness in the frame of urban mass consumer culture that flourished in the postwar era. Specifically, the massive modernization of the parks promoted under the NPS Mission 66 program would redesign and reconceptualize the parks as rationalized modern consumer landscapes—an extension of postwar planned suburbs, shopping malls, and the expanding interstate highway system. Despite the emergence of environmentalism during the postwar era, Mission 66 fully institutionalized maximum public enjoyment of park wilderness, providing the infrastructure and management policies that solidified park wilderness as consumer spectacle.

The Malling of Park Wilderness

Launched in 1956, the same year as Eisenhower's Interstate Highway Act, Mission 66 was a ten-year, multimillion-dollar, comprehensive plan to upgrade and expand the National Park System in time for the fiftieth anniversary of the National Park Service in 1966. Although the National Park System and infrastructure had benefited from New Deal spending—most notably the Civilian Conservation Corps, which supplied the parks with a cheap and continuous source of labor for maintenance and infrastructure development— American entry into World War II shifted money and resources to the war effort. Government funding for construction projects dried up, annual budgets were severely cut, visitation declined precipitously, and staffing was drastically reduced. Although the Park Service succeeded in protecting the parks from wartime profiteering, in effect the parks were mothballed during the war years. After the war, as park visitation resurged, Park Service administrators estimated that 80 million people would travel to the national parks in 1966. Mission 66 provided a plan to increase park funding, upgrade facilities, and modernize the National Park System to accommodate this postwar travel boom.[25]

In the immediate aftermath of World War II, a new culture of abundance literally and figuratively transformed the landscape of American culture. As wartime production shifted back to domestic manufacturing, the economy boomed. Individual earnings rose dramatically and more and more Americans attained the comforts of middle-class living—two cars, a house in the suburbs, and a television set. Increasing affluence combined with the five-day workweek, paid vacations, and an expanding interstate system that enticed and enabled Americans to take to the road in search of leisure and recreation. In 1960, Americans spent almost $19 billion on recreation, up from $4 billion in 1940.[26] Automobile and travel advertising, such as General Motors' popular "See the U.S.A. in Your Chevrolet" campaign, promised a wonderland of scenic adventures for automobile tourists. Despite these enticements, visitors to the national parks (99 percent of whom were now arriving in the parks by automobile) found deteriorating roads, dangerous trails, insufficient accommodations, lack of service facilities, inadequate staffing, and traffic. The Park Service was completely unprepared to manage the postwar travel boom.

In the immediate aftermath of the war, after travel restrictions were lifted in August 1946, the director of the Park Service, Newton B. Drury, reported, "the floodgates of travel opened immediately. For months thereafter all previous monthly records for numbers of visitors were broken." Drury described it as "an unprecedented wave" of park visitors.[27] Visitors to Yellowstone had reached the 1 million mark in the summer of 1948, almost double the number of those who came in the summer of 1941 before the U.S. entered the war. By 1955, visitation to Yellowstone had increased again by more than 25 percent; overall visitation to the parks had topped 50 million, up from 17 million in 1940.[28] In the meantime, funding and facilities in the parks remained at prewar levels. In a scathing 1953 *Harper's* essay, writer and historian Bernard Devoto lamented, "a lack of money has now brought our national park system to the verge of crisis."[29] He suggested closing the crown jewel parks if funds were not available to improve visitor services.

Conceived by NPS director Conrad Wirth, Mission 66 promised to transform the National Park System, to bring the parks in line with the larger transformation taking place in American culture. Son of a noted municipal park superintendent and trained as a landscape architect, Conrad Wirth came to the National Park Service in 1931 to work under Horace Albright. As chief land planner in the Park Service, Wirth managed the Civilian Conservation Corps state park programs and national park camps. He cut his teeth developing a national recreation plan for public lands during the late 1930s and early 1940s. Appointed as director of the National Park Service in 1951, he would bring to the position his bureaucratic and political expertise and a strong commitment to public parks and recreation.

Through Mission 66 he sought to upgrade the national parks to meet the recreational needs of white, suburban, middle-class Americans.[30] Mission 66 both responded to and reflected the postwar transformation of American culture, specifically the increasing dependence on the automobile, rapid suburbanization, a growing middle class, rising incomes, expanded opportunities for consumption, recreation and leisure, and a growing population.

Mission 66 is best understood as a comprehensive modern planning initiative. It did not simply seek to expand and upgrade park facilities to accommodate the growing number of visitors, it sought to put forward a national recreation infrastructure and policy plan to address widespread economic, technological, and social change which was transforming American culture. In other words, it sought to fully integrate the parks into the emerging mass consumer culture of the postwar era. The accomplishments of Mission 66 bear witness to this extensive transformation. They include 2,767 miles of new and rehabilitated roads; 936 miles of new or rehabilitated trails; 1,502 new parking areas; 575 new campgrounds; 535 new water systems; 271 new power systems; 521 new sewer systems; 218 new utility buildings; 221 new administrative buildings; 1,239 new employee housing units; and 110 new visitors' centers.[31] In addition, Mission 66 added twenty-seven new units to the Park Service, which included two significant park types—national seashores and national recreation areas. These statistics do not include the contributions made by park concessionaires, which provided new guest cabins, motels, and commercial buildings. Beyond the physical improvements to the parks, Mission 66 was also responsible for increasing park staffing, augmenting interpretation facilities, providing additional interpretative literature and information, redesigning the park logo, professionalizing staff training, and dramatically expanding the Park Service annual budget. It ushered the Park Service into the modern era.

Yellowstone's Canyon Village perhaps best reflects the modern consumer landscape set in place through Mission 66 development. Located on the Grand Loop Road near the Yellowstone Grand Canyon, Canyon Village served as one of the flagship projects for Mission 66. Developed as a public/private partnership between the Park Service and Yellowstone's chief concessionaire, the Yellowstone Park Company, the new village was meant to upgrade and replace the facilities available at the Old Canyon Inn. Through the Mission 66 planning process, park administrators had determined that the Old Canyon Inn, a 1911 structure designed in a rustic style by Old Faithful architect Robert Reamer, was not only outdated but also encroached on the scenic beauty of Yellowstone Canyon. The proposal called for the demolition of the inn and surrounding cabins, to be replaced by a modern park village consisting of 500 motel units, a modern motor lodge with cafeteria, coffee bar, and restaurant, and employee dormitories. The Yellowstone Park Company contracted the noted Los Angeles architecture firm of Welton Becket and Associates, renown for its modern shopping center designs and suburban housing developments, to design the lodge and motel cabins. The Park Service provided the site work and village infrastructure as well as the employee dorms and a new visitor center equipped with a post office. Two other park concessionaries hired Becket to design a general store and a photography shop to complete the development.[32]

As the first Mission 66 project to break ground on June 25, 1956, Canyon Village epitomized the modernist consumer vision of Mission 66. The design, scale, function, and layout of the village mirrored that of a comprehensive suburban shopping and residential development. The completed village included a Park Service entrance building; Welton Becket's motor lodge which included a cafeteria, restaurant, and coffee shop; Hamilton's general store, also designed by Becket; Haynes photography shop; and a Park Service visitor center, all situated around a U-shaped parking lot. Behind this central complex were three loops of prefabricated motel cabins and two employee dormitories.

The village plan as well as the individual buildings reflected recent trends in modernist design and planning. Becket's motor lodge and the commercial spaces included large expanses of glass set off by minimalist structures of wood and concrete. Canyon lodge featured a dramatic asymmetrical gable roof with extended eaves that culminated in "glu-lam" roof beams extending to the ground. The other large commercial spaces, also designed by Becket, reinforced this "contemporary look" with expansive pitched roofs, large plate-glass windows, high ceilings, and wide-open floor plans. A wide sidewalk connected the large buildings situated around the U-shaped parking lot, giving the village the feel of a suburban shopping plaza. The motel cabins, which consisted of prefabricated modules with flat roofs situated in "radial clusters," were set off in the woods removed from the main commercial part of the village, accentuating a suburban feel.[33]

The visitor center, designed by the Park Service to complement Becket's scheme, completed the modern village plan. As architectural historian, Sarah Allaback has argued, "The Mission 66 visitor center remains today as the most complete and significant expression of the Park Service Modern style." Conceived by Park Service planners as a new building type "to serve as a control point for . . . 'visitor flow,'" visitor centers reflected new trends in integrated planning that sought to accommodate the expanding automobile culture by centralizing convenient "one-stop" services, which allowed for more efficient land use while facilitating easy access by automobile. As Allaback explains, "Like the shopping center, the visitor center made it possible for people to park their cars at a central point, and from there have access to a range of services or attractions."[34] In the same way that the suburban shopping mall of the 1950s embodied a new building type that made consumer products readily accessible in an enjoyable modern atmosphere, the visitor center was meant to offer the same kind of "one-stop" convenience for park wilderness.[35] Conceptualized as the "hub of the park interpretive program," visitor centers housed administrative offices, reception and information areas, exhibition spaces, auditoriums, public restrooms, and other service amenities.[36] The idea, according to Ethan Carr, was to concentrate "services in a central location from which the surrounding landscape was viewed, often through a large window or from a structured terrace." There, visitors could be conveniently oriented to the park experience, learning what to see and why to see it. Carr argues that park planners believed that "while this increasingly alienated perspective farther removed people from the landscape both emotionally and literally, it also enabled larger numbers to 'enjoy' the park while producing less impact upon it."[37] In other words, the interpretive program made manifest in park visitor centers served to further abstract wilderness into a consumer spectacle, readily available for the park visitor to "enjoy."

Visitor centers went hand in hand with a more structured approach to park interpretation. Not only was a new division of interpretation created in the Park Service, but interpretation became one the most important parts of the Mission 66 initiative. New interpretative programs taught visitors about park history, geology, wildlife, scenic attractions, and conservation.[38] They were also directed to an array of new park amenities that made wilderness more accessible, including illustrated maps, nature guides, ranger programs, and roadside displays. Visitor centers, like the one in Canyon Village, became the central dissemination point for packaged park wilderness, culminating the display of wilderness as a consumer spectacle.

The Wilderness Niche

Mission 66 was quickly challenged by wilderness advocates such as the Sierra Club and the National Parks Association for its extensive development program and lack of attention to scientific wilderness management and preservation. As early as 1957, when the first Mission 66 projects were under construction, critics began to question everything from new road improvements in the parks to the modernist architecture. Historians have generally followed this critique, dismissing Mission 66 as a misdirected artifact of 1950s expansionist planning that was eclipsed by the emerging environmentalist movement before it was even completed. However, as Ethan Carr has persuasively argued in the first book-length study of the program, "[T]o a significant degree, as far as the visitor experience is concerned, the national park system and the Park Service still function as artifacts of Mission 66." The modern park designed to accommodate the automobile tourist and serve large numbers of visitors, and to allow for the display and consumption of the spectacle of wilderness with efficiency, comfort, and ease remains the norm across the National Park System. As Carr concludes: "Mission 66 park development remains today as much a part of the federal public landscape as its counterpart and contemporary, the interstate highway system."[39]

Historians and critics have generally characterized the battle over Mission 66 as a turning point in NPS wilderness policy, marking the shift from "aesthetic conservation" and "façade management," to a more scientific and ecologically based management policy. The general assumption has been that the policies and practices of wilderness preservation put in place by the Wilderness Act were dialectally opposed to Mission 66 and its modernist conception of park management. Environmental historian Paul Sutter has provided a detailed assessment of the genesis of this shift in wilderness preservation and its critique of postwar urban industrial consumer culture in his book *Driven Wild*. In this frame, Mission 66 development and attention to public access gave way to the Wilderness Act of 1964 and a turn toward the preservation and protection of untouched nature. As Sutter explains, "What made modern wilderness distinct, separate from the national park ideal, was the *critique* of consumerism that was central to it."[40]

Yet, the two mindsets shared more than might appear. Despite the commitment of the Wilderness Act to protecting lands "where the earth and its community of life are untrammeled by man," it also framed wilderness in many ways as the pinnacle of consumer desire.[41] For all its attention to promoting a more "ecological," "primitive," or "natural" conception of wilderness, in legislating the preservation of pristine and primitive wilderness, the Wilderness Act also gave wilderness a new kind of allure, elevating it to the level of the sacred, imbuing it with aura and authenticity. At the very moment when advertising and marketing professionals began to deploy new strategies of market segmentation, niche marketing, and high-end styling to expand and differentiate a saturated one-dimensional market and titillate consumer desire in a culture of increasing affluence, the Wilderness Act officially designated wilderness in similar exclusive and alluring terms. Just as Mission 66 democratized wilderness, providing easy access to the national parks for the expanding middle class, the Wilderness Act sought to distinguish and designate wilderness as something rarer and more remote than its recreational counterpart on display in the nation's national parks. In these terms, wilderness reflected the very consumer desires and values Wilderness Act advocates sought to mitigate. These values are clearly reflected in the language the Wilderness Society used to frame its core principles: "primitive" landscapes, "Superlatively Scenic Areas," "an environment of solitude," or undeveloped places "which are sufficiently spacious that a person may spend at least a week in travel in them without crossing his own tracks."[42] In reacting against the malling of national park wilderness, the Wilderness Act simply promised an alternative consumer experience—more exclusive, more dramatic, more authentic wilderness.

The founders of the Wilderness Society could not entirely escape consumer-oriented visions of landscape either, linking wilderness with "adventure," and "emotional thrill."[43] As Wilderness Society founder Aldo Leopold explained, "Our ability to perceive quality in nature begins, as in art, with the pretty. It expands through successive stages of the beautiful to values as yet uncaptured by language."[44] Wilderness—real wilderness—is like an artistic masterpiece, a one-of-a-kind experience imbued with an un-nameable aura available to those few who have the desire, the means, and the will to attain it. High-end, one-of-a-kind consumer products are marketed using this same kind of allure.[45] In other words, the Wilderness Act did not present a break from National Park Service policy and practice, nor did it affect a rejection of consumerism. Rather, it marked an extension and refinement of the consumerist frame firmly established and institutionalized in national park wilderness.

This story of national park wilderness underscores the larger connections between the ideal of wilderness and the aspirations and desires of urban industrial consumer culture. It suggests that in our culture the concept of wilderness in many respects has been shaped and defined by the logos of consumption—the desire for authentic, one-of-a-kind, self-fulfilling experiences. And what this story of Park Service wilderness reveals is that as wilderness became increasingly available as a consumer product, as it became a mass-produced consumer experience, wilderness advocates sought to preserve and enhance its consumer allure by making it more remote, more authentic, and more sacred. But perhaps more importantly, what this story suggests is that the distinction we make between civilization and wilderness—urban vs. wild—is in fact a false dichotomy. Wilderness is, as the Park Service well understood, a "state of mind," dependent on the socioeconomic, technological, and cultural structures that have come to define urban industrial life over the past century. The act of conceiving and preserving wilderness as a distinct place with fixed characteristics—be they its spectacular or pristine qualities—is simply part of the process of contextualizing and ordering natural landscape for modern uses, both physical and metaphorical.

What this alternative history of national park wilderness suggests is that perhaps we ought to pay more attention to those performing bears in Yellowstone. What they reveal is that wilderness and consumption go hand in hand. The structures and meanings that order our modern urban-industrial world define and encompass our national parks and wilderness preserves as well. Pitting the one against the other blinds us to the implications of our ambivalent cultural love affair with wilderness. And until we are able to see beyond the spectacle of wilderness to our own desires and actions, we will not be able to conceptualize a viable policy of preservation that might sustain the natural world we inhabit and share.

Notes

I would like to thank Phoebe S. Kropp for her insightful comments on how to improve this essay.

1. Alice Wondrak Biel, *Do (Not) Feed the Bears: The Fitful History of Wildlife and Tourists in Yellowstone* (Lawrence, KS: University Press of Kansas, 2006), 20.

2. Ibid. Quotations on pages 19, 20, 22, and 12.

3. U.S. Statutes at large, 17(1872), 32–33, quoted in Alfred Runte, *National Parks: The American Experience,* #d. ed. (Lincoln, NE: University of Nebraska Press, 1997), 46.

4. The Wilderness Act, in *America's National Park System: The Critical Documents,* ed. Lary M. Dilsaver (Lanham, MD: Rowman and Littlefield, 1994), 278.

5. The literature on the history of National Parks is too vast to cite in its entirety. For the defining historical narrative see Roderick Nash, *Wilderness and the American Mind,* rev. ed. (New Haven, CT: Yale University Press, 1973). See also Runte, *The National Parks,* and Richard W. Sellars, *Preserving Nature in the National Parks: A History* (New Haven, CT: Yale University Press, 1997). Paul Sutter is the latest historian to follow this historiographical trend; see Paul S. Sutter, *Driven Wild: How the Fight Against Automobiles Launched the Modern Wilderness Movement* (Seattle, WA: University of Washington Press, 2002).

6. Howard R. Stagner, "Preservation of Natural and Wilderness Values in National Parks," March 1957, unpublished draft report, National Park Service, Denver Service Center Library, quoted in Ethan Carr, *Mission 66: Modernism and the National Park Dilemma* (Amherst, MA: University of Massachusetts Press, 2007), 269–70.

7. For example, in addition to Biel, *Do (Not) Feed the Bears,* see Marguerite S. Shaffer, *See America First: Tourism and National Identity, 1880–1940* (Washington, DC: Smithsonian Institution Press, 2001), 40–92; Mark Daniel Barringer, *Selling Yellowstone: Capitalism and the Construction of Nature* (Lawrence, KS: University Press of Kansas, 2002); Chris J. Magoc, *Yellowstone: The Creation and Selling of an American Landscape, 1870–1903* (Albuquerque, NM: University of New Mexico Press, 1999); Marta Wiegle and Barbara A. Babcock, eds., *The*

Great Southwest of the Fred Harvey Company and the Santa Fe Railway (Phoenix, AZ: Heard Museum, 1996); Mark Neumann, *On the Rim Looking for the Grand Canyon* (Minneapolis, MN: University of Minnesota Press, 1999).

8. For a history of the emergence of a national consumer culture, see Susan Strasser, *Satisfaction Guaranteed: The Making the American Mass Market* (New York: Pantheon Books, 1989).

9. U.S. Statutes at large, 17(1872), 32–33, quoted in Runte, *National Parks,* 46.

10. Leah Dilworth, "Discovering Indians in Fred Harvey's Southwest," in Weigle and Babcock, eds., *Great Southwest,* 163.

11. "New Playground for Americans," *St. Paul Pioneer Press Dispatch,* 17 April 1910.

12. The National Park Service Organic Act (16 U.S.C. l 2 3, and 4. Aug. 25, 1916 (39 Stat. 535. http://www.nps.gov/legacy/organic-act.htm).

13. Keith Olson, *Biography of a Progressive: Franklin K. Lane, 1864–1921* (Westport, CT: Greenwood Press, 1979), 13.

14. Sellars, *Preserving Nature in the National Parks,* 5 and 88.

15. For biographical information on Stephen Mather see Robert Shankland, *Steve Mather of the National Parks,* 3rd ed. (New York: Knopf, 1970).

16. Quote from Franklin K. Lane, secretary of the interior, in "Testimonial to Awarded 'Father of National Park,'" Stephen Tyng Mather Clippings, Carton 1, Stephen Tyng Mather Papers, Bancroft Library, University of California, Berkeley, California. Hereafter cited as Mather MSS.

17. "Millionaire Works for Pay as High-Class Clerk in Government Service," *New York Sun,* 27 June 1915. Scrapbook, Volume 8, Personal Clippings, 1915–1928, Mather MSS.

18. See Strasser, *Satisfaction Guaranteed.*

19. See clippings in scrapbooks, Volume 4–7, Mather MSS.

20. "Colorado—A Game Sanctuary," *Rocky Mountain News,* 26 March 1915; and "Trying to Turn Travel to Wonderlands of the U.S." Scrapbook, Volume 4, Clippings Re Public Official Career, 1915–1916, Mather MSS.

21. "National Parks to Parks Highway Association." Scrapbook, Volume 4, Clippings Re Public Official Career, 1915–1916, Mather MSS.

22. Albright to Wilbur, March 5, 1929, quoted in Sellars, *Preserving Nature in the National Parks,* 59.

23. Ibid., 24.

24. Franklin K. Lane to Stephen T. Mather, 13 May 1918, in *America's National Park System: The Critical Documents,* edited by Lary M. Dilsaver (Lanham, MD: Rowman and Littlefield, 1994), 49–50.

25. For estimated visitation numbers for 1966, see National Park Service, *Mission 66: To Provide Adequate Protection and Development of the National Park System for Human Use,* Washington, DC: U.S. Dept of the Interior, 1956, n.p. Note that this estimate was off by 47 million. In 1966, 127 million people traveled to the parks; see Carr, *Mission 66,* 127.

26. Susan B. Carter et al., eds., *Historical Statistics of the United States,* Millennial Edition, Vol. 3 (New York: Cambridge University Press, 2006), 253–54.

27. Newton B. Drury quotations from National Park Service, *Annual Report from the Director of the National Park Service to the Secretary of the Interior 1946* (Washington, DC: Government Printing Office, 1946), 307–10.

28. Carr, *Mission 66,* 4.

29. Bernard DeVoto, "Let's Close the National Parks," *Harper's* 207, no. 1241 (Oct. 1953): 49–52.

30. Conrad Wirth, *Parks, Politics, and The People* (Norman, OK: University of Oklahoma Press, 1980).

31. Sellars, *Preserving Nature in the National Parks,* 184; See Sarah Allaback, *Mission 66 Visitors Centers: The History of a Building Type* (Washington, DC: U.S. Department of the Interior, 2000), 256, for the number of visitor centers. Note that Sellars says there were 114.

32. For the history of Mission 66 project in Canyon Village see "Constructing Suburbia in America's Oldest National Park: Conrad Wirth, Welton Becket, and Mission 66 at Yellowstone's Canyon Village" (master's thesis, University of Wyoming, 2006).

33. Carr, *Mission 66,* 238–39.

34. Allaback, *Mission 66 Visitors Centers,* 24–25.

35. Carr, *Mission 66,* 220.

36. *Mission 66: To Provide Adequate Protection and Development of the National Park System for Human Use,* National Park Service, 1956, quoted in Allaback, Mission 66 Visitors Centers, 27.

37. Carr, *Mission 66,* 221.

38. Barry MacIntosh, *Interpretation in the National Park Service* (Washington, DC: Department of the Interior, National Park Service, 1986).

39. Carr, *Mission 66,* 224.

40. Sutter, *Driven Wild,* 16.

41. The Wilderness Act, in Dilsaver, ed., *America's National Park System,* 277.

42. Quotations from "The Wilderness Society," January 21, 1935, The Wilderness Society Papers, Denver Public Library, Denver, Colorado, Box 11, Folder 14, quoted in Sutter, *Driven Wild,* 242–47.

43. Ibid., 247.

44. Aldo Leopold, "Marshland Elegy," in *A Sand County Almanac* (New York: Oxford University Press, 1949), 96.

45. For the ways in which consumer products are infused with one-of-a-kind allure see Collin Campbell, *The Romantic Ethic and the Spirit of Modern Consumption* (Oxford: Basil Blackwell, 1987).

The Devil in the Cathedral

Sewage and Garbage in Yosemite National Park

CRAIG E. COLTEN AND LARY M. DILSAVER

Yosemite National Park is unquestionably one of the "crown jewels" of the United States National Park System.[1] Beyond the stunning geologic grandeur of its glacially carved valley, the park received adoring praise from the pen of John Muir who beckoned others to come worship in the wilderness cathedral.[2] The combination of natural wonder and promotional prose spurred urban residents from the San Francisco Bay Area and beyond to make Yosemite a destination. The millions who subsequently have visited the park's 761,000 acres have scarcely left a trace on the park's rugged landscape.[3] Yet as visitor numbers rose throughout the twentieth century, officials voiced concern over unleashing the devil in this pristine chapel.[4] The devil in this case was waterborne disease that could contaminate the pilgrims and downstream communities, and garbage that could attract pests and transform paradise into a refuse heap. While countless hiking boots have failed to mar the park's scenery, one cholera outbreak could have spoiled the public's view of the park as a pristine retreat and equated the park with an urban slum.

Hal Rothman has written about an inherent conflict faced by communities near national parks or other tourist destinations. Seeking to reap the benefits of tourist dollars, they sacrifice control over their local economies and even their authenticity: "Locals must be what visitors want them to be in order to feed and clothe themselves and their families, but they also must guard themselves, their souls, and their places from people who less appreciate its special traits."[5] This conflict is what he appropriately referred to as the "devil's bargain."

Yosemite faced a slightly different situation. Since it is a national park, it did not seek the same rewards as shop owners in tourist towns, but the Park Service has measured success by visitor numbers. With a mandate to permit access, officials desired campers and hikers to make national parks their destinations, and agency culture commonly responded to increasing congestion with infrastructure improvements, in an escalating cycle of repair and upgrade.[6] Because Yosemite was successful in producing a steady increase in visitor numbers during the 1910s and 1920s, as a consequence, sewage and garbage became major concerns particularly during the peak summer months when a city's worth of temporary residents crowded into the valley.

Yosemite was not the only park that faced public-health pressures from a swelling seasonal population, but it provides an excellent vantage point to view the Park Service's attempts to balance its mandate to allow access and yet still maintain the all-important scenery that attracted visitors. The park's efforts to expand its sewage, garbage, and water services to accommodate spiraling numbers of visitors was at the same time carried out through an evolving policy that sought to protect scenic landscapes by sequestering intrusive features; public-health concerns fused with landscape aesthetics. By the 1930s these practices became part of the standard tool kit of park planners and continued to guide development in Yosemite and across the park system. World War II interrupted park development, and although new design principles and environmental priorities guided infrastructure development after 1945, efforts persisted to conceal the infrastructure necessary to contain the devilish influences of growing numbers of visitors.

The idea of hiding human infrastructure in a natural or wilderness setting developed more than a century before Yosemite's establishment as a state park in 1864 and followed picturesque landscape traditions emanating from Britain.[7] When California asked Frederick Law Olmsted for recommendations on the operation of Yosemite Valley, his 1865 reply contained a lengthy statement of philosophical and practical ideals that the state should pursue in managing an unspoiled, hence inherently picturesque, landscape: "The first point to be kept in mind then is the preservation and maintenance as exactly as possible of the natural scenery; the restriction, that is to say, within the narrowest limits consistent with the necessary accommodation of visitors, of all artificial constructions and the prevention of all constructions markedly inharmonious with the scenery or which would unnecessarily obscure, distort or detract from the dignity of the scenery."[8] By the time Congress established Yosemite as a park in 1872, a philosophy of romanticism would demand that managers screen infrastructure in a picturesque scene, especially those elements "inharmonious" with a wilderness enclave.

Although California's Yosemite Park Commission did not aggressively pursue Olmsted's ideals in Yosemite Valley, the Department of Interior ultimately adopted them when it took over the site.[9] On the eve of the Park Service's inception in 1916, Mark Daniels, its first landscape engineer, declared a formative concept about landscape preservation. "Natural phenomena," such as great canyons and waterfalls had "an educational value that cannot be estimated." As such, they were worthy of protection. Additionally, one of the fundamental functions of parks was to further "knowledge and *health*" [emphasis added]. And finally, he included in his "general policy" the statement that "to foster tourist travel it will be necessary to develop the roads, trails, and other accommodations in the parks to a point where the traveler will not be subjected to serious discomfort."[10] Comfort included lodging and food services, but also the removal of nuisances and health threats by way of water, sewerage, and garbage service.

In Yosemite's early years, destructive landscape changes as well as improper sanitation and the specter of disease received little attention. By the 1890s, the U.S. Army took charge of most of Yosemite from the state of California. The commander's instructions included steps to deal with degradation being caused by trespassing grazers, lumberjacks, and miners, along with disfigurement caused by legitimate visitors. Col. S. B. M. Young, the army commander, in 1896 reported that "The majority of campers are careless and negligent about extinguishing their fires and policing their camp grounds when leaving. The spectacle of empty tins that had contained preserved fruits, soups, vegetables, sardines, etc., together with offal from the cook fire, and other more objectionable [wastes], is detestable anywhere, but is abominable in the superlative degree when included in the view of a beautiful mountain stream skirted with meadows luxurious grasses and gardens of wildflowers."[11] Although the army commanders noticed deteriorating conditions in the campgrounds, they focused their principal attention on the large-scale damage caused by outlawed land uses.

The first assessment of Yosemite's sanitary condition was carried out following the late nineteenth-century "sanitary awakening" in American cities and at a time when the fundamental conflict between scenery preservation and public sanitation had become obvious.[12] The park's acting superintendent noted in 1907 that river pollution was a problem; campers were taking their water from a polluted stream.[13] M. O. Leighton, the U.S. Geological Survey's chief hydrographer, visited Yosemite in 1907. He claimed that "the most important consideration with maintenance of Yosemite Valley as a tourist resort is the water supply."[14] Sewage releases at the scale common to a small city were seen as an urban intrusion into the wilderness and were wholly unacceptable in a rural national park. Leighton pointed out that "below the hotel the water is grossly polluted and the superintendent of the park properly refused to permit campers to occupy any of the sites along the lower portion of the valley."[15] He acknowledged that it would be impossible to completely restore the river's pristine condition and that the river would have to carry some sewage. Consequently, the park could not rely on the river for its potable water supply. In addition, he argued that since visitors and downstream communities continued to use the foul water that it was essential to treat sewage to minimize risk.[16] In keeping with urban remedies for a nature overwhelmed, Leighton recommended turning to more remote pure water supplies and its delivery to the places where people congregated.

Work on a "collecting well" that would capture spring water and feed it into a delivery system for Yosemite Valley began in the summer of 1911, and installation of a new set of delivery pipes took place the following year.[17] There was virtually no discussion about the landscape impacts of these improvements; instead public health concerns were the driving force. By 1913 the increased water supply was overwhelming cesspools and impacting park streams. "In consequence of these conditions, the waters of the Merced River, which is a beautiful mountain stream, and should be maintained by the United States, are polluted."[18] Human wastes were despoiling nature and bringing what had been largely urban nuisances into the wilderness.

The initiation of National Park Service management of Yosemite led to a tremendous rise in visitor use. Summer populations rose from 31,000 in 1915 to over 460,000 in 1928. In 1916, there were as many as 5,000 visitors at any given time in the valley, two-day populations in 1929 were as high as 25,000.[19] To preserve the scenery and public health, the Park Service had to undertake major renovations of its water, sewerage, and garbage infrastructure. Unlike in cities, park planners had to take exceptional steps to minimize the visible intrusion of these essential features.

Yosemite's superintendent noted in 1915 that work on an improved water supply system was nearing completion. With increased water use, sewage had become a more pressing issue and he called for a new sewerage system and disposal plant to replace the existing septic tanks in 1915. In alignment with Leighton's 1907 assessment, he noted that water below the hotel was polluted with sewage.[20] The following year, R. B. Marshall, superintendent of the national parks (his title would change to director with the 1916 creation of the National Park Service), visited Yosemite with J. A. Hill, an authority on hotel sanitation, and declared that public-health conditions were deplorable. Urging adequate funding for a new sewerage system, he proclaimed, "I shudder at the probability of an epidemic of typhoid or some other common epidemic that could be directly charged to the lack of proper sanitation."[21]

Congress was slow to fund sanitation, and the park superintendent continued to recommend sewerage improvements through the 1910s. A particularly adamant appeal appeared in 1919. W. B. Lewis pointed out that the septic system at one camp in the main valley failed completely during the high water season, which corresponded with the peak travel period when the soil had no capacity to absorb the effluent. Consequently, "The entire sewage discharge from a community of 1,000 people . . . goes to the pollution of the river."[22] Despite warnings from the Park Service, visitors continued to use tainted water from the Merced River for cleaning and cooking purposes and exposed themselves to great risk. The superintendent warned "that these conditions exist is most unfortunate, and it is not pleasant to cogitate on what might happen in the way of a serious epidemic within the valley or in any of the settlements along the river outside the park that are dependent upon the river for their supply of drinking water if these conditions are allowed to continue."[23] To further strengthen his case, he noted that the California Board of Health had indicated that the only way to contend with the problem was to install a sewage treatment plant. The fear of an epidemic emanating from Yosemite ultimately convinced Congress to appropriate funds for improvements; and with those appropriations the Park Service carefully installed those improvements to avoid scenic distractions. While the superintendent proclaimed in 1920 that river pollution was worse than in previous years and that "the public health of the valley was being seriously endangered," construction of a new sewerage system was underway.[24]

Here Park Service engineers faced a major infrastructural challenge that threatened the scenery and, hence, the image of the park. The site selected for the treatment facilities was below the village complex and near the Merced River in the midst of a pine grove. This location adhered to the landscape engineer's standard policy to "screen" industrial structures.[25] Behind a roadside border of trees, the Park Service cleared about ten acres of forest to make room for the Imhoff tanks and settling beds. According to Donald Tresidder, one of the principal concessionaires in Yosemite, the Park Service came under sharp criticism for this forest removal. He claimed that "from the trails and points of the rim of the Valley the beds are very prominent and mar the landscape."[26] Ironically, visitor awareness of infrastructure could result from nonvisual senses. Odors from the plant began to intrude on visitor comfort and enjoyment of the stunning scenery. The consulting sanitary engineer from the Public Health Service, H. B. Hommon, was summoned in 1925 because the "odors arising from the concrete settling tank at the sewer farm have been obnoxious . . . ever since the plant was put in operation."[27] Again in 1927 Hommon visited to try to remedy the odor problem.[28] Despite visual screening, offensive odors drew people's attention to what was already an overtaxed infrastructure.

The odors stemmed from the fact that the sewage treatment plant was under-sized for the demands placed on it. Designed to handle wastes of about 6,000 people, it was receiving the effluent of as many as 25,000 visitors during peak periods. Furthermore, the Park Service never expanded the plant beyond its original specifications. In 1927 H. B. Hommon began deliberations with park personnel on ways to alleviate the odor problem. An obvious solution was simply to enlarge the existing plant. According to Hommon, there "was vigorous objection by everyone to cutting down timber and clearing five more acres in the forest and this plan was abandoned."[29] Ultimately, Hommon, a panel of outside experts, the landscape engineer, and other interested parties put forward a plan to close the old facility and build an entirely new sewage treatment works further down the Merced River valley. This process reveals a most deliberate effort to take landscape matters into consideration. Hommon pointed out three requirements for the new facility: (1) sterile effluent, (2) no odor, and (3) *concealment from the highway* [emphasis added].[30] In a subsequent publication, Hommon elaborated that "the landscape engineers of the National Park Service required that the plant be so designed and located that it could not be seen from the two highways that paralleled Merced river on the floor of the valley or from the two highways that pass out of the valley along the north and south walls."[31]

Visits to prospective sites by Hommon and John Wosky, the park's landscape engineer, led to the selection of a relatively flat floodplain tract near Bridalveil Falls. According to Hommon, "at this location the plant will be about 300 feet from the two highways that parallel the river and it will be fairly well hidden from view by trees."[32] Indicating the importance of landscape in construction decisions, Hommon's letter accompanying his draft plans stated that "since this is a preliminary plan, it does not seem necessary to have it approved by the Director and the Landscape Division. If the appropriation is made available for the plan, detailed plans will be prepared and these will be submitted for approval in the usual manner."[33]

During construction, the Park Service went to considerable lengths to preserve the landscape and situated the new facility amid trees. When laying the sewer lines, crews sometimes had to tunnel beneath roots to preserve trees.[34] In addition, workers received instructions to backfill trenches promptly so that construction work would not be visible from roadways.[35] Following an inspection by O. C. Hopkins of the Public Health Service, the park superintendent remarked that "landscape minded engineering is showing very gratifying results in the general appearance of the sewer system construction work now engaging the work of a large crew of men."[36] The park superintendent praised the efforts of the construction team in his November 1930 monthly report: "Special mention should be made of the exceptional landscaping and eradication of construction marks being effected on this project. Even though it has been necessary to lay this line across one of the most beautiful meadows not a scar will remain when this work is finally completed."[37]

Removal, or eradication to use the park's term, of the old sewage plant followed completion of the new facilities in 1931. During the spring and summer of 1932, crews demolished the Imhoff tanks and the old sewer farm. By June the Park Service had removed all the old concrete structures and landscaping was underway to erase any trace of the old facilities.[38]

Consideration of landscape intrusions continued with the formal articulation of a Park Service policy in 1935. John Wosky, Yosemite's resident landscape architect in the early 1930s, noted the continuing influence of the famous landscape architecture family: "As you know, Mr. [Frederick Law] Olmsted [Jr.] is very interested in screening the campers from the views of the main road."[39] Screening often required planting trees to hide many "unnatural" features. The Park Service graded and planted trees to obscure the view of a borrow pit near the Yosemite Lodge.[40] More planting accompanied the construction of comfort stations in Yosemite Valley.[41] Sometimes "concealing" paint colors were used, as with the new water storage facility installed in 1930.[42] Nearly ubiquitous use of the National Park Service brown helped obscure many structures, signs, and other landscape features.

In 1935, the National Park Service published its policy to sequester infrastructure in a design handbook, in part to guide the state parks undergoing rapid construction by the Civilian Conservation Corps. Arno Cammerer, the service's director, clearly asserted this position in a manual on construction for parks: "In any area in which the preservation of the beauty of Nature is a primary purpose, every modification of the natural landscape, whether it be by construction of a road or erection of a shelter, is an intrusion. A basic objective of those who are entrusted with the development of such areas for the human uses for which they are established, is, it seems to me, to hold these intrusions to a minimum and so to design them that, besides being attractive to look upon, they appear to belong to and be a part of their setting."[43] The authors pointed out that structures did not add to a park's beauty, but to its use. Thus they acknowledged that the Park Service viewed its constructions as intrusions and that such "trespasses" should be executed with as much "grace" as possible.

While roads and lodgings were necessary and the steps taken to blend them into the local landscape have received extensive discussion, the most intrusive artifacts to accompany park development were its utilities, in particular the above-ground water, sewerage, and garbage facilities.[44] In the handbook park planners, designers, and sanitary engineers noted that they confronted some of the same problems as urban public-works directors, but had to install their infrastructure under very different circumstances. Water-storage facilities function best when placed on high ground above the service territory, but unlike in cities, where a silver tower standing high above the city represented tax dollars well spent, national parks had to disappear their tanks into the surrounding landscape; park personnel painted storage tanks to make them blend in with the natural scenery or disguised them as observation towers.[45]Sewage treatment plants, like their urban counterparts, had to occupy downstream locations. In some mountainous parks, this meant siting them along roads leading into a park from more populated lowlands—hardly an auspicious greeting to the public. H. B. Hommon, the U.S. Public Health Service engineer who assisted with the design of sanitation facilities in western parks, stated that park policy called for adequate sewage treatment to avoid downstream problems, and that his staff also had to "conform to the high standards of the Park Service in relation to architecture and preservation of the natural scenery in the parks."[46] To achieve this objective, designers employed vegetative screening or use of tributary basins to sequester potentially offensive facilities.[47] Garbage dumps or incinerators had to be set apart as well. The 1935 report on park structures offered the following guidance on garbage facilities: "Incinerators should be located conveniently near to the intensively used areas, yet must be decently retired so that their nuisance quality is minimized. . . . Tree growth and other natural screening from view are only advantageous if they do not also become obstructions to draft."[48] Vitally important to successful park operations, these utilities demanded basic engineering and aesthetic treatment—which meant that the public should never see them and that they must not interfere with the natural scenery. Ironically, at Yosemite and other western parks, feeding bears garbage became such popular attractions that the Park Service had to construct bleachers to accommodate the throngs of visitors who wanted to view the daily entertainment. By the late 1930s, however, incinerators had largely replaced the bear-feeding spectacle.

Incinerators were among a larger group of maintenance structures that challenged park planners. One of the most explicit passages in the 1935 report dealt with such maintenance buildings. Obviously essential, these structures were not intended for public view. The Park Service offered these suggestions: "its location is off the track beaten by park patrons, and is an isolated and well-obscured one, where this stepchild among park structures need not suffer unfavorable comparison with necessarily more self-conscious and better groomed neighbors. . . . If such a site is not available, then the service building must go in for protective coloration."[49] This basic guidance applied not just to maintenance equipment sheds and garages, but to stables, pump houses, and power plants. When possible, the guidebook suggested that service buildings assume a "hollow square" arrangement. Plain outer walls would form a palisade around an internal courtyard where service activity could take place and the building itself became a screen. The propose of this was to "mask" intrusions that might diminish from the "eye appeal" of the park's scenery.[50]

In the years following World War II, park officials voiced shrill concern with the growing need for basic facilities. Between 1931 and 1948, visitor numbers multiplied nearly ten times—from 3.5 million to nearly 30 million. By 1955, that number rose still higher to 50 million. Visitors were overwhelming the prewar infrastructure. In response to the deterioration of facilities, Newton Drury, director of the Park Service, described the parks as "victims of the war." Others argued the parks were at risk of losing the "nature" that served as their fundamental purpose and attraction.[51] In response to this critical situation, the Park Service embarked on an ambitious plan known as Mission 66 to upgrade the system's infrastructure and meet the expanding demands on lodges, campgrounds, and comfort stations.

This effort ushered in an entirely new view towards structures and scenery preservation. According to park historian Linda McClelland, Mission 66 "brought an end to the pioneer and indigenous models, handcrafted appearances, and subtle naturalistic harmonies that marked the park architecture of the 1920s and 1930s." Indeed, William G. Carnes, head of the Mission 66 staff, instructed his employees to "disregard precedent, policy, present operating and management procedures, traditions and work habits."[52] While this suggests a complete rejection of the notion of secluding intrusive features, Mission 66 buildings were "intended to blend into the landscape, but through their plainness rather than identification with natural features," according to historian Sarah Allaback.[53] Use of modern designs employing steel and glass placed greater emphasis on utility. Nature was increasingly on view from inside structures even if the new buildings were not intended to resemble their surroundings or completely retire from view. Despite a shift toward modern design for public facilities, such as the newly important visitor center, the park continued to keep the public works sequestered from the public's eye. Ultimately, Mission 66 received credit for completing 521 new sewer systems and 535 new water systems throughout the national park network, most of which received adequate screening to minimize their visual impact.[54] With such im-provements, visitor numbers continued to climb, while environmentalists criticized the Park Service for unleashing negative impacts on nature contrary to its mission.

Stresses and strains on park utilities were reported in many western parks, leading at least one superintendent at Joshua Tree National Park to dump garbage in abandoned mines and wells to conceal it from view.[55] At Yosemite, postwar demands for potable water prompted the Park Service to seek assistance from the Public Health Service. The health service recommended the installation of two new storage reservoirs. Given the necessity of positioning the reservoirs up gradient from Yosemite Valley where consumers congregated, the report acknowledged the conflict between practical and aesthetic objectives. The optimal location for one tank would be in direct sight of the Glacier Point overlook. Nonetheless, the Public Health Service noted that "it is believed that the reservoir could be partially buried, screened by trees, and camouflaged to such an extent that most viewers from Glacier Point would never see it, and the hydraulic advantages outweigh the esthetic [sic] deficiencies."[56] Practicality dominated the potential siting decision, but screening techniques would offset any visual impacts. Without explanation, the Park Service chose not to build the storage reservoirs.[57]

As Yosemite began its Mission 66 planning to upgrade facilities, it included two very explicit statements about preserving scenery. A 1956 report noted that the park had experienced visitor numbers swelling from 640,000 in 1946 to 1.1 million in 1956 and this demanded a major expansion of facilities. Nonetheless, Yosemite staff sought to continue scenery preservation. Any additions, they wrote, would have to follow guidelines that would afford "maximum protection of the scenic, scientific, wilderness, and historic resources."[58] In addition they would have to be "so designed and located as to reduce the impact of public use on valuable and destructible features."[59] The report also called for shifting two older public works facilities outside the existing park. Because the incinerator and the sewage treatment works were in the Yosemite Valley, where there was also the greatest concentration of visitors, planners proposed shifting both facilities twelve miles down the Merced River to the El Portal service facility.[60]

The old 1931 sewage treatment plant continued to operate through the Mission 66 period, but by 1970 consulting engineers brought in to assess utility needs pointed out it was "deteriorating rapidly." They also observed it was odorous, and posed a potential public health problem. Urging its relocation out of the valley, the engineers argued that the "treatment plant is in a very scenic part of the Valley and has precluded development of this area for visitor use as a picnic area or campground."[61] A follow-up study performed by the U.S. Geological Survey monitored continuing water quality concerns emanating from the old sewage plant.[62] The park had already shifted its garbage incinerator to the El Portal site, and the engineers recommended building a regional sewage treatment plant at the same site. This would effectively reposition the most obvious infrastructure well beyond the park's boundaries and offer the ultimate seclusion. The regional sewage treatment plant eventually replaced the old treatment works in 1977, and park crews have removed all traces of the former facility, just as they had done with the original plant.

Across the western region in the 1970s, parks once again had to assess the adequacy of their public works following the completion of Mission 66 projects and a consequential surge in visitors. Responsibility for designing public works for the parks shifted from the long-standing relationship with the U.S. Public Health Service to a diverse set of private engineering firms. These consultants did not bring the same attention to scenery preservation as the Public Health Service engineers had done, and they supplanted those traditional priorities with basic engineering and regulatory parameters. For example, a 1973 solid-waste management study observed that, "It would seem that with the apparently unlimited open spaces one finds in Glacier National Park, the disposal of solid waste would be a very simple matter. This, however, is not the case. The geology of the Park is such that trying to find a suitable site for a sanitary landfill within the park is virtually impossible."[63] Suitability depended on the appropriate geology for constructing a landfill and not sequestering it from public view. Likewise, the same consulting firm recommended exporting the wastes outside the limits of Sequoia and Kings Canyon due to the lack of a geologically suitable landfill site there.[64] While preserving scenery was not mentioned, removing the landfills from park property certainly functioned in accord with that traditional mission.

When considering sewage facilities, outside consultants also emphasized compliance with new state and federal environmental regulations.[65] Public health remained a primary concern with sewage, although protection of wildlife and the streams and lakes themselves rose in importance—reflecting the environmental concerns of the times. Nonetheless, at Yellowstone consultants acknowledged the traditional concern with concealing infrastructure from view. "Treatment areas should be removed as far as practical from populated areas and screened from general view by vegetation or topography." In addition, they advised locating plants in open areas to avoid clearing existing forests.[66] At Muir Woods, where septic fields provided sewage treatment, concern with overloading the existing system and the creation of potentially offensive conditions prompted discussions of linking into a larger regional treatment plant in the early 1970s.[67] This would have also transferred treatment outside that park's boundaries.

Water quality regulations and geologic suitability for landfill sites increasingly shaped siting decisions for utilities, mounting pressure on parks; traditional concerns with screening infrastructure gradually pushed most of those activities outside park boundaries. Shifting Yosemite's incinerator and later its sewage treatment facility to a downstream location exemplify this overall trend during the environmental era of the 1970s.

Rooted in earlier romantic notions of picturesque park design, Park Service landscape architects practiced methods to preserve scenery through various forms of concealment or screening. While the sanitation infrastructure and utility buildings were not to wear façades, nature hid them from public view. Plantings of native species or concealment in narrow valleys or behind massive boulders sequestered the intrusive utilities. When Thomas Vale argues that human intrusion in Yosemite has been negligible, perhaps he testifies to the effectiveness of this strategy.[68] In addition, the presence of the essential public-works infrastructure, while largely invisible to the public, has helped the Park Service avoid serious outbreaks of disease that early park administrators feared.

Although the Park Service has contained the devil in the form of disease, its ever-expanding public-works facilities have enabled the ballooning of visitor numbers. Some have argued in recent years the parks have taken on an urban feel with traffic congestion and even air pollution. Lary Dilsaver and William Wyckoff have shown that new infrastructure lead to increased visitation, which in turn requires further expansion in a cycle of cumulative causation.[69] In a sense, park officials have made a bargain with the devil in terms of access. Yet, strictly in terms of public works, the Mission 66 projects and the more recent regulation-driven sewage and garbage facilities have not seriously degraded the landscape of Yosemite or other parks. Transferring those activities outside the park perpetuates the traditional concept of secluding intrusive features from public view, even if that is no longer the primary motive.

Notes

We want to acknowledge Julie Tuason who was a partner in our initial work on this project and a key contributor to two preliminary public presentations on the subject. Support for this work came from the National Register, History, and Education Division of the National Park Service and an LSU Council on Research, Faculty Research Grant. We are extremely grateful for the generous assistance of the staffs at the Denver Service Center, the Yosemite National Park Library, and the National Archives-Western Division, San Bruno, California. We also thank Alyson Greiner and the two anonymous reviewers whose comments greatly improved the initial paper stemming from this research. Portions of this paper previously appeared under the title "The Hidden Landscape of Yosemite National Park" in the *Journal of Cultural Geography* 22 (2005): 27–50 and are re-reprinted here with permission.

1. Alfred Runte, *National Parks: The American Experience,* 2nd ed. (Lincoln: University of Nebraska Press, 1987), and Alfred Runte, *Yosemite: The Embattled Wilderness* (Lincoln: University of Nebraska Press, 1990).

2. John Muir, "The Treasures of the Yosemite," *The Century Magazine* 40 (August 1890): 483–500 and John Muir, "Features of the Proposed Yosemite National Park," *The Century Magazine* 40 (September 1890): 656–67.

3. Thomas and Geraldine Vale, *Time and the Tuolumne Landscape: Continuity and Change in the Yosemite High Country* (Salt Lake City: University of Utah Press, 1994), 138.

4. Runte, *Yosemite;* Stanford Demars, *Tourist in Yosemite* (Salt Lake City: University of Utah Press, 1991); Robert Pavlik, "In Harmony with the Landscape: Yosemite's Built Environment, 1913–1940" in *Yosemite and Sequoia,* eds. Richard Orsi and Alfred Runte (Berkeley: University of California Press, 1993), 97–109; and Ethan Carr, *Wilderness by Design: Landscape Architecture and the National Park Service* (Lincoln: University of Nebraska Press, 1994).

5. Hal K. Rothman, *Devil's Bargains: Tourism in the Twentieth-Century American West* (Lawrence: University of Kansas Press, 1998), 12.

6. Lary M. Dilsaver, "Stemming the Flow: The Evolution of Controls on Visitor Number and Impacts in National Parks," in *The American Environment,* eds. Lary M. Dilsaver and Craig E. Colten (Lanham, MD: Rowman and Littlefield, 1992), 235–56; and Lary M. Dilsaver and William Wyckoff, "Agency Culture, Cumulative Causation, and Development in Glacier National Park," *Journal of Historical Geography* 25:1 (1999): 75–92.

7. Craig E. Colten and Lary M. Dilsaver, "The Hidden Landscape of Yosemite National Park," *Journal of Cultural Geography* 22 (2005): 27–50; Humphry Repton, *An Enquiry into the Changes of Taste in Landscape Gardening* (London, UK: J. Taylor, 1806); Andrew Jackson Downing, *A Treatise on the Theory and Practice of Landscape Gardening Adapted to North America* (New York: A. O. Moore & Company, 1859).

8. Frederick Law Olmsted, "The Yosemite Valley and the Mariposa Big Tree Grove," printed in *America's National Park System: The Critical Documents,* ed. Lary M. Dilsaver, (Lanham, MD: Rowman and Littlefield, [1865] 1994), 12–27, 22–23.

9. Runte, *Yosemite,* 28–29.

10. Mark Daniels, "Report of the General Superintendent and Landscape Gardener," in *Reports of the Department of the Interior, 1915,* V. 1, (Washington, DC: Government Printing Office, 1915), 843–906, 846.

11. U.S. Congress, House Doc. 5, 54th Cong. 2nd sess. "Report of the Acting Superintendent of Yosemite National Park," in *Report of the Secretary of the Interior,* V. 3 (Washington, DC: Government Printing Office, 1896), 736.

12. J. B. Jackson coined the term in *American Space: The Centennial Years, 1865–1876* (New York: W. W. Norton, 1972); and Martin Melosi fully explores the revolution in urban public works in *Sanitary City: Urban Infrastructure in America from Colonial Times to the Present* (Baltimore: Johns Hopkins University Press, 2000).

13. U.S. Department of the Interior, "Report of the Acting Superintendent of Yosemite National Park," on *Reports of the Department of Interior, 1907,* V. 1, (Washington, DC: Government Printing Office, 1907), 557–66, 563.

14. M. O. Leighton, "Sanitary Conditions and Water Supply, Yosemite National Park," in *Reports of the Department of Interior, 1908,* (Washington, DC: Government Printing Office, 1908), 437–42.

15. Ibid, 438.

16. Ibid, 438.

17. U.S. Department of the Interior, "Report of the Acting Superintendent of Yosemite National Park," in *Reports of the Department of Interior, 1911,* V. 1, (Washington, DC: Government Printing Office, 1912), 585–97; and U.S. Department of the Interior, "Report of the Acting Superintendent of Yosemite National Park," in *Reports of the Department of Interior, 1912,* V. 1, (Washington, DC: Government Printing Office, 1913), 659–68.

18. U.S. Department of the Interior, "Report of the Acting Superintendent of Yosemite National Park," in *Reports of the Department of Interior, 1907,* V. 1, (Washington, DC: Government Printing Office, 1914), 715–31, 723.

19. U.S. Department of the Interior, "Yosemite National Park," in *Annual Report of the Superintendent of National Parks, 1916,* (Washington, DC: Government Printing Office, 1916), 14, 41–46, 44; and U.S. Department of the Interior, *Report of the Director of the National Park Service, 1930* (Washington, DC: Government Printing Office, 1930), 31–32, 32 198–200.

20. U.S. Department of the Interior, "Yosemite National Park," in *Annual Report of the Superintendent of National Parks, 1916* (Washington, DC: Government Printing Office, 1916), 909–10.

21. U.S. Department of the Interior, "Yosemite National Park," in *Annual Report of the Superintendent of National Parks, 1916* (Washington, DC: Government Printing Office, 1916), 14–15, 15, 41–46.

22. U.S. Department of the Interior, "Yosemite National Park," in *Report of the Director of the National Park Service, 1919* (Washington, DC: Government Printing Office, 1919), 182–200, 195.

23. Ibid, 196.

24. U.S. Department of the Interior, "Yosemite National Park," in *Report of the Director of the National Park Service, 1920* (Washington, DC: Government Printing Office, 1920), 92–97, 234–41, 241, 331–37.

25. Ibid, 95.

26. Donald Tresidder, "The National Park: A Public Health Problem," (master's thesis, Stanford University School of Medicine, 1927), 114–15.

27. Yosemite National Park, Superintendent's Monthly Report, October 1925, 3, Yosemite National Park Library.

28. Yosemite National Park, Superintendent's Monthly Report, March 1927, 2, Yosemite National Park Library.

29. H. B. Hommon, Report on Sewage Disposal for Floor of the Valley, Yosemite National Park, 1929, 1–3, Record Group 79, Records of Superintendent Yosemite National Park, 1910–53, Box 70, Folder 660-03.41, National Archives, San Bruno, California.

30. Ibid, 3.

31. H. B. Hommon, "Yosemite Valley Activated Sludge Plant," *Journal, California Sewage Works Association* 4 (1931): 51–62, quote at 55.

32. H. B. Hommon, Report on Sewage Disposal for Floor of the Valley, Yosemite National Park, 1929, 6, Record Group 79, Records of Superintendent Yosemite National Park, 1910–53, Box 70, Folder 660-03.41, National Archives, San Bruno, California.

33. H. B. Hommon, Report on Sewage Disposal for Floor of the Valley, Yosemite National Park, 1929, 1–3, Record Group 79, Records of Superintendent Yosemite National Park, 1910–53, Box 70, Folder 660-03.41, National Archives, San Bruno, California.

34. Yosemite National Park, Superintendent's Monthly Report, March 1931, Yosemite National Park Library.

35. F. A. Kittredge, Memo of Conference and Inspection Trip, Yosemite National Park, June 2, 1931, 3, Record Group 79, National Park Service, Records of Superintendent 1910–1953, Box 6 Yosemite, Folder 204—Inspections and Investigations. National Archives, San Bruno, California.

36. Yosemite National Park, Superintendent's Monthly Report, August 1930, n.p., Yosemite National Park Library.

37. Yosemite National Park, Superintendent's Monthly Report, November 1930, n.p., Yosemite National Park Library.

38. Yosemite National Park, Superintendent's Monthly Report, April, June, August 1932, and September 1931, Yosemite National Park Library.

39. J. B. Wosky, Report of Chief Architect through Superintendent, Yosemite National Park, May 27, 1930, 3, Landscape Files, Yosemite National Park Library.

40. Ernst Davidson, Report of Chief Landscape Architect through Superintendent of Yosemite National Park, December 1930, 2, Landscape Files, Yosemite National Park Library.

41. J. B. Wosky, Report of Chief Architect through Superintendent, Yosemite National Park, May 27, 1930, Landscape Files, Yosemite National Park Library.

42. Yosemite National Park, Superintendent's Monthly Report, September 1930, n.p., Yosemite National Park Library.

43. U.S. Department of the Interior, *Park Structures and Facilities* (Washington, DC: U.S. Department of the Interior, 1935), 1.

44. Carr, *Wilderness by Design;* and Linda F. McClelland, *Building the National Parks* (Baltimore: Johns Hopkins University Press, 1998).

45. U.S. Department of the Interior, *Park Structures and Facilities,* 5 and 128; also Albert H. Good, *Park and Recreation Structures, Part 1, Administration and Basic Services Facilities* (Washington, DC: U.S. Department of the Interior, National Park Service, 1938).

46. H. B. Hommon, "Treatment and Disposal of Sewage in the National Parks," *American Journal of Public Health* 25 (1935): 128–44, quote at 193.

47. U.S. Department of the Interior, *Report of the Director of the National Park Service, 1930,* (Washington, DC: Government Printing Office, 1930), 31–33, 199–200.

48. U.S. Department of the Interior, *Park Structures and Facilities,* 240.

49. Ibid, 239.

50. Ibid.

51. Sarah Allaback, *Mission 66 Visitor Centers: History of a Building Type* (Washington, DC: U.S. Department of Interior, National Park Service, 2000), 1; and McClelland, *Building the National Parks,* 462.

52. Quoted in McClelland, *Building the National Parks,* 464.

53. Allaback, *Mission 66 Visitor Centers,* 12.

54. Sellars, *Wilderness by Design,* 184.

55. Frank Givens, Memo to Regional Director of the National Park Service, 17 November 1950, RG 79, Box 264, National Archives, San Bruno, California.

56. U.S. Department of Health, Education and Welfare, *Report on Yosemite Valley Water System: Yosemite National Park California* (San Francisco: U.S. Public Health Service, 1955), 37.

57. Metcalf and Eddy Engineers, *Report on Improvements and Additions to Water and Sewerage Systems at Yosemite Valley, Yosemite National Park California* (Washington, DC: U.S. Department of Interior, National Park Service, 1970), 32.

58. National Park Service, *Mission 66 for Yosemite National Park* (Washington, DC: U.S. Department of the Interior, 1956), 5.

59. Ibid, 5.

60. Ibid, 8.

61. Metcalf and Eddy Engineers, *Report on Improvements and Additions to Water and Sewerage Systems at Yosemite Valley,* xxii.

62. R. J. Hoffman, A. E. Dong, and G. L. Keeter, "Water Quality Study of a Reach of the Merced River in Yosemite National Park and Vicinity California, April 1973–September 1974," (Menlo Park, CA.: U.S. Geological Survey, Open File Report 76-326, 1976).

63. Consoer, Townsend & Associates, Glacier National Park: Solid Waste Management Study (Washington, DC: U.S. Department of Interior, National Park Service, 1973), 4.

64. Consoer, Townsend & Associates, Sequoia and Kings Canyon National Parks: Solid Waste Management Study (Washington, DC: U.S. Department of Interior, National Park Service, 1972), 4.

65. National Park Service, Status of Major Environmental Sanitation Facilities in the National Park Service (Washington, DC: National Park Service-Public Health Service, 1974).

66. Metcalf and Eddy Engineers, *Master Sewerage Study: Yellow Stone National Park Wyoming* (Washington, DC: U.S. Department of Interior, National Park Service, 1968), 3-3–3-4.

67. Brown and Caldwell, *Muir Woods National Monument: Waste Water Treatment and Disposal Study* (Washington, DC: U.S. Department of Interior, National Park Service, 1972).

68. Thomas Vale, "The Myth of the Humanized Landscape: The Example from Yosemite National Park," *Natural Areas Journal* 18:3 (1998): 231–36.

69. Dilsaver and Wyckoff, "Agency Culture."

Sleeping Outside

The Political Natures of Urban Camping

PHOEBE S. KROPP YOUNG

On a warm Saturday night in June 2005, three young men arrived at their carefully chosen campsite. They pitched their North Face tents, unrolled their sleeping bags, and sat down to enjoy an evening in the out of doors. Friends and successful entrepreneurs from New York City, this group of campers appeared to be following a well-beaten path—temporarily escaping their urban lives for adventure and solace in nature. Where they departed from the millions of Americans who annually head out on a camping vacation, however, was in their selection of setting: not woods, lake, or mountains, but Times Square, mid-town Manhattan. Camping in the capitol of pavement-and-neon civilization—what were they doing there?

Their explicit reasons were simple, without any stated political, environmental, or artistic motivations. They thought it would be cool. As they wrote in their blogs the next day, the experiment met expectations. "The night was spectacular," one entered. He went on to describe their plans and experience: "We chose the traffic median at 44th Street because it is a wide island right in the middle of Times Square with plenty of room for our tents to sprawl. It was noisy and bright, but the LEDs replaced the stars nicely and the skyscrapers couldn't have imitated sequoias any better." The campers seemed happy to converse with the crowds that gathered, pose for photos, and to accept the pizza a stranger brought them. While they noted that no less than ten different police officers came to investigate their camp, the men prided themselves on successfully negotiating their way out of an order to disperse. Posing either as photographers for the North Face company or as fans waiting on line for concert tickets, they managed to keep their site until morning.[1]

The appeal of this scene, to campers, crowds, and cops alike, centered on its apparent novelty. The image of tents on a traffic island looked so incongruous as to be entirely whimsical. The reflexive connection of camping with wilderness left viewers unable to assimilate the Times Square bivouac as anything but anomaly. As one individual responded, "This was a very thought-provoking experiment. . . . If people can camp in public places such as state and national parks, then why should they not be able to camp in Times Square?"[2] Urban streetscapes and rural parklands may both be public spaces, but they are public in different ways. People do not, in fact, camp freely in either, and must adhere to different sets of regulations. Nonetheless, camping on the street is not the same as camping in national parks. Yet, despite the extraordinary urban location, the norms of wilderness-style camping still seemed to govern. The tight cultural bond between camping and nature allowed the campers to imagine skyscrapers as Sequoias, an improbable metamorphosis that the tents seemed to invite. Online reactions echoed this refrain, using wilderness camping as the operable referent. One joked, "Excellent spot. How far did you have to hike to find it?" while another added only "i have the same north-face tent." Whether judging them exquisitely hip or unfathomably crazy, what most found provocative was the urban simulation of a nature experience, if quoted only in the form of branded camping equipment.[3]

Comparatively few, and none of the campers, remarked upon the other potentially volatile comparison to those who camped in the city on a regular basis—the homeless. Had several disheveled and itinerant men set up camp in Times Square not with Gore-Tex and digital cameras but shopping carts and old blankets, the conversations with authorities and passersby were likely to have had a different tenor. The campsites of the homeless are not urban anomalies, no matter how scarce city officials have tried to make them. The novelty of the stunt, then, rested not in the idea of urban camping, but the identities of the campers who practiced it. Middle-class urbanites sleeping outside with the help of purchased gadgetry represented a recognizably safe image, even if practiced in an unusual location. One of the few to query this discrepancy, a user posted, "Don't get me wrong. I'm all for Starwars fans and Apple freaks (I'm one) and you guys camping out on the streets in high traffic areas. Heh, it's all the rage these days, but when exactly did the police stop enforcing loitering laws?"[4] Sleeping outside in the city, he reminded, is legally defined as abnormal. For those in pursuit of consumption or attention, playing the scofflaw is part of the appeal. For those seeking shelter, these connotations are more hazardous.

Sleeping outside brings the body in direct contact with nature—with earth, water, and air. Like the cheeky Times Square tents, it also illuminates key points of contact between nature and the city—intersections that shape social discourse about class and camping, the home and the homeless. Simply put, the meaning of sleeping outside has a history, one that resides not only in nature's playground, but also in the culture and politics of the city. This long history is the subject of this brief essay. Since it first became a popular leisure pursuit in the late nineteenth century, camping's raison d'être centered upon relieving the pressures of urban life. In the minds of many it served as a prime outlet for escaping the confines of the city and "getting back to nature." Even as people continued to camp in the city for various reasons—economic need, political statement, consumer desire—it is the wilderness vacationers that became normative. The more camping became socially endorsed and state-subsidized as a wholesome jaunt into nature, by the 1920s and 1930s, the more the idea of urban camping, out of necessity rather than choice, appeared socially threatening, even deviant—a division that reappeared with great force near the end of the twentieth century. In other words, sleeping under the stars in the woods has often conjured notions of tranquility, freedom, adventure, pleasure, and health; sleeping outdoors in the city implied filth and illness—the more ominous side of nature—and more often conjured police surveillance. The act of camping appears to prompt either an image of wholesome national pride or a symbol of suspicion and shame. To seek the root of this duality is to ask how cultural understandings of nature have played into historical experiences of class and civic belonging.

"A Temporary Home in the Wilds"

Through much of the nineteenth century and before, camping in America existed as a form of ordinary travel practice. If travelers made note of their outdoor habitations in areas when then came upon scarce lodging, they did not highlight the occasion as a significant departure from daily life. Moreover, when migrants, miners, farmers, naturalists, surveyors, trappers, and revivalists—not to mention Native Americans—camped, they did so for reasons other than the desire for a "wilderness experience," which would later come to define the activity. Moments when mass camping was impossible to ignore—in overland wagon trains or the foothills of gold rush California, for example—the camping was a means to another ends.

It would be another set of Americans who would begin to fashion camping as noteworthy. Soldiers on both sides of the Civil War bedded down in tents for many seasons and became as skilled at making camp as waging war. Though they camped for military purposes rather than themselves, as veterans they spent many more years recalling the camp life itself with nostalgia—the brotherly camaraderie, the masses of white canvas peaks, the domestic haven from battle. A good number took opportunities to revisit the experience, with a few peacetime adjustments: training their rifles on game and hopefully avoiding dysentery. As veterans walked out of town and into the woods, they came to serve in the vanguard of both leisure campers and tramps in America. They did not necessarily share a simple, "unquenchable and irresponsible wanderlust acquired during the war," as some contemporary observers alleged. Camp memories could represent purpose and labor as well as respite. Tramps in particular fulfilled key roles in the expanding industrial economy. Many worked and lodged outdoors, embodying a mobile, fluid labor supply for the fluctuating post–Civil War business cycles.[5] Whether intentionally sought or not, means of life or recreational choice, camping acquired a new visibility, often suggesting a departure from the expectations of social and working life in an era of accelerating urban industrialism."

A small but growing set of urbanites became attracted to the concept of a hiatus in the form of temporary camping for leisure. Their camping was deliberate, often chosen as an alternative to a vacation at a resort hotel, which despite typically serene rural settings harbored the purported faults of urban overcivilization. As such, leisure campers in the late nineteenth and early twentieth centuries made the escape from city to wilderness the defining arc of their travel. Horace Kephart's 1906 guide de rigeur, *Handbook for Vacation Campers and Travelers in the Wilderness,* gave voice to an emerging logic. The woodsman spoke for many of his devotees in suggesting that camping lent one both nature experience and a chance to slip the reins of civilization. "To many a city man there comes a time when the great town wearies him. He hates its sights and smells and clangor.... There come visions of green fields and far-rolling hills, of tall forests and cool, swift-flowing streams." Kephart urged the city-bound man to "go where he can hunt, capture, and cook his own meat, erect his own shelter, do his chores." This, he suggested, provided simultaneously "freedom from care," "unrestrained liberty of action," and "proud self-reliance." The satisfaction of camping for Kephart and many of his generation lay equally in the beauty of nature and in its challenge. As such, camping adhered to the "strenuous life," a program of physical and mental rehabilitation Theodore Roosevelt had prescribed to what he saw as a sickly nation, suffering from the effects of too much urban civilization.[6] By imagining social and personal redemption in "roughing it," these campers differentiated themselves not only from resort vacationers but also from those who camped for less philosophical reasons.

Still, while many leisure campers touted the physical and moral rewards of camp work, they described the goal of their labors in terms of domestic comforts as often as they did manly strength. As a writer for *Outing Magazine* in 1898 suggested, "There is, to most men, if they would only realize it, a real pleasure to be found in the very act of making a temporary home in the wilds comfortable and attractive."[7] The attraction to the concept of a temporary home is telling. Campers might have been roughing it, but they imagined themselves as creating little islands of civilization in the wilderness. Campers admired their abilities to produce comfort and found that doing the work of camp, making the beds and tending the fire, was in itself comforting.

Sleeping arrangements suggested the shift from deprivation to domestic comfort. In the era before foam mats and down sleeping bags were common, camp beds usually consisted of hammocks, hay, or an improvised pile of tree boughs, leaves, and blankets. New Yorker Grace Mitchell approached her first camping trip in 1906 with trepidation, wondering how sleeping outside, bedless in the chilly air, would affect her body. Yet, she was surprised to report, after her first night on pine boughs, "we were obliged to confess that we had never slept sounder on the finest of beds.... From the standpoint of health, a life in the real outdoors is unsurpassed." Mitchell was not alone in her praise for the health, restfulness, comfort, and pleasure of outdoor slumber. A writer for *Country Life in America* suggested that the person who could not sleep upon a two-foot bed of spruce or hemlock—if properly made—"as soundly and refreshingly as he did in his childhood, has need to consult his medical advisor." One camper suggested that the "charm of camp life" affected the interpretation of physical comfort. "You go to camp and sleep on a bed that would rouse your indignation at home—of common straw, it may be, with no sheets or pillows. . . . You disregard dust and dirt, and the lack of a thousand little conveniences. And without hypocrisy, you say you enjoy all these things." The bed itself, he surmised, would induce not only "deep and quiet sleep," but also the desire to "lie awake from sheer enjoyment of the novelty of it, to look at the stars, or listen to the gentle breathing of the night wind in the boughs over head."[8] Sleeping outside lay at the center of the leisure camping experience in its formative years; it marked the distance urbanites had traveled from their indoor worlds.

For many practitioners, the act of sleeping outside—and declaring it comfortable—represented a litmus test for authentic wilderness experience. One woman scorned in 1910 "the expensive kind of so-called camping in the Adirondacks, where one can live in a house with every luxury the whole summer through." This was not, she argued, "real camping. For the genuine thing, you must sleep in the open or in tents in some wild spot several days from civilization." Sleeping arrangements, that is, whether one's roof was stars and canvas or tin and shingle, made a crucial difference, but not the only one. Bodily contact with a nature understood to be "wild" came to define the social practice of leisure camping.[9]

The oxymoronic challenge of roughing it in comfort was embodied in an intensifying focus on the consumption of specialized leisure camping equipment. Private purveyors of camping gear and supplies like L.L. Bean and the Coleman Company, established in the first years of the twentieth century, tapped into an avid market.[10] Despite the investment in the rhetoric of self-reliance and wilderness experience, leisure campers eagerly consumed an array of gadgets designed especially to ease their forays into the wilderness. Many of these collapsible, multifunction, new material items were conspicuous precisely because their purpose was limited to the leisure camp—they had no use, or were deliberately not used, in leisure campers' modern homes, and they were too specialized or expensive for itinerant campers. It was indeed the material culture of camping that allowed leisure campers to perform a specific identity. Along with the automobile, which quickly became a preferred camping vehicle, the "outfitting"—both for self and site—marked the difference between camper and itinerant. In this way, camping evolved as a cultural style one might display, which suggested class positions, urban identities, and intellectual outlooks.[11] Indeed, the very possession of camping gear framed camping as a vacation, both heightening and normalizing the sense of departure from daily life.

By the turn of the twentieth century, leisure camping had become a relatively popular form of vacationing. Nonetheless, these urbanites on holiday did not have the woods to themselves. In addition to hoboes and laborers whose peregrinations often drew comments of concern during this era, families like that of Alphonso Reeves employed camping as part of a subsistence strategy. Between 1900 and 1906, the Reeves family slipped easily between house living and tent camping. For a time they would take lodging in small Wyoming, South Dakota, and Montana towns, and when work or welcome ran out, as a group they would venture out in the wilds for months at a time in search of new opportunities. Trapping for fur, hunting wolves and coyotes for bounty, or serving as game wardens, camp living allowed them to earn and save money not available to them in town. Their camp equipment and methods resembled that of leisure campers, but their motives and interpretations differed a good deal. For the Reeveses, camping did not appear a grand escape from daily life or civilization. Although there are episodes where the family took time for pleasure experiences in nature—hiking to see a view, for example—it is clear that they did not choose a life in the wilds for affective reasons; nor was it always pleasant. They were there neither to rough it nor to marvel at making comfort. Rather, their path represented what historian Eric Monkonnen has argued about tramps during this era in general, "a rational response to underemployment as well as unemployment."[12] However atypical the Reeveses may have been in their use of camping as a family strategy, they suggest that camping as a practice could contain a range of motivations and relationships to nature.

The more successful city dwellers envisioned camping as an escape, the more their definitions began to narrow the social norms of sleeping outside. Over time, it was the Reeveses and those who camped for reasons other than leisure that began to appear curious. The split in camping correlated with a national discomfort that grew in the years after the Civil War with a persistently, even determinedly rootless section of the population. Despite the fact that much of the labor market and economy at the turn of the twentieth century, particularly in the West, depended upon the very willingness of workers not to establish permanent residence, the practice aroused suspicion. Concerned press coverage of tramps often sensationalized those who chose to dwell in outdoor "jungles"—group encampments on the outskirts of cities and towns—over the majority looking for work and housing in "the main stem" of urban neighborhoods catering to transients. Homeless tramps, traveling hoboes, itinerant workers, or resourceful families appeared to engage in what one scholar has called "a practice of casual lodging that challenged reigning middle-class conceptions of home" and the sense of order and stability they connoted.[13] The heightened contrast between leisure- or nature-driven camping and functional outdoor transience framed the latter as culturally anachronistic in a modern society of homes.

Yet in some respects the phenomenon of tramping was central to the cultural as well as economic transitions of the era. When tramps explained their choices as a critique of urban-industrial order, as a few did, their complaints echoed the words of Horace Kephart in describing the men who chafed at the bonds of the modern city. Not all tramps would have agreed with the one who reported in 1902, "I think this nomadic life is a healthy life."[14] Leisure campers, on the other hand, heartily endorsed such a sentiment, offering it nearly verbatim in many publications, though the nomadism they imagined took a distinctly different, temporary, and more comfortable form. If bemoaning the pressures of industrial civilization was a key cultural narrative, then sleeping outside represented a vehicle for this grievance. What separated the forms of camping, and the campers themselves, embodied shifts not only in structures of class but also in visions of nature as a space for leisure, consumption, and domestic comfort.

"How to Motor Camp Without Hoboism"

By the 1920s, for most, camping represented a departure from normal life, acceptable because it was temporary; if camping became one's normal mode of living, then it appeared marginal. This separation increased throughout the twenties and thirties with the spread of automobile ownership and the widespread establishment of municipal, state, and federal campgrounds to accommodate auto camping. These features made camping more popular among the middle class. Initially, campers used their cars in search of the same kinds of rugged wilderness excursions as an earlier generation had practiced. But campgrounds closer to town, with more amenities—indoor plumbing, community spaces, functional kitchens—grew in popularity. By the early 1930s, tenting was on the wane. As a sociologist observed in 1931, "Tourists are a bit weary of pitching and breaking camp and generally playing Indian." Still, he believed, average tourists preferred the domestic freedoms of camping, which offered a sense of being "at home and . . . at ease," to hotels, which made those of modest means "feel like a bum."[15] These assessments were anchored in the social context of the 1930s, which gave leisure campers new points of comparison. Their counterparts were no longer mannered resort loafers but the ill-housed third.

Campers in this era were less concerned with achieving authentic experiences in nature than in avoiding the feeling or appearance of a bum. This was not merely idle dread. The onset of the Great Depression found an increasing number of people sleeping outside with something other than nature or leisure on their minds. Early in the spring of 1933, researcher Nels Anderson conducted a one-day census of homeless, producing a conservative estimate that 1.5 million Americans spent the night in public shelters or slept outdoors. Despite the resemblance to earlier tramps, these transients were different and newly shocking. Industrial tramping had been on the wane in the 1920s, as the rise of corporate capitalist welfare made it both a less likely individual economic strategy and less essential to the broader economy. Earlier cultural suspicions of tramps notwithstanding, they fit a certain niche that evaporated by the 1930s. The plight of the unemployed homeless and the dust bowl migrants now evoked social tragedy, especially in the context of the construction of a modern welfare state.[16]

With so many of the down-and-out sleeping outside, in full public view, the divide between camping as a form of privilege and camping as a function of poverty became a critical, contentious space. The fundamentally temporary hiatus that animated leisure camping symbolically reinforced the settled home to which campers returned. Camps of Depression-driven homeless often figured in the reports of observers, whether sympathetic or not, as the troubling negation of home itself.[17] Turned away from overwhelmed urban systems of public lodging, transients often took up temporary residence in Hoovervilles, extant hobo jungles, and auto camps. The same auto camps described for tourists as modern and homelike acquired an unsavory cast when populated by migrants. According to the 1937 report of Labor Secretary Frances Perkins, the "Living conditions for most migrants are deplorable. . . . At night they sleep by the road-side, in squatter camps, or crowd into one- or two-room cabins in low-priced tourist camps" which were "frequently crowded, inadequately equipped, and unsanitary." Elsewhere praised for its healthful and restful effects, Perkins found that "exposure in camp life" posed major health hazards, especially to children.[18] That these campers squatted in public parks, on private grounds, and near riverbanks was nothing new; before regulated campgrounds, leisure campers squatted, with or without automobiles, as a matter of course with little suggestion of social or physical repercussions. The emergence of a public consumer landscape for leisure camping served to highlight and isolate those on its margins. While public sympathy motivated some to advocate for the needs of the migrant poor, the interpretive assumptions that the homeless were outcasts, without resources, community, or political standing would have lasting implications.[19]

One of the most visible events where camping evoked the costs and tensions of the Depression was the mass encampment of the "bonus army" of 1932. Thousands of World War I veterans joined together to urge the federal government to grant their service bonuses several years early due to the economic emergency. Members of what became known as the Bonus Expeditionary Force, in true hobo fashion, hopped freight trains in places all over the nation on their way to Washington. They set up camp in tents and other makeshift dwellings in places like Anacostia Flats, near the Potomac River, where homeless had already established a settlement. Leaders of the bonus march, as historian Todd DePastino argued, imposed army-style order to camp life in an effort to "combat the impression that the campers were disreputable bums, tramps and hoboes looking to feed from the public trough." Moreover, veterans posed for photographs showing themselves maintaining neat, ordered families within canvas houses and peddled the prints in the street to generate income and allies. Though their pleas garnered support across the nation, their camp did not entirely escape suspicion. To many observers the camps "suggested less an army bivouac than 'an immense hobo jungle.'"[20]

Whether it added to or undercut the veterans' political challenge, the camp itself clearly put a great deal of pressure on the Hoover administration. Camping with a purpose, beyond pleasure or survival, the bonus army embodied the latent potential for social unrest among the transient. Thus, even after the bonus bill failed, Hoover was intent upon dispersing the camp itself, and in late July ordered the U.S. Army to clear out the flats. The camp became a battleground, as troops employed tanks and tear gas and then "applied the torch to the shacks in which the veterans lived." Though veterans defended their positions with weapons improvised from the ground itself, "the disordered camp" the New York Times reported, quickly became "a mass of flames as the bonus seeking veterans set fire to their own miserable shacks."[21] The violent destruction of the encampment proved a fatal blow to Hoover's reelection chances, but the episode also suggested that, away from the woods, camping could represent a threat to the social order.

Whether sleeping outside with political goals or with no place else to go, disordered urban camping caused alarm. Social conditions, however, were not always as desperate as the physical arrangements implied. Some observers found a semblance of community and camp camaraderie, and—not unlike the tourists who preferred the auto camp to the hotel—more than a few transients expressed a preference for the independence of these lodgings to the social regimentation of public facilities. [22] Transients or their camps did not always conform to the expectation of wretchedness or deviance. In fact, some officials worried that for those struggling to hold onto settled lives, these new hoboes might be modeling an attractive method of dealing with economic woes. As New Dealer Harry Hopkins observed, transients appeared "a cross between a carefree gypsy and a fugitive from justice," and thus presented a difficult social problem to address.[23] The lore of hoboism and camping alike contributed to a strain of romanticism that rendered itinerants as poor but freed from the responsibilities of civilization. At the end of the 1936 film *Modern Times,* hand in hand with Paulette Goddard, Charlie Chaplin's lovable tramp simply walked away from urban, industrial civilization.[24] That few could or would follow this example and abandon their homes for the promise of a supposedly freer life outside the city did not lessen the cultural tensions around transience in the era.

Leisure campers were not immune from this tension. On the road and at auto camps vacationers sometimes made camp not far from the functionally transient. Money matters dictated that both vacationers and migrants cluster around inexpensive facilities. References to camping as an affordable vacation increased during the 1930s. The suggestion that camping was an economical pursuit was not new; advocates in earlier eras were fond of remarking on the cost benefits of "plain American camping," particularly "for moderately poor people at least, who cannot afford yachting trips and the like." By the Depression years, the language had changed. In defending her choice of a camping vacation, one woman wrote, "I have an idea that the medical profession might disapprove of a camping trip for a baby. But upon finding themselves with a vacation sans salary, a six months' old son, a dilapidated coupe, and almost exactly no money, what is a young couple to do?" The remainder of her article was devoted to proving how they were able to have a wholesome and relaxing vacation on a small budget. The baby, she argued, profited especially, "never had a day of illness . . . , and cried not more than twice on the whole vacation."[25] The claim of health was particularly significant. With auto camps being declared health menaces, a practice that had once represented an escape from the problems of city life now appeared squarely in the middle of such urban issues as transience and sanitation.

Trailers, equipment relatively new to the camping scene, typified this tension. They appeared in the 1920s as custom-built automobile accessories, "a handier and cheaper means of making a vacation camping trip; all of the smaller comforts of home in a neat portable package." Within a decade trailers became more ambitious. Envisioned as an entire, collapsible "mobile metal house," the trailer attracted a sizable following among campers who found comfort and convenience more appealing than roughing it. Grand gadget that it was, trailers had opponents with multiple complaints. Those who continued to practice old-fashioned styles of tent camping saw trailers as corrupting the essential wilderness experience. For others, trailers warned of the possibility of semipermanent transience. What would happen if people began to use trailers to live in rather than vacation? How would the nation account for these wanderers, "living briefly here and there as squatters, rootless as air plants, paying no taxes, creating a new kind of motor slums?" Despite industry assurances that trailers were designed "to be a vehicle, not a permanent address," migrants and others did find them to be workable homes on wheels, though not in the feared numbers.[26] Trailer camping thus came under suspicion from one side for obviating the need to sleep outside, and from the other for providing a way to sleep anywhere.

Trailers may not have been quite camping, but more to the point was the way they allowed one to be transient without appearing homeless. To a much greater degree than in previous eras, leisure campers worried about "how to motor camp without hoboism."[27] Differentiating themselves from itinerants was an imperative task for vacationers, and trailers offered a useful tool. A writer for *Sunset Magazine* hedged her cost-conscious appeal with instructions on how to be well equipped. "Camping with the family is less work than living at home, less expensive even and a tonic for soul and body. . . . Take a trailer if you must, but do make your camp comfortable and your meals lavish." Even though they raised suspicions of their own, trailers created different physical and social impressions than the disheveled appearance of Hoovervilles. As the manager of a luxurious Miami tourist camp on Biscayne Boulevard quipped, "If people wanted to raise hell, they wouldn't go to a trailer camp."[28] The amenities made all the difference between the appearance of comfort and contentment and the suggestion of desperation and disorder.

The camping equipment industry offered an ever-increasing array of products for leisure campers to buy, use, and display. A 1937 survey in the *New York Times* testified to the innovation in gadgetry. "During the past year many novel and useful additions have been made to the long lists of gadgets and devices already available for those lovers of the outdoors desiring a homelike touch to their temporary dwellings erected in the open. The city-dweller who pitches a tent in the woods not only wishes to feel that he is 'roughing it,' but also seeks the simple physical comforts and conveniences which help to make life in the out-of-doors more pleasant."[29] The desire of city dwellers to rough it in style, and to create temporary homes in the woods reinforced the dominant logic of leisure camping. Immersed in an effort to camp without appearing homeless, the material of one's "outfit" took on greater symbolic significance. Whatever the practical improvements, the accumulation of gadgets emphasized one's leisured status as much as it provided new functions.

Whether or not leisure campers could afford to outfit themselves with the latest gear, they began to discover a newly organized and subsidized camping landscape. Camping advocates detailed their enjoyment of new United States Forest Service and National Parks public campgrounds. Both the affordability and federal imprimatur attracted campers like Leonora Philbrook, who "hiked, camped, fished, and saw the wonders of the Sierra National Forest for almost nothing. It was an inexpensive vacation, but the most enjoyable one we ever had."[30] Several governmental agencies were engaged in campground construction throughout the era, setting up predictable public facilities in wilderness settings. The irony was that at the same time it was aggressively subsidizing leisure camping, the federal government was elsewhere breaking up homeless encampments and resisting the construction of migrant camps.

The state thus invested in the divisions between normative and nonnormative camping. The logic seemed in part to hinge on the location: urban camping appeared socially and physically deleterious, while the wilderness was restorative for citizens and the civic body alike. The Civilian Conservation Corps offered the prime example of this, as recruits not only developed wildlands for recreational use, but also placed special emphasis on virility and manhood achieved through physical labor in the outdoors. Even though most enrollees came from small towns and rural areas rather than cities, CCC rhetoric maintained its claim of rescuing weakly city men and rehabilitating them in the wilderness. Those infamous urban campers, the bonus marchers, became prime candidates for recruitment to President Roosevelt's tree army. Veterans were allowed to enroll in the corps regardless of age, with special preference given to those who had joined the bonus expedition. Who better to transform than these men? The official mantra of the CCC prescribed the wilderness camping cure: "Let them breathe clean fresh air. Let them work outside with their hands digging dirt and planting trees. And let them sleep under the stars."[31]

Both the disease and the remedy, sleeping outside had come to carry significant cultural and political weight in the 1930s. Where, with whom, and with what equipment one camped could give the appearance either as suspiciously marginal or solidly mainstream. In an era where the accumulated standards of middle-class home living appeared vulnerable to prolonged national poverty, camping was not an inconsequential activity. When it continued, as it had before, to reinforce and replicate the domestic comforts of home, camping found public and popular endorsement. When sleeping outside embodied homelessness in the heart of urban America, it elicited public sympathy but created little ground upon which to claim public voice.

"Warning: Sleeping on the Streets May Make You Look Homeless"

The presence of homeless urban campers in American cities persisted during the many decades following the Great Depression. If their numbers and social salience waned in mid-century, by the 1980s homelessness began to be seen as an epidemic without precedent. A set of historical and political developments converged to create a spike in the homeless population and while a new "politics of compassion" packaged it as a wholly new crisis, historical understandings of what it meant to camp persisted.[32] Whether observers rendered the homeless as a human tragedy or a visual nuisance, they shared a belief that people should not be sleeping outside—unless by choice, in nature, and with a waiting roof at home. Advocacy for the homeless often prioritized bringing outdoor lodgers inside. Simultaneously, urban redevelopers have worked to make outdoor public urban spaces less hospitable for sleeping. Homeless-proof benches, among other innovations of public design, testified to the enforcement of a proper and an improper way to inhabit the city. Increasingly restrictive urban rules about space have made homeless camping not only suspicious but nearly impossible.[33]

Some thirty-two blocks south of Times Square sits a site more noted for urban camping. Tompkins Square, a ten-acre park in the Lower East side, was a prime destination in the 1980s, and not for the likes of twenty-something entrepreneurs out for a lark. A regular population of one to three hundred gathered there, and a sort of settled community had begun to emerge. The neighborhood surrounding the park had been for many years a foot-in-the-door kind of place—economically marginal but home to waves of new immigrants trying to make it. As the area began gentrifying, residents of low-rent apartments found themselves literally on the curb. Nathaniel Hunter Jr., evicted in 1983 from a building going co-op, had tried to fight the change, but lost heart and much of his resources. He decided, instead of giving up his neighborhood, to move into the adjacent green space in Tompkins Square. Using language reminiscent of campers bound for wilderness sojourns, he recalled that, "I just wanted to be left alone, to find a spot in space to cool my head out. So I came here. I found a sanctuary, really, trees, open space, solitude." He wasn't the only one. New Yorkers without housing came from all parts of the city and began to build semipermanent settlements—tents, shacks, outdoor kitchens.[34]

By 1988, when a violent clash between homeless people, other protestors, and the police left thirty-eight injured, Hunter found himself once again in the middle of a very public struggle over his space. The community there was far from ideal—in the year following the riots, one woman burned her neighbor to death in his tent, and a soup kitchen started for the residents degenerated into an "open-air drug bazaar." Hunter worried that the city had disturbed the park's natural refuge: "now we have cook fires burning, political activists yelling, police around, all the things I had been running away from. Now I'm worried about my actual eviction from the park."[35] He had cause to be worried—for several years, city officials had continuously changed their minds about enforcing the official 1:00 a.m. curfew. Periodically, they came to raze the residents' structures, often to great protest; within days, people came back to rebuild their tents and shacks.

In December 1989, city officials decided upon a "compromise." Once again, "city and park police officers mounted a long planned, long announced operation of nearly military complexity" to remove all the shelters from the park. But they also lifted the curfew, making Tompkins Square the only public park in New York City without one. An officer made it clear that one could still sleep there overnight: "If they want, the homeless people can come back later with blankets and sleeping bags. They just won't have the structures." And just as before, some did, despite the 18-degree weather. A few set up tents nearby in vacant lots, complete with Christmas lights, which staked a defiant claim upon the place. The owner of the decorated tent stated resolutely, "We're going to rebuild tent city. Until they come up with a better alternative to city run shelters, we're going to stay." Others set fire to their own tents in protest, while most tried to stuff as many belongings as they could into the city-furnished plastic bags. As one woman walked away with a small, brittle, Charlie-Brown-style Christmas tree, she grumbled, "At least we saved our tree."[36]

The ensuing months saw an uneasy compromise develop, where police allowed the residents to put up their tents at night so long as they broke down the camp in the morning, but this too was short lived. In 1991, the city government announced that it would "no longer tolerate the use of public parks as living spaces." Tompkins Square was closed for an eight-month renovation, during which 24-hour police patrols were its only denizens. The redesigned park included a permanent police station as well as a spatial reorganization that discouraged the reestablishment of a homeless community there. The struggle for space waged up until that point involved a complex, overlapping set of political, economic, and cultural trends. That the battle was joined not only by police and homeless, but also by landlords and squatters, developers and renters, suggests the ways in which the act of sleeping in Tompkins Square became a focal point for a shift in civic identity and the wrenching changes in housing expectations it implied.

Homeless people figured meaningfully into this broader history, not least in the ways in which they attempted to reassert a place for themselves in the city. The tenacity with which many returned to their spots suggests that despite the unsettled nature of a tent "that must be collapsed every morning at seven, . . . for many people [it] was far better than the dangerous, atomized, prison-like conditions in city shelters." A hobbled choice perhaps, but evidence suggests that at least some homeless people preferred the hazards of independent outdoor life to the rigid state controls of public shelters.[37] Sleeping outside attested as much to a desire for civic voice and standing as it did to the apparent loss of social and economic power that had led them there.

"In the now decades-long debate over the meanings and methods of sleeping outside," New York City adopted a division between shelter and sleep earlier than most. Recent legal tactics to clamp down on homeless settlements have followed its lead, specifically targeting "urban camping." Responding to the Supreme Court's unwillingness to allow municipalities to criminalize the act of merely sleeping in public, cities have instituted restrictions on unauthorized camping. Defined as the act of erecting and inhabiting tents, shacks, or other improvised dwellings, urban camping has become part of the criminal code, the bureaucratic label for the homes of the homeless.[38] As legal shorthand, the term relies upon a century-long accrual of meaning that imbued the practice with a sense of deviance.

Despite the legal bans, urban camping has become something of an underground fad among some students and young professionals. While some do camp out in the city with certain purposes—in line for tickets or television shows or to save money—many appear to pursue it for similar reasons as wilderness camping: as a distinctive form of leisure, an escape from the usual expectations of urban life, a little adventure.[39] An entry on the WikiHow website for "How to Urban Camp," suggests the approach and methods this privileged brand of urban campers employs. Step one is straightforward: "Determine the proper site for your urban camping adventure," while step five is more tricky: "Find lodging at night. This can be a really tough [thing] to do safely without spending money. You obviously can't set up a tent in the middle of the sidewalk." (Obviously, WikiHow authors hadn't met the Times Square gang.) The site suggests instead, "You could go into alleys or just sleep whereever [sic] the homeless people sleep. Have people stay watch at night to guard your stuff." Make sure, it adds, to bring a "Small legal non-ranged personal weapon for self defense. Pocket knife, pepper spray and stun guns all would work to prevent mugging." The site does not suggest interacting or sharing resources with homeless people themselves. Instead, the emphasis remains upon how to distance oneself from a homeless identity. Listed under "Warnings" is the caveat that "Sleeping on the streets may make you look homeless." Recommended items to pack include a number intended to prevent such mistaken identification. In addition to a backpack, tent, and sleeping bag, one ought to bring their gym membership (for the locker room facilities) and a portable music player. The latter, WikiHow warns, can make one more vulnerable to mugging and thus the personal digital and personal defense accessories go hand-in-hand.[40] As it was for Depression-era campers who tried to camp without hoboism, the gadgets make all the difference in displaying the identity of campers rather than homeless.

From one perspective, these intrepid campers—or perhaps even the homeless themselves—look like pioneers, or perhaps merry pranksters, interrogating our cultural assumptions about cities and nature. If unintentionally, they pose the question: why not camp here? Is the sunset not also beautiful? What makes some experiences in nature more natural than others? Leisure campers may continue to anchor the normative encounter with nature, as one quintessentially about wild places and consumer products, but moments spent in wilderness offer only part of the story.[41] Sleeping outside in the city muddies the presumed separation of urban and natural spaces, just as it makes visible the ways in which the poor are scoured from parts of the civic landscape.

The tent cities that swelled in number and population in the difficult economy that arrived in 2008 raise these issues as well. Made homeless by financial hardship, some deliberately sought out spaces of urban nature to pitch their tents and ride out their own economic storm.[42] Many of the foreclosed and unemployed, in fact, relied upon an array of camping equipment—lanterns, coolers, tents—marketed and perhaps originally purchased for leisure purposes. Though this repurposing attracted little attention, it came in a context where camping and gear received positive press as a less expensive alternative for family vacations in tough economic times. Perhaps this irony contains the seeds of a political dialogue about the uses of technology and nature.[43] Instead, sympathetic observers, profit-minded developers, and conservationists alike tended to describe tent cities as a misuse of natural space. Many painted tent cities as distressing "third worlds" in America with homeless residents poignant visual symbols of a public tragedy, both human and environmental.

Homeless people may make the choice to camp under some kind of duress, but defining the predicament need not be the end of the analytical road. If we focus as much on the choice to sleep outside as on the constraints under which it is made, new historical questions emerge. Whether for industrial tramps, Depression migrants and marchers, or contemporary homeless people, asking why tents and parks and riverbanks appear to have supplied recurring options might point to more than the tragic symbols of troubled times. These episodes demand analysis of how citizens, homeless and otherwise, envision relationships between urban and natural space and how those relationships affect civic and political participation. How nature fits in modern American culture has had significant effects, on people and landscapes alike. How Americans fit—or appear not to fit—in modern conceptions of nature has shaped shifting visions of home, modernity, class, citizenship, and the state.

Notes

The author would like to thank John Herron, Peggy Shaffer, and Bryant Simon for the insightful perspectives they lent to this essay. I am also grateful to Carl Abbott for his comments, to Peter Blodgett for archival materials, and to Char Miller for asking me to do something urban with my camping research. I am honored to be included in this volume for the chance to acknowledge my personal and intellectual debts to Hal Rothman, though I could never repay them.

Initial quotations in this chapter are taken from online blogs, which may include irregular punctuation, spelling, grammar, and/or capitalization.

1. Zach Klein, "Times Square . . . Check," Flickr.com, June 12, 2005, http://www.flickr.com/photos/zachklein/18841510/in/set-445224/ accessed August 19, 2007.

2. Scott Johnson, posting, on "Pitch Camp—Urban Camping in Times Square," Amit Gupta's Blog, June 12, 2005, http://amitgupta.com/blog/shoebox/2005/06/12/pitch-camp-urban-camping-in-times-square/ accessed August 19, 2007.

3. "Lukky" and "andyisoutside," postings, on "Pitch Camp," Amit Gupta's Blog, June 12, 2005.

4. MichaelMeiser, posting on Klein, "Times Square . . . Check."

5. Eric H. Monkkonen, "Introduction," in *Walking to Work: Tramps in America, 1790–1935,* ed. Eric H. Monkkonen (Lincoln and London: University of Nebraska Press, 1984), 6–9. On tramps, see also Todd DePastino, *Citizen Hobo: How a Century of Homelessness Shaped America* (Chicago and London: University of Chicago Press, 2002), 17–21. For discussion of the emergence and early travels of leisure campers, see Cindy S. Aron, *Working at Play: A History of Vacations in the United States,* (New York: Oxford University Press, 1999), ch. 5. For an example of a Civil War veteran's involvement in camping, see John Mead Gould, *How to Camp Out: Hints for Camping and Walking* (New York: Scribner, Armstrong & Co., 1877).

6. Horace Kephart, *Camping and Woodcraft: A Handbook for Vacation Campers and for Travelers in the Wilderness,* vol. 1: Camping, (1906; Knoxville: University of Tennessee Press, 1988), 17–21. For discussion of Kephart's influence, see Jim Casada, "Introduction," to *Camping and Woodcraft,* vii–xxxiii. On Theodore Roosevelt and the strenuous life, see Gail Bederman, *Manliness and Civilization: A Cultural History of Gender and Race in the United States, 1880–1917* (Chicago: University of Chicago Press, 1996).

7. H. A. Hill, "Camping in Comfort," *Outing* 32 (August 1898): 505. For an expanded discussion of this stage of leisure camping, see Phoebe S. Kropp, "Wilderness Wives and Dishwashing Husbands: Comfort and the Domestic Arts of Camping Out, 1880–1910," *Journal of Social History* 43, no. 1 (Fall 2009): 5–30.

8. Grace Olney Mitchell, "Two Women Outdoors in Idaho," *Country Life in America* 10 (June 1906): 199, 201; Charles E. Ingalls, "How to Enjoy a Vacation," *Country Life in America* 16 (May 1909): 128, 130; Charles S. Greene, "Camping in Mendocino," *The Overland Monthly* 22, no. 130 (October 1893): 346–47.

9. Mrs. Larz Anderson, "Camping for Women," *Country Life in America* 18 (June 1910): 180. The body, as historian Christopher Sellers noted, is "a paradigmatic site where our humanity entangles with a nature at once 'us' and 'other' from us." Christopher Sellers, "Thoreau's Body: Towards an Embodied Environmental History," *Environmental History* 4, no. 4 (October 1999): 486–514.

10. Sheldon Coleman, *The Coleman Story: The Ability to Cope with Change* (New York: The Newcomen Society in North America, 1976); Leon Gorman, *L.L. Bean: The Making of an American Icon* (Boston, MA: Harvard Business School Press, 2006); M. R. Montgomery, *In Search of L.L. Bean* (Boston, MA: Little, Brown and Company, 1984).

11. My understanding of camping as a space of consumption and a form of taste draws in part from Jennifer Price, *Flight Maps: Adventures with Nature in Modern America* (New York: Basic Books, 1999); Matthew W. Klingle, "Spaces of Consumption in Environmental History," *History and Theory,* Theme Issue 42 (December 2003): 94–110; and Pierre Bordieu, *Distinction: A Social Critique of the Judgment of Taste,* Richard Nice, trans. (Cambridge, MA: Harvard University Press, reprint ed., 2007).

12. Mrs. Alphonso Reeves, Diary of family's travels in South Dakota, Wyoming, and Montana, 1900–6 (HM 53214), Henry E. Huntington Library; Monkkonen, "Introduction," 3–6. Several things set the Reeves family apart even from most tramps, notably the fact that they traveled as a largely nuclear group and, most remarkably, the existence of the diary.

13. DePastino, *Citizen Hobo,* 138, 68–71; Eric H. Monkkonen, "Regional Dimensions of Tramping, North and South, 1880–1910," in Monkkonen, ed., *Walking to Work,* 207; Carlos Schwantes, *The Pacific Northwest: An Interpretive History* (Lincoln: University of Nebraska Press, 1989), 250–65; Paul Groth, *Living Downtown: The History of Residential Hotels in the United States* (Berkeley: University of California Press, 1994), ch. 5.

14. John C. Schneider, "Tramping Workers, 1890–1920: A Subcultural View," in Monkkonen, ed., *Walking to Work,* 219–20. The "nomadic life" quotation appeared originally in

John J. McCook, "Leaves from the Diary of a Tramp: VI," *Independent* 54 (February 6, 1902): 337.

15. F. E. Brimmer, quoted in Norman Hayner, "The Auto Camp as a New Type of Hotel," *Sociology and Social Research* (1931): 369. The best scholarly work on this transition between individualized camping in cars and predictable auto camps is Warren Belasco, *Americans on the Road: From Autocamp to Motel, 1910–1945* (Cambridge, MA: The MIT Press, 1979). He terms the earlier stage not "playing Indian" but "Gypsying," both renderings which were, obviously, full of ethnic commentary.

16. Nels Anderson, *Men on the Move* (Chicago: University of Chicago Press, 1940), 66; Groth, *Living Downtown*, ch. 5; Monkkonen, "Introduction," 4–8.

17. DePastino, *Citizen Hobo*, 17.

18. Frances Perkins, quoted in Anderson, *Men on the Move*, 100; Joan M. Crouse, *The Homeless Transient in the Great Depression: New York State, 1929–41* (Albany: State University of New York Press, 1986), 75, 97–98.

19. David Wagner, *Checkerboard Square: Culture and Resistance in a Homeless Community* (Boulder, CO: Westview Press, 1993), 3–4.

20. DePastino, *Citizen Hobo*, 195–200. For additional discussion of the Bonus Army, see also Roger Daniels, *The Bonus March: An Episode of the Great Depression* (Westport, CT: Greenwood Publishing, 1971). Anderson discussed bonus marchers in terms of migrancy and suggested that most of the men who marched east to encamp in the District of Columbia had previously migrated west in similar fashion, camping and "'bumming' their way, but they went singly or in small groups. Their moving caused no alarm." Only when massed and moving east were they feared. Anderson, *Men on the Move*, 54.

21. "Hoover Orders Eviction," *New York Times*, July 29, 1932, p. 1.

22. Crouse, *The Homeless Transient*, 100–101.

23. Ibid., 194–95

24. DePastino, *Citizen Hobo*, 165.

25. Ernest Ingersoll, "Practical Camping," *The Outlook* 56 (June 5, 1897): 324; Leta Foster Ide, "Camping with a Fresh Little Heir," *Sunset* 72 (May 1934): 24.

26. "200,000 Trailers," *Fortune* (1937): 105–6. For the development of trailer camping, see Belasco, *Americans on the Road*; for an opponent's view, see Emilio P. Meinecke, "The Trailer Menace," typescript, April 1, 1935, United States Department of Agriculture, Bureau of Plant Industry.

27. F. W. Leuning, *Motor Camping* (Milwaukee, WI: Milwaukee Journal Tour Club, 1926), 1.

28. Doris Hudson Moss, "Ye Who Enter Here Leave All Boiled Shirts Behind," *Sunset* 73 (July 1934): 9; Ollie Trout, manager of Biscayne Boulevard tourist camp, quoted in, "200,000 Trailers," 229.

29. "'Collapsible' Idea Rules Camp Items: Ingenious Gadgets for Outdoors Designed to Conserve Space in Autos and Tents," *New York Times*, February 21, 1937, p. 69. See also, "New

Things in City's Shops: Rush for Children's Camping Equipment," *New York Times*, June 12, 1938, p. 51; Helga Iversen, "Fish are Biting—Let's Make Camp!" *Sunset* 75 (August 1935): 19.

30. Leonora Philbrook, "Camping in the Sierra National Forest," *Sunset* 72 (February 1934): 22.

31. DePastino, *Citizen Hobo*, 207–8; Daniels, *The Bonus March*, 222–33; Bryant Simon, "'New Men in Body and Soul': The Civilian Conservation Corps and the Transformation of Male Bodies and the Body Politic," in Virginia J. Scharff, ed., *Seeing Nature Through Gender* (Lawrence: University Press of Kansas, 2003), 80–102; Neil M. Maher, *Nature's New Deal: The Civilian Conservation Corps and the Roots of the American Environmental Movement* (New York: Oxford University Press, 2007).

32. Wagner, *Checkerboard Square*, 4–5.

33. For discussions of urban space and design and the homeless, see Mike Davis, *City of Quartz: Excavating the Future in Los Angeles* (New York: Vintage, 1990); Joanne Passaro, *The Unequal Homeless: Men on the Streets, Women in Their Place* (New York: Routledge, 1996); Groth, *Living Downtown*, 16–17. For the trend of "shelterization," see Wagner, *Checkerboard Square*.

34. John Kifner, "Worlds Collide in Tompkins Square Park," *New York Times*, July 31, 1989. For a history of Tompkins Square, the surrounding neighborhood, the gentrification and "housing panic" of the 1980s, and the battles of police, homeless, squatters, and residents over the park, see Anthony Marcus, *Where Have All the Homeless Gone?: The Making and Unmaking of a Crisis* (New York: Berghahn Books, 2005), ch. 6.

35. Robert D. MacFadden, "Park Curfew Protest Erupts Into a Battle and 38 are Injured," *New York Times*, August 8, 1988; Stephen A. Holmes, "A Neighborhood Battle: Apartments or a Park?" *New York Times*, December 18, 1989; Kifner, "Worlds Collide."

36. John Kifner, "Tent City in Tompkins Square Park Is Dismantled by Police," *New York Times*, December 15, 1989, p. B1.

37. Marcus, *Where Have All the Homeless Gone*, 135; Wagner, *Checkerboard Square*, 17–18; Talmadge Wright, *Out of Place: Homeless Mobilizations, Subcities and Contested Landscapes* (Albany: State University of New York Press, 1997), 4–7.

38. Rob Teir, "Restoring Order in Public Spaces," *Texas Review of Law and Politics* 2 (1998): 255–91; Harry Simon, "Towns Without Pity: A Constitutional and Historical Analysis of Official Efforts to Drive Homeless Persons from American Cities," 66 *Tulane Law Review* (March 1992): 631–76.

39. An overview of leisure camping as family activity in the post–World War II era can be found in Susan Sessions Rugh, *Are We There Yet?: The Golden Age of American Family Vacations* (Lawrence: University Press of Kansas, 2008), ch. 5. See also Peter Boag, "Outward Bound: Family, Gender, Environmentalism and the Postwar Camping Craze, 1945–1970," *Idaho Yesterdays* 50 (Spring 2009): 3–15."]

40. "How to Urban Camp," wikiHow.com, June 1 2007, http://www.wikihow.com/Urban-Camp accessed, August 19, 2007. As its creators define the site: "wikiHow is a collaborative

writing project aiming to build the world's largest how-to manual. Our mission is to provide free and useful instructions to help people solve the problems of everyday life."

41. This is not to romanticize the homeless as leading some sort of ideal outdoor life, but rather to suggest that stigmatizing their uses of urban nature does little to address the historical questions prompted by acts of sleeping outside. William Cronon opened up new debate about the split understandings of nature and divisions in environmental consciousness in "The Trouble with Wilderness; or Getting Back to the Wrong Nature," in *Uncommon Ground: Toward Reinventing Nature,* ed. William Cronon (New York: Norton, 1995), 65–90. Rebecca Solnit meditated on the relationship of natural beauty to moments of coercion and places of degradation in several essays in her collection, *Storming the Gates of Paradise: Landscapes for Politics* (Berkeley: University of California Press, 2007), 2–3, 135–39, 172–75, 225–53.

42. Sacramento's tent city aroused a great deal of national commentary in the winter and spring of 2009, appearing in major media outlets from National Public Radio to *Oprah.* Katharine Q. Seelye, "Sacramento and Its Riverside Tent City," *New York Times,* March 11, 2009, http://thelede.blogs.nytimes.com/2009/03/11/tent-city-report/?apage=2, accessed March 11, 2009; Maria L. La Ganga, "In Sacramento's tent city, a torn economic fabric," *Los Angeles Times,* March 20, 2009, http://www.latimes.com/news/local/la-me-tent-city20-2009mar20,0,3125317.story?page=2, accessed March 20, 2009; Jesse McKinley, "Cities Deal with Surge in Shantytowns," *New York Times,* March 26, 2009, http://www.nytimes.com/2009/03/26/us/26tents.html, accessed March 26, 2009; Richard Gonzales, "In Sacramento, Tent-City Dwellers Want to Stay," National Public Radio, April 16, 2009, http://www.npr.org/templates/story/story.php?storyID=102448047, accessed April 16, 2009.

43. For insightful discussion of the cultural representations and politics of nature and technology, see John P. Herron, "The Call in the Wild: Nature, Technology and Environmental Politics," in *The Political Culture of the New West,* ed. Jeff Roche (Lawrence: University Press of Kansas, 2008), 310–31. For an example of the promotion of camping as a frugal vacation alternative see John D. Sutter, "In a slump, camping comes into vogue," CNN.com, March 26, 2009, http://www.cnn.com/2009/TRAVEL/03/26/camping.economy.index.html, accessed March 26, 2009. Identification of camping equipment, from Coleman lanterns to REI tents, derived from images included in the newspaper and media reports cited in note 42 as well as the following photo galleries: "Tent City in Sacramento, California," *The Guardian,* March 20, 2009, http://www.guardian.co.uk/world/gallery/2009/mar/20/tent-city-homeless-sacramento-california?picture=344877292, accessed March 26, 2009; "Tent City," sfgate, Home of the *San Francisco Chronicle,* March 6, 2009, http://www.sfgate.com/cgi-bin/article.cgi?f=/g/a/2009/03/06/Tent_City.DTL, accessed March 26, 2009.

City

Boundary Issues

Clarifying New Orleans's Murky Edges

ARI KELMAN

At first, there were just tiny ridges flanking the river, barely perceptible piles of Big Muddy's mud. Then, over millennia they grew, as the Mississippi deposited layers of soil during flood seasons. It happened like this: when the swollen river spread from its channel, the unconstrained torrent slackened. Without a current carrying it, suspended material sank. The heaviest sediment dropped closest to the river, with lighter silt falling farther away. So the Mississippi built its banks, earthen ramps descending gradually from its shores. We know these accretions as the river's natural levees.[1]

Eventually, the levees became useful for people, a consequence of local topography and continental geography. Native Americans knew the riverbanks as the highest, driest ground in the flat, damp delta. They shared their knowledge with Europeans who settled Louisiana. For these people, the Mississippi and its levee embodied the New World's promise. The river gathered the waters of thousands of smaller streams crisscrossing its valley, an expanse stretching from the Rockies' eastern face to the Alleghenies' western slope. More than 15,000 miles of navigable waterways make up the Mississippi system, a funnel whose spout would, it seemed, shunt trade inexorably toward the Gulf of Mexico. For boosters, the Mississippi was God's signature carved into the valley; they saw in the turbid river images of empire. And the levee was more evidence of a divine plan: an elevated spot on which to build an entrepôt where produce gathered from the North American interior could arrive at market near the river mouth.[2]

Such visions of benign nature, working in concert with imperial aspirations, prompted the French to place New Orleans on a crescent-shaped stretch of the levee in 1718. Four years later, Pierre-François-Xavier de Charlevoix, a Jesuit priest, visited. "Rome and Paris had not such considerable beginnings," he wrote, "were not built under such happy auspices, and their founders met not with those advantages on the Seine and the Tiber, which we have found on the Mississippi, in comparison of which, these two rivers are no more than brooks." Geography was destiny. The river would inevitably make New Orleans great. But not even faith in environmental determinism allowed Charlevoix to overlook grim features of the local scene: "Imagine to yourself two hundred persons, who have been sent out to build a city, and who have settled on the banks of a great river, thinking upon nothing but putting themselves under cover from the injuries of the weather." So from the first, New Orleans had a strained relationship with its environs, which seemed to guarantee and cloud its future.[3]

Geographers sum up this tension as a disparity between "site"—the particular land a city occupies—and "situation"—a more abstract measure of a metropolitan area's advantages relative to other places. New Orleans, in this formulation, was (and, to some extent, still is) blessed with a near-perfect situation. As Charlevoix noted, its location, when compared to other cities, is among the finest imaginable. The French built New Orleans on the east bank of the nation's greatest river, near its outlet, in an era before technologies began circumventing the vagaries of geography. Without railroads, cars, or planes annihilating space, the rivers of the Mississippi system were the region's principal commercial highways, leaving New Orleans in command of a vast hinterland. Just downstream from the city lay the Gulf of Mexico, which provided access to the Atlantic world of trade. River traffic was the city's economic lifeblood.

New Orleans's site may be equally bad. The city was built on sediment, the long ramp of the Mississippi's levee. The highest ground is found along the river frontage. From there the land slopes down—roughly fifteen feet over a distance of about one and a half miles—until it craters at the city's rear, where much of the ground is below sea level. Through the start of the twentieth century, a cypress wetland, known locally as the backswamp, stretched from there to the shore of Lake Pontchartrain, several soggy miles away, where the terrain climbs to the peak of the lake's levee. New Orleans, then, is a bowl ringed by bodies of water, which stare down into town like voyeurs. And because the city is surrounded by levees and sits on a high water table, there is no natural drainage, a hazard in a place that averages nearly sixty inches of rain annually. The delta, finally, is a fertile disease environment; some of the nation's deadliest epidemics have prostrated New Orleans. If Charlevoix worried over the fate of two hundred colonists seeking shelter from inclement weather in 1722, who can now forget images of thousands of New

Orleanians huddled in the Superdome, clinging to rooftops, or pleading for help following Katrina, the latest chapter in the city's long disaster history.[4]

The disjuncture between site and situation in New Orleans has always generated anxiety, much of it centered on the city's borders, especially the levees. Levees are supposed to form a boundary between the human and nonhuman worlds in New Orleans. On one side of the river levee, for instance, the Mississippi roils by the metropolis it helped create. During flood seasons, especially, the river looms high above. Onlookers crane their necks and gaze over the levee at the Mississippi, their benefactor/antagonist. On the levee's other side sits New Orleans, designed as the very antithesis of wild nature: rectilinear, orderly, a beacon of progress. But the boundary between the city and its surroundings has never been stark. A tourist visiting New Orleans in 1859 captured the juxtaposition, sublime and terrifying: "it was a fearful sight to see the vast river, more than a mile wide, rising inch by inch until it reached the top of the levee, when hundreds of ships and steamers were floating far above the level of the streets—as high, indeed as the roofs of the houses in the back streets of town." Nature and culture mingle in New Orleans, an environmental borderland where site and situation collide.[5]

The city's residents have never been satisfied with this uncertain state of affairs. Theirs is a commercial metropolis, a for-profit concern. And commerce abhors chaos, preferring predictable markets. At the same time, wild nature is a dangerous neighbor. As a result, New Orleanians have struggled to reinforce the lines dividing their city from its environs. They have, in doing so, tried to overcome problems of site to realize the promise of situation. These efforts have often focused on the levee and date back to the earliest period of settlement. In 1719, for instance, New Orleans flooded, and engineers suggested augmenting the levee to keep the city dry. They hoped to confine the Mississippi in its channel, making the river more reliable by building it artificial banks. By 1727, laborers had constructed a mound, eighteen feet wide and a yard high, stretching for a mile fronting the city. But New Orleans still flooded—including in 1735, 1775, and 1783. So throughout the French and Spanish colonial periods, workers further improved the artificial levee. Around the period of the Louisiana Purchase, flood control works snaked downstream from Baton Rouge to just below New Orleans.[6]

As for the Purchase (I'm speaking here about the Louisiana Purchase, not the purchase of Louisiana, thus the upper-case makes sense.) itself, Thomas Jefferson's interest in New Orleans had nothing to do with the specifics of the city's site and everything to do with the implications of its situation. For Jefferson, New Orleans would serve as what then was known as the West's—the Ohio and Mississippi valleys—

great metropolis. For decades, American settlers in the region had clamored for access to New Orleans, recognizing that their economic prospects depended on a so-called right of deposit in the city. Westerners had, on several occasions early in the nation's history, gone so far as to threaten to secede if federal authorities could not secure such right for them. Jefferson, then, understood what the Mississippi meant to the region, which is why he dispatched ministers to Paris to try to purchase New Orleans. When news filtered back to Washington in 1803 that Robert Livingston and James Monroe had purchased all of Louisiana, including the city of New Orleans, Jefferson believed that his vision for settling the West could finally come to fruition, because the United States now controlled the Mississippi River.[7]

But even after the Purchase, it still seemed possible that rather than sweeping the city to greatness the Mississippi might instead wash it away. Unwanted water sometimes seeped into New Orleans during flood seasons early in the American period, dimming the city's commercial prospects and threatening its citizens. The *Conseil de Ville* (city council) responded by regularizing levee improvements—the city often used enslaved African Americans, another commodity bought and sold at New Orleans's vibrant markets, for this backbreaking labor—and taxing ships docked at the waterfront to help pay for the work. Still the river would not be contained. On May 4, 1849, the levee broke fifteen miles upstream. The resulting flood submerged two hundred blocks of New Orleans and forced ten thousand people from their homes. For six weeks, low-lying parts of the city remained under water, totally obscuring New Orleans's already uncertain edge. Laborers only sealed the breach in mid-June, and water slowly receded from the city.[8]

The 1849 flood had far-reaching implications, ushering in an era of federally subsidized public works on the Mississippi. Congress passed the Swamp Land Act of 1850 and sponsored scientific surveys of the lower Mississippi undertaken by an army engineer, A. A. Humphreys, and a civilian, Charles Ellet. Although the Swamp Land Act had little impact in New Orleans, the surveys reshaped the city's levee and landscape. Ellet filed first. He suggested that human endeavors, upstream development, and levees that climbed ever skyward exacerbated the flood menace. Ellet offered a multi-tiered alternative: more levee improvements; building outlets or spillways to shunt floodwater from the river; and constructing massive reservoirs, artificial wetlands, to soak up excess rain before it ran off into the Mississippi. In highlighting the impact people had on their environment, Ellet's visionary conclusions long prefigured George Perkins Marsh's findings in *Man and Nature,* a core text for American conservationists.[9]

Andrew Atkinson Humphreys took longer than Ellet to publish. But when he did in 1861, his work had greater sway, influencing generations of hydrologists,

engineers, and politicians. Humphreys's *Physics and Hydraulics* is a hybrid document: part scientific treatise, part broadside. It is deeply researched, richly detailed,
and terribly wrong in its conclusions, which were spurred as much by Humphreys's
ambitions as his data. Humphreys hated Ellet for threatening the standing of military engineers. *Physics and Hydraulics,* consequently, undermines nearly all of
Ellet's insights, summarily dismissing outlets and reservoirs before arguing that
only "an organized levee system [can] be depended upon for the protection against
floods in the Mississippi Valley." And when Humphreys became chief of the U.S.
Army Corps of Engineers, he had a pulpit from which to help craft an enduring
policy known as "levees only."[10]

With federal agencies setting standards and absorbing two-thirds of construction costs, the city's levees reached new heights. The building boom, though, hit
high gear when Progressive city planning ideologies linked with industrial technologies. Beginning in 1890, with the formation of the Orleans Levee Board, engineers
believed they could rationalize the city's environment, finally clarifying where the
messy natural world ended and regulated spaces of urban life began. Under the
aegis of the levee board, workers moved millions of cubic yards of earth to the
waterfront. New levees rose at least three feet higher than any previous flood; at the
crown they were four to ten feet across, at the base six to seven times as wide again.
These massive public works, emblems of state power, dwarfed any flood control
efforts previously undertaken in the city. New Orleans began to resemble a village
barricaded against an impending invasion.[11]

As New Orleanians struggled to remake the levee, another boundary proved as
irksome. The backswamp confined the city to a thin strip of the Mississippi's levee:
the sliver by the river. For New Orleanians this was a problem twice over: first,
because their city could not grow, except to stretch longer; and second, because
they viewed the swamp not just as a hindrance but a danger, a source of disease.
Starting in the Spanish era, New Orleanians had tried in vain to drain the wetlands'
"deadly contents." Then, as yellow fever nearly decimated the city in 1853, it became
known as a "wet graveyard," prompting more futile drainage initiatives. As late as
1887, with rival cities embracing sanitary reform, Charles Dudley Warner visited
New Orleans on assignment for *Harper's.* He was stunned by "gutters green with
slime . . . canals in which the cat became the companion of the crawfish, and the
vegetable in decay sought in vain a current to oblivion." New Orleans had become
a joke, a city stuck in the mud.[12]

Civic leaders, buoyed by a heady combination of Progressive optimism and New
South boosterism, hoped to redeem the city's reputation by reclaiming its wetlands.
They promised that with improved artificial levees standing sentinel at the front

door and the backswamp gone from the rear, New Orleans could grow while staying dry and healthy. To do so, the city needed a "scientific system of drainage." Then
the climate abetted the reform impulse when a storm dumped more than one billion gallons of rain on New Orleans on August 13, 1894. Lacking adequate drainage,
New Orleans's bowl filled with water. There were "high tides" throughout town, and
"regattas could have been rowed on Canal Street." Just six months later, members of
the New Orleans Drainage Advisory Board presented detailed findings about how
the city could expand off the high ground of the natural levee and spread out without flooding, even during downpours.[13]

The board called for improved street gutters. The gutters would flow into branch
drains. The branch drains would lead into larger main drains. The main drains
would travel into a network of canals, some as wide as forty feet across. The canals
then would lead to a central outflow channel and would be gravity fed. The channel would be sited on the lowest point in the city to take advantage of the natural
slope leading into it. In this way, the city's topography, declining away from the
high ground on the river and lake levees, would impel the drainage inside the
new system. And pumping stations located strategically along the system's length
would maintain a powerful current for the drainage within, until a final set of huge
pumps raised the contents over the artificial levee and into a bayou that ultimately
would drain into a nearby lake.[14]

In some respects, there was nothing new about the drainage board's suggestions.
New Orleans needed to domesticate its landscapes, to secure the border between
itself and its surroundings by ensuring that water would remain where people
wanted it: either outside the levees or within the neatly delineated confines of the
drainage system. Once more New Orleans would improve its site to capitalize on
its situation. But the method for accomplishing this was new and ironic. The city
would build an artificial river system in its midst: brooks (gutters) linked to tributaries (branch drains), feeding larger tributaries (main drains), joining still bigger
tributaries (branch canals) of a trunk stream (the main channel), flowing into a
major body of water (a nearby lake). The key difference lay in the city's concave
shape. River systems must follow the earth's layout; Newtonian physics promises
that water flows downhill. New Orleans's drainage system, by contrast, would
employ artifice to control nature, using pumps to overcome the inconvenience of
gravity and the misfortune of the city's slope.

After protracted wrangling over funding, including an election in which women,
ostensibly keeping house on a municipal scale, voted in New Orleans for the first
time, construction began in 1900. Each year after that, the city advanced and the
backswamp retreated. By 1909, forty miles of canals crossed New Orleans, and

even the acid-tongued author George Washington Cable marveled: "the curtains of swamp forest are totally gone. Their sites are drained dry and covered with miles of gardened homes." Then, in 1913, A. Baldwin Wood invented screw pumps—many still operate—bearing his name, allowing the drainage works to suck up still more wetlands. A rise in assessed property narrated the system's growth and the swamp's decline: in 1890, New Orleans's tax rolls included $132 million worth of property; by 1914, that number had nearly doubled. The same year, triumphant sanitarians noted that the death rate had plummeted, from twenty-seven per one thousand at the turn of the century, to below twenty per one thousand.[15]

Observers celebrated the city's scientific management of space, both the huge levees and drained districts where new homes sprouted like kudzu. One correspondent exclaimed: "it is a transformation from medieval conditions to the standards of the twentieth century." Louisiana's state engineer, Henry Richardson, boasted: "Risk can be reduced to almost any extent." Adding: "It is only a matter of labor and cost to build levees . . . that will remain impregnable against any flood." Reformers and technocrats had seemingly cleaned up the city's muddy border with nature. Because of their good work New Orleans would be safer, prettier, and could stay open for business.[16]

It was a pipe dream, of course, born of misplaced faith in technology and willful forgetting. The levees, designed to eliminate overflows, often made things worse—as Charles Ellet had realized half a century before. With development in the Mississippi Valley ongoing, and artificial banks confining more runoff inside the channel, the river set new high-water marks in 1912, 1913, and 1922. But in each year the Mississippi carried less water than it had in earlier, lower flood seasons. New Orleans remained dry. But the city was in more danger. At the same time, the drainage system exacerbated threats it supposedly had eliminated. Wetlands, including the backswamp, though long reviled as wasted land or worse, had actually served as huge sponges—again, as Ellet had noted. Without wetlands absorbing seasonal rains, and with more paved surface area in the city each year creating more runoff, New Orleans increasingly relied on its drainage system to remove excess water. If the pumps stopped, the city would fill.[17]

Across the twentieth century, New Orleanians, surrounded by levees and beholden to drainage technologies, lived in a prison of their own making. But few people realized the danger because the city's borders with nature appeared more secure than ever. The levee hid the river. And the urban wetlands were gone. Only during catastrophes were New Orleanians forced to reckon with the peril. During the 1927 flood, for instance, the city filled with rain after the drainage system failed. New Orleans responded by dynamiting the levee downstream, a spectacle designed to reassure onlookers that the city was safe, and building improved flood-control mechanisms, including an upstream spillway. Next came Hurricane Betsy, which slammed into New Orleans in 1965. Betsy pushed a storm surge into Lake Pontchartrain, overtopping and breaching levees. It left low-lying parts of the city, including the Ninth Ward, under water for more than a week.[18]

In the years between those two disasters, the city struggled to maintain the illusion of safety. Engineers improved the drainage system, swallowing up the last of the urban swamps, and constructed miles of new levees and floodwalls. By mid-century, it seemed New Orleans had finally sorted its spaces: the city here and nature there. Which allowed for another kind of segregation: racial and socio-economic. New Orleans had been a cultural as well as environmental borderland, where rich, poor, white, and nonwhite, often lived side by side—if not by choice then necessity. Bound to the sliver of the levee for two centuries, there had been little room for exclusive enclaves. By the 1960s, though, elevated freeways connected the city with suburbs, many of which had been built on drained land. New Orleans stratified, with the poor and people of color often occupying lowlands in the city while whites fled town for new developments.[19]

Then came Katrina, whose apocalyptic particulars are too well publicized and too complicated to be entirely knowable: high winds, another storm surge, failing levees, muddy floodwater stagnating for weeks, and no clear line between the city and its surroundings. And yet some members of the committees charged with planning New Orleans's recovery still ignore the warnings written into the city's disaster history. It now appears New Orleans will try again to engineer itself out of harm's way, once more attempting to improve its levees and drainage system. The various committees seem captivated by the notion that is possible to separate the city from its surroundings, a myth that will not die, no matter how many of New Orleans's residents do.

Notes

1. Charles R. Kolb and Jack R. Van Lopik, "Depositional Environments of the Mississippi River Deltaic Plain," in Martha Lou Shirley, ed., *Deltas in their Geologic Framework* (Houston: Houston Geologic Society, 1969), 17; Roger T. Saucier, *Geomorphology and Quaternary Geologic History of the Lower Mississippi Valley* (Vicksburg: U.S. Army Corps of Engineers Waterways Experiment Station, 1994), 136–41.

2. Tristam Kidder, "Making the City Inevitable: Native Americans and the Geography of New Orleans," in Craig Colten, ed., *Transforming New Orleans and Its Environs: Centuries of Change* (Pittsburgh: University of Pittsburgh Press, 2000), 9–21; Christopher Morris, "Impenetrable But Easy: The French Transformation of the Lower Mississippi Valley and the Founding of New Orleans," in Colten, ed., *Transforming New Orleans,* 22–44.

3. François Xavier Charlevoix, *Journal of a Voyage to North America*, II, ed. and trans. Louise Phelps Kellogg (Chicago: Caxton Club, 1923), 258, 272.

4. Peirce F. Lewis, *New Orleans: The Making of an Urban Landscape* (Cambridge, MA: Ballinger Publishing, 1976), 17.

5. Quote from: T.L. Nichols, *Forty Years of American Life* (London: Longmans, Green, & Co., 1874), 132.

6. Donald W. Davis, "Historical Perspective on Crevasses, Levees, and the Mississippi River," in Colten, ed., *Transforming New Orleans*, 84–106; Benjamin G. Humphreys, *Floods and Levees of the Mississippi River* (Washington: The Mississippi River Levee Association, 1914), 19.

7. E. Merton Coulter, "The Efforts of the Democratic Societies of the West to Secure Navigation of the Mississippi," *Mississippi Valley Historical Review*, 9 (December 1924): 378–88; Ari Kelman, *A River and Its City: The Nature of Landscape in New Orleans* (Berkeley: University of California Press, 2003), 29–40.

8. George Washington Cable, *The Creoles of Louisiana* (New York: Charles Scribner's Sons, 1884), 276–84; Craig Colten, *An Unnatural Metropolis: Wrestling New Orleans from Nature* (Baton Rouge: Louisiana State University Press, 2005), 26–27; Davis, "Historical Perspectives on Crevasses," in Colten, ed., *Transforming New Orleans*, 96–97; George E. Waring and George Washington Cable, "History and Present Condition of New Orleans, Louisiana," in *Tenth Census, Report on the Social Condition of Cities*, XIX, Part 2 (Washington, DC: Government Printing Office, 1887), 249.

9. John Barry, *Rising Tide: The Great Mississippi Flood of 1927 and How it Changed America* (New York: Simon and Schuster, 1996), 36–91; Charles Ellet, *Report on the Overflows of the Delta of the Mississippi*, Senate Ex. Doc. 20, 32nd Cong., 1st Sess., 27–36; Charles Ellet, *The Mississippi and Ohio Rivers* (Philadelphia: Lippincott, Grambo, and Co., 1853), 132–134.

10. Barry, *Rising Tide*, 36–91; A. A. Humphreys and H. L. Abbot, *Report Upon the Physics and Hydraulics of the Mississippi River* (Washington, D.C.: Government Printing Office, 1867), 155, 162, 173, 176 (quote appears on page 192); Martin Reuss, "Andrew A. Humphreys and the Development of Hydraulic Engineering: Politics and Technology in the Corps of Engineers, 1850–1950," *Technology and Culture*, 26 (1985): 1–33.

11. *Act No. 93 of 1890 Creating the Orleans Levee District* (New Orleans: Hyatt Company, 1891). For the levees' growth, see *Report of the Board of State Engineers*, various years.

12. Quote one from *New Orleans Daily Picayune*, September 14, 1853. Quote two from B. Dowler, "On the Necropolis of New Orleans," *New Orleans Medical and Surgical Journal*, 7 (1850): 277. Quote three from Charles Dudley Warner, "New Orleans," *Harper's New Monthly Magazine*, XXIV (1887): 186.

13. Quote one from *Address from the Executive Committee of the Citizens Drainage and Paving Ass'n to the People of New Orleans* (New Orleans: A.W. Hyatt, 1889), 1. Quotes two and three from *New Orleans Daily Picayune*, August 14, 1894, 3. *Report on the Drainage of the City of New Orleans, by the Advisory Board* (New Orleans: T. Fitzwilliam & Co., 1895), 11, 15, 17, 34, 48–51, 71–72.

14. *Report on the Drainage of New Orleans,* 23–38.

15. Quote from George Washington Cable, "New Orleans Revisited," *The Book News Monthly,* 27 (April, 1909): 560. Martin Behrman, *New Orleans: A History of Three Great Public Utilities* (New Orleans: Brando Print, 1914), 5. For the drainage system's growth, see *Semi-Annual Report of the Sewerage and Water Board of New Orleans,* various years.

16. Quote one from Frank Putnam, "New Orleans in Transition," *New England Magazine,* XXXVI (1907): 234. Quote two from *Report of the Board of State Engineers from April 20, 1896, to April 20, 1898* (Baton Rouge: News Publishing, 1898), 119.

17. Barry, *Rising Tide,* 157–166; Colten, *Unnatural Metropolis,* 32–46, 82–107.

18. Barry, *Rising Tide,* 188–192, 228–257; Colten, *Unnatural Metropolis,* 145–46.

19. The Brookings Institution Metropolitan Policy Program, "New Orleans after the Storm: Lessons from the Past, a Plan for the Future," (October 2005), 1–42; Colten, *Unnatural Metropolis,* 149–61.

The Nature and Business of War

Drilling for Oil in Wartime Los Angeles

SARAH ELKIND

In 1942, Seaboard Oil Company proposed to drill for oil beneath Elysian Park in Los Angeles, arguing that the wells would help supply the war effort. Although support for the war ran very high, protests erupted immediately. Oil had brought a great deal of wealth to Los Angeles, but the petroleum industry had also caused a lot of damage: well-landscaped neighborhoods had turned into industrial zones, derricks loomed over cemeteries, and drilling took place in streets.[1] Prospecting caused such destruction that Los Angeles outlawed oil wells near city parks almost as soon as the city's oil industry began production in the early 1890s, and by the 1940s zoning laws protected parks and residential neighborhoods from drilling and its related development. Seaboard's proposal should have had little hope of success.

But World War II created an unusual context for American industries. Many land-use, labor, and industrial regulations seemed counterproductive, even quaint, amid total war. Federal agencies relaxed regulations and environmental protections to help the military or increase supplies of vital materials, eventually permitting salt mining in Death Valley National Monument and tungsten mining in Yosemite National Park, and loggers almost gained a free hand in Olympic National Park.[2] In changing national environmental regulations, World War II also undercut local resistance to industrial production, opening the way in Los Angeles for oil drilling even in its densest neighborhoods. This set the stage for a postwar rollback of the regulatory state and an increase in industry's dominance of the policy making at all levels of government.

Oil development had begun in Los Angeles in 1892, when Edward L. Doheny drilled a shallow well about a mile from Los Angeles's City Hall. Over the next eight years, more than a thousand wells were drilled in what became known as

the Los Angeles City Field. By 1909, California was the nation's leading oil producer, and Los Angeles oil fields were among the state's richest.[3] While oil development brought incredible wealth to the city, it also caused a myriad of problems.
New strikes brought stampedes for leases and drilling rights. Natural-gas explo-
sions, runaway wells, noise, odor, and sprayed or spilled oil befouled the community and lowered residential property values. Fires raged out of control amongst
tightly packed wooden derricks, open oil tanks, and spilled crude. One resident
who stayed in Huntington Beach despite the bedlam there, complained: "These oil
men have taken everything except the food in the icebox. . . . My back yard is an oil
well, a sump hole. My fence is gone and the inside of my house is a mess."[4]

To curb the worst excesses of oil development, in 1897 the Los Angeles City
Council passed an ordinance that prohibited drilling within 800 feet of Elysian
Park or Echo Park, or within 1,800 feet of Los Angeles's other city parks.[5] Subsequent rules forced oil companies to reduce the danger, odors, noise, and other nuisances associated with production. By the late 1920s, zoning regulations limited
where oil companies could drill in Los Angeles but, as soon became clear in Venice
Beach, these regulations could not withstand the onslaught of a rich oil strike.

In 1929, oil was discovered at Venice Beach, which Los Angeles had annexed
just three years earlier, ensuring that its industrial regulations applied there. But
these were ignored in the rapid and chaotic drilling that followed. This was in
part because locals fought against the implementation of those protective codes.
In January 1930, some five thousand Del Mar and Venice residents attended mass
meetings and public hearings to demand unrestricted drilling in the Venice-Del
Mar oil field. Thousands more signed petitions urging the city planning commission to ignore rules which would have limited drilling in residential areas. Venice's former city attorney, who sought to lease his own land in the 1930s, claimed
oil drilling was "possibly one of the most popular issues with the greatest unanim-
ity of opinion in the area as has ever been heard of."[6] The Los Angeles City Council buckled before the pressure; according to the *Los Angeles Times*, "the desire to
drill became so great in that district" that the city council could no longer refuse.[7]
Derricks, tanks, and pump houses quickly displaced homes. The remaining residents faced life in a noxious industrial zone. The consequences of almost unrestricted drilling quickly shifted public opinion.

When opposition to drilling in the Venice–Del Mar field did arise, objections
focused more on the distribution of oil wealth than on drilling itself. Oil companies did not lease all properties in an oil field. Landowners who could not lease
their property suffered all the costs of oil development but enjoyed none of its
benefits. One proposed solution was the community lease, in which a group of

homeowners leased their land as a block and shared royalties. In 1930, Venice's city council member B. M. Hansen proposed a system of community leases that would have allowed homeowners within Venice to approve or reject drilling city block by city block. This system, he argued, would protect property values within Venice, and give all residents a voice in oil development near their homes. In addition, by slowing the rate of oil pumping, community leases could increase total production from the Venice–Del Mar field by conserving the natural gas pressures necessary for extracting oil.[8]

In November 1931, Ramsey Petroleum requested that the Los Angeles City Planning Committee rezone five acres of land so it could drill diagonally, or whip-stock, from a neighborhood just north of Elysian Park into oil sands it believed lay underneath the city park.[9] All but a few of the abutting property owners supported the request and in December 1931, the city planning committee voted to allow the company to drill. The *Los Angeles Times* criticized Ramsey Petroleum's test well as "adverse to the public interest and the welfare of the city, though pleasing to particular, though short-sighted, property-owners."[10] A superior court judge soon joined the opposition, as did the city's playground and recreation commission, water and power commission and fire department, the League of Women Voters, the Los Angeles Chamber of Commerce, the Los Angeles Municipal League, and a host of neighborhood improvement associations. They constantly referred to the "fiasco at Venice" as a key reason for opposing what the *Los Angeles Times* labeled an "absurd wildcatting scheme."[11]

The public hearing on the Ramsey Petroleum's test well was raucous. Nine hundred people attended, hissing, booing, and breaking out in "wild cheering and dismal groans at every opportunity." The "hostile mob" even hooted down Charles H. Randall, the city council president whose district included the old Los Angeles City Field and Elysian Park, and who proposed rejecting the permits. A year earlier, those who insisted that land ownership included the freedom to drill for oil had won the debate; now, those neighbors who considered oil drilling an "invasion of property rights" and a threat to property values had triumphed. As opposition to the Elysian Park project grew. Randall and the *Los Angeles Times* proposed, but still could not pass, an outright ban on oil drilling in residential Los Angeles.[12]

In the early 1930s, Angelenos disagreed about whether the right to drill for oil on private property trumped the rights to abutters to protect their property from the nuisances and dangers of oil drilling; about how to resolve the competing mineral rights of all property owners in an oil field; and about the relationship between individual property rights and the communal benefit from zoning and industrial regulation. Opponents of the Venice and Elysian Park projects also emphasized the importance of real estate values and the community's prosperity. As the 1930s wore on, however, attention shifted from questions of property and community to the behavior and intentions of the oil companies themselves. Oil development on California's beaches put the industry at odds with the public.[13] A series of scandals from the early 1920s through the late 1930s—Teapot Dome; the Julian Petroleum stock fraud; and two inquiries into price fixing and violations of the Sherman Anti-Trust Act—increased public antipathy toward oil companies.[14] In all, the oil industry did not appear very trustworthy by the time World War II gave prospectors a new opportunity to look for oil in the heart of Los Angeles.

Yet the war created a state of emergency that opened the doors to unprecedented oil exploration. After all, the military's trucks, tanks, ships, and planes required unprecedented amounts of oil, just as hostilities cut the United States off from foreign supplies. The U.S. did not face a nationwide oil shortage during the war. Secretary of the Interior Harold Ickes freely acknowledged that he had imposed gasoline rationing to save rubber, not fuel. Nevertheless, the Southern California oil fields were the primary source of fuel for the navy's Pacific fleet. The war sustained those calling for aggressive oil exploration in Los Angeles. The oil industry responded briskly to wartime calls for more oil. In just two months in 1942, California producers opened one hundred new wells and increased the state's oil flow by 6 percent. One company invested so much money in drilling and exploration that it could not pay its employees.[15] Firms in Los Angeles renewed proposals for wells in protected residential sections of the city. Even though their support for the war would precipitate a reassessment of urban drilling, Angelenos remained skeptical of the oil companies' motives, and quite concerned about their city and their property values. The conflict between the need for oil and the desire to protect neighborhood integrity was central to debates over urban drilling in the 1940s, as Angelenos struggled to decide if drilling was truly necessary for the war effort or if oil companies were taking advantage of the emergency to gain access to oil that local regulations had placed off limits.

The first of the wartime urban drilling proposals came before the Los Angeles City Council a month after Pearl Harbor. In January 1942, J. E. Elliot and Shell Oil proposed a deep well in an unincorporated corner of land called the Gilmore Island, between the La Brea Tar Pits and West Hollywood. Even though Gilmore Island was unincorporated county land, the city of Los Angeles claimed the right to approve Shell's project because the wells would affect residential neighborhoods within city limits. Under pressure from the city council, Shell developed a plan for Gilmore Island that would have made it a model urban oil well. To reduce noise and odors, Shell Oil promised to house all drilling and pumping equipment inside an attractive concrete structure; to eliminate dangerous storage tanks Shell intended to transport oil to the refinery in underground pipes.[16]

Los Angeles officials faced enormous pressure to approve the Gilmore Island well. Shell consistently defended the project as necessary for the war.[17] The Secretary of the Navy, Frank Knox, and the federal Office of Production Management wrote to Los Angeles city officials urging them to approve new development of the Los Angeles city fields generally and the Gilmore Island project specifically. Residents of the neighborhoods around Gilmore Island, however, were "unimpressed" by Knox's letter, and rejected the new wells as "nothing more . . . than a wildcat oil scheme."[18] Two hundred and fifty of its residents spoke against the oil wells at a public hearing in June 1942. Mayor Fletcher Bowron initially agreed with them, vetoing the ordinance that would have annexed Gilmore Island and permitted drilling there, on the grounds that Shell's project threatened the rights of the city and the interests of nearby property owners.[19]

Bowron was outraged that oil companies wanted to use the war emergency to circumvent hard-won regulations, and he was incensed that federal officials sided with the oil companies. He also wanted to replace the existing project-by-project review of oil well permit applications with standard regulations to protect property near oil wells. Bowron did not have enough support on the city council to implement these plans. Only one city council member consistently supported Bowron on the oil issue. Roy Hampton, whose district included Elysian Park, used every parliamentary procedure he could to block projects like Gilmore Island, and continued his campaign against urban drilling when he left office. Their early opposition was trumped when late in 1942 the council narrowly approved a drilling permit for a residential neighborhood near Los Angeles harbor and overrode Bowron's previous Gilmore Island veto. Outvoted, Bowron reluctantly approved both projects, but he vowed to see to it that Shell fulfilled its promises to "eliminate noise and other nuisances" and that its wells did not "detract from the value of residents' property."[20] Shell found no oil at Gilmore Island, which saved its neighbors from ongoing operations.[21]

The green light at Gilmore Island unleashed a small flood of applications for nine new oil projects, mostly in residential areas where the council had previously—sometimes repeatedly—refused to let oil companies drill. Seaboard Oil Company's proposal for Elysian Park was typical.[22] Its plans were almost identical to Ramsey Petroleum's 1931 proposal, and Seaboard may have begun seeking oil leases for this project starting in 1937. Like Ramsey Petroleum before it, Seaboard sought permission to erect a test well on an eleven-acre site northwest of Elysian Park, near the intersection of Riverside Drive and Dallas Street, from which Seaboard hoped to whipstock under the park. The company promised to pay the city 21 percent of the revenue from oil extracted out from under city property; additional sums would go to the property owners who leased their land to the company. Like Shell at Gilmore Island, Seaboard promised to enclose its derricks and machinery to protect nearby homes from noise and damage.[23] Seaboard justified drilling under Elysian Park to help win the war, thus giving the project the same patriotic sheen that Shell had employed in its Gilmore Island bid. With these assurances, and hoping to profit from oil royalties, two thousand homeowners signed leases with Seaboard.[24]

Seaboard then brought the plan before the Los Angeles City Park Commission, which approved the Elysian Park well in late February 1943. Within a week, opponents organized a mass meeting with Mayor Bowron, the city planning commission, and council member Roy Hampton.[25] The controversy over urban drilling became a major campaign issue in least four city council races that March. Candidates Wilder W. Hartley, David Stannard, John Baumgartner, and Robert L. Burns faced constituents who held "indignation mass meetings" if their representatives endorsed a drilling project in their neighborhoods, as well as oil companies that "vowed vengeance" if a council member or candidate opposed oil wells. Hartley and Stannard both decided to take on the oil companies rather than the voters. Harley declared himself opposed to new wells in the residential areas of his Wilmington district, while Stannard, of Venice, tried to ban new oil wells within a half mile of all the beaches in the city of Los Angeles and adjacent communities.[26]

The council elected that March included more opponents of city drilling than had sat on the previous council, but the newly elected representatives did not take office until July 1943. In the interim, the lame-duck city council continued to approve drilling permits. They insisted they would not let drilling "affect the rights of residential property," but their votes on urban-drilling proposals seemed to place greater emphasis on the development of oil supplies. Mayor Bowron blocked their actions with his veto and began drafting a new uniform ordinance on urban drilling.[27]

The most controversial paragraph in Bowron's May 1943 proposal required all new wells in residential areas to close six months after the end of the war, and gave the city's zoning administrator power to prohibit oil operations that he or she judged would "cause grave harm to" or "diminish seriously the value or detract from the use" of adjacent property.[28] Many public officials did not think Bowron's draft went far enough. The city planning commission, for example, wanted to ban urban drilling outright, and yet accepted its spirit "because the Federal government had stated that the oil industry must produce great quantities of oil for war purposes at the earliest possible date."[29]

Oil companies accepted regulations requiring them to reduce the impact of their wells on nearby property, but they adamantly opposed time limits on oil production. Accordingly, they pushed through amendments that extended their operating window first to three and then to seven years after the war ended. They insisted as well that they needed to operate wells for many years to recover construction costs, and that modern drilling technology made such strict limits unnecessary. The industry organ, *Petroleum World,* published articles that insisted that only initial well drilling caused any significant disruption, and public fears were entirely unfounded because modern drilling practices would never produce another oil field as chaotic and dangerous as Venice, or the even more notorious Signal Hill field.[30]

Angelenos who had experienced the bedlam of residential oil drilling in the 1920s and 1930s had ample reason for skepticism about these rosy predictions, but the oil industry had so much support in Washington that their critics had trouble implementing Bowron's proposed regulations. In addition to Secretary of the Navy Knox, whose calls for more oil "to win the battle of the Pacific" gave the petroleum industry a critical military justification for expanded oil production, the industry enjoyed support from Harold Ickes and from the Petroleum Administration for the War (PAW). Ickes and PAW rejected Los Angeles's proposed regulations, and PAW wanted to streamline the permitting process for new oil wells and decentralize regulatory oversight to increase oil production.[31] Ickes had staffed the agency with petroleum-industry experts, three-quarters of whom came from oil companies, and then put the organization in the hands of a former vice president of Standard Oil of California. Industry influence was compounded by the PAW's dependence upon a group of oil executives, the Petroleum Industry War Council, for policy recommendations.[32] This type of industry-government collaboration was not unusual during World War II, and was seen as essential to secure industry cooperation with the federal government's unprecedented intervention in the economy. But the integration of oil executives into the federal policy-making apparatus gave them far greater influence over Los Angeles's oil regulations than their local opponents enjoyed.

That is why Bowron and his two main allies against urban drilling, city council member Roy Hampton and attorney Marshall Stimson, found the oil industry's influence in Washington and military and strategic justifications for oil-production drilling equally impervious to their opposition. Hampton and Bowron agreed that approving oil wells in residential neighborhoods, even to win the war, set a dangerous precedent that threatened to turn the whole city into an oil field.[33] When Hampton said this, he was recalling what happened in Venice in the 1930s, but

Bowron was also thinking of Oklahoma City, a city he visited in 1943 and where oil wells had spread rapidly from unincorporated territory on the outskirts of town through poor neighborhoods then into rich residential districts, and finally onto the grounds of the state capitol itself.[34] Bowron and Hampton also concurred that oil companies should not drill in residential areas unless absolutely necessary, and that the federal government had neither fully exploited alternatives nor proven that the Navy really needed Los Angeles's oil.[35]

Marshall Stimson took an even harder line against urban drilling. He owed his prominence in Los Angeles to his role in breaking the Southern Pacific Railroad's monopoly over Los Angeles harbor.[36] He shared with his allies an acute sense that oil drilling initiated an "endless damaging chain" that allowed drilling to spread, with devastating consequences for the community. But Stimson also challenged the prodrilling side's property-rights arguments, repeatedly citing cases of absentee landowners who profited from oil from afar, damaging resident landowners' property and investments with impunity. Stimson clearly sympathized with the actual residents of oil-producing neighborhoods, and implied that their wishes had far more legitimacy than those of absentee landowners.[37]

He also argued that oil wells caused damage "to the city as a whole [that] would far outweigh any possible gain that might arise from drilling in certain limited areas," and demanded that before the Los Angeles oil fields were tapped the U.S. Navy should open the Elk Hills Naval Petroleum Reserve; finally, Stimson believed that the paw should ease production restrictions in rural areas.[38] "The Government will get quicker oil and more of it by removing these restrictions than by drilling in the City of Los Angeles," he argued, "and any citizen of Los Angeles has a right to demand that that be done first." The fact that the Department of the Interior and the Petroleum Administration for the War had refused to do this, was evidence, Stimson believed, that major oil companies just wanted to use the war to gain access to oil that had been off-limits during peacetime; and that the nation's largest oil firms controlled federal oil policy, to the detriment of small oil producers, Los Angeles, and the public interest.[39]

Even with articulate and aggressive critics like Hampton and Stimson speaking out against urban drilling, Mayor Bowron had to walk a fine line when challenging the oil industry and paw; he moved cautiously, often delaying and moderating his position until he had a clear sense of public opinion and of the real options open to the city. In addition, he and the city council jockeyed for political influence, which prompted the mayor to veto ordinances that he had sponsored and to convene multiple public hearings on urban drilling while claiming to have no fixed opinion on the question. Bowron needed public opinion behind him if he was to take on

PAW. His actions in the summer of 1943 reflect the delicate balance he struck to marshal public opinion against new drilling in residential Los Angeles.

In late June, the lame-duck city council passed Bowron's model ordinance and linked it to a drilling proposal for an abandoned golf course in Westwood, and the mayor then held a series of public hearings on drilling that July and August. Many opponents of drilling warned that city-sanctioned oil wells would start the city down a slippery slope; they disputed the navy's claims that it needed oil from residential areas; they complained that oil production would devastate property values; and questioned the oil industry's motives, insisting that oil production end when peace returned. The Angelenos who spoke at these hearings regarded the oil industry as "a selfish type of enterprise," and called upon city officials to protect their real estate investments.[40] Others, such as the spokesperson for residents of Elysian Heights, drew a sharp line between the public good and the interests of the oil companies. Urban drilling, he declared, would "set up a monopoly by the oil companies *not* in the best interests of the majority of the citizens." He raised the specter of political corruption, too, reasoning that if the city controlled oil drilling through a political process, the oil companies would have no choice but to enter politics as the railroads had decades earlier. Perhaps the most damaging sentiment was voiced by the secretary-manager of the Beverly Hills Chamber of Commerce who feared "that there is a group hiding behind the American flag, working for a selfish interest."[41]

Ironically, in the summer of 1943 Bowron vetoed his own model ordinance to pursue regulations that would force the oil companies to close oil wells at the end of the war.[42] Harold Ickes rejected Bowron's proposals, and Herbert R. Gallagher, director of the Los Angeles office of PAW told the city council that he wanted "every field and pool in the state, including those within the city of Los Angeles" developed as swiftly as possible.[43] Under pressure from Ickes and Gallagher, Bowron reluctantly changed his position and approved Seaboard's Elysian Park well. The city council approved the Elysian Park well a few months later, but not before Seaboard Oil's attorney accused one council member of threatening to "impose conditions so stringent that no private enterprise could undertake drilling at any time."[44] Residents of the neighborhood were deeply disappointed; some four hundred property owners had demanded that the city limit oil operations to the duration during public hearings on the Elysian Park well.[45] Bowron's hopes for a uniform oil ordinance were frustrated, but oil executives were convinced that the Elysian Park well would be so "unobjectionable" that opposition to urban drilling would soon "dissipate." They reassured the Los Angeles public that "The company recognizes its responsibility to the public and will conform with the provisions of farsighted city planning."[46]

After Bowron signed the Elysian Park ordinance, approval of additional oil wells soon followed, but the long delays from repeated public hearings and careful manipulation of parliamentary procedure allowed a sense of urgency to settle around the oil-drilling issue. In November 1943, council member John Baumgartner's frustration erupted: "Oil that geologists are certain is underlying the Fox Hills area might well be on the way right now to our boys fighting the Japs in the Pacific if it were not for these kind [sic] of tactics." Council member Carl Rasmussen joined him, calling his colleagues "dilatory."[47] Apparently, the California State Assembly agreed; a special assembly interim committee convened hearings on Los Angeles's oil policies in mid-November 1943. The Citizen News, one of Los Angeles smaller newspapers, blamed Bowron and quoted city council member Ira J. McDonald excoriating Bowron for "using the oil issue as a political football." Meanwhile, Seaboard began drilling the Elysian Park well in May 1944, despite a lawsuit that former city council member Roy Hampton had filed.[48] In mid-June, Seaboard discovered that it had sunk hundreds of thousands of dollars, and a lot of political capital, on a "duster" that would produce no more oil than the so-called model well at Gilmore Island.[49]

Bowron claimed to have signed the Elysian Park ordinance only because of "a conviction, based upon indisputable evidence, that there is a shortage of oil for war purposes, particularly on the West Coast," but his correspondence with the city council reflected his continued opposition to urban drilling on principle, and his belief that the companies applying for urban drilling permits were "not actuated by purely patriotic motives but by expectation of profit," because no company yet had offered to limit production to the duration. He never really believed that the oil shortage was as desperate as the PAW claimed; supporting this contention was PAW's decision to limit production from some California oil wells in November 1943. He also thought that the Department of the Interior and the navy should have reduced the fuel sent to surplus butadiene and aluminum production rather than permit the oil industry to ruin his city. Not long after Seaboard received final permission to drill at Elysian Park, Bowron announced that he would oppose any further urban oil wells until the question of urban drilling was submitted to voters for their approval.[50]

It is unclear which way a referendum on urban oil drilling would have gone. Strong opposition to oil wells continued in most affected neighborhoods, but commitment to the war effort tempered that opposition. Some Angelenos remained adamant that sacrificing everything, including their homes and communities, to defeat the Axis was not worth it; others who opposed drilling in residential areas in principal expressed some willingness to accept oil wells if oil companies also sacrificed. These comments by homeowners were typical: "If the government really needs the oil, I will let them drill in my front yard and turn the proceeds over to the Red Cross, if they will agree to stop when the war is over."[51] Another fumed: "The Government took my son and can take my oil—but why should I ruin my home to make an oil company richer?"[52] In this, Angelenos merely carried the oil companies' and the PAW's claims of a war emergency to their logical conclusion. Even those willing to accept oil wells as an emergency measure could not countenance "wrapping the flag" around urban drilling for profit, and as long as the oil companies fought all time limits on production from urban wells, these Angelenos could not accept urban drilling.

Others believed that the war justified expanded oil production. This position was clearly demonstrated by a series of letters printed in the *Los Angeles Times* in February 1944, which the newspaper had solicited to gauge public opinion. In an editorial introducing the letters, the *Times* reported that 90 percent of correspondents favored urban drilling for the war effort, but also noted that a local oil company had published a circular urging Angelenos to show their support for oil wells. The letters were, if anything, enthusiastic about the war, but less sanguine about the oil wells. In the most poignant of these, Ora E. Knight argued: "There are so many things we have had to put up with and endure because of the war effort that it seems positively infantile nonsense to make such a fuss over aesthetics. If I could have a seat on the bus every day, for instance, I would be happy to sit in the shadow of an oil well. If I could only have my friends and relatives back from the service an oil well even within a few hundred yards would not make me unhappy."[53] She was probably not the only one to feel this way.

Debate over urban drilling dragged on for several more years. The city council did not pass uniform rules governing drilling within the city limits until February 1945. In the meantime, the Westwood golf course was rejected again in August 1944. Seaboard sought and received permission to drill what turned out to be a modestly productive well in Chavez Ravine, a far poorer and politically weaker community than Westwood, in September 1944.[54] The Wilmington wells, which Bowron had vetoed in 1942, received necessary zoning variances in February 1945. A few months later, the Dumm Brothers Petroleum Corporation secured permission to drill in the Lincoln Heights neighborhood, about two miles east of Chavez Ravine.[55] Oil companies continued to press for oil development of residential neighborhoods after the war. They could no longer cite the war, so they argued for new wells near the airport and in Boyle Heights on the grounds that the city's and state's future depended upon "oil, oil and more oil."[56]

World War II changed oil politics in Los Angeles and the nation by introducing patriotism into what had been a conflict over property rights, zoning, and urban environmental regulations. Between 1942 and 1945, in speeches, public hearings, and newspaper articles, the oil companies and their opponents each tried to depict themselves as more patriotic than other stakeholders. The oil companies clearly had the upper hand in this rhetorical conflict; they simply had to describe their plans as necessary for the war effort to make their case; the navy, Ickes, and PAW all supported these claims. This consigned Bowron, Stimson, and their allies to questioning the oil companies' motives, or attempting to redefine patriotism to include protecting the community from uncontrolled industrial development. Thus in a 1943 letter to Ickes, Stimson declared, "I know there is no patriotism in their efforts to open up the City of Los Angeles" for oil drilling.[57] Likewise, Bowron used the oil companies' objections to his model ordinance against them, arguing that if Los Angeles residents had to sacrifice their homes to fuel the navy, the oil industry should be willing to risk economic loss to win the war. That they worked so hard to protect their profits, Bowron insisted, proved that they were motivated by greed not patriotism. City council president Remsen D. Bird acknowledged a different use of patriotism in these debates when he complained that the oil companies' and federal officials' constant references to the war put him "in the position of being unpatriotic" if he sought to restrict drilling.[58]

The attempts to connect urban drilling and its regulation to patriotism cast local resource policy issues in terms which quelled opposition and undermined industrial regulations. World War II not only allowed the oil industry to gain access to areas that Los Angeles had placed off-limits to it, but wartime policy changes and institutions also allowed American businesses to redefine national policy goals. During and after the war, a new emphasis on economic growth overshadowed prewar policies designed to mitigate corporate influences. In Los Angeles, this policy realignment extended far beyond oil, as city and county officials instituted air-pollution control policies that rigidly controlled household pollution but emphasized technological change and cooperation with industries, and flood-control structures that sacrificed recreation and small-scale agriculture to protect industry. Given the explosive growth of industry, industrial jobs, and population in Los Angeles during World War II, elected officials' attention to industrial prosperity is understandable. However, the story of urban drilling in Los Angeles also reveals the ways in which a national emergency can undermine legal protections that communities establish to limit powerful interests, protect minorities and civil rights, or shape their environment. This was true during World War II, it was true during the Cold War anti-Communist campaigns, and it is equally true now.

Notes

1. On the impact of the migration of Texas and Oklahoma oil workers on Los Angeles society, see Douglas Flamming, *Bound for Freedom: Black Los Angeles in Jim Crow America* (Berkeley: University of California Press, 2005). Works on oil regulation range from Hugh Gorman's excellent study of federal oil pollution regulation, *Redefining Efficiency: Pollution Concerns , Regulatory Mechanisms, and Technological Change in the U.S. Petroleum Industry* (Akron, OH: University of Akron Press, 2001) and J. G. Clark's *Energy and the Federal Government: Fossil Fuel Policies, 1900-1946* (Cambridge: Knopf, 1987), to William R. Freudenberg and Robert Gramling, *Oil in Troubled Waters: Perceptions, Politics, and the Battle over Offshore Drilling* (Albany: State University of New York Press, 1994) and Robert Engler, *The Politics of Oil: A Study of Private Power and Democratic Directions* (New York: Macmillan, 1961). Other works on the history of oil in the United States include Gerald D. Nash, *United States Oil Policy, 1890-1964* (Pittsburgh: University of Pittsburgh Press, 1968); Roger M. Olien and Diana Davids Olien, *Oil and Ideology: The Cultural Creation of the American Petroleum Industry* (Chapel Hill: University of North Carolina Press, 1999); and Daniel Yergin, *The Prize: The Epic Quest for Oil, Money, and Power* (New York: Simon & Schuster, 1991). For more information on the Los Angeles city fields and the impact of oil on the development and politics on Los Angeles, see Fred W. Viehe, "Black Gold Suburbs: the Influence of the Extractive Industry on the Suburbanization of Los Angeles, 1890-1930," *Journal of Urban History* 8:1 (1981): 3-26; and Nancy Quam-Wickam, "'Cities Sacrificed on the Altar of Oil': Popular Opposition to Oil Development in 1920s Los Angeles," *Environmental History* 3:2 (1998): 189-209. For an excellent study of the California oil industry, see Paul Sabin, *Crude Politics: The California Oil Market, 1900-1940* (Berkeley: University of California Press, 2005).

2. Gerald Nash, *World War II and the West: Reshaping the Economy* (Lincoln: University of Nebraska Press, 1990), 158-60; Clayton Koppes, "Environmental Policy and American Liberalism," *Environmental History* 7 (1983), 23, 27. According to Robert Engler, the oil industry has consistently sought rights to drill for oil on public lands. See Robert Engler, *The Politics of Oil: A Study of Private Power and Democratic Directions* (New York: McMillan, 1961), p. 3.

3. Freudenberg and Gramling, *Oil in Troubled Waters*, 15, 72-73; Yergin, *The Prize*, 25, 28-9.

4. The *Los Angeles Times* (hereafter *LAT*) contains many descriptions of the chaos and filth that accompanied oil development. Los Angeles city leaders repeatedly sought to curb the impact of oil development. See for example "Measures to Stop the Oil Nuisance," *LAT*, 3 May 1901; "War to Bar Oil Leaks in Sea Starts," *LAT*, 9 Nov. 1926; "Oil Pollution Evil Banished," *LAT*, 21 March 1929; Proquest. For residents' reactions to Huntington Beach drilling, see Jim Combs, "Another Oil Boom Brings Chaos to Huntington Beach," *Fortnight* 18:6 (16 Mar 1953), 11-13. Although this resident protested oil development, according to Combs, most Huntington Beach residents were so money-struck that they welcomed oil in spite of the chaos and

filth it brought to their neighborhoods. Even the oil company acknowledged the impact of drilling on property values, particularly when it affected oil company-sponsored residential real estate development or the value of oil executives' homes. See for example, "Obsequies of Oiley Oozers," *LAT*, 19 Nov. 1905, and "Oil Spoils Country Places," *The Oil Age* 8:3 (March 1917): 17. See also Yergin, *The Prize*, 219-20.

5. "That Oil Ordinance," *LAT*, 25 Jan. 1897. From Proquest.

6. Mrs. R. Blum to Los Angeles City Council, 5 Feb. 1930, City Archives Box A435, Communication #1319; Bertha S. Edwards to Los Angeles City Council and Planning Commission, 10 Feb. 1930, City Archives Box A435, Communication #1307. George Acret, "Summary of the Venice Oil Situation," City Archives Box A434, Communication #879; Spencer H. Horner to Councilman E. Webster, "Resolution" 8 Feb. 1930, City Archives Box A435, Communication #1308.

7. "Venice Rushes to Drill," *LAT*, 31 March 1930, from Proquest.

8. B. M. Hansen to Los Angeles City Council, 6 Feb. 1930, City Archives Box A434, Communication #1167. For complaints by property owners denied leases, see Mrs. R. Blum to Los Angeles City Council, 5 Feb. 1930, City Archives Box A435, Communication #1319; Bertha S. Edwards to Los Angeles City Council and Planning Commission, 10 Feb. 1930, City Archives Box A435, Communication #1307.

9. "New Municipal Oil Hunt Pends," *LAT*, 26 Jan. 1931, from Proquest. For some years, geologists had postulated that "rich oil stratum" that might out produce the legendary Signal Hill field lay under the park. In 1937, a crevasse opened in the bluff of Elysian Park that looms over Riverside Drive. The city engineers blamed the impending landslide on seepage from the nearby Elysian Park reservoir, but the *Los Angeles Times* reported a theory that high gas pressures associated with oil deposits under the park had caused the problem. See "Landslide Peril Nearer," *LAT*, 20 Nov. 1937, Proquest.

10. "Oil Drillers' Hearing Rests," *LAT*, 12 Dec. 1931; "Oil Test Voted Near Park Site," *LAT*, 30 Dec. 1931. For the *Los Angeles Times*'s criticism of Ramsey Petroleum's test well, see "Unwise Oil Drilling Plan," *LAT*, 2 Jan. 1932, in Proquest.

11. "Yankwich Protests Oil Plans," *LAT*, 14 Jan. 1932; "Hearing Slated on Oil Drilling," *LAT*, 18 Jan. 1932; "Women Add Protest on Oil Drilling," *LAT*, 19 Jan. 1932; "Oil Aftermath Clean-Up Asked," *LAT*, 20 Jan. 1932; "Clamour Raised at Oil Hearing," *LAT*, 22 Jan. 1932, all in Proquest; "Against Drilling in Residential Districts," *The Municipal League Bulletin* 9 (20 Jan. 1932), 3-5; "Hearing Slated on Oil Drilling," *LAT*, 18 Jan. 1932; "That Oil-Drilling Scheme," *LAT*, 19 Jan. 1932, both in Proquest.

12. "Clamour Raised at Oil Hearing," *LAT*, 22 Jan. 1932; "Oil Aftermath Clean-Up Asked," *LAT*,, 20 Jan. 1932;"Oil Drilling Move Killed," *LAT*, 29 Jan. 1932; "Oil Drilling Scotched," *LAT*, 30 Jan. 1932; "Randall Would Restrict Areas for Oil Drilling," *LAT*, 30 Jan. 1932; "Oil Drilling Ban Favored," *LAT*, 4 Feb. 1932. News coverage of residential drilling and control of oil drilling diminished significantly over the course of the spring of 1932. The issue reappeared, briefly, after the city planning committee approved an oil drilling permit for the Del Rey Hills near

Loyola University, and again in 1936, with drilling proposals for Redondo Beach. See "Stop that Oily Business," *LAT*, 27 July 1932, in Proquest; "City Council Takes Stand Against Town Lot Oil Drilling," *Redondo Reflex*, 1 May 1936.

13. For a description of some of the conflicts that arose with oil development along the beaches, see Sarah S. Elkind, "Black Gold and the Beach: Offshore Oil, Beaches and Federal Power in Southern California," *Journal of the West* 44:1 (2005), 8–17.

14. "Mamma Spank," *Time*, 18 Oct. 1937, 63; "Oil Price Fixing: Sixteen Companies Convicted under the Sherman Act," *Newsweek*, 31 Jan. 1938, 31–32; "War Stills Oil Turmoil," *Business Week*, 16 Sept. 1939, 17–18. For a detailed account of the Julian Petroleum scandal, see Jules Tygiel, *The Great Los Angeles Swindle: Oil, Stocks and Scandal during the Roaring Twenties*, (Berkeley: University of California Press, 1994). Allegations surfaced before Pearl Harbor that the large oil companies' anticompetitive practices caused local shortages. See Michael Straight, "Double-Cross in Oil," *New Republic*, 20 Oct. 1949, 501–2.

15. "California Petroleum Situation—December 1942," 8 Feb. 1943, in "Statistics: California Situation," Petroleum Administration for the War Records, Box 138, National Archives, Laguna Niguel, California. According to this memo, in December 1942 California drillers had 18,500 wells producing 774,000 barrels of oil per day. This was the largest output since November 1929. "Minutes of the Annual Meeting of Shareholders of Burnoel Petroleum Corporation," 31 July 1942, in Burnoel Petroleum Company Papers, Huntington Library.

16. Howard Kegley, "California Oil News," *LAT*, 21 Feb. 1942; "Gilmore Island Oil Drilling Plea Supported by Knox," *LAT*, 27 May 1942; "Gilmore Area Addition Seen," *LAT*, 9 Oct. 1942, all in Proquest. The A. F. Gilmore Company was part of a local business empire that included a dairy farm, oil company, real estate, and sports facilities including the city's first baseball arena. The A. F. Gilmore Company survives today as the owner and operator of an upscale shopping mall and what it bills as "the original Farmer's Market" at Fairfax Boulevard and Third Street. For Shell Oil's involvement at Gilmore Island, see "Oil Drilling Vote Deferred," *LAT*, 27 June 1942.

17. "Gilmore Island Oil Drilling Opponents Ask for More Time," *LAT*, 4 June 1942; "Proposed Gilmore Strip Oil Drilling Debated," *LAT*, 18 June 1942, Proquest.

18. Proposed Gilmore Strip Oil Drilling Debated," *LAT*, 18 June 1942, Proquest. The *Los Angeles Times* listed the Wilshire District Civic League, the Miracle Mile Association, and an "oil man" named Byron D. Seaver among the opposition. For federal support for Gilmore Island drilling, see "Gilmore Island Oil Drilling Plea Supported by Knox," *LAT*, 27 May 1942; O. P. M. Urges Permit to Drill for Oil on Gilmore 'Island,'" *LAT*, 28 May 1942, both in Proquest.

19. "Mayor Vetoes Oil Ordinance," *LAT*, 22 Sept. 1942, Proquest.

20. "Gilmore Island Oil Drilling Program Speeded," *LAT*, 30 Oct. 1942, Proquest. For an example of Roy Hampton's campaign, see "Oil Drilling Vote Deferred," *LAT*, 27 June 1942, Proquest.

21. "Oil Muddle in the City of Los Angeles," *Petroleum World*, August 1943, 21; and "Oil Drilling Policy Sought," *LAT*, 19 May 1943.

22. Howard Kegley, "California Oil News," *LAT*, 5 Nov. 1942, Proquest. In the aftermath of the approval of Gilmore Island, oil companies came forward with proposals to drill in the Salt Lake Field, the Sherman field, Fox Hills Country Club, the Westwood Hills Golf Course, on La Cienaga at Third Street, near the Chatsworth Reservoir on Woodlake Avenue, west of LAX airport, and at Soto and Valley Blvd near the site of the Ascot Speedway. See "Oil Drilling Interest Soars," *LAT*, 15 Dec. 1942; "Oil Drilling Vote Deferred," *LAT*, 27 June 1942, Proquest.

23. Howard Kegley, "Oil News," *LAT*, 4 Sept. 1937, from Proquest. "Ruling on Elysian Park Oil Drilling Deferred," *LAT*, 11 Aug. 1943; "Oil Decision Put Off Again," *LAT*, 18 Aug. 1943; "Planning Board Backs Elysian Park Oil Test," *LAT*, 25 Aug. 1943, all in Proquest.

24. "Standard of California's War Program," *Petroleum World*, 40 (Aug. 1943): 22; "Oil Shortage Facing State, Says Attorney," *LAT*, 2 Sept. 1943; "Ruling on Elysian Park Oil Drilling Deferred," *LAT*, 11 Aug. 1943, both from Proquest.

25. "Elysian Park Oil Drilling Offers to Be Sought Today," *LAT*, 25 Feb. 1943; "Bowron and Hampton to Address Meeting," *LAT*, 2 March 1943, both from Proquest.

26. "Oil Becomes Factor in City Elections," *LAT*, 29 March 1943; "Council Asked to Ban Beach Oil Drilling," *LAT*, 26 Feb. 1943; "Attack on Oil Drilling Move Proves Futile," *LAT*, 17 April 1943, both from Proquest.

27. "Council Defers Action on Wilmington Drilling," *LAT*, 6 May 1943; "Oil Drilling Law Backed," *LAT*, 12 June 1943. On Bowron's ordinance, see "Oil Drilling Policy Sought," *LAT*, 19 May 1943, Proquest. On the impact of the March 1943 elections on the city's oil policy, see "Oil Drilling Veto Upheld by Councilmen," *LAT*, 10 July 1943; "Oil Becomes Factor in City Elections," *LAT*, 29 March 1943; "Oil-Drilling Ordinance Brings Fight in Council," *LAT*, 22 June 1943 all in Proquest; and "Council Balks Oil Drilling in Westwood," *Los Angeles News*, 29 Aug. 1944, in Clippings, Bowron Collection.

28. "Oil Drilling Law Backed," *LAT*, 12 June 1943, Proquest.

29. Ibid.

30. "Oil Muddle in the City of Los Angeles," *Petroleum World*, 40 (Aug 1943): 21. *Petroleum World* articles were frequently reprinted in the *Los Angeles Times* and cited in city council meetings, which helped the oil industry shape public debate over wartime drilling policy in Los Angeles. "A Noiseless Well in the Heart of the City," *Petroleum World*, 40 (Mar 1943), 30–40ff.; "Exploration for Oil Planned without Disturbing Sites," *LAT*, 14 Feb. 1943, Proquest. On the industry's reaction to protests in an earlier decade, see "Los Angeles Oil Wells in Danger of Stoppage," *The Oil Age* 15:2 (Feb. 1919): 32. For a description of the chaos that followed the discovery of oil at Signal Hill, see Yergin, *The Prize*, 219–20.

31. Carrington King, "PAW Gives California the Green Light," *Petroleum World* 40 (April 1943): 18. For the secretary of the navy's position, see Martin Van Couvering, "Searching for Oil in the City When Los Angeles Was Young—and Now!" *Petroleum World* 40 (March 1943): 56.

32. Engler, *The Politics of Oil*, 278–79. See also Harold Ickes, *Fightin' Oil* (New York: Alfred A. Knopf, 1943). On industry influence on the federal government during World War II more generally, see Alan Brinkley, *The End of Reform: New Deal Liberalism in Recession and War* (New York: Alfred A. Knopf, 1995); Alan Brinkley, *Liberalism and Its Discontents*, (Cambridge: Harvard University Press, 1998); Louis Galambos, *The Public Image of Big Business in America, 1880–1940* (Baltimore: Johns Hopkins University Press, 1975); and Koppes, "Environmental Policy and American Liberalism." These historians trace the eclipse of Progressive Era industrial regulation by mid-century policies that emphasized economic growth and cooperation between government and industry to World War II and the federal government's dependence upon industry executives to mobilize the nation's businesses for the war effort. There is, however, considerable debate over the roots of mid-twentieth-century policy shifts. In his 1962 volume, *Americans for Democratic Action* (Westport, CT: Greenwood Press, 1985), Clifton Brock attributed the changes to the influence of conservative Southern Democrats in Congress. John L. Broesamle, in *Reform and Reaction in Twentieth Century American Politics* (Westport, CT: Greenwood Press, 1990), focused on the emergence of interest-group politics and the growth economy after World War II. Lizabeth Cohen likewise emphasizes the impact of the growth economy on federal policy, although her book, *A Consumers' Republic: The Politics of Mass Consumption in Postwar America* (New York: Vintage Books, 2004), unlike Broesamle's, explores the grassroots of the new federal emphasis on material prosperity. Furthermore, a number of authors dispute that World War II substantially changed the relationship between government and business, but note instead that industry and the largest corporations benefited enormously from Progressive regulation. See for example, Samuel P. Hays, *Conservation and the Gospel of Efficiency: The Progressive Conservation Movement* (Cambridge: Harvard University Press, 1959); Nash, *United States Oil Policy, 1890–1964*; and Oliver Zunz, *Making America Corporate, 1870–1920* (Chicago: University of Chicago Press, 1990).

33. "Oil Drilling Vote Deferred," *LAT*, 27 June 1942, Proquest; "Other City Drilling Programs Proposed," *Petroleum World* 40 (Aug. 1943): 64; Marshall Stimson is quoted as criticizing the major oil companies' influence in the PAW in "Council Defeats Move to Repeal Drilling Action," *LAT*, 21 July 1943.

34. Bowron to the city council, 31 Jan. 1944, box 56, Bowron Collection. On the spread of oil wells throughout Oklahoma City and even onto the grounds of the state capital there, see Morris P. Moore, "Zoning against Oil Wells," *American City* (Sept. 1930): 157–58; and David S. Robertson, "Oil Derricks and Corinthian Columns: The Industrial Transformation of the Oklahoma State Capital Grounds," *Journal of Cultural Geography*, 16:1 (1996): 17–35.

35. "Lone Bid Submitted in Park Oil Project," *LAT*, 26 March 1943, Proquest.

36. Robert Gottlieb and Irene Wolt, *Thinking Big: The Story of the Los Angeles Times, Its Publishers, and their Influence on Southern California* (New York: G. P. Putnam's Sons, 1977), 68–71; "Marshall Stimson, Lawyer, Dies at 75," *LAT*, 28 Dec. 1951, Proquest.

37. Marshall Stimson, "Statement," 9 Feb. 1944, Box 1, "Oil Drilling in the City of Los Angeles," in Marshall Stimson Collection, HEH.

38. Marshall Stimson, "Statement," 9 Feb. 1944, Box 1, "Oil Drilling in the City of Los Angeles," in Marshall Stimson Collection, HEH; "Attack on Oil Drilling Move Proves Futile," *LAT,* 17 April 1943, from Proquest.

39. Stimson to Ickes, 19 June 1943, Box 1, "Oil Drilling in the City of Los Angeles," in Marshall Stimson Collection, HEH. See also, "Council Defeats Move to Repeal Drilling Action," *LAT,* 21 July 1943, Proquest.

40. "Notes Taken at Public hearing on the Oil Drilling Ordinance, Thursday Afternoon, July 1, 1943," 3-4, in Box 56, Bowron Papers. See specifically comments by Mr. Leland Reeder, Immediate Past President of California Real Estate Association, Mrs. Gold, and Bruce Murchison.

41. "Mr. Springer—Speaking for a Group of Neighbors in Elysian Heights,," and J. O. Smith, secretary-manager of Beverly Hills Chamber of Commerce, in "Notes Taken at Public hearing on the Oil Drilling Ordinance, Thursday Afternoon, July 1, 1943," 3-4, in Box 56, Bowron Papers.

42. "Mayor Vetoes Ordinance for Westwood Oil Drilling," *LAT,* 8 July 1943, Proquest. Bowron also vetoed the Westwood Golf Course oil well in July 1943. The council voted again on the Westwood Hills golf course proposal in January 1944, narrowly approving it. See "O. K. Oil Drilling in West L. A. Tract," *Los Angeles Herald Express,* 26 Jan. 1944; "Council Asks Oil Drilling," *Los Angeles Examiner,* 27 Jan. 1944; "Council Backs Drilling on Old Golf Course," *LAT,* 27 Jan. 1944, all in clippings, Bowron Collection.

43. As quoted in "'Every Field and Pool Must Be Drilled,'—PAW," *Petroleum World* 40:8 (August 1943): 21. See also "Mayor Asks Council's Views on Oil Drilling," *LAT,* 7 July 1943; "Mayor Proposes Safeguards for City Oil Drilling," *LAT,* 15 July 1943, both in Proquest; Ickes to Bowron, 19 Jan. 1943, 3, in Box 56, Bowron collection.

44. Bowron, as quoted in "Oil Drilling Deadlock in City May Be Broken," *LAT,* 6 Aug. 1943, Proquest; William Rains quoted in "Final Oil Hearing Set," *LAT,* 25 Sept. 1943. See also, "Oil Shortage Facing State, Says Attorney," *LAT,* 2 Sept. 1943; "Council to Get Drilling Issue," *LAT,* 24 Sept. 1943, all in Proquest.

45. "Ruling on Elysian Park Oil Drilling Deferred," *LAT,* 11 Aug. 1943, Proquest.

46. As quoted in "Elysian Park Drilling Voted," *LAT,* 9 Nov. 1943, in Proquest.

47. "Mayor Signs Oil Measure," *LAT,* 28 Nov. 1943; "Delay on Oil Issue Ends," *LAT,* 17 Nov. 1943, Proquest. After Elysian Park, the city council gave the Huntington Land & Improvement Company permission to drill Los Angeles's next urban oil well next to the Ascot Speedway at the corner of Soto Street and Valley Boulevard. Bowron vetoed the Ascot project, arguing that the city council should wait until it saw whether the Elysian Park well proved as problem-free as promised, but the council overrode his veto the next day. On the council's initial vote on Ascot, see "Council Approves New Drilling Site," *LAT,* 2 Dec. 1943. For Bowron's

veto and the council's override, see "Nullify Veto on Ascot Oil Drilling," *Los Angeles Herald,* 25 Jan. 1944; and "Council Votes Oil District," *Los Angeles Examiner,* 26 Jan. 1944, both in clippings files, Bowron Collection.

48. "Urged Red Tape Be Cut in L. A. Oil Drilling," *Los Angeles Herald Express,* 16 Nov. 1943; "Oil 'Politics' Laid to Mayor," *Citizen News,* 30 Aug. 1944, both in clippings, Bowron collection. Superior Court Judge Emmet H. Wilson decided the lawsuit in favor of drilling under the park in late January 1943, but he forbade any operations within the park itself. See "Approves Drilling Outside of Park," *Daily News,* 25 Jan. 1944; "Elysian Oil Warning Given," *Los Angeles Examiner,* 25 Jan. 1944; "Park Whipstock Well Approved," *LAT,* 25 Jan. 1944, all in clippings files, Bowron Collection. For the rest of the story on Hampton's lawsuit, see "Elysian Drilling Injunction Asked," *LAT,* 18 Dec. 1943; "Park Drilling Must Wait," *LAT,* 18 Jan. 1944; Howard Kegley, "California Oil News," *LAT,* 16 Jan. 1944; "Elysian Park Oil Project Approved," *LAT,* 28 Jan. 1944; Howard Kegley, "California Oil News," *LAT,* 12 Feb. 1944; Howard Kegley, "California Oil News," *LAT,* 6 May 1944; "Soundproof Oil Drills Start in Elysian Park," *LAT,* 24 May 1944, all in Proquest.

49. "Elysian Park Test Oil Well Proves 'Duster,'" *LAT,* 23 June 1944, Proquest.

50. Bowron to the city council, 31 January 1944, 3, Box 56; "Oilmen Denounce Ickes Output Cut in Gas Crisis," *LAT,* 17 Nov. 1943; "Mayor Urges Special Ballot on Oil Drilling," *LAT,* 1 Feb. 1944; "Mayor Urges Special Ballot on Oil Drilling," *LAT,* 1 Feb. 1944, all in Clippings, Bowron Collection. See also, "Mayor Signs Oil Measure," *LAT,* 28 Nov. 1943, Proquest

51. As quoted in "Larger Reserve of Oil Urged at Council Hearing," 24 June 1943, Proquest. For readers' letters on the subject of urban drilling, see R. G. Winter, "Why the Delay;" Mrs. A. L. Gribling, "Wells Favored;" Kenneth J. McIntosh, "Why Limit It;" Olga Dickenson, "Produce it Quickly," and P. J. Yorba, "Permission Favored," all in *LAT,* 14 Feb. 1944, Proquest.

52. D. G. Springer (Save Your Homes Association) to Stimson, 8 March 1943, Box 1, Marshall Stimson Collection, HEH.

53. "Oil Drilling in City Backed," *LAT,* 14 Feb. 1944. Ora E. Knight, "'Nonsense to . . . Fuss,'" *LAT,* 14 Feb. 1944, in Clippings, Bowron collection. The *Los Angeles Times* filled the editorial page of the February 14 issue with letters on the oil question; only two of the dozen or so letters opposed urban drilling. Marshall Stimson wrote one of these.

54. "Model Oil Drilling Ordinance Passed," *LAT,* 9 Feb. 1944. The 1944 model ordinance passed 11–2, with a majority strong enough to override a mayoral veto. "Council Backs Drilling on Old Golf Course," *LAT,* 27 Jan. 1944, both in Proquest; "Council Balks Oil Drilling in Westwood," *Daily News,* 29 Aug. 1944; "Westwood Oil" *Los Angeles Herald,* 28 Aug. 1944, both in Clippings, Bowron Collection. On Chavez Ravine, see "Council Okays Request for Oil District," *Citizen News,* 12 July 1944; "Oil Wells," *Los Angeles Herald,* 12 July 1944; "Chavez Ravine Drilling Asked," *Los Angeles Examiner,* 13 July 1944, all in Clippings, Bowron Collection; Howard Kegley, "California Oil News," 15 Sept. 1944; "Test Drilling Gets Approval," *LAT,* 10 Oct. 1944, both in Proquest. Seaboard struck oil in Chavez Ravine in September 1945

(Howard Kegley, "California Oil News," 26 Sept. 1945, Proquest.) By February 1946, Seaboard had abandoned this "small pumper of heavy oil" and its other Chavez Ravine leases (Howard Kegley, "California Oil News," 8 Feb. 1946).

55. "Oil Drilling Sanctioned in Wilmington Area," *LAT*, 11 Feb. 1945; "Amended Application to Drill Oil Granted," *LAT*, 10 July 1945, both in Proquest.

56. Continental Oil Co. executive, as quoted in "Oil Well Showdown," *Daily World,* 21 June 1946, in Clippings, Bowron Collection.

57. Stimson to Ickes, 19 June 1943, Box 1, "Oil Drilling in the City of Los Angeles," in Marshall Stimson Collection, HEH.

58. See, for example, "Mayor Vetoes Ordinance for Westwood Oil Drilling," *LAT,* 8 July 1943; "Mayor Proposes Safeguards for City Oil Drilling," *LAT,* 15 July 1943; "Mayor Vetoes Oil Ordinance," 22 Sept. 1942, all in Proquest. For Resmen Bird's reactions, see "City Planners Adopt Oil Well Time Extension," *LAT,* 19 June 1943, in Proquest.

Stand by Your Brand

Vail, Colorado, and the Consumer Roots of Popular Environmentalism

WILLIAM PHILPOTT

Vail, Colorado, is an environmental disaster. At least, that is how many people see it today. An overgrown corporate megaresort, it has turned a scenic alpine glen into an ugly jumble of towers and condominium blocks, crowding the valley floor and clawing up the slopes on either side. It has metastasized westward down the Eagle River, spawning several more urban tumors, cluttering once-glorious expanses of ranchland with golf courses, gated subdivisions, box stores, and trailer parks. It now sprawls more than twenty miles from end to end—nearly forty if you count the growth still farther down valley, around Gypsum and Eagle—and stretching longer each year; a giant waste of scenery, energy, water, and habitat. And along the interstate highway that forms its spine, traffic roars incessantly, dirtying the air, shattering the mountain quiet, exacting a murderous toll on wildlife, and clogging rivers with sandy, oily runoff. Vail is, in the words of one recent documentary, "the epitome of mountain development run amok."[1]

But there was a time, back in the 1960s and early 1970s, when many saw Vail as just the opposite: an environmental *ideal*. Attractively designed, Vail kept development to a human scale and complemented the high country's alpine beauty. Carefully planned, Vail integrated transportation and recreation, efficiently accommodating masses of vacationers in a compact space. As a full-service resort amidst one of America's most scenic landscapes, Vail made it easy for people to escape the city and get back to nature. And as a highly profitable enterprise in the "clean" industry of recreation, Vail showed that there was economic value to outdoor beauty, creating an incentive for Coloradans to take better care of their mountain landscapes. Far from reviling Vail, many people thought the best thing that could happen to the mountains would be to have *more places just like it*.

Some might wonder, "What were they thinking?" But if we posit that these people were sincere in idealizing Vail this way, we open a new window on popular environmental thought after World War II. In particular, Vail's experience focuses our attention on a powerful but largely unnoticed influence on Americans' environmental thinking: the business practice, increasingly pervasive in the postwar era, of packaging and marketing places.[2] Vail's case shows how promoters made places: how they constructed settings to attract and accommodate consumers, and how they encouraged consumers to envision and enjoy these settings in certain ways. Vail also demonstrates how, when consumers bought into the qualities of place that tourist promoters sold them, it could kindle in them a fierce desire to guard those qualities against perceived threats. In short, what began as a product could become a popular environmental cause.

Vail's creation story has become a big part of the resort's mystique.[3] It begins in the 1950s, when a local man named Earl Eaton "discovered" a sprawling mountain just west of Vail Pass, recognized it as prime ski terrain, and revealed it to Pete Seibert, the manager of the ski area where Eaton worked. Seibert, a former ski racer and veteran of the army's famed Tenth Mountain Division, then hatched the "vision" (as the creation story always calls it) that became Vail. He got Forest Service permission to develop the mountain for skiing, and with help from well-connected Denver friends, he bought the ranchland at the mountain's base and recruited more investors to finance the building of a full-scale resort village there. *Vail*, he and his partners named it, not just because it was the name of the nearby pass, but because they thought it crisp and catchy. In other words, Vail, more than a place name, was a *brand name*, the land's very labeling chosen with marketing in mind.[4] Seibert's investment pitch stressed Vail's "natural competitive advantages": its dazzling snow conditions and ski terrain, and its readily accessible location, right on U.S. Highway 6, a direct link to Denver and the recently designated route of future Interstate 70.[5]

The creation story tells how a whole new town appeared almost magically, in this quiet Rocky Mountain valley where only a sawmill, sheep pasture, and lonely two-lane road had once been.[6] Construction began in spring 1962, and after crews spent a frenzied summer and fall—cutting ski trails; installing a gondola and two chair lifts; building a lodge; and laying gas, sewer, water, and electrical utilities—Seibert's company, Vail Associates (VA), managed to open the resort on schedule on December 15. Also built in time for the inaugural season were a motel, dormitory, gas station, delicatessen, liquor store, drugstore, ski boutique, restaurant, and twenty-seven houses.[7] By its third year, Vail could already boast a full range of lodges, shops, services, dining, and diversions, not to mention a fast-growing collection of houses and condominiums for a growing populace of seasonal and permanent residents.[8]

Vail's sudden appearance awed Coloradans, with many comparing it to the boomtowns of gold and silver rush days.[9] But in fact its closest historical ana- logue was something less romantic: the suburban development, built from scratch by a corporate entity and marketed as a ready-made community. Vail especially resembled the species of postwar western suburb that historian John Findlay has termed the "magic land." This was an enclave, like Disneyland or the original Sun City, whose development was elaborately planned, and whose design was scripted around some unifying theme, lending visual and functional cohesion and allowing the magic land to be marketed as a refuge from urban chaos and suburban sprawl.[10] Vail was not suburban, of course. But it *was* planned by a corporation, marketed as a refuge, and crafted around a carefully chosen set of marketing themes. Not by accident would its critics often deride it as more theme park than real community.

Vail's theme-park feel came, more than anything else, from its faux-Alpine design, variously described by fans and detractors as "neo-Salzburgian," "Plastic Bavaria," or "Wisconsin Swiss."[11] Whatever one called it, the village unabashedly aped Alpine ski hamlets like Zermatt and St. Anton, which Pete Seibert adored, as did his design partner, Milwaukee architect and VA partner Fitzhugh Scott Jr. In keeping with the popular image of a little Swiss town, the two men made Vail Vil- lage a tangle of picturesque little lanes, and they insisted that all buildings conform to an Alpine theme. Usually that meant gabled roofs with heavy overhangs, earthy or "natural" colors, and exteriors of stone, stucco, brick, or wood. It also meant no building could loom more than four stories, for anything taller might dwarf pedes- trians and ruin the cozy Alpine feel. To enforce the Alpine theme, VA set up an architectural committee, which had to approve the building plans before a buyer could secure title to a lot in Vail Village.[12] This explains why early Vail boasted so many chalet-like buildings with German names—the Gasthof Gramshammer, the Sitzmark, the St. Moritz. But the architectural committee also approved a Scandi- navian inn, "Normandy chateaux," an Olde English tavern, and a replica of a Kitz- bühel casino, right on Bridge Street.[13] Vail's Europeanness seemed hokey to some, but it was one of VA's main marketing themes. "The moment you set boot in Vail," suggested one ad, "you've crossed an ocean.... Come to Vail. It's where Europe is."[14]

Swiss chalets might seem far removed from suburbia—which was, of course, much of the point. But Vail was also scripted around some very suburban themes. Most basically, it catered to the suburban yearning to escape the troubles of the city. VA banned a number of city trappings from Vail Village, including tall build- ings, rooftop TV antennas, overhead wires, parking meters, traffic lights, neon signs, and "diners that come in the shape of frankfurters." VA even barred automobiles from some streets, leaving the cozy lanes to pedestrians and horse-drawn sleighs.

Restricting cars seems ironic, with VA's business plan so heavily premised on Interstate 70 access, but again, the idea stemmed from the overarching desire to make Vail a refuge from urban ills.[15] As Bob Parker, VA's marketing manager, explained, Vail's founders predicted that "Americans would be delighted to get away from smog and noise and speed and the frantic bustle of our modern urban existence." Vail's first mayor called the chance to "escape asphalt jungles" and other city worries "Vail's very excuse for existence."[16]

Social exclusivity was another suburban yearning that Vail openly indulged. It quickly became known as a haven for the rich—not the morally dubious celebrity rich, as in Aspen, but more the conservative CEO kind. "[Y]ou may rub ski poles with the presidents of IBM, Motorola, Sundstrand, and other large corporations," gushed one travel writer.[17] VA cultivated this image from the start—for example, by offering house lots to early investors (which resulted in many executive types building homes in Vail) and by basing the resort's summer business on "high class convention and group meetings" instead of "off highway tourism" (which, boosters feared, would turn Vail into a cheap tourist trap).[18] Though Seibert would later deny ever wanting to build an elites-only resort, it is clear from VA's early marketing that attracting elites was a goal—and with it, keeping out what the local newspaper editor called "undesirables."[19] Vail's carefully crafted brand was not about glitz or glamour. Instead, like the affluent suburbs that most of its guests called home, Vail stood for conservatism, respectability, and upward mobility: exclusivity of the most buttoned-down kind.

Convenience was another of Vail's defining themes. The village was designed to maximize visitor convenience, especially by making it convenient for visitors to spend money.[20] Trading on Vail's "natural advantages," the ski mountain and the interstate-to-be, Seibert and Scott plotted a parking lot next to the highway, a gondola terminal at the foot of the mountain, and a compact walking village in between. The plan made it easy for guests to walk from their cars to their lodges, their lodges to the lifts, ski back to their lodges when the lifts closed, then spend the après-ski hours strolling around the village, spending as they went.[21] Cleverly, Seibert and Scott made Bridge Street—the one that led from the parking lot to the gondola—the main shopping street too, so to get from their cars to the gondola, visitors would *have* to walk past shops and restaurants along the way. Seibert and Scott threw in another sly twist—literally—by making Bridge Street bend to the left as it sloped uphill to the gondola. The bend added Alpine charm, but even more, it subliminally induced visitors to consume. The two men calculated that the bend would pique visitors' curiosity, make them want to walk up the street to see what lay around the curve. As they walked, they would pass by all those shops and bistros, and succumb to the temptation to spend.[22]

Still, for all its convenience, exclusivity, and Europeanness, Vail's ultimate appeal came down to recreation. In fact, you might say outdoor recreation was Vail's defining theme, for it shaped this town like no other in Colorado. By the 1960s, many old mining or ranching towns, like Aspen, Steamboat, and Breckenridge, had developed tourist trades. But in Vail alone, recreation dictated *everything* from the very start: the choice of townsite, the design of all the buildings, the layout of the streets. Moreover, Vail (unlike, say, Aspen) had no history of resource extraction; it had never related to its environs in anything but recreational terms. Indeed, the intimate intertwining between town and recreational surroundings was one of Vail's most marketable attributes. va's winter advertising showed the ski slopes that, unlike in most ski towns, ran right down into the village, while "SummerVail" ads interspersed images of golf, tennis, and other in-town activities with pictures of scenery and leisure in the surrounding vacationland. Marketing imagery for both seasons blurred together town and mountain landscape, fostering the notion that to vacation in Vail was to immerse oneself utterly in recreational nature.[23]

To say the marketing of Vail worked well would be an understatement. During its first decade, Vail boomed far beyond its founders' dreams, drawing over half a million skier visits by its tenth season.[24] Each year brought millions of dollars' worth of new construction—not just in the village, but in the "suburbs" that began sprouting up- and down-valley, mostly anchored by condominium complexes, as developers raced to cash in on Vail's cachet.[25] A mighty entrepreneurial zeal ("blind enthusiasm and blind optimism," one man remembered it) energized the place in those years.[26] va's policy of selling village lots and relying on the buyers to start their own businesses, rather than controlling all the businesses itself in classic company-town fashion, paid rich dividends. Even as business owners competed for customers, they also, by all accounts, felt a shared faith in the package va was selling, and a shared determination to help sell it. The local newspaper, the *Vail Trail*, exhorted every Vailite to become a walking chamber of commerce, ready to pump the nearest visitor's hand and ply him with talking points about Vail's attributes. To teach the talking points, Vail's chamber of commerce held sales training seminars for locals. The goal, explained the *Trail*, was to "bring about 100% saturation of all people in Vail who have contacts with our guests, so that the wonderful, magical, interesting story of Vail can be passed on with complete authenticity."[27]

For people who had pulled up roots to start anew in Vail, working to build a business, a village, and an economy from scratch could be all-consuming. But work and profits were not the only reasons people made the move. Many loved the idea of living in a small town; others liked the suburban-style promise of raising their children in a wholesome, healthy environment. The environmental side of the suburban dream was, in fact, a powerful draw for Vail residents. Like a suburban developer, VA marketed the chance to live in open space, free from urban ugliness, with outdoor recreation and reminders of nature close at hand. And many early transplants parroted these themes in explaining why they liked Vail. "I happen to prefer spruce to smog," averred one early comer, explaining why she had made the move. "[Y]ear round mountain living offers something more than life in the cement canyons of a smog-smothered city."[28] For her, the product that VA sold to vacationers—the chance to escape for a spell from the city, relax and spend money for fun, and interact recreationally with the Rocky Mountain outdoors—had become a full-time way of life.

Some in Vail even became convinced that VA's package represented a sort of environmental ideal: the perfect integration of natural beauty and human use. VA marketing manager Bob Parker, for one, took a keen interest in protecting the high-country environment, and he was convinced that fostering more development like Vail was the way to do it. A thriving outdoor-recreation industry would mean "Not less trout water, but more!" Parker wrote in 1967. "Not more freeways, but more ski trails! . . . Not tarpaper shacks and trailers, but attractive, planned resorts!"[29] In this vision, large-scale recreational development would create the incentive to take better care of the high country; economic development and environmental stewardship would go hand in hand. Environmental utopia could be Colorado's if Coloradans opted for "attractive, planned resorts" over the destructive industries of the past.

It was a self-serving argument, coming from a VA executive. Yet Parker was right: investing in Vail did indeed turn many locals into environmentalists. A number of locals, including Parker himself, became active in wilderness politics in the late 1960s, at one point suing to stop the Forest Service from allowing logging next to a primitive area near Vail. Logging would "jeopardize the businesses and economic welfare of residents and investors in the Vail area," the locals argued—for as a spokesman for the town wilderness group explained, "Much of Vail's success . . . is because of the beauty of our natural surroundings and the use of the land for outdoor recreation."[30] There was the direct link Parker had predicted, between Vail-as-product and the perceived need for environmental protection.

Soon many others in Vail would become invested in environmental issues too, though wilderness was not the worry that brought them there. Instead, matters of land-use planning, open space, and the built environment were at the core of their concern, and the triggering events took place right in Vail itself. Already by the late 1960s, locals were grumbling that the small-town summer quiet was being lost to the clamor of construction and the swelling golf and convention trade. Interstate 70's arrival raised fears too. Just a few years earlier, VA had touted the interstate as one of the resort's "natural advantages." But when construction of I-70 reached the valley in 1967, no less than Pete Seibert worried about the effect it would have on the scenery and "the desirability of the Vail resort location," and the usually boosterish *Trail* fretted that the traffic and noise might "become a monster."[31] Then growth began to remake the appearance of the cozy little Alpine village itself. Imposing new buildings started going up—a seven-story shopping center in 1968, an eight-story hotel tower the next year—and threatened to overwhelm the modest scale of Vail Village and ruin the impression of escaping the city.[32] That had been a core attribute of VA's package, and judging from locals' agitation over the prospect of losing it, they saw it as a core attribute of their Vail lifestyle too.

Two developments in 1969 sent Vailites over the edge. First came the "Mountain Haus," a six-story, sun-blocking hulk that appeared in an uncomfortably visible spot: right at the village entrance, where visitors left their cars, crossed a little covered bridge, and ostensibly entered into Alpine Fantasyland.[33] Then came "LionsHead," a whole new village that VA began developing just west of the original one. This time, instead of crooked lanes and Swiss chalets, VA's design plan called for angular, brutish edifices, arranged stiffly around concrete plazas. It made sense from a fashion viewpoint (the architecture mimicked the supermodern resorts then in vogue in the French Alps) and a market one too (Vail's astronomical real estate prices generated enormous pressure for denser development).[34] But locals were horrified. The twin shocks of LionsHead and the Mountain Haus were "the two things that got people thinking about density and about growth," one town official later recalled. "All of a sudden, they saw these big buildings going up, and everybody said, 'Wait a minute, this isn't what we perceived Vail to be.'"[35] The threat to VA's carefully packaged townscape jeopardized the entire lifestyle Vailites had bought into, and apparently not even VA could be trusted to defend it.

Increasingly, Vailites turned to the insights of the emerging environmental movement. Letter writers to the *Trail* began to echo some of the core ideas of late-1960s environmentalism: that scenic beauty and a sense of connection to nature were vital to human welfare; that these were in imminent danger of destruction at the hands of selfish profiteers; and that bigger was not always better, that society should no longer let the quest for growth and profits run roughshod over the quality of life.[36] Vail's town government, which in its first few years had functioned mostly as an arm of the booster machine, began to act on the new thinking. The town imposed its first zoning and subdivision controls in 1969, annexed land up- and down-valley in hopes of curbing "suburban" sprawl, and levied a fee on building projects, with the money going to buy open space and develop parks and recreational facilities. Championing these policies was town manager Terry Minger, who came to Vail from Boulder, a city known for its aggressive efforts to limit growth.[37] In 1971 Minger also launched the Vail Symposium, an annual event that brought in outside experts to talk to towns-people about the issues facing Vail, and he organized the first two symposia around environmental themes. The planners, politicians, foresters, architects, environmen-talists, and others in attendance injected still more environmentalist ideas into the local discourse, for example when former interior secretary Stewart Udall, keynoting the 1972 symposium, called for a "*value* revolution" (a favorite exhortation of envi-ronmentalists) and urged Vailites to "define their limits to growth" (echoing the title of a bestselling book, released earlier that year, that forecast the exhaustion of the world's resources).[38]

But even as Vail's environmentalism echoed the national environmental move-ment, it also took on a distinctive local flavor. Of course that was going to be true anywhere, as environmental sentiment drew from each community's unique his-tory, qualities of place, and mix of people laying claim to the landscape. In Vail's case, environmental debate centered on issues like open space preservation, land-use zoning, wilderness designation, the conservation of view corridors and recre-ational amenities, the regulation of architectural character—in short, on matters of leisure, visual design, and the organization of space. This is suggestive, because those were the same matters Vail Associates had stressed in the initial packaging of the resort. Vail's brand of environmentalism was taking its lead from VA marketing. Again and again, when Vailites tried to describe the qualities of place they hoped to save, they invoked imagery from VA advertising, or harked back to the design ele-ments VA had used to give Vail Village its original "theme-park" character.

With recreation the only industry in town, all locals had an economic stake in what VA was selling. But as consumers of the Vail product, they had a lifestyle stake too. That became clear when, during the 1966 mayoral campaign, candidate Ted Kindel declared that serving guests should be town officials' top priority. No, another man countered; the "first obligation" should be "establishing a pleasant . . . and protective community *for the people living here.*" And when Kindel accused growth critics of "selfish escapism," of wanting "a quiet little community with inter-minable play hours for its residents," three locals retorted that Vail was "not just . . . a product that is to be sold, but . . . a place to raise families and lead the good life that our brochures so attractively promise."[39] They could not have been any franker about how fully they had bought into VA's marketing. For them, the "good life" that VA marketed had become a full-blown lifestyle, very much worth defending.

And that explains why threats to Vail's carefully packaged atmosphere angered locals like no other environmental issue. The quaint Alpine walking village, the heart of VA's package, had become the heart of the Vail lifestyle too, so preserving it became the heart of the local environmental agenda. The symposium encouraged this way of thinking when speaker after speaker praised Vail Village's selling points: its "human scale," its effort to "keep the people and cars separate," its use of "wood and natural building materials," its ban on "ticky-tacky, unattractive, uncoordinated" growth.[40] In fact, at the first two symposia, a local consensus jelled that VA's original package—low-rise, clustered, tightly controlled development that integrated the built landscape with its recreational surroundings—was the best recipe for growth in the fragile high-country environment. What had started as a resort-marketing formula had become nothing less than a blueprint for environmentally farsighted planning.[41]

Some symposium speakers took it a step further, declaring mountain resorts like Vail the last hope for people to escape modern metropolitan chaos and rediscover harmony with nature. By this line of thinking, Vailites owed it *to humanity* to keep that hope alive. They were, in Terry Minger's words, "the trustee of the last remnants of our natural heritage." If they let Vail grow out of control, it would not only despoil one of the last pristine landscapes, but sever the intimate interconnection between nature and human community that people came to the mountains to find. Saving the wilderness meant preserving the human scale of Vail.[42]

So in 1973 the Town of Vail moved to claim the mantle of village planning and architectural control that VA had once held, while updating it for the Environmental Decade. New zoning rules required all building projects to undergo an "environmental impact review"—a stipulation that revived VA's old design-review requirement but also took inspiration from the National Environmental Policy Act of 1969.[43] Likewise, the town's new master plan, the 1973 "Vail Plan," gave each of VA's old selling points an environmentalist twist. For example, VA's ban on city trappings now extended to the car: under the plan, all visitors would be made to park in a huge underground garage before strolling up a refreshingly traffic-free Bridge Street. (As a bonus, the earthen berm covering the garage, landscaped with grasses and flowers, would screen the village from the exhaust and engine roar of Interstate 70.) And VA's Alpine design theme got a new "natural" look, as the plan called for the entire village to be landscaped with greenbelts, rock walls, log benches, and trees—thousands of trees, creating the impression of "the adjacent forests creeping in from the hillsides, over the roadway, into the village itself." Thus would "the impact of man within the Valley of Vail be softened," the plan promised, showing its environmentalist stripes. "The time in Vail for man to work in harmony with nature is now."[44]

It might sound like a striking departure, this declaration of a new environmental mission for Vail. But for all the bold notes, it bears repeating that the Vail Plan drew much of its inspiration from an old resort-marketing formula, and for that reason, the environmentalist agenda that it articulated was essentially conservative. This becomes clearest when you consider two more elements of the marketing formula that found voice in the Vail Plan: exclusivity and entrepreneurialism. The Vail Plan did nothing to render Vail any more affordable or less socially exclusive, and in that sense it served to uphold that particular marketing theme. And rather than raise serious questions about the environmental costs of aggressive entrepreneurialism, the plan recognized that Vail existed to make money off visitors. Indeed, it suggested ways the town might accommodate *more of them*. It proposed the parking garage in this spirit, as well as a major expansion of park and recreational facilities, which, it was claimed, would serve tourists as well as residents, and "attract summertime activity."[45] Nowhere did the Vail Plan say growth should be stopped or slowed for environmental reasons. Instead, it held out hope that protecting environmental quality would, by enhancing Vail's visitor appeal, *further* its growth. In this sense, the Vail Plan's brand of environmentalism echoed the vision that VA's Bob Parker had floated in the mid-1960s: a vision in which environmental stewardship and large-scale tourist development went hand in hand. Maybe that is why locals backed the Vail Plan so heartily: because even as it took their environmental concerns seriously, it also acknowledged their desire to make money, recognizing that entrepreneurialism was as basic to Vail's identity as the ski slopes and Swiss village.

What, in the end, can we learn from the environmental debates in early Vail? On the surface it seems such a peculiar place that perhaps its experience cannot be generalized. Yet Vail was not so strange at all. Yes, it was a manufactured place; corporate-built, thematically designed. But so were the suburban subdivisions, retirement villages, office parks, and shopping centers that proliferated across the postwar American landscape. All of them catered to consumers of at least some means, and all of them indulged the escapist fantasies of postwar America, the obsession with leisure, the desire to feel close to nature without giving up modern comforts. Vail may have been more blatantly packaged than most. But with government agencies, chambers of commerce, airlines, auto clubs, and countless others all trying to persuade people to vacation here, or move their families, factories, or headquarters there, it is fair to say that a great many postwar places were packaged in some way or another. Such marketing played an increasingly powerful role in molding Americans' sense of place—if not of Vail, then of the Colorado high country, Las Vegas, Southern California, Florida, or any of a number of other cities, regions, or states that were marketed as ideal places to vacation, do business, work, or live.

Promoters tried to get people to relate to these places as consumers: to buy into the notion that spending time and money there would bring fulfillment and a stronger sense of self.[46] And as Vail's case shows, consumers could indeed find surprisingly powerful personal meanings in the settings that were packaged for them, sometimes even molding their lifestyles and identities around the marketed qualities of place. When they did, they found themselves with a personal stake in saving those qualities. They found themselves invested in environmental protection.

True, the environmental agenda that Vailites pursued would have seemed frivolous to people fighting toxins in their drinking water or nuclear power plants in their backyards. But therein lies another lesson. Environmentalism, we are reminded, was not a monolithic phenomenon. It assumed different forms, focused on different problems and priorities, in different settings. Of course there were many reasons for this, from the peculiarities of local demographics and culture, to the functioning of the local economy and the nature of the local ecology. But Vail's story alerts us to another key influence we have mostly missed: the distinctive ways a place was packaged and advertised. Paying heed to this can help us grasp why environmentalism took on such divergent forms in different places—and why some places seemed not to register with environmentalists at all. It can also help us better understand why environmentalism, for all its revolutionary potential, did so little to challenge the culture of endless growth, all too often reflected rather than rejected social exclusivity, and in general ended up as one of the more conservative social movements of the 1960s and 1970s.

Conversely, even as consumerism limited environmental protest, it was a major reason why many Americans protested at all. When people became attached to certain landscapes as consumers, it might not have turned them into ecologists, but it did spur many of them to care. In this sense, it does not cheapen popular environmentalism to suggest that it took some of its cues from advertising. It simply sheds more light on the complicated mediating role consumer culture played between twentieth-century Americans and the natural and physical world around them.

Notes

The author would like to thank Greg Summers and Ari Kelman for thought-provoking feedback on a very early incarnation of this story; and Shelby Balik for her close reading and help in refining the analysis. Many thanks also to Char Miller for the invitation to contribute to this tribute volume. Most of all, the author would like to acknowledge the late Hal Rothman for his keen interest in, and early and energetic support for, this research on corporate resort building.

1. *Resorting to Madness: Taking Back Our Mountain Communities,* DVD, directed by Hunter Sykes and Darren Campbell (Olympic Valley, CA: Coldstream Creative, 2007).

2. On the commercial packaging and marketing of places, much of the scholarship is by sociologists and geographers who are interested in tourism and other forms of place

consumption; an example I have found especially helpful is John Urry, *Consuming Places* (London: Routledge, 1995). There is also an enormous body of "best practice" literature aimed at marketing professionals, tourism planners, and others who are interested in promoting places to tourists, investors, and the like, but this literature is of limited use to anyone interested in the *histories* of the practices. Historians themselves have so far paid rather little attention to commercial place making, but one very important exception is the ground-breaking book by western urban and cultural historian John Findlay, *Magic Lands: Western Cityscapes and American Culture After 1940* (Berkeley and Los Angeles: University of California Press, 1992). There is also a small but growing body of historical scholarship on state efforts to "brand" places for tourism and other commercial purposes; see Susan Sessions Rugh, "Branding Utah: Industrial Tourism in the Postwar American West," *Western Historical Quarterly* 37:4 (Winter 2006): 445–72; Frieda Knobloch, "Creating the Cowboy State: Culture and Underdevelopment in Wyoming Since 1867," *Western Historical Quarterly* 32:2 (Summer 2001): 201–21; and Michael Dawson, *Selling British Columbia: Tourism and Consumer Culture, 1890–1970* (Vancouver: University of British Columbia Press, 2005). The germinal work, and jumping-off point, for all studies of the creation of spaces and places is Henri Lefebvre, *The Production of Space,* trans. Donald Nicholson-Smith (Oxford, England: Blackwell, 1991).

3. For versions of the Vail creation story, including Eaton's "discovery" and Seibert's "vision," see: Sandra Dallas, *Vail* (Boulder, CO: Pruett, 1969), 9–20; June Simonton, *Vail: Story of a Colorado Mountain Valley* (Dallas: Taylor, 1987), 58–75; Peter W. Seibert with William Oscar Johnson, *Vail: Triumph of a Dream* (Boulder, CO: Mountain Sports Press, 2000), 45–49, 52, 58–60, 64–71, 74–5, 78–81; and Dick Hauserman, *The Inventors of Vail* (Edwards, CO: Golden Peak Publishing Co., 2000), 16–76.

4. On the choice of Vail as a name, see Simonton, *Vail: Story of a Colorado Mountain Valley,* 19, 66; Seibert and Johnson, Vail: *Triumph of a Dream,* 38; Hauserman, *The Inventors of Vail,* 30. At least one early VA partner wanted to use the old Ute name for the Rockies, "Shining Mountains," but Seibert vetoed the idea, arguing that "shining" might suggest icy ski trails—anathema to lovers of powder or "ballroom" skiing. This anecdote is further evidence that marketing considerations played heavily into the naming decision.

5. Vail Associates, Ltd., prospectus (August 14, 1961), 5–6, 8.

6. For examples of the "magic" trope, see: Curtis Casewit, "Miracle out of a Meadow," *Ford Times* (December 1967): 7, 10; and "Vail Gondola Operating," *Eagle Valley Enterprise* (December 13, 1962): 1.

7. Simonton, 67–75; Curtis W. Casewit, "Victory at Vail," *Success! Unlimited* (January 1967): 43; Rod Slifer, interview, Vail, Colorado, August 30, 1993; Paul Hauk, *Chronology of the Vail Ski Area* (Glenwood Springs, CO: U.S. Forest Service, White River National Forest, 1979), 1, 6; Pasquale Marranzino, "Vail Ski Pass Starts Fast," *Rocky Mountain News* (January 8, 1963): 29; Robert Parker, interview, January 12, 1994.

8. Vail Associates, Ltd., brochure, 1964–5 ski season, personal collection of Paul Hauk, Glenwood Springs, Colorado.

9. See, for example, Jack Foster, "White Gold Makes A Gleaming City," *Rocky Mountain News* (March 10, 1963): 53.

10. Findlay, *Magic Lands,* especially his explanation of the concept on 5–6.

11. Judith Axler Turner, "One Vail of No Tears," *Washington Post* (January 24, 1974): D11; Richard Schneider, "Plastic Bavaria II on tap, thanks to Forest Service," *Rocky Mountain News* (September 8, 1974); Dallas, *Vail,* 24. "Wisconsin Swiss" apparently referred to the Milwaukee origins of architect Fitzhugh Scott.

12. Peter Seibert, interview, Vail, Colorado, January 6, 1994; Seibert and Johnson, Vail: *Triumph of a Dream,* 98–9; Fitzhugh Scott, interview, Vail, Colorado, August 27, 1993; Robert Parker, interview, January 12, 1994; Slifer, interview; Hauserman, *The Inventors of Vail,* 44–5; David Sage, interview, Vail, Colorado, July 22, 1993. A third partner, Aspen architect and Tenth Mountain veteran Fritz Benedict, also consulted on Vail's design in the early stages, but his proposed village layout and architectural theme (a modern take-off on old mine and ranch buildings) were both rejected. He did stay on to serve on VA's architectural control committee.

13. The quotation is from Lois Hagen, "Vacation House Steps Down the Mountain," *Milwaukee Journal Women's Section* (February 6, 1969): 6. For more on the Euro-eclecticism of Vail architecture, see: Belle Forrest, "Happy Vail Pass: Our Never Land," *Rocky Mountain News Festival* (February 19, 1967): 1; Foster, "White Gold Makes a Gleaming City"; Pat Hanna, "Super Supper Club Set for Vail," *Rocky Mountain News* (December 18, 1964): 114; "Plush, New Night Club Opens in Vail Village," *Denver Post* (December 20, 1964): 67; "Vail," in Colorado Ski Country USA, *Manual of Colorado Skiing and Winter Sports, 1964–1965* (Denver: Colorado Ski Country USA, 1964), 37–9.

14. Vail Associates, Ltd., advertisement in *Skiing* (October 1968). For an amusingly critical view, see Turner, "One Vail of No Tears."

15. The quotation is from Curtis W. Casewit, *United Air Lines Guide to Western Skiing* (New York: Doubleday, 1967), 30; see also "Town Council Passes Next Year's Budget," *Vail Trail* (October 11, 1968): 8; David Sage, interview.

16. Bob Parker, "Parker Pens" column, *Vail Trail* (February 17, 1967): 10, boldface in the original; Ted Kindel, "A Christmas Message from Our Mayor, Ted Kindel," *Vail Trail* (December 23, 1966): 1.

17. Casewit, *United Air Lines Guide,* 36–7.

18. Vail Associates Inc., Executive Committee, minutes, August 10, 1967, Box 1, Vail Associates papers, Collection #715, Denver Public Library Western History Department (hereafter VAP); see also Florence Steinberg, "Conventioneers Cognizant of the Complete Resort," *Eagle Valley Enterprise* (September 5, 1968): 5. The places where the Vail Resort Association, the local chamber of commerce, ran its summer ads—in publications like *Venture, Status,*

National Geographic, Diplomat, and *The New Yorker*—further suggested the affluent, educated clientele they were trying to reach. See "It's A Small World—We Made It That Way!" *Vail Trail* (October 4, 1968): 2.

19. Seibert, interview; Sharon Brown, "Profile: Image Maker, Bob Parker," *Vail Trail* (April 16, 1971): 7; George Knox, "It Always Helps to Know," *Vail Trail* (July 28, 1967): 2.

20. The British sociologist of tourism and leisure John Urry has termed such a setting, structured to facilitate or encourage spending, a "consuming place"; see Urry, *Consuming Places,* especially his explanation of the term on 1–2.

21. Seibert, interview; Parker, interview, January 12, 1994; Scott, interview; Roger Ritchie, "A Cozy Place to Ski . . . Vail," *Flightime: The Air Travelers Magazine* (January–February 1968): 16. Seibert saw Vail's mountain-village integration as a key feature, setting the resort apart from rival Sun Valley in Idaho. Sun Valley's developer, the Union Pacific Railroad, had built its resort village from scratch, much like VA did with Vail. But at Sun Valley, some three miles separated the village from the ski facilities—meaning visitors had to rely on cars or buses to get from their accommodations to the slopes.

22. Seibert and Johnson, Vail: *Triumph of a Dream,* 98–9; Seibert, interview; Scott, interview; Parker, interview, January 12, 1994. Seibert later claimed the idea for Bridge Street also came from Zermatt. "You get off the train in Zermatt," he told me, "and then to go to the mountain you have to walk up this main street. It was obvious that there were important commercial advantages to having kind of a dog bone [Bridge Street, bent a bit like a dog leg] and having the shaft of the bone be the shopping area." VA marketing director Bob Parker, on the other hand, recalls that the plan to funnel customers up Bridge Street was Fitzhugh Scott's. Scott did, in fact, design the street layout, but since participants' memories have faded over time, it seems safest to conclude that the village design was a collaborative effort.

23. Vail Associates, Ltd., prospectus, April 25, 1961, p. 11; Vail Resort Association, "SummerVail" brochure, n.d. (1960s), author's personal collection.

24. Memorandum, Vail Corporation, November 1960, GPCP; Vail Associates, Inc., annual report (1968), 11; Vail Associates, Inc., annual report (1972), 2.

25. Photograph and caption on the Bighorn subdivision, *Eagle Valley Enterprise* (December 26, 1963): 1; Willard Haselbush, "Spectacular Vail Village Rises in Colorado Sheep Pasture," *Denver Post* (December 29, 1963): 1D; "Alpine-type Village Going Up In Gore Creek Valley Area," *Rocky Mountain News* (December 29, 1963): 45; "Contemporary High Rises Will Go Up At Lion's Ridge," *Vail Trail* (October 5, 1969): 10; Olga Curtis, "Vail: There is also a summertime," *Denver Post Mountain Living* (May 24, 1970): 30; "Vail Building Boom Moving Westward," *Vail Trail* (July 30, 1971): 19.

26. Slifer, interview.

27. Sharon Brown, "Profile: Ted Kindel, Town Pioneer," *Vail Trail* (November 2, 1971): 8; George Knox, "Smile—You're On PR," *Vail Trail* (December 16, 1968): 2; "VRA Sponsors Employer-Employee Refresher Session," *Vail Trail* (December 9, 1966): 1.

28. Slifer, interview; Marcia Sage, personal interview, Vail, Colorado, July 22, 1993; Lillian Miller, "Lift Lines" column, *Vail Trail* (December 16, 1966): 4; Miller, "Lift Lines" column, *Vail Trail* (February 10, 1967): 4. The quotation is from the second Miller column.

29. Bob Parker, "Parker Pens" column, *Vail Trail* (January 13, 1967): 1, 7. Parker expressed the same sentiments in a letter to the *Denver Post*, which was reprinted in the *Eagle Valley Enterprise* (October 14, 1965): 8.

30. Brief for the Federal Appellants; U.S. Court of Appeals, 10th Circuit; Nos. 404–70, 405–70, 406–70; Robert W. Parker, et al., *Appellees v. USA*, Clifford Hardin, Edward P. Cliff, David S. Nordwall, James O. Folkestad, Kaibab Industries, Appellants, p. 5; James Kemp, vice chairman of the Eagles Nest Wilderness Committee, quoted in "Wilderness . . . or Lumber?" *Colorado Magazine* (July–August 1969): 13.

31. On the loss of summertime serenity, see, for example, "Vail Having $15 Million Boom in Quiet Economy," *Denver Post* (August 2, 1970): 1G. On the interstate, see Pete Seibert, quoted in "State Hiw'y Dept Charged With 'Bad Faith,'" *Eagle Valley Enterprise* (July 28, 1966): 5; "It's The Time For—," *Vail Trail* (December 30, 1968): 2. In fairness, Seibert's negative view was surely exacerbated by the fact that he was locked in a legal dispute with the state highway department at the time over the question of how much VA should be compensated for land lost to the interstate right-of-way. Predicting that the highway would damage Vail's attractiveness was one way VA could justify asking for more compensation.

32. "New CROSSROADS of VAIL Project Inspired by Vail Growth Progress," *Vail Trail* (April 19, 1968): 4; "Restored And Enlarged Lodge (Broadmoor) At Vail To Be Greatest," *Vail Trail* (September 7, 1969): 5.

33. "Vail Complex to Replace Lodge," *Denver Post* (December 7, 1969): 4M; "Vail Construction To Total $12 Million," *Vail Trail* (June 1, 1969): 10; Connie Knight, "Vail's Summer Construction Underway," *Vail Trail* (May 31, 1970): 5.

34. Information on the thinking behind LionsHead is from Joe Macy, personal interview, Vail, Colorado, September 1, 1993; Morten Lund, "Their New Alps Versus Our New Alps," *Ski* (November 1971): 85–91ff; Terry Minger, personal interview, Denver, Colorado, August 23, 1993; Seibert, interview; David Sage, interview; "Vail's 1969 Expansion Plan Detailed," *Vail Trail* (February 24, 1969): 1. Seibert also claimed VA was motivated by its ongoing dispute with the state highway department over the value of 110 acres of VA land the department had condemned for construction of Interstate 70. By selling LionsHead land for high-density development, Seibert later explained, VA hoped to "justify the value of the land they [the highway department] were taking." Seibert, interview; see also "State Hiw'y Dept Charged With 'Bad Faith,'" *Eagle Valley Enterprise* (July 28, 1966): 1; "Land Award Is Set For Vail Associates," *Denver Post* (November 15, 1967): 34; "Road Dept. Appeals Vail Award Ruling," *Denver Post* (November 3, 1968): 36.

35. Slifer, interview.

36. For some good examples, see Walter McC. Maitland, letter to the *Vail Trail* (December 22, 1972): 54; Gordon Brittan, quoted in Sharon Brown, "Profile: Gordon Brittan: Actively

Retired Vailite Challenges the Young," *Vail Trail* (July 16, 1971): 19; Willis M. McFarlane, letter to the *Vail Trail* (October 27, 1972): 26.

37. On Minger's role, see, for example, Terry Minger and Sharon Hobart, "The Home Rule Charter Plan," *Vail Trail* (April 7, 1972): 26; Town of Vail, Board of Trustees, minutes, February 1, 1972; "Voters Okay Home Rule Commission," *Vail Trail* (April 21, 1972): 1; "Home Rule Charter Vote Draws Comments from Voters," *Vail Trail* (September 8, 1972): 25; "Home Rule Charter Passes," *Vail Trail* (September 15, 1972): 1; Celia Roberts, "A Look At Annexation From Town & County," *Vail Trail* (August 31, 1973): 27.

38. Stewart L. Udall, quoted in "Colorado: growing, growing, gone?" *Colorado Investor Fact Sheet* 1:9 (September 5, 1972): 1, 2, 3, emphasis in the original. See also Rigomar Thurmer, "The Second Vail Symposium . . . they listened and became aware!," *Vail Trail* (August 11, 1972): 8–9; Donella H. Meadows, Dennis L. Meadows, Jorgen Randers, and William W. Behrens III, *The Limits to Growth* (New York: Universe Books, 1972).

39. Ted Kindel, "Kindel for Mayor," *Vail Trail* (October 14–21, 1966): 7; John McBride, letter to the editor, *Vail Trail* (November 4–11, 1966): 1, emphasis added; Kindel, "Candidate for Mayor Makes Final Bid;" and Ron Fricke, Christopher B. Hall, and William H. Duddy, letter to the editor, *Vail Trail* (November 4–11, 1966): 1, 4, 7.

40. Robert W. Knecht, "Local, State and Federal Policies on Land Use," *The First Vail Symposium: "The Role of the Mountain Recreation Community"* (Vail, CO: Town of Vail and Vail Resort Association, [1971]), 15 (first two quotations); Desmond Muirhead, quoted in "Colorado: growing, growing, gone?," *Colorado Investor Fact Sheet* 1:9 (September 5, 1972): 5; Thomas A. Corcoran, "A Developer's View of Mountain Recreation Communities," *The First Vail Symposium*, 35.

41. *The First Vail Symposium* passim; "Colorado: growing, growing, gone?"

42. This line of thinking appears in a number of the speeches in *The First Vail Symposium*. See especially "Preface," i; John A. Dobson, "Welcome Speech," 2–3; Knecht, "Local, State and Federal Policies," 15; Corcoran, "A Developer's View," 34–5. The quotation is from Minger, "Keynote Speaker Introduction," 4.

43. Town of Vail, Ordinance No. 8, Series of 1973, Article 16.

44. Royston, Hanamoto, Beck & Abey, and Livingston & Blayney, *The Vail Plan*, prepared for the Town of Vail, August 1973; Bob Ewegen, "Automobile Target of Vail Bond Issue," *Denver Post* (August 14, 1973): 18; Minger, personal interview. The quotations are from *The Vail Plan*, 6A.

45. *The Vail Plan*, 5. The parking garage, like the bend in Bridge Street, was even slyly designed to induce spending. Newly arrived visitors descending from the upper levels would encounter a series of terraces with commanding views of the village, where they would gape at all the options before them, and presumably be tempted to indulge. *The Vail Plan*, 3; Livingston and Blayney, "Vail Planning Study: Parking: Preliminary Concepts," memorandum, n.d. [1973].

46. My understanding of consumerism here draws most directly from Gary Cross, *An All-Consuming Century: Why Commercialism Won in Modern America* (New York: Columbia University Press, 2000); Colin Campbell, "Consuming Goods and the Good of Consuming," *Critical Review* 8 (Fall 1994): 503–20; and the classic essay by T. J. Jackson Lears, "From Salvation to Self-Realization: Advertising and the Therapeutic Roots of the Consumer Culture, 1880–1930," in Richard Wightman Fox and T. J. Jackson Lears, eds., *The Culture of Consumption: Critical Essays in American History, 1880–1980* (New York: Pantheon, 1983), 1–38. On tourism as a means for consumers to construct personal and collective identities, see Ellen Furlough, "Making Mass Vacations: Tourism and Consumer Culture in France, 1930s to 1970s," *Comparative Studies in Society and History* 40: 2 (April 1998): 247–86; and the essays in Shelley Baranowski and Ellen Furlough, eds., *Being Elsewhere: Tourism, Consumer Culture, and Identity in Modern Europe and North America* (Ann Arbor: University of Michigan Press, 2001). On consumers' propensity to use natural things to define, excite, relax, please, or reassure themselves, see Jennifer Price, *Flight Maps: Adventures with Nature in Modern America* (New York: Basic Books, 1999); and Susan G. Davis, *Spectacular Nature: Corporate Culture and the Sea World Experience* (Berkeley and Los Angeles: University of California Press, 1997).

The *Whole Earth Catalog,* New Games, and Urban Environmentalism

ANDREW G. KIRK

"Soylent Green is people!" Charleton Heston screamed at the climax of the 1973 environmental science fiction cult film *Soylent Green.* The movie appeared during a period of scarcity-fueled apocalyptic nightmares, climaxing with the Arab oil embargo and the energy crisis. *Soylent Green* was just one example of a subgenre of 1970s sci-fi B movies that refashioned the technophobia of the 1950s and gave it a *Mod Squad* twist. Inspired by the urban dystopian science fiction of writers like Phillip K. Dick and Robert Heinlein, the films of this genre often concluded with a hopeful journey away from the technologically demented city into a pristine countryside devoid of humans and their tainted technologies. This escape-to-nature theme was in tune with the environmental advocacy of the day even if it was out of step with an American culture that was building cars like the giant gas-guzzling Ford Galaxie. Yet, while Heston dramatically fought technology gone wrong in *Planet of the Apes* (1968), *Soylent Green,* and the *Omega Man*(1971), *Whole Earth Catalog* founder Stewart Brand and a cohort of Bay Area innovators were articulating an alternative vision of pragmatic technologically—enthusiastic environmentalism aimed at Americans who lived in and around cities and planned on staying.

If Brand were the hero in a *Whole Earth*–inspired film (there was a proposal for a Broadway show) he might have shouted, "Counterculture green is people!" Because his version of environmentalism was all about people, culture, and technical innovation aimed at ecological living in the places were people were, not preserving the choice morsels of wilderness where they weren't. He and his peers believed that any version of a sustainable future would have to include innovative people working on human-centered environmental solutions in the cities and suburbs where they lived. This film might have concluded with Brand and crew leaving the countryside and driving back to the city with a trailer full of windmills, solar panels, an "Earth Ball," and blueprints for how to build a rammed earth home, "living machine," or rooftop urban garden.

The *Whole Earth Catalog* captured a new alchemy of environmental concern, small-scale technological enthusiasm, design research, and innovative outdoor recreation. Initially aimed at countercultural communes, and remembered best as the bible of the back-to-the-land movement, *Whole Earth* moved quickly away from these enthusiasms and became one of the most significant forums for urban environmentalism. Unlike the Bay Area environmentalism of the Sierra Club that encouraged members to leave the city to commune with and recreate in the nature of the Sierras or elsewhere, *Whole Earth* provided a forum for those ecologically minded Bay Area residents who wanted to find ecology within the city and its immediate hinterlands.

Behind the scenes of *Whole Earth* was The Point Foundation. Brand founded Point with the substantial profits from his National Book Award–winning *Last Whole Earth Catalog* (1972). Point was an effort to create a model for foundation organization and philanthropic activism informed by the social context of the counterculture. Brand's "anti-foundation" became a means for exploring what board member and *The Seven Laws of Money* (1974) author Michael Phillips called, "way-out money schemes," grounded in careful considerations of right livelihood, simple living, and British economist E.F. Schumaker's "economics as if people mattered."[1] Looking back, environmentalist and Point board member Huey Johnson said the efforts at Point were a "classic and important way" to think about philanthropy.[2] Further, Point was a meaningful attempt to support social causes, mainly in the Bay Area, related to quality of life and social justice. Most importantly, Point represented a directed effort to help convert the constellation of alternative environmentalism presented on the pages of *Whole Earth* into something resembling a coherent movement.

The history of American philanthropy in the twentieth century raises complex questions about wealth and power in a country that has never resolved the issue of private versus state responsibility for social welfare. As Waldemar Nielsen argued in his monumental survey of twentieth-century foundations: "In the great jungle of American democracy and capitalism, there is no more strange or improbable creature than the private foundation."[3] In 1971 Point was posed to add a new species of strange creature to this improbable world, one that better represented the tradition of American foundations to act as benefactors to innovative "seekers of root causes" and creative solution finders than the "gaseous foundation world of the 1960s." Point became an example of how philanthropy could be changed by a new and enlightened generation.[4] "Being a counter-foundation," Brand explained, meant "Dealing individual-to-individual rather than institution-to-project, pursuing leanness, rigor, and surprise in good-doing."[5] For board member Huey Johnson, Point provided an opportunity to create an alternative to a granting system he abhorred. As someone who worked extensively in the foundation world, Johnson was eager for a gutsy, mold-shattering experience in philanthropy that would emphasize what he called "radical giving," an alternative to "the enduring trend to safe traditional educational, religious or medical giving," that he found "disheartening" and "costly to society."[6] The work of Point, though often disorganized and frustratingly underplanned, exemplified the root meaning of the word philanthropy—love of humanity. It was the love and respect for people and their products that differentiated Point from most environmentally minded foundations and organizations of the period. One of the most interesting environmental efforts funded by Point was the New Games Tournament.[7]

Brand had a long interest in games, recreation, and exploring how creative play might be used to release aggression without real conflict. He spent a considerable amount of his Point Foundation time and money exploring alternative outdoor recreation and sponsored a series of events exploring new forms of outdoor recreation to encourage the Bay Area community "to relate to its natural environment in a new and creative way."[8] His first idea was for something he called "Softwar," a "conflict which is regionalized (to prevent injury to the uninterested), refereed (to permit fairness and certainty of a win-lose outcome), and cushioned (weaponry regulated for maximum contact and minimum permanent disability)."[9] He discussed these ideas with friend George Leonard, author of the 1970s classic, *The Ultimate Athlete* (1974).[10] Leonard was a leading advocate of alternative sports and enthusiastic supporter of Brand's idea for an alternative recreation event in the Bay Area.

Recreation appeared in all the *Whole Earth Catalogs* under the heading "Nomatics." These sections celebrated traditional forms of recreation such as backpacking, camping, rock climbing, and water sports, and highlighted the recreational activities of the Sierra Club, among others. A closer look at the Nomatics sections reveals strong support for a diversity of recreational activities geared more toward urban parks and less mobile urban populations who were unlikely to be participants in the Sierra High Trip school of Bay Area recreation or have the time or inclination to spend weeks hiking the John Muir Trail. Brand's thinking about Softwar motivated him to think hard about how his version of Nomatics and outdoor recreation in general might better serve the diverse population of the Bay Area. Prior to the publication of the first *Whole Earth*, Brand designed an event titled "World War IV," a scenario game for "the peaceniks I was dealing with," who, according to Brand, "seemed very much out of touch with their bodies in an unhealthy way."[11] Later, his work chronicling the rise of the early computer game, *Spacewar,* for *Rolling Stone* elicited a long run of thoughtful pieces on the role that recreation and games play in shaping culture and quality of life. Both of these experiences convinced Brand to further explore alternative recreation as a means of working on cultural differences, increasing awareness of environmental issues, bringing together diverse groups of actors and, of course, to have fun. The New Games tournaments became the vehicle for Brand to explore these interests and promote them to a wide audience.

The New Games idea grew from a ferment of environmentalism, small-scale technology, design, marketing, and Bay Area culture. As he started planning New Games, Brand also launched a new publishing venture, the *CoEvolution Quarterly* (1974). Brand's thinking about urban ecology and recreation found their most subtle expression on the pages of *CoEvolution Quarterly. CoEvolution* provided a forum for many of the organizers, community leaders, and participants of New Games to elaborate on their evolving notions of outdoor recreation and urban environmentalism. One of the most frequent criticisms of the counterculture was its obsession with leisure and play at the expense of productive contributions to society. But a close look at the Nomatics of *Whole Earth* and accomplishments of New Games in particular reveals that even beneath the counterculture quest for leisure, recreation, and fun lurked a promising effort to provide a framework for pragmatic ecological living. As Hal Rothman pointed out in his detailed study *The New Urban Park: Golden Gate National Recreation Area and Civic Environmentalism,* San Francisco and its remarkable collection of urban open spaces exemplified changing perceptions about the relationship between recreation and public lands during a period when "the nation grappled with urban uprisings, and empowered constituencies," searching for positive outlets for urban aggression.[12] More than any other single event, New Games exemplified the nexus of thinking about economy, sport, pragmatic environmentalism, and social activism that was emerging from northern California in the early 1970s and the granting efforts of the Point Foundation and the network of *Whole Earth* publications that supported it.[13]

The New Games Tournament was held on two consecutive weekends in October 1973 at the Nature Conservancy's 2,200-acre Gerbode Preserve, just north of the Golden Gate Bridge. Organized by Brand and sponsored by the Point Foundation, with particular support from Point board member and then-president of The Trust for Public Land (TPL), Huey Johnson, New Games was an opportunity for the "community to relate to its natural environment in a new and creative way."[14] Interestingly, this event most clearly demonstrated the ways that the pragmatic environmentalism implicit in *Whole Earth* and explicit in the activities of Point sometimes diverged from the mainstream environmental movement of the early 1970s. Brand had encountered some resistance to proposals to hold events—like a series of *Whole Earth* jamborees that became a fondly remembered Bay Area tradition—in Golden Gate Park from the newly formed Golden Gate National Recreation Area Citizens Council, and he turned to Huey Johnson's Trust for Public Land to provide a large open space within easy striking distance to the city.

Johnson founded TPL in 1972 to provide a more urban-focused model of the land-banking model he helped perfect as the first Nature Conservancy representative in the American West, and New Games was an excellent showcase for his innovative efforts. Johnson's success with the Nature Conservancy and intense work with Point encouraged him to break out on his own and form The Trust for Public Land to further his model of market savvy environmental advocacy.[15] A central feature of Johnson's environmental philosophy was his belief that "unless we can make the cities more livable it is going to be very difficult to preserve natural areas."[16] His work with Point, which brought him into closer contact with grassroots urban environmentalism, alternative technology proponents, and alternative design activists, convinced him that "city dwellers are really going to be the ones making the decisions on the use of natural resources," and "that unless some traditional environmentalists moved into the urban areas and helped the cities," larger goals of preserving the "integrity of the total environment" would fail.[17]

Johnson's new focus provided a bridge between urban ecological design pioneers like the "New Alchemists" and Bay Area innovators like Helga and Bill Olkowski, who were working on urban design issues, and foundations and advocates who supported more traditional environmental preservation activities.[18] Through his activities at the Point Foundation and The Trust for Public Land, Johnson became an articulate spokesman for the "livable communities" movement that helped shape a civic environmentalism and emerging ecological design philosophy, which influenced trends in new urbanism, urban ecological design, and green consumption in the coming decades. In the early 1980s, he worked to organize the American Green Party to bring his ideas more directly into the political sphere.[19] By the end of the 1990s, The Trust for Public Land had banked 1.3 million acres of open space in American urban centers. Johnson counted New Games as among the most important of his efforts in the 1970s.

On those two weekends of the first New Games Tournament, over 6,000 Bay Area adventure seekers paid $2.50 to gather in the beautiful Gerbode Valley for a remarkable celebration of alternative nature recreation.[20] Onlookers perched on the rolling hillsides could watch hang gliders silently swooping over crowds of players intently balancing on beams while being pummeled with gunny sacks in a game of "Tweezli-Whop," or head-banded and bearded participants diving for a high flying "Schmerltz." Large groups, sometimes numbering in the hundreds, played "Slaughter," "Caterpillar," "Vampire," "Hagoo," "Planet Pass," "Orbit," and "Siamese Soccer." Parachutes fluttered in the wind around smaller groups working on inventing their own new games or quietly playing the Native American inspired "Bone Game." Nothing drew more of a crowd than the game that became the icon of the New Games movement, "Earth Ball."

At six-feet in diameter, painted as a globe, the giant rubber and canvas Earth Ball was the focal point of the New Games Tournament. Participants used the ball for many games, from balancing on it to crawling under it. But mostly the ball was the object of rushing crowds who hoisted and threw it, chased it, rolled it, and piled on it. The primary Earth Ball activity was a loosely structured game where two sides worked to push the giant ball across a boundary marker with the goal of keeping the game going as long as possible; there were no winners in the traditional sense. Participant William deBuys remembered wallowing in the mud under the Earth Ball at the bottom of a pile of jubilant New Gamers, having the time of his life.[21] Prior to the event, the ball drew curious onlookers as it was slowly inflated at a San Francisco gas station. Then large crowds chased the bounding ball down San Francisco streets where curious onlookers kept joining the parade, a trend that came to be known as "snowballing"—building a crowd like one builds a snowball. Kids in particular loved the Earth Ball, and versions of the ball and the noncompetitive sports ideal it represented found their way to gym classes all over America in the late 1970s.

The tournaments were a major success and received significant national news coverage, including a live broadcast with Walter Cronkite and a feature article in *Sports Illustrated.*[22] The sight of a large bunch of hippies, grandmotherly types, children, and a nice multiracial mix of Bay Area citizens playing weird new games in a beautiful setting was a no-lose proposition for the media. The coverage for the most part, however, did not parody and succeeded in capturing the thoughtful ideas that drove the event. *Sports Illustrated* reporter Keith Power carefully explained the unusual event, Brand's motives, and the countercultural context for a reevaluation of sport and urban open-space use. While he concluded that "This is obviously not the kind of constructed diversion apt to catch on with the average American in pursuit of New Leisure," he nonetheless captured the spirit of an event that was more than a stunt.

New Games exemplified the convergence of alternative sport, environmentalism, and urban social activism that drove the granting efforts of the Point Foundation and provided the intellectual framework for a generation of Bay Area counterculture environmentalists who used recreation as a spearhead for a pragmatic everyday environmentalism. Community organizer and New Games planner Pat Farrington made it clear that "one of our major goals is to make people aware of public lands and promote using them in an ecologically sound manner."[23] The New Games and Point Foundation efforts in the Bay Area during the mid-1970s highlighted the ways that technologically enthusiastic environmentalists were building new coalitions of recreationalists and conservationists while reaching out to new urban constituencies long ignored by the mainstream environmental movement.

Not all approved of the New Games scope and some worried about the enthusiasm for technologically oriented new sports that were changing the tone of open-space use in the Bay Area during the 1970s. For those accustomed to viewing the Marin hills free of crowds, or quietly walking or hiking the valleys, New Games might have seemed like an invasion. New Games also brought with it lots of toys and tools, from hang gliders to the Earth Ball and big colorful parachutes causing the "bare hills of Gerbode, covered only with the parched grasses of summer" to "burst into color."[24] Most of the technologies deployed during New Games, however, were simple and left little lasting impact on the land. Huey Johnson thought the potential for New Games to link the preservation of wild and scenic lands surrounding San Francisco with innovative community building addressing pressing urban social and environmental issues of the early 1970s easily outweighed concerns about new and expanded use. Further, the hang gliders and other simple tools for New Games were in perfect keeping with long-established trends in technologically facilitated nature use, and were only more obvious because they were being deployed in the new urban parks where their use was visible to millions.

The history of American outdoor recreation in the twentieth century is, to a certain degree, a history of leisure tool enthusiasm. Outdoor sports have always wielded influence inversely proportional to their purity; in other words, sports with lots of cool toys tended to gain power because of the wider appeal and the marketing clout of outfitters. The tools of recreation linked constituents to the market and gave certain groups greater access to political power than the purists enjoyed. The mainstream environmental movement has been so influential that we tend to assume that most Americans must have envisioned a disconnect between nature and technology; however, in reality, the natural and technical worlds were very much entwined in American thinking and *Whole Earth,* and the events like New Games that it sponsored, appealed to that latent connectedness. New Games struck such a chord precisely because the incongruity between nature and culture championed by the wilderness crowd was not actually the mainstream of American thought. Because we assume that only environmentalists (and especially wilderness advocates) spend a great deal of time thinking about nature, we tend to make assumptions about the role wilderness proponents played in shaping American thinking about the relationship between nature (as sublime and natural) and technology (as intrusive and artificial); but, in fact, most Americans probably think about nature a good deal, and especially about ways to avoid being killed by it, enjoy it, adjust to it, and master it. The environmental recreation on display at New Games was a needle entering a rich vein of ubiquitous everyday nature thinking. As Hal Rothman reminded us in *Devil's Bargains: Tourism in the Twentieth-Century American West* (1998), American tourists and outdoor recreationalists have long embraced the very ambiguities and contradictions between technology, nature, and consumption that the history of outdoor recreation reveals.[25] In 1968, the same year that *Whole Earth* was founded to foster connections between technology, culture, and nature, the American environmental movement was beginning to distance itself from the recreationalists who constituted a key constituency of the movement throughout the twentieth century. The beginnings of the break with recreation coincided with the culmination of the most dramatic expansion of recreational tourism in American history and the rise of the outdoor sports technology industry.[26]

Whole Earth celebrated the symbiosis between technologically enhanced recreation, thoughtful consumption, and nature appreciation through its Nomatics sections. Dick Raymond, *Whole Earth*'s patron saint, started his career as a recreation economics consultant at the Stanford Research Institute, and Nomatics editor J. Baldwin began his career in industrial design building tents for Bill Moss. Recreation and leisure loom large in the history of the counterculture and play a significant role in shaping the cultural context for environmentalism in the 1960s and 1970s.[27] It was no coincidence that Baldwin, the publication's long-time technology expert and editor, was also the editor of the Nomatics section. As an early recreational designer, Baldwin knew firsthand about the relationship between recreation tech and environmental concern.

The work of emerging companies—like Yvon Chouinard's Great Pacific Iron Works (the forerunner of Patagonia)—that were presented to readers of *Whole Earth* the same year as Brand was conceiving New Games later demonstrated through their success the power of the countercultural model of green economics and alterative recreation.[28] Chouinard's first catalog came out in 1972, the same year as *The Last Whole Earth Catalog,* and was clearly modeled on Brand's most popular publication.[29] The *Last* featured Chouinard and Tom Frost's young company in the Nomatics section as a source for high-quality, high-tech mountain gear, but also as a source of history and environmental philosophy.[30] Like *Whole Earth,* it was much more than a listing of products; it was a work of art and an articulation of an emerging philosophy of outdoor recreation and environmentalism. Chouinard in particular, along with several business-savvy partners including climbing pioneer Tom Frost, linked extreme sports, environmental advocacy, and consumerism in a manner similar to *Whole Earth*. Chouinard's corporate success was built on the countercultural recreation ethos that New Games celebrated.

Historian Joseph Taylor has observed "an emerging tension within environmental culture" that came about in the late 1960s. It centered on the growing split between those who embraced the ambiguous area of American culture that accepted the fact that human technology, human culture, and ecology were inexorably linked, and those who wished to draw the line between nature and culture more sharply.[31] For the environmental movement, this debate emerged most clearly in the discussion of new trends in outdoor recreation and tourism that were supplanting resource extraction as the primary interaction between the American public and the public lands. Some in the environmental movement, like Sierra Club director David Brower, concluded that the outdoor recreation culture of the late 1960s, "in which marketing and play go hand in hand," no longer fit with the politically energized environmental movement.[32] Stewart Brand provided a counter argument to this view through all of his publishing ventures, but even more directly with his work on the New Games tournaments.

While Brower and the Sierra Club were worried about the impact of dramatically expanding interest in outdoor recreation, federal land-management agencies like the National Park Service were working, as they had since 1916, to reconcile preservation and recreation in keeping with the trends of the day. Under the leadership of Stewart Udall, the National Park Service shifted responsibility for recreation management to a new agency, the Bureau of Outdoor Recreation (BOR), created in 1962 as part of a larger federal effort to rethink outdoor recreation and the public lands with a special emphasis on providing urban recreational opportunities.[33] The newly formed BOR played a particularly significant role in the Bay Area where Point Reyes National Seashore had been recently established and the groundwork for the "New Urban Park" was coalescing around the spectacular Golden Gate open spaces that formed the heart of San Francisco and Marin. The BOR expressed early interest in helping promote the New Games Tournament as an example of the type of creative urban recreation the agency was created to foster.[34] The involvement of the BOR in New Games and favorable press in the agency's publication *Outdoor Recreation Action* helped legitimize the event and its countercultural version of urban outdoor recreation.

The subtle conflicts surrounding New Games and other similar events, like the *Whole Earth* jamborees, demonstrated the persistence of conflicting ideas about what constituted environmentalism even among groups with similar concerns about the same place. Specifically, the New Games tournaments highlighted differences between the urban and human-centered environmentalism of *Whole Earth*, the Point Foundation, and the national environmental groups that were late in recognizing the importance of making outdoor recreation meaningful and viable for diverse urban populations.[35] It also demonstrated class and generational conflicts within the Bay Area community of outdoor enthusiasts. Supporters of hiking, walking, and traditional forms of urban and suburban leisure often reacted against emerging forms of alternative recreation like mountain biking, hang gliding, and mass participatory events—such as the giant tug of war or "Earth Ball" mayhem—that New Games facilitated. While traditionalists might have viewed New Games as nothing more than a weird distraction from nature communion, the event was a harbinger of critical changes in the recreational economy and the culture of outdoor sports.

The second New Games Tournament, held a year later and again sponsored with Point Foundation funds from Huey Johnson and Stewart Brand, was advertised in Spanish and Chinese and actively sought to move far beyond the normal constituency for outdoor recreation; its planners wanted to bring together players "across diverse social, ethnic and economic backgrounds" so that they might better relate "socially through play."[36] Huey Johnson articulated the environmental importance of the event nicely: "As a professional environmentalist," he wrote, "I feel it is urgent that we reach the urban center. Our origins are WASP in funding, energy and direction. If there is one lesson we have learned in the last few years, it is that inherent in the meaning of 'ecology' and 'human ecology' is the awareness that environmental relationships do not stop at 'boundaries,' be they nations, wilderness areas, cities or neighborhoods."[37]

Johnson was one of the most consistent and eloquent voices for this view among his generation of environmentalists. He refashioned the earlier efforts of pragmatic conservationists, such as Arthur Carhart and Edward Hilliard, who worked against the trend in environmental advocacy to compartmentalize land and activities and sought instead to craft an environmental ethic that could appeal to a broader spectrum of American society.[38] In keeping with the mission of The Trust for Public Land, Johnson emphasized the importance of shifting the focus of the environmental movement to the "urban center" which he thought would "give a much-needed diversity," and "modernize a movement still based on the early conservation philosophy of Thoreau and Leopold."[39] Johnson and the New Games promoters understood, ahead of many, that the "city dweller feels removed from the land," and traditional environmental issues like wilderness were too often an abstraction for the bulk of urban Americans.

The New Games movement is fondly remembered as a positive moment in the fading years of the Bay Area countercultural moment. New Games peaked in the Bay Area with the second tournament, but spread quickly across the nation and by 1976 became an international trend spawning several popular books and significant changes in the way recreation was perceived by a new generation of outdoor enthusiasts. Interest in New Games faded in the 1980s, but not before leaving a legacy of enthusiasm for new forms of urban outdoor recreation, many of which still endure in urban parks everywhere.

Notes

1. Michael Phillips to Stewart Brand, May 17, 1974, *Whole Earth Catalog* Records, M1045, 3:4, Department of Special Collections, Stanford University Libraries. Schumaker quote is from the subtitle of *Small is Beautiful: Economics as if People Mattered* (New York: Vintage, 1993). Some of what follows, in revised form, draws from my book, *Counterculture Green: The Whole Earth Catalog and American Environmentalism* (Lawrence: University Press of Kansas, 2007).

2. Huey Johnson interview with author, San Francisco, 2/14/06.

3. Waldemar A. Nielsen, *The Big Foundations: A Twentieth Century Fund Study* (New York: Columbia University Press, 1972), 3. See also, Mark Dowie, *American Foundations: An Investigative History* (Cambridge: The MIT Press, 2001).

4. Mark Dowie, *American Foundations*, x.

5. Stewart Brand, "Agent Report," January 1972, Point Foundation Records, M1441, 2:22, Department of Special Collections, Stanford University Libraries.

6. Huey Johnson, "Point Departure Paper," Huey Johnson Papers, Resource Renewal Institute, San Francisco, California.

7. Andrew Fluegelman, ed., *The New Games Book* (San Francisco: Headlands Press, 1976); *More New Games* (New York: Doubleday, 1981). Pat Farrington, "New Games Tournament," *The Coevolution Quarterly* 2 (Summer 1974): 94–101.

8. Fluegelman, *The New Games Book*, 9.

9. Ibid.

10. George Leonard, *The Ultimate Athlete* (New York: Viking Press, 1974).

11. Fluegelman, *The New Games Book*, 8. Quotes are from Stewart Brand Journal, 1973, 97–110, Stewart Brand Papers, M1237, Department of Special Collections, Stanford University Libraries. See also Sam Binkley, *Getting Loose: Lifestyle Consumption in the 1970s* (Durham: Duke University Press, 2007), 230–36

12. Hal Rothman, *The New Urban Park: Golden Gate National Recreation Area and Civic Environmentalism* (Lawrence: University Press of Kansas, 2004), 97.

13. Point veteran Bill Bryan also became a pioneer in significant changes in outdoor recreation when he founded a pioneering ecotourism company in the early 1980s, where

he worked with industry leaders to create a responsible travel movement aimed at coming up with best practices for sustainable/ecotravel. William L. Bryan, Jr., "Appropriate Cultural Tourism—Can It Exist? Searching for an Answer," in Hal K. Rothman, ed., *The Culture of Tourism, The Tourism of Culture: Selling the Past to the Present in the American Southwest* (Albuquerque: University of New Mexico Press, 2003), 140–63. For information on Bryan's work in environmentally minded tourism see "Off The Beaten Path" at www.offthebeatenpath .com and www.adventurecollection.com for responsible tourism guidelines.

14. Andrew Fluegelman, ed., *The New Games Book* (New York: Dolphin Books, 1976), 10–11.

15. Huey Johnson to Michael McCurry, December 23, 1975, *Whole Earth Catalog* Records, 5:1, Department of Special Collections, Stanford University Libraries. For background on The Trust for Public Land, see www.tpl.org.

16. Huey Johnson to Ivah Deering, December 11, 1973, Huey Johnson Papers, Resource Renewal Institute, Point Grants, Vol.1.

17. Ibid.

18. Nancy Jack Todd, *A Safe and Sustainable World: The Promise of Ecological Design* (Washington, DC: Island Press, 2005). Helga Olkowski, Bill Olkowski, Tom Javits, and the Farallones Institute Staff, *The Integral Urban House: Self-Reliant Living in the City* (San Francisco: Sierra Club Books, 1979).

19. Cynthia F. Lambert, "Huey D. Johnson: The Green Party," *Mother Earth News* 84(November/December 1983).

20. Ibid.

21. William deBuys, conversation with author, 2/28/07.

22. Keith Power, "Searching for Brand New Earth Games," *Sports Illustrated* (January 7, 1974): 30–31. William O'Brien, "A Gamut of Games Scheduled for Marin," *San Francisco Examiner,* Friday, October 12, 1973, 4. Susan Benson, Kathryn Meyer, Pat Farrington, "The Energy Crisis and New Games: A Challenge and an Answer," *Outdoor Recreation Action* (Spring 1974): 44–46. New Games materials can be found in *Whole Earth Catalog* Records, M1045, 25:5–8, Department of Special Collections, Stanford University Libraries.

23. Fluegelman, ed., *The New Games Book,* 13.

24. Ibid, 11.

25. Hal Rothman, *Devil's Bargains: Tourism in the Twentieth-Century American West* (Lawrence: University Press of Kansas, 1998), 23–24.

26. Ibid.

27. Peter Braunstein and Michael William Doyle, "Historicizing the American Counterculture of the 1960s and 1970s," in the same authors' *Imagine Nation: The American Counterculture of the 1960s and 1970s* (New York: Routledge, 2002), 8–12. Nice concise discussion of 1960s leisure and the counterculture.

28. Chouinard, "On Corporate Responsibility" in *Patagonia: The Edge Book Winter 2004 Catalog* (Winter 2004): 36–37; Yvon Chouinard, *Let My People Go Surfing: The Education*

of a Reluctant Businessman (New York: Penguin Press, 2005), 129–33 for specifics on catalog politics.

29. Galen Rowell points out the link between *Whole Earth* and Chouinard in his review of Yvon Chouinard and Tom Frost, "Chouinard Equipment," *American Alpine Journal* (1973): 522–23.

30. Drew Langsner, "Chouinard Equipment for Alpinists," in Stewart Brand, *The Last Whole Earth Catalog,* 257.

31. Joseph E. Taylor, "On Climber, Granite, Sky," *Environmental History* 11:1 (January 2006): 130–33. Taylor points to the divisions within the Sierra Club between David Brower and a group of influential Yosemite climbers over the environmental vs. recreation coverage in the *Sierra Club Bulletin.* Rothman, *The New Urban Park,* 12.

32. Ibid, Taylor, 133.

33. OUTDOOR RECREATION FOR AMERICA—ORRRC REPORT, 1962 OUTDOOR RECRE-ATION FOR AMERICA: A Report to the President and to the Congress by the Outdoor Recreation Resources Review Commission, Laurence S. Rockefeller, Chairman, January, 1962.

34. Susan Benson, Kathryn Meyer, Pat Farrington, "The Energy Crisis and New Games: A Challenge and an Answer," *Outdoor Recreation Action* (Spring 1974): 44–47.

35. Huey Johnson, "New Games—Some Thoughts From An Environmentalist," Huey Johnson Papers, Resource Renewal Institute, Point Grants, Vol. II.

36. New Games Report, Point Foundation Report for 1974, Point Foundation Records, M1441, 1:2, Department of Special Collections, Stanford University Libraries.

37. Johnson, "New Games."

38. For the best statement about problems with too restrictive classifications of nature see William Cronon, "The Trouble With Wilderness; Or, Getting Back to the Wrong Nature," in William Cronon, ed., *Uncommon Ground: Toward Reinventing Nature* (New York: W.W. Norton & Company, 1995), 69. For a remarkably similar argument against elevating a mythically pristine wilderness at the expense of the rest of the environment, see Arthur Carhart, *Planning for America's Wildlands* (Harrisburg, PA: The Telegraph Press, 1961). Carhart has often been criticized for his failure to support the wilderness bill at a time when his influence and access to a national audience was at a high point. Carhart argues, convincingly, that wilderness as defined by the Wilderness Society did not really exist in any pure state; it was an "experience," a construct that lived "within your mind" rather than in a particular place. Carhart refused to support the Wilderness Bill in 1964 because he felt that arguing for wilderness purity would be a de facto concession to those who sought to develop lands not considered pristine. For information on the philosophy and activism of Edward Hobbs Hilliard, see Andrew Kirk, *Collecting Nature: The American Environmental Movement and the Conservation Library* (Lawrence: University Press of Kansas, 2001), 83–107.

39. Johnson, "New Games."

Escape to the West/
Return to the East

The Lure of the City Familiar

JOEL A. TARR

I'm an eastern and midwestern urbanite, born and educated in Jersey City, New Brunswick, and Chicago, and now a long-time resident of Pittsburgh. I am habituated to eastern industrial cities! Twice in my lifetime, however, I tried to acclimate myself to living in western urban environments—specifically, Tucson, Arizona, and Long Beach, California—but each time I scurried back east to more familiar urban places.[1] Obviously, in reversing my trek, I went contrary to the vast westward migration in the second half of the twentieth century of those easterners and midwesterners seeking sun, space, and access to natural environments and playgrounds.[2]

In contrast, Hal Rothman, who was two generations or more younger than me, embraced the western experience that his position at Las Vegas offered him and spent much of his scholarly life exploring and writing about it. He had grown up and lived in a consumer-oriented suburban environment that was moving away from the earlier, more industrialized American city that I had experienced in my lifetime. He believed that in the West one could see the impact of human action on the environment more clearly than in "humid climes." He perceived that Las Vegas particularly embodied the new urban synthesis of service and leisure, and held the key to the future, as cities moved into a postindustrial world.[3]

A whole new generation of historians including Patricia Limerick, Richard White, and John Findlay began to conceptualize an alternative vision of the West. In his book, *Magic Lands: Western Cityscapes and American Culture After 1940,* for instance, John Findlay notes that westerners tried "to set their cities and their region apart from the East." The cities of the West were perceived of as "virgin," compared to the tired and jaded cities of the East, and this perspective, whether correct or not, had the effect of convincing potential migrants and residents that they could find a better life in that region. Other historians, sociologists, and novelists who have written about migration to western cities agree on the lure of the "Golden West," however misguided it was to think of the West as a single environment.[4]

I have no doubt that I shared the perception that Findlay notes when I embarked in 1952 for Tucson to attend the University of Arizona at the tender age of eighteen. The Jersey City where I grew up personified all that western urban migrants sought to escape from in the eastern city: crowded housing and slums, factories, dirty streets, and air laden with smoke and fumes. Turf battles between ethnic and racial groups were frequent, and one had to be careful not to walk down the wrong street or utter the wrong answer to a challenging question. Although the city's political boss Frank "I am the law" Hague was finally out of the mayor's office after thirty years, he left a tradition of corruption and machine politics that plagued the city for decades.

I remember boarding the train in Jersey City to take the long trip to Tucson, accompanied by my best friend from high school who was also attending the university. His family had previously migrated to Los Angeles to join relatives who had moved there in 1931 to open a Kosher-style delicatessen, counting on the patronage of other migrants who missed the ethnic foods of the eastern cities.[5] The trip to Tucson seemed endless, as the train sped through the midwestern plains and the desert landscapes of the Southwest. I remember staring out the window at the distant horizon, marveling at the large jackrabbits that raced alongside the train. For a kid who had barely been out of the congested environs of Jersey City, it was an eye-opening experience, introducing me to the vast open spaces that were a prime feature of the western landscape.

When I arrived in Tucson it had just over 45,000 inhabitants and was unlike any city that I had experienced. The city was essentially flat, with a small downtown and a scant skyline. Most of the buildings were relatively small, with numerous white or multicolored, one-story bungalows, sometimes of adobe, with weird devices on their roofs (solar hot water heaters and evaporative coolers). Palm trees, the first I had ever seen, lined the streets, while majestic stands of cacti stood guard over the desert floor and marched up into the foothills. The city spread out into the desert and so-called suburban "ranchettes" had begun to move into the hills. Everything looked parched except for the flooded lawns of the university buildings that I initially mistook for swimming pools![6]

My closest friends became the native Arizonians who attended the university and who disdained the playboy habits of most of the out-of-state students. Outdoor sports were high on the Arizonian's list of activities, as was hunting rabbits in the desert. In an attempt to fit in, I purchased a single-shot .22 as a ticket to their desert adventures, but never came close to hitting anything. I was surprised at the easy entry to the natural environment, both desert and hills, compared to the dense metropolitan area where I had grown up and where open country, aside from the vast swampy meadowlands near the city, was difficult to access.

In spite of the variety of new experiences or perhaps because of them, I became increasingly unhappy, missing my family and, oddly enough, the familiarity of dense and diverse Jersey City. The virtues of the western environment had passed me by, and much of my free time was spent listening to classical music or reading in the library. To my Arizona friends, I was a strange bird—why did I cloister myself when the outdoors beckoned? One of them took pity on me at Thanksgiving break and took me to his home in Scottsdale, then a town of small bungalows of just over 2,000, but now with a population of over 200,000 residents and still growing! In retrospect, Scottsdale personifies the explosive growth potential of western urban environments for me as Las Vegas did for Hal. I am sure that he would have been more attuned to the features of Tucson that I found odd (solar hot water heaters, evaporative coolers, and residential sprawl) and would have understood them as necessary adaptations to the desert climate or reflections of personal housing preferences. But I could not foresee this future nor did I want to embrace it, and I decided to return to New Jersey to attend Rutgers University.

That June, back in New Jersey, I drove down the newly opened Garden State Parkway to see the Rutgers campus in New Brunswick for the first time. I was struck by its colonial character (founded in 1766) and wondered how I could have rejected the history and tradition reflected in its hallowed buildings ("Old Queens") for what I then saw as the newness and crassness of the desert city and its university. It was there that I became enthralled with the study of history, benefiting from professors such as John Higham, Richard L. McCormick, and Henry Winkler.

Four years later in 1957, armed with two history degrees, I again ventured west, but only as far as Evanston and Chicago, to take my PhD at Northwestern University. I found Chicago almost as difficult to live in as Jersey City. The "city of big shoulders," as the writer Nelson Algren entitled it, was monumental and ugly. Its streets were as dirty as those in Jersey City and its politics almost as corrupt, as the daily newspapers and my dissertation research on William Lorimer, a Chicago political boss, revealed.[7] During my time in the "Windy City," its weather was especially harsh and its winters fierce, with snow and ice often clogging the streets. Although a student at Northwestern, I lived in Hyde Park on the city's South Side for three years since my then wife was doing her graduate work in psychology at the University of Chicago. Chicago in those years was torn by racial conflict, as a large stream of African American migrants from the South encountered strong resistance in their attempts to move into white neighborhoods. The strife was especially intense in the areas around Hyde Park.[8]

Chicago was an extraordinary city but living there was not easy and in 1961, when I began job hunting, I felt ready to move on to a less-demanding locale. That spring I received a job offer from Long Beach State College (now California State University at Long Beach). Fed up with Chicago winters and urban tensions, I decided to discard the bad memories of my Tucson experience and escape for a second time to the Golden West. I would join those millions of Americans moving westward from snowbelt cities to the sunlit promised land.

Within a few years, however, I realized that my earlier perception that I was not meant to be a western urbanite had been correct. Long Beach had some attractions, but it appeared to me that the city's and Los Angeles County's most rapidly developing features were the construction of new freeways and mile after mile of tract homes complete with shopping malls (I had never seen one before living in California). The region's almost total dependence on the automobile produced smog that often obscured the nearby mountains. At the time there was little ethnic diversity at the college or in Long Beach, which seemed to be inhabited primarily by escapees from Iowa farms seeking the combination of consumption and leisure that Hal had written about ("Iowa By The Sea")[9] Tradition was absent in most of these new areas and signs that proudly boasted, "founded in 1950," were the source of merriment to us easterners.

The college itself, founded in 1949, grew rapidly in terms of students and faculty. Making new friends was attractive but at the same time those with whom I became friendly often moved on to other colleges and universities, frequently in the East. Sun and beach were great, but to have my career advance I needed freedom from distractions and more time in the library—hedonism clearly had its limitations. The East again beckoned, and in 1967 I moved to Carnegie Mellon University in the "Renaissance City" of Pittsburgh.

Although in the midst of dramatic change, Pittsburgh was still an industrial city and had many of the same urban problems and features as Jersey City and Chicago. At one time known as the "Gateway to the West," it dated back to the eighteenth century. Ethnically diverse with many identifiable neighborhoods, it had a very prominent downtown and miles of large steel mills lining the rivers. Air quality was much improved over what it had been before 1946 or so, but it was still only fair. The rivers were great assets but also suffered from pollution. The hillsides along the rivers were picturesque and often built up with small worker-built houses; two inclined plane railroads (there had been seventeen at one time) connected the hilltop residences with factories and mills clustered on the banks of the Monongahela River. Wonderful architecture existed in the downtown and in the neighborhoods, but there were also large slum areas and a sharp racial divide between whites and blacks. A public/private coalition had accomplished considerable improvement in the city's environment, its infrastructure, and its downtown, but residents were becoming increasingly restive about the operations of the top-down coalition. Beautiful countryside existed outside the city but it had often been scarred by mining and industry.[10]

What was unusual about Pittsburgh in those years was that it was the first major industrial city to attempt to renew itself, hence, the title "Renaissance City." That is, one had a very visceral sense that things were changing positively in many respects even in the face of the city's population decline. It was also a manageable environment, relatively easy to negotiate by walking or by using the decent public transportation system. That is, unlike the western cities, one was not totally dependent on the automobile for mobility. In addition, one did not have to cope with endless miles of freeways and tract homes, although suburbanization was speeding up. Yet, because of inherited institutions and habits, change was not easy to accomplish. The city became my permanent home and the subject of a considerable part of my research.

From an analytical point of view, what can be gleaned from this memoir to help provide a broader understanding of the differences as well as the similarities between western and eastern cities? Coming from an eastern background with a strong set of roots in the history and character of the industrial city, I did not make the adjustment to the western urban environment as easily as did many other eastern migrants. The attractions of climate and of the diverse natural environments of ocean, desert, and mountains did not provide a strong enough pull to hold me in the West as it did for so many others.

Hal, on the other hand, embraced his new environment in Las Vegas, shaped by a different set of influences than mine. He had lived, as he noted, in "service-oriented" postindustrial rather than industrial communities.[11] His research identified the shift from resource exploitation to a world of service and consumption that he maintained was a new type of urban reality. He predicted that Las Vegas and other western tourist towns were a forecast of the future shape of American cities: "Las Vegas now symbolizes the new America, the latest in American dream capitals. As New York once defined the commercial economy and Chicago . . . epitomized the industrial city, Las Vegas illustrates one of the pillars of the postindustrial, postmodern future . . . Las Vegas has become an icon."[12] Earlier forms would be discarded for a new set of consumption values and a culture that focused on hedonistic choice.

Many of the changes in western cities that Hal described had occurred during the years after I first journeyed to the West.[13] The mountains, the desert, and the ocean are still there today, as is the sunny and often benign weather, but humans have modified them in significant ways for good and for ill. The greatest change in past decades in the West has been the spread of the built environment over large areas of the formerly untouched landscape in the form of housing developments, shopping malls, interstate highways, airports, and other forms of infrastructure.

Some western metropolitan areas, such as Los Angeles, have become denser than those in the East in terms of population. While the typical residence is still the single-family home, multi-unit condominiums are appearing at a rapid rate. Population is now much more ethnically diversified compared to the past, and in this regard it is more similar to eastern cities. The regional economy has also greatly changed, becoming much less oriented towards resource exploitation and driven by factors such as consumerism, tourism, and computer-related electronics.[14]

In many ways, in the same decades, many eastern cities have become more like those in the West. While western cities were the first to experience suburban sprawl, eastern cities have followed suit, especially in their newer suburbs. Peripheral growth and sprawl in eastern cities has often been accompanied by central-city decline. In eastern cities the density distinction between city and suburb has diminished, although major income and racial differences persist.[15] No longer does one think of eastern cities as polluted and western cities as pristine. Cities in both regions share issues relating to air and water quality, water supply, flooding, and landscape transformation. The question of adequate water provision is especially severe in western cities in arid areas, such as Hal's Las Vegas. Western and eastern cities may have more in common today than they did forty or fifty years ago, brought about by a common desire for suburban living and consequent automobile dependence.[16]

In the future will similarities between eastern and western cities increase or decrease? Or, as Hal suggested, might uniformity be replaced by a series of novel urban adaptations fitted to locality and culture and based on factors such as environment, technology, and personal preferences? History is not always predictable and in an age of ballooning gasoline prices and water scarcity, a different urban model may yet emerge. Undoubtedly, if Hal had lived, he would have been quick to perceive the change and to modify his urban predictions.

Notes

I wish to thank Jeffrey Stine, Anthony Penna, and Char Miller for their helpful suggestions in regard to this essay.

1. I do not count a year spent as a visiting assistant professor at the University of California, Santa Barbara, 1966–67.

2. A Brookings Report recently noted that from 2007 to 2008 the U.S. migration rate reached its lowest point since World War II. States in the intermountain West and the Southeast, were especially effected. See, William H. Frey, "The Great American Migration Slowdown: Regional and Metropolitan Dimensions," at http://www.brookings.edu/multimedia/video/2009/1209_migration_frey.aspx.]

3. "Interview: Hal K. Rothman," *Environmental History* (Jan. 2007) 12:143; Hal Rothman, *Neon Metropolis: How Las Vegas Started the Twenty-First Century* (New York: Routledge, 2002).

4. John M. Findlay, *Magic Lands: Western Cityscapes and American Culture After 1940* (Berkeley: University of California Press, 1992).

5. For an environmental history of Tucson and of Phoenix, see Michael F. Logan, *Desert Cities: The Environmental History of Phoenix and Tucson* (Pittsburgh: University of Pittsburgh Press, 2006).

6. Canter's Delicatessen and Restaurant is a famous Los Angeles eating place. In 2003 the family opened a Canter's Deli in Las Vegas. See, http://www.cantersdeli.com/aboutcanters/.

7. Joel A. Tarr, *A Study in Boss Politics: William Lorimer of Chicago* (Urbana: University of Illinois Press, 1971).

8. Arnold R. Hirsch, *Making the Second Ghetto: Race and Housing in Chicago, 1940–60* (Chicago: University of Chicago Press, 1998).

9. See Chad Greene, "'From Iowa by the Sea' to International City, A Look at Long Beach's Changing Demographics," *Long Beach Business Journal Archives* (1/7/06) for changes in Long Beach's demographic composition; Rothman, *Neon Metropolis*.

10. Roy Lubove, *Twentieth-Century Pittsburgh: Government, Business, and Environmental Change* (New York: John Wiley & Sons, 1969; Joel A. Tarr, ed., *Devastation and Renewal: An Environmental History of Pittsburgh and Its Region* (Pittsburgh: University of Pittsburgh Press, 2003, 2005).

11. "Interview: Hal K. Rothman," 143.

12. Rothman, *Neon Metropolis*, xxvii.

13. For the newest Western metropolitan growth areas, including Las Vegas, see Robert E. Lang, Andrea Sarzynski, Mark Muro, "Mountain Megas: America's Newest Metropolitan Places and a Federal Partnership to Help Them Prosper," Brookings, July 20, 2008, http://www.brookings.edu/reports/2008/0720_mountainmegas_sarzynski.aspx.

14. Carl Abbott, *The Metropolitan Frontier: Cities in the Modern American West* (Tucson: University of Arizona Press, 1993); Findlay, *Magic Lands, 265–303;* and William Fulton, Rolf

Pendall, Mai Nguyen, and Alicia Harrison, *Who Sprawls Most? How Growth Patterns Differ Across the U.S.* (Washington: The Brookings Institution, 2001).

15. See, Robert Bruegmann, *Sprawl: A Compact History* (Chicago: University of Chicago Press, 2005).

16. See, for instance, William Deverell and Greg Hise, *Land of Sunshine: An Environmental History of Metropolitan Los Angeles* (Pittsburgh: University of Pittsburgh Press, 2005), 67–200; Char Miller, *On the Border: An Environmental History of San Antonio* (Pittsburgh: University of Pittsburgh Press, 2001).

CONTRIBUTORS

KATHLEEN A. BROSNAN is an associate professor of history at the University of Houston and the author of *Uniting Mountain and Plain: Urbanization, Law and Environmental Change along the Front Range* (2002).

CRAIG E. COLTEN is the Carl O. Sauer Professor of Geography at Louisiana State University. He is the author of *An Unnatural Metropolis: Wresting New Orleans from Nature* (2005) and *Perilous Place, Powerful Storms: Hurricane Protection in Coastal Louisiana* (2009).

LARY M. DILSAVER is professor of historical geography at the University of South Alabama. He has authored or edited five books and many articles on the National Park System and various topics on the western United States.

SARAH S. ELKIND is an associate professor teaching environmental, political, and urban history at San Diego State University. Her first book, *Bay Cities and Water Politics* (1998), explored regional public works and political reform in Boston, Massachusetts, and Oakland, California, and won the Abel Wolman Award in 1999.

ARI KELMAN teaches history at the University of California, Davis, and is author of *A River and Its City: The Nature of Landscape in New Orleans*.

ANDREW G. KIRK is professor of environmental and western history and director of the Public History Program at the University of Nevada-Las Vegas. His most recent book is *Counterculture Green: The Whole Earth Catalog and American Environmentalism* (2007).

MATTHEW KLINGLE is associate professor of history and environmental studies at Bowdoin College in Brunswick, Maine. He is the author of *Emerald City: An Environmental History of Seattle* (2007), along with numerous articles and essays.

PHOEBE S. KROPP YOUNG is an assistant professor of history at the University of Colorado at Boulder, where she teaches and writes about the cultural and environmental history of the modern United States and the American West. She is the author of *California Vieja: Culture and Memory in a Modern American Place* (2006).

WILLIAM L. LANG is professor of history at Portland State University, where he teaches environmental and public history courses. Lang is author or editor of six books on Northwest history, including *Great River of the West: Essays on the Columbia River* (1999) and *Two Centuries of Lewis & Clark* (2004).

MARTIN V. MELOSI is distinguished university professor of history and director of the Center for Public History at the University of Houston. His research interests include urban environmental history, energy history, and public history. If you have room you can add: Melosi is author or editor of 16 books and more than 70 articles and book chapters.

CHAR MILLER is director of the environmental analysis program and W. M. Keck Professor of Environmental Analysis at Pomona College; he is author of *Gifford Pinchot and the Making of Modern Environmentalism* and editor of the companion volumes *Water in the 21st-Century West* and *River Basins of the American West.*

WILLIAM PHILPOTT is an assistant professor of history at the University of Denver, specializing in environmental, suburban, and western history. He is the author of *The Lessons of Leadville; or, Why the Western Federation of Miners Turned Left* and of the forthcoming *Vacation Land,* a study of tourism after 1945 and its influence on popular environmental culture and politics.

MARGUERITE S. SHAFFER is the director of American studies and an associate professor of American studies and history at Miami University in Oxford, Ohio. Her work focuses on popular environmentalism and public culture. She is the author of *See America First: Tourism and National Identity* and the editor of *Public Culture: Diversity, Democracy, and Community in the United States.*

JOEL A. TARR is the Richard S. Caliguiri University Professor of History and Policy at Carnegie Mellon University. He recently published, with co-author Clay McShane, *The Horse in the City: Living Machines in the 19th Century* (2007), and edited *Devastation and Renewal: An Environmental History of Pittsburgh and Its Region* (2005). In 2008 the Society for the History of Technology awarded him its Leonardo da Vinci Medal for outstanding contributions to the history of technology.

JESSICA TEISCH received her doctorate in geography from the University of California, Berkeley. She is currently an environmental consultant and managing editor of *Bookmarks* magazine.

INDEX

Burns, Robert L., 210
Bush, George H. W., 4
Bush, George W., 4

Cable, George Washington, 201
California, 4, 112; agriculture, in northern,
35–37, 40, 43; land settlement plans
for, 24, 26, 27; Napa city, 35, 36, 38, 44,
47; St. Helena, 35, 38, 41, 45, 46–47;
suburban development, of northern,
6, 35–37, 42–43, 50; water supply and,
117, 118, 120, 121, 126; Williamson Act of
1965, 6, 37, 40. *See also* Bay Area; Los
Angeles; Napa County; San Francisco;
San Jose; Santa Clara County; sugar
industry; Yosemite National Park
California and Hawaiian Sugar Refining
Corporation, 19, 23
California Board of Health, 158
California Court of Appeals, 42
California Environmental Quality Act,
49
California Land Conservation Act of
1965. *See* Williamson Act of 1965
California State Water Quality Control
Board, 45
California Sugar Refinery, 18, 23
California Supreme Court, 119
California Water Service Company, 123,
126
Calistoga (Calif.), 35, 47
Cammerer, Arno, 160
Campen, Alden, 124
camping: automobiles and, 1920s to 1930s,
177–79, 180–83; camping gear, 175–76,
181–82, 186; as good for health, 175, 177,
180, 182; hoboes and, 9, 176, 178–79,
180, 181; homelessness and, 9, 172, 177,
178–79, 181, 182, 183–85, 186–87; nine-
teenth- and early-twentieth-century,
173–77; as sleeping outside, 9, 172–73,
179, 180, 186–87; subsistence and,
176–77; in Times Square, 171–72, 183;
Tompkins Square Park, N.Y., 183–85;
urban camping, 180, 182, 183–86; wil-
derness and, 172, 173, 174–76, 178, 181,
182, 186; in Yosemite National Park,
156, 158, 163
Carhart, Arthur, 251
Carlin, Debbie, 83
Carnegie Mellon University, 258
Carnes, William G., 162
Carr, Ethan, 148, 149
Carson, Joseph, 106
Carson, Rachel, 62
Carter, Glen, 107
Cascade Mountains, 102
"Cascadia," 81
Cedar River, 76, 78–80, 85; salmon habitat
conservation plan, 79, 82, 84
Celilo Falls, 102
Changing Places (Lodge), 4
Charles Krug winery, 44
Charlevoix, Pierre-François-Xavier de,
195–96
Chicago, 3, 18, 19, 257–58
Chinese immigrants, in Hawaii, 20, 22, 23,
28–29
Chouinard, Yvon, 249–50
Citizen News, The (Los Angeles), 214
Citizens for the Preservation of Thornton
Creek, 78
Citizens' League on Government and
Taxation of Santa Clara County, 122,
123
Civilian Conservation Corps (CCC), 144,
145, 160, 182
Civil War, camping and, 173–74
Clean Water Act, 105
Clifford, James, 63
climate change, 85, 87
Clinton, Bill, 4
CoEvolution Quarterly, 245
Cold War, 77, 216
Coleman Company, 175
Colten, Craig, 9
Columbia River, 106, 108; commercial
development on, 98, 102, 103; dams
for hydroelectric power and, 102–3;
dredging of, 98, 99, 102; flooding,

May 1948, 103–4; importance to
Portland, 8, 96–97, 98, 109; recreational
development and, 101, 104–5. *See also*
Portland; Willamette River
Columbia River Fishermen's Association,
106
Columbia-Willamette seaway, 97, 98, 99,
100, 102
Committee for the Preservation of the
American Way of Life, 124
Community Coalition for Environmental
Justice (Seattle), 83
Conlin, Richard, 85
conservation, 58. *See also*
environmentalism
Continental Divide, 141
Cooke, George P., 17, 24, 26
Coppola, Francis Ford, 48
Country Life in America, 175
"Coyote Creek Battle of 1903–1905,"
118–19
Crockett (Calif.), 19, 23
Cronkite, Walter, 247
Cronon, William, 18
Cross, Virginia, 80

The Dalles, 102
Daniel, John, 41, 42
Daniels, Mark, 156
Daphnia, 78
Davies, Jack, 41
Davis, Richard Harding, 2
Death Valley National Monument, 205
deBuys, William, 5, 247
Denegri, D. M., 119
Denver, 2, 3, 226
DePastino, Todd, 179
*Devil's Bargains: Tourism in the
Twentieth-Century American West*
(Rothman), 249
Devoto, Bernard, 145
Dick, Phillip K., 242
Dilsaver, Lary, 9, 165
Dinosaur National Monument, 138
Dodson, W. B., 102

Doerr, Robert, 124
Doheny, Edward L., 205
Do (Not) Feed the Bears (Biel), 137
Driven Wild (Sutter), 149
Drury, Newton B., 145, 162
Dumm Brothers Petroleum Corporation,
215
Duwamish River, 75, 78, 88
Duwamish Waterway, 75–76, 83

Eagle (Colo.), 225
Eagle River, 225
"Earth Ball," 11, 247, 248, 251
East Maui Irrigation Company, 19
East Side County Water District, 122
Eaton, Earl, 226
Echo Park, 138
Eddie Bauer, 76
Edwards Aquifer recharge zone, 67
Eisenhower, Dwight D., 144
Elk Hills Naval Petroleum Reserve, 212
Elkind, Sarah, 10
Ellet, Charles, 198–99, 201
Elliott, J. E., 208
Elliott Bay, 76, 88
Elsman, Ralph, 123, 124
Endangered Species Act: listing, salmon,
74, 82, 83–84, 108; of 1973, 74, 79
enology. *See* wine industry
environmentalism: Lady Bird Johnson
and, 61–62; logging in Seattle and,
79–80; in Napa County, 41, 49;
National Park Service and, 8–9,
138, 139, 142–44, 162; New Games
Tournament and, 11, 244–45, 247–48,
249, 251; Portland and, 105, 107–8; recreation and tourism and, 247–48, 250;
salmon in Seattle and, 78, 80, 81–82,
83–84, 87–90; urban environmentalism, 242–43, 245, 246, 251; in Vail,
Colo., 226, 229–30, 231–34, 235; *Whole
Earth Catalog* and, 242–43, 245–46,
249–51
Environmental Protection Agency, 108
ethnic diversity, 258, 260

Mitchell, Grace, 175
Mitchell, H. G., 122
Modern Times (movie, 1936), 180
Mondavi, Robert, 44
Monkonnen, Eric, 176
Monongahela River, 259
Monroe, James, 198
Montgomery, Louis, 119
Moran, Thomas, 139, 140
Moses, Stan, 80
Moss, Bill, 249
Muckleshoot Indian Tribe, 80–81, 82, 85
Muir, John, 154
Muir Woods, 164
Multnomah dredge, 99
Municipal Ownership League (San Jose),
  119

Napa (Calif.), 35, 36, 38, 44, 47
Napa County: agricultural preserve
  of, 6–7, 34, 38, 40–44, 45, 47, 49–50;
  environmentalism in, 41, 49; general
  agriculture in, 6, 34–35, 36–37, 40–41,
  48; Hispanic population of, 47; local
  government development and, 39–40,
  50; Measures to preserve agriculture,
  43–44; population, 35, 36; proposed
  highway, 1961, 38, 43, 47; soil erosion, 45–46, 48–49; vineyards in, 34,
  36–37, 38–39, 41, 43, 45–46, 48–49;
  Williamson Act of 1965 and, 37–38;
  wineries vs. vineyards, 45, 48, 49. *See
  also* tourism; wine industry
Napa County Board of Supervisors, 38,
  42, 43, 45, 48
Napa County Conservation,
  Development, and Planning
  Commission, 35
Napa County Resource Conservation
  District, 49
Napa River, 34, 43, 45–46
Napa Sustainable Winegrowing Group, 49
Napa Valley Foundation, 46
"Napa Valley National Vineyard," 39
Napa Valley Vintners Association, 44

Nash, Roderick, 138
National Cattleman's Association, 40
National Environmental Policy Act of
  1969, 105, 233
National Geographic, 107
National Marine Fisheries Service, 73,
  108
National Parks Association, 148
National Park Service, 64, 182; bears and,
  8–9, 137–38, 151, 161; environmentalism and, 8–9, 138, 139, 142–44, 162;
  establishment of, 141, 156; garbage disposal, 161–62, 163; infrastructure and
  landscaping, 9, 157, 158, 159–62, 164–65;
  infrastructure within parks, 143, 144,
  145, 146–47; Mission 66 program, 144,
  145–49, 162, 164; potable water for
  visitors, 161, 162; public health issues
  in parks and, 155, 164, 165; roads within
  parks and, 143, 144, 146; sewage disposal, 160–61, 162, 164; visitor centers,
  147–48, 162; visitor numbers and, 144,
  145, 154, 157, 162, 165; wilderness for
  consumers and, 138–51; wilderness
  preservation and, 143–44, 148–51, 158,
  160, 165, 250. *See also* Yellowstone
  National Park; Yosemite National
  Park
National Park Service Organic Act of
  1916, 141
National Society of the Colonial Dames
  of America, 60
Native Americans, 66, 195; Blackfeet
  Indians, 141; at Grand Canyon, 140–41;
  Muckleshoot Indian Tribe, 80–81, 82,
  85; of Puget Sound, 75, 79, 83, 85
Native Plants magazine, 66
natural gas, 206, 207
Nature Conservancy, 245, 246
Nature's Metropolis (Cronon), 18
Neon Metropolis (Rothman), 12
Nevada, 4
New Age, 11
New Deal, 103, 144, 180
Newell, Frederick H., 22–23